TROPE

ABOVE & ACROSS PHILADELPHIA

EDITED BY

MICHELLE FITZGERALD

KENDRA HUSPASKA

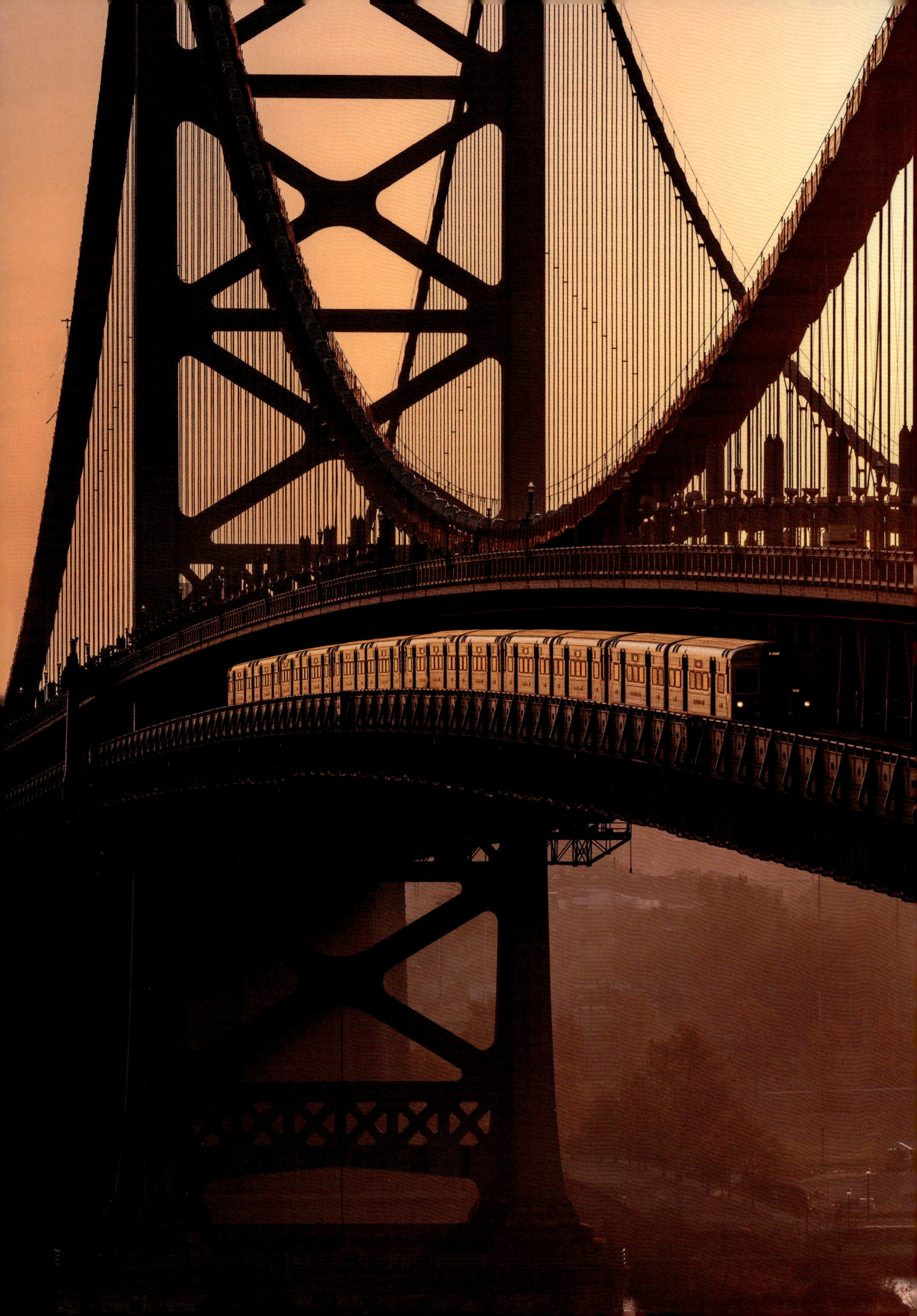

PHOTOGRAPHS BY

ANDY D'ANGELO

BRETT GROSS

BRIAN FISHMAN

DANIEL MORENO

GREG ADAMS

KIM SLOUF

LICHAO LIU

LUKE CUCCURULLO

NATHANIEL BAYONA

THOM CARROLL

TREVOR W. ADAMS

FOREWORD BY

PAUL STEINKE

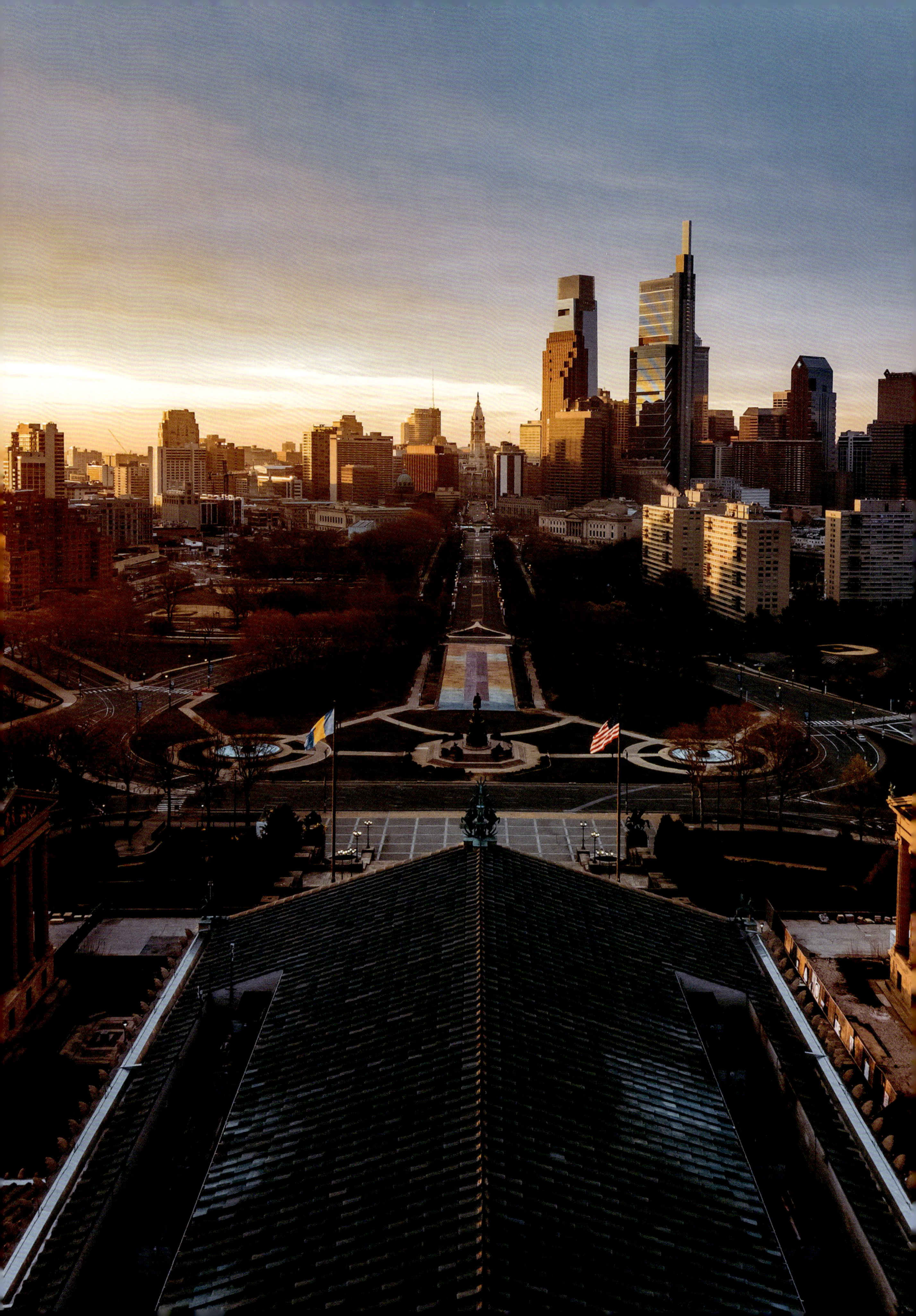

"This is Philadelphia. This is the birthplace of freedom, liberty and democracy."
— Michael Nutter, Former Mayor of Philadelphia

Above & Across Philadelphia is a curated collection of 140 aerial photographs of Philadelphia taken by 11 independent photographers.

Philadelphia is known as the birthplace of America and is known for its historical landmarks, rich history, and vibrant culture. A city of contrasts, Philadelphia's architecture is a blend of colonial heritage, industrial expansion, and modern urbanism, where centuries-old cobblestone alleys lie just a few blocks from modern skyscrapers.

Philadelphia is a city rooted in history, yet constantly moving forward. From the Philadelphia Museum of Art with its Greek Revival architectural style and famous "Rocky Steps" to the modern architectural marvel of the Comcast Technology Center, an ultra-modern glass skyscraper that is the tallest building in both Philadelphia and the state of Pennsylvania, Philadelphia offers something for everyone. The photographs in this collection, taken from helicopters, from observation decks and atop buildings, and with the use of drones, capture the juxtaposition of time — presenting Philadelphia from a new perspective.

Let *Above & Across Philadelphia* transport you and experience the breathtaking beauty of Philadelphia — from above & across.

Michelle Fitzgerald & Kendra Huspaska
Editors

"Philadelphia is an incredible city. We have world-class educational institutions and healthcare facilities. We have a thriving downtown, an amazing and diverse food and restaurant scene, world-renowned museums, and great arts and culture. We have wonderfully vibrant neighborhoods that are the lifeblood of our city."
—Cherelle L. Parker, Mayor of Philadelphia

In 1682, when London-born William Penn decided where he would locate his New World colony's principal city, he settled on a flat, well-watered expanse of land between the Delaware and Schuylkill Rivers. "Philadelphia," he named it, from the Greek for City of Brotherly Love. As a Quaker who suffered persecution from his intolerant British peers, Penn wanted his city to be a place of religious freedom. And as a survivor of the devastating London fire of 1666, he envisioned a city with rectilinear, intersecting streets flanking square building plots, each of which would hold a single house surrounded by gardens — the better to prevent fire from spreading from one building to another.

William Penn's 17th century urban form has survived to this day, nearly 350 years after he first stepped ashore from his ship, *Welcome*. Remarkably, modern Philadelphia is still arrayed along the same rectilinear, intersecting streets, albeit with dense development that quickly filled in the garden plots as Penn's city grew to an extent he could have never imagined. Penn's original gridiron plan reserved four supersized plots as green spaces, which today are public parks named after George Washington, Ben Franklin, James Logan (Penn's secretary), and David Rittenhouse (a renowned astronomer and inventor). A fifth plot at the geographic center of the gridiron was reserved for public buildings where today, an enormous bronze statue of William Penn stands atop City Hall tower, erected in 1894. From his lofty perch 548 feet above the street, the city's founder surveys his urban creation.

Thus was formed the nucleus of a great American city, a downtown that Philadelphians call "Center City." Situated in a broad, mostly flat river valley, Philadelphia lacks the backdrop of mountains, lakes, or oceans that set the tone for other iconic cityscapes — although the surprisingly broad Delaware River offers an appealing aqueous perspective of the cityscape. Nor is the city defined by its tall buildings, although several skyscrapers soar to more than respectable heights.

What I have found to be Philadelphia's secret power is the power of small. Its streets were laid out in the horse and buggy days and now seem impossibly small and narrow. This may be the bane of motorists, but it's pure joy for pedestrians in this most walkable of cities. What's more, the busy east-west and north-south arteries are interlaced with even narrower lanes and alleys, many lined with tiny little row houses, private clubs, hidden taverns, and eateries. The most famous of these, Elfreth's Alley, is the oldest continually occupied residential street in America.

Emanating from the urban core are blocks and blocks of row houses in every direction: north, south, west, and — well, not east, because there lies the Delaware River and New Jersey. But in neighborhood after neighborhood outside of Center City, the red brick row house reigns supreme. Philadelphia has more attached dwellings by far than any other city, sometimes as many as 120 per block (60 per side). At the corners can often be found taverns, hair salons, groceries, and other neighborhood-serving shops and services.

But it's not all asphalt, brick and concrete. Starting at City Hall, a wide, tree-lined boulevard cuts across the grid: the Benjamin Franklin Parkway,

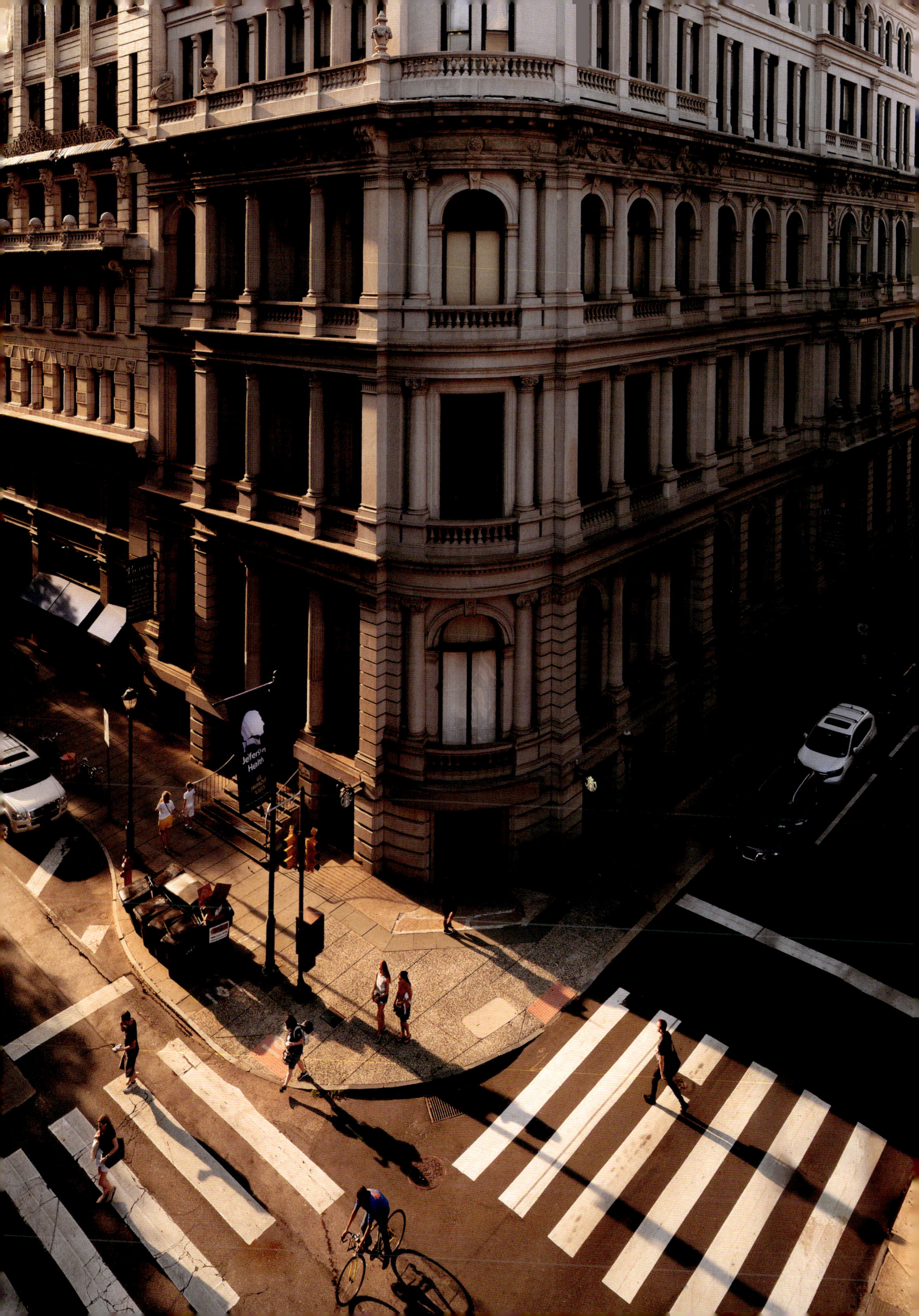
Health

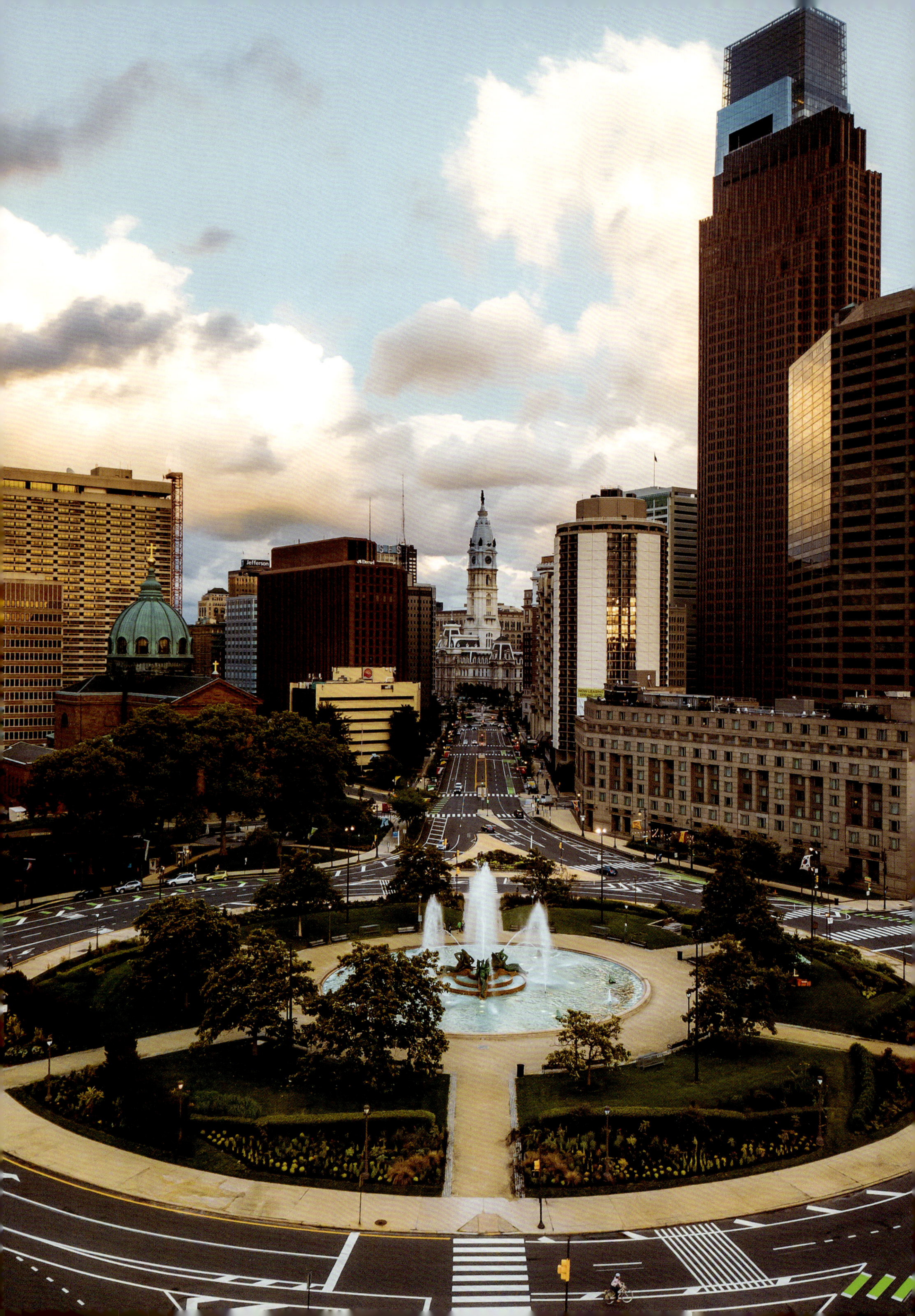

inspired by the Champs-Élysées. At its terminus rises an amber-colored limestone temple housing the city's incredible art museum. Stretching out behind it is the broad, green expanse of Fairmount Park, flanking the Schuylkill River, embracing nearly 5,000 acres on both sides of the river. The park, among the largest in the United States, provides a verdant backdrop for the scullers rowing to and from Boathouse Row who were immortalized by Thomas Eakins. The park extends north and west along the river to the mouth of the Wissahickon Creek, which cuts its way through a magnificent, deep gorge that for centuries has inspired naturalists, painters, and even Charles Dickens.

The city is not all row houses, either. Its built environment reflects centuries of great American architecture. William Strickland started the national craze for Greek Revival design in the 1820s, giving rise to Philadelphia's 19th century reputation as the "Athens of America." Later, Frank Furness created a muscular Victorian-era architectural style that defined the cityscape during Philadelphia's industrial heyday. In the 20th century, architects like Louis Kahn, Aldo Giurgola, Robert Venturi, and Denise Scott Brown devised the so-called Philadelphia School of modern architecture that resonated not just in this city but around the world.

The sum total is a joy to experience from the bird's eye, despite the absence of snow-capped peaks or great lakes. But to truly appreciate Philadelphia is to simply walk its streets, many of which were traversed in bygone days by the founding fathers, determined abolitionists, civil rights champions, and great patriots who helped to forge the great American story.

Paul Steinke
Executive Director, Preservation Alliance
for Greater Philadelphia

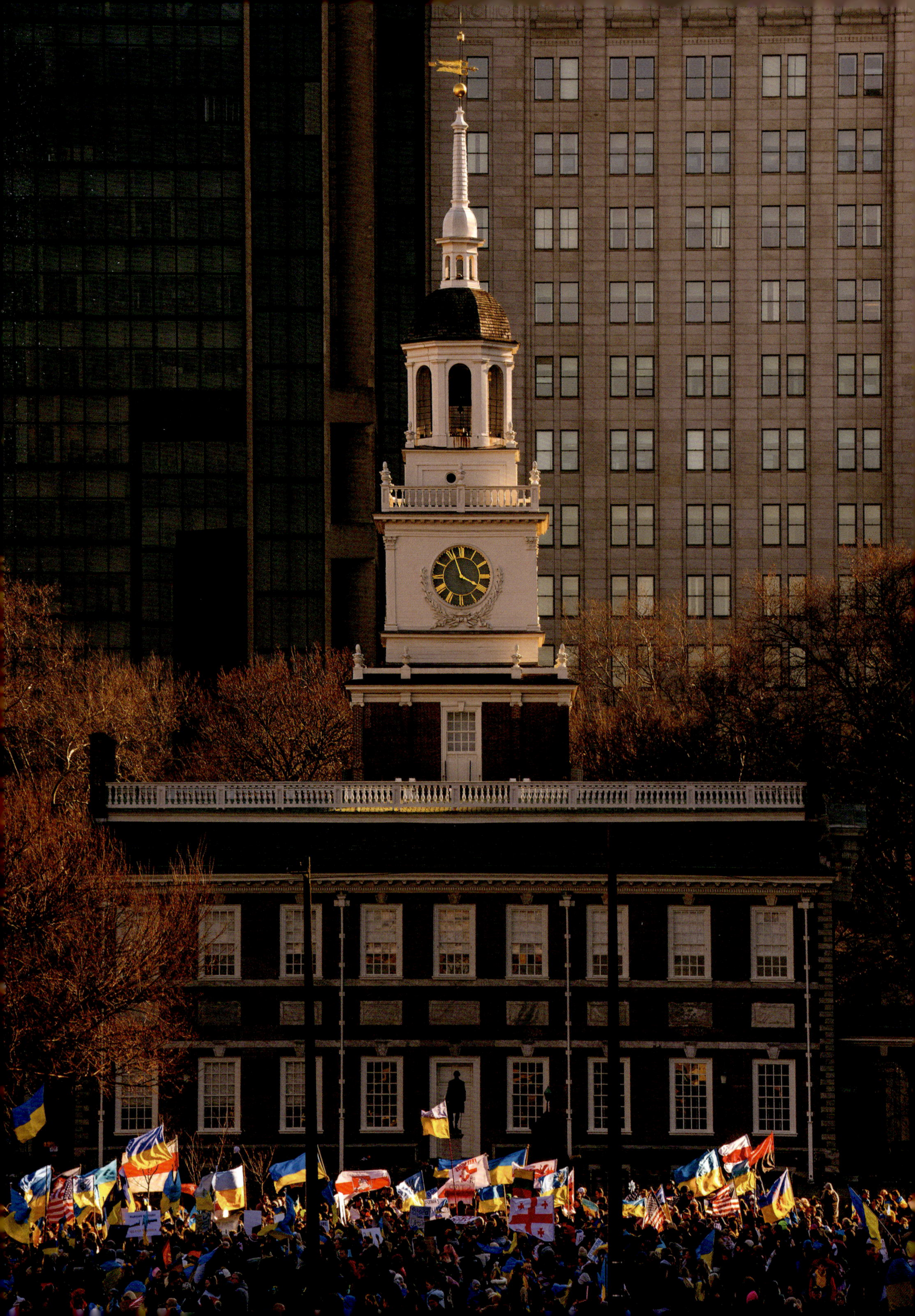

Birthplace of America ★ Philadelphia is known as the "Birthplace of America" due to its central role in the American Revolution and the founding of the United States. Modern Philadelphia was founded in 1682 by William Penn, an English Quaker who received a land grant from King Charles II as repayment for a debt owed to his father. Penn envisioned a "holy experiment" in religious freedom and fair governance, naming the city Philadelphia, meaning "City of Brotherly Love." ★ Penn designed the city using a grid pattern — one of the earliest in America — with wide streets and five central squares. This innovative plan focused on public space, order, and health. Philadelphia grew quickly into a major colonial city due to its strategic location for trade and shipping, religious and cultural tolerance, and its role as a center for government and education. ★ Located in the Old City neighborhood, Independence Hall is best known as the site where both the Declaration of Independence and the United States Constitution were debated and adopted. Designed in Georgian style and originally built as the Pennsylvania State House, Independence Hall initially housed the colonial government of Pennsylvania. Serving as a central meeting place for revolutionaries during the American Revolution, the Declaration of Independence was adopted in the Hall's Assembly Room on July 4, 1776. In 1787, the Constitutional Convention was held in Independence Hall. The U.S. Constitution was debated, drafted, and signed in the same Assembly Room. Designated as a UNESCO World Heritage Site in 1979, Independence Hall attracts millions of visitors each year and remains a symbol of freedom and democracy.

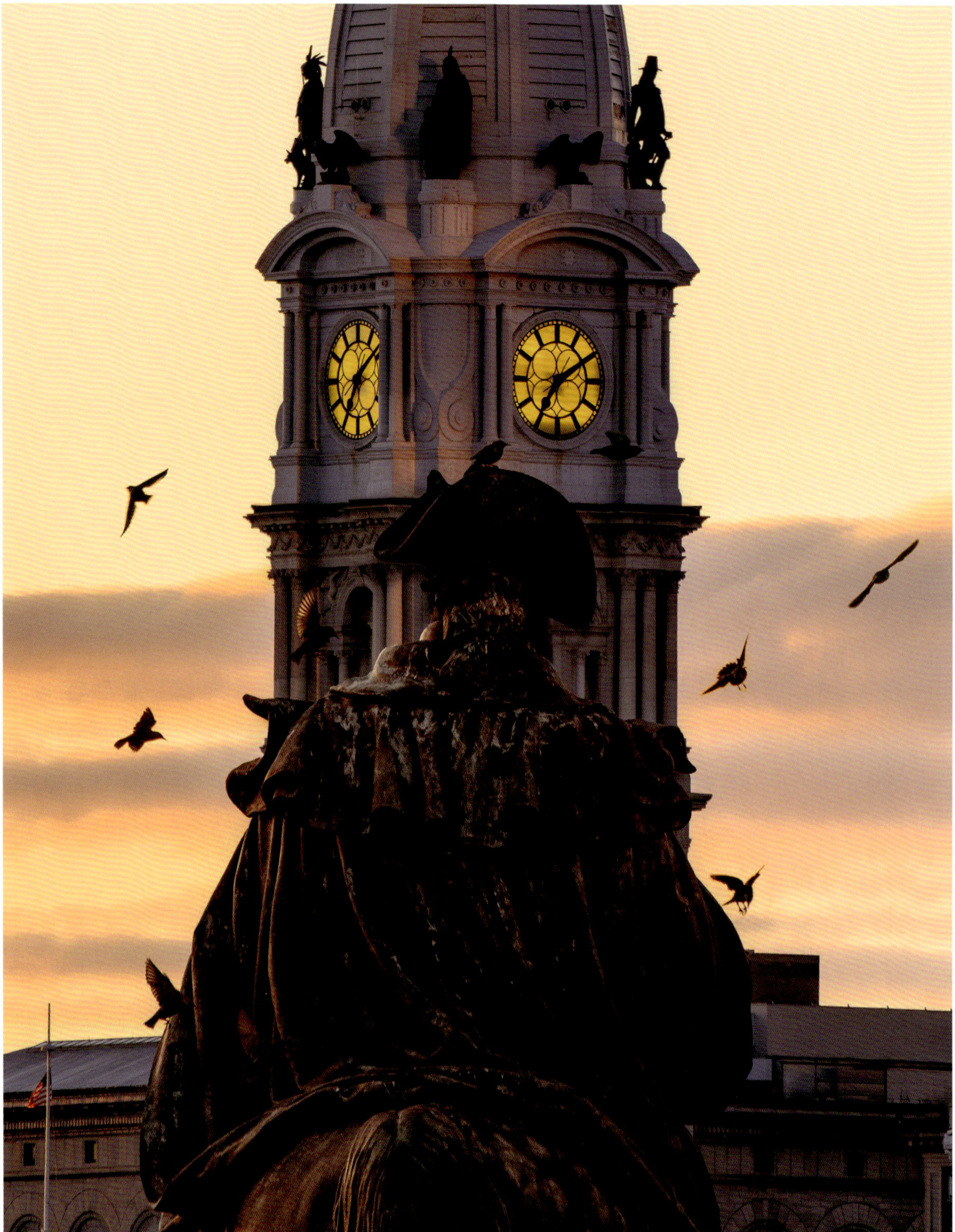

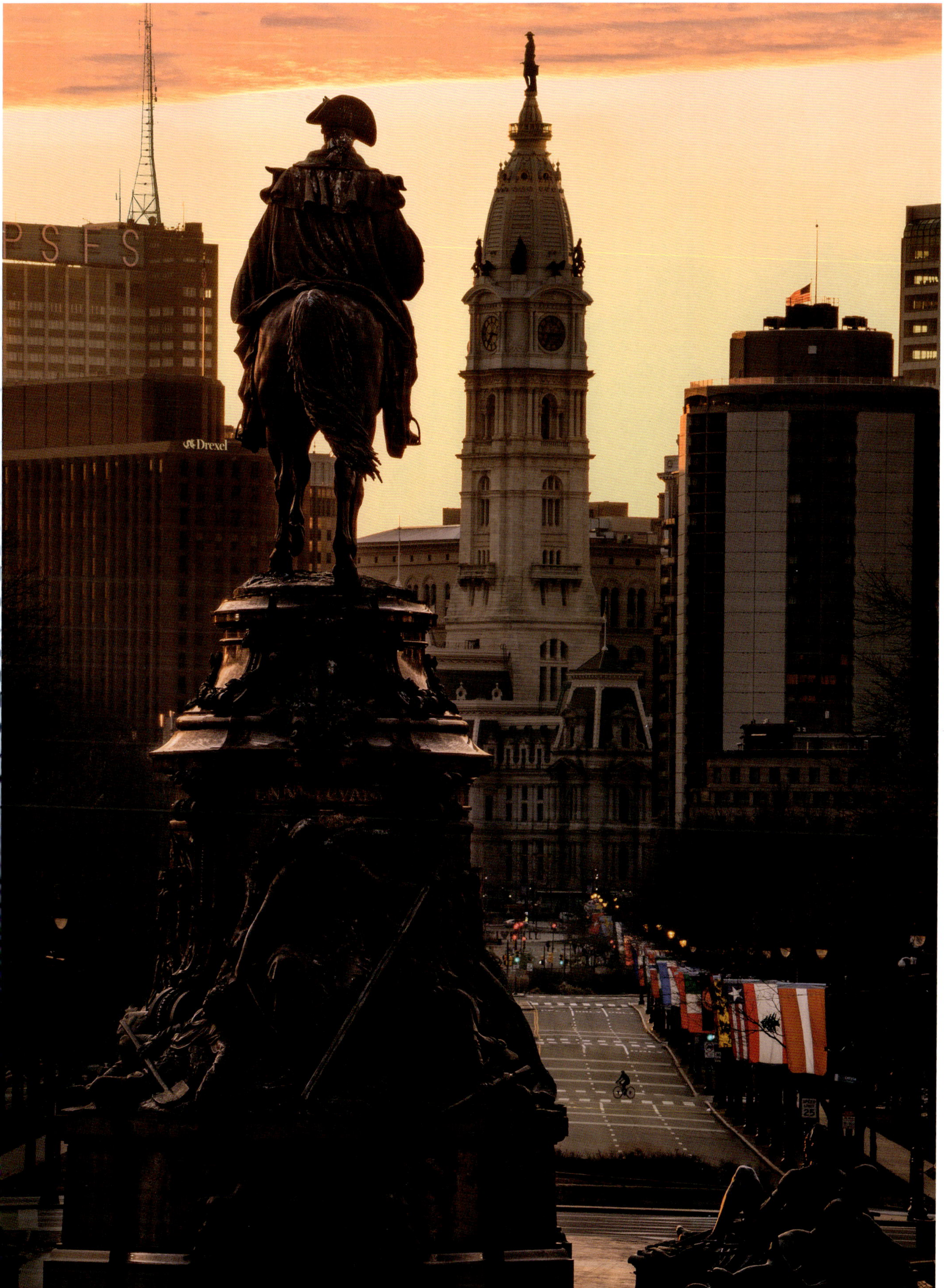
PSFS
Drexel

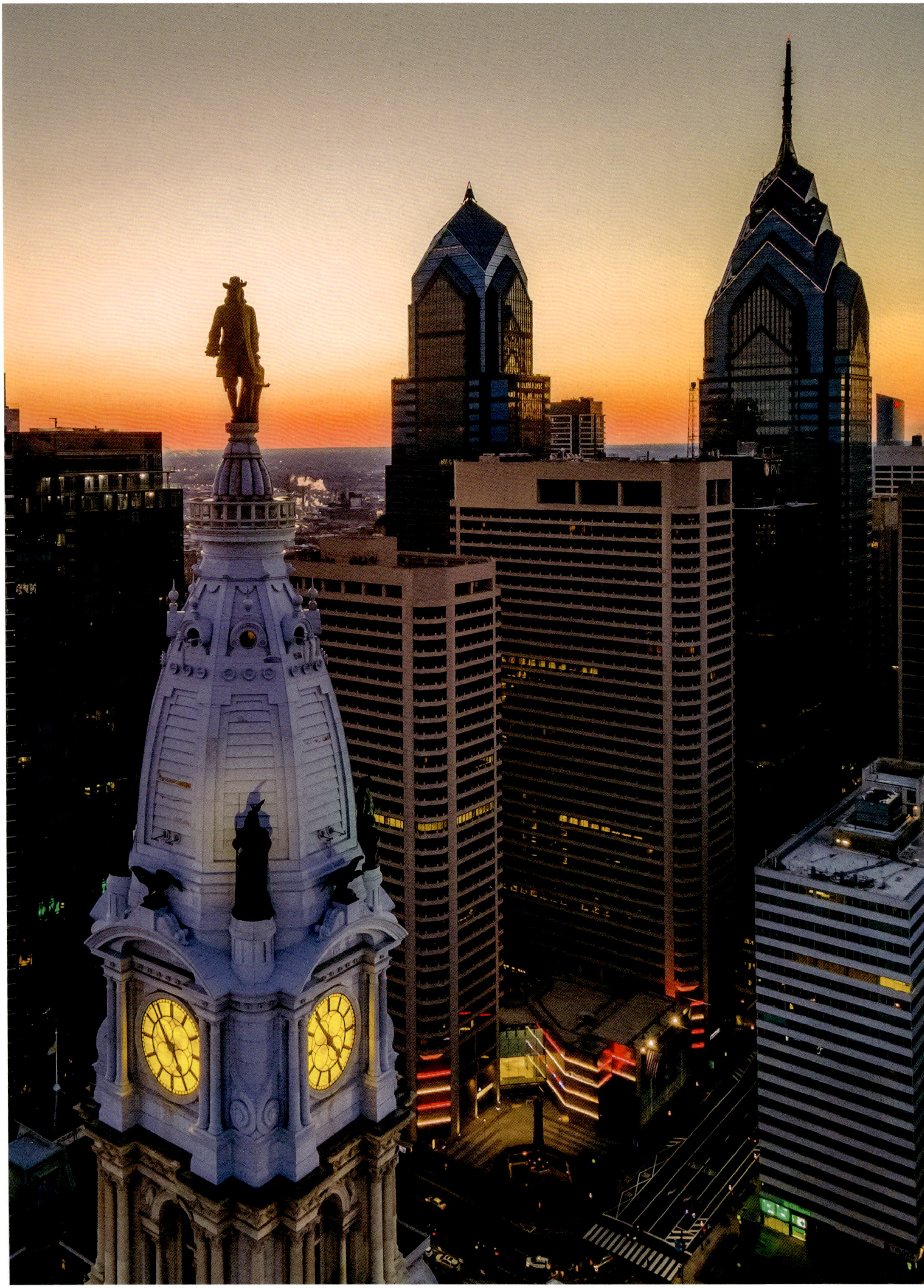

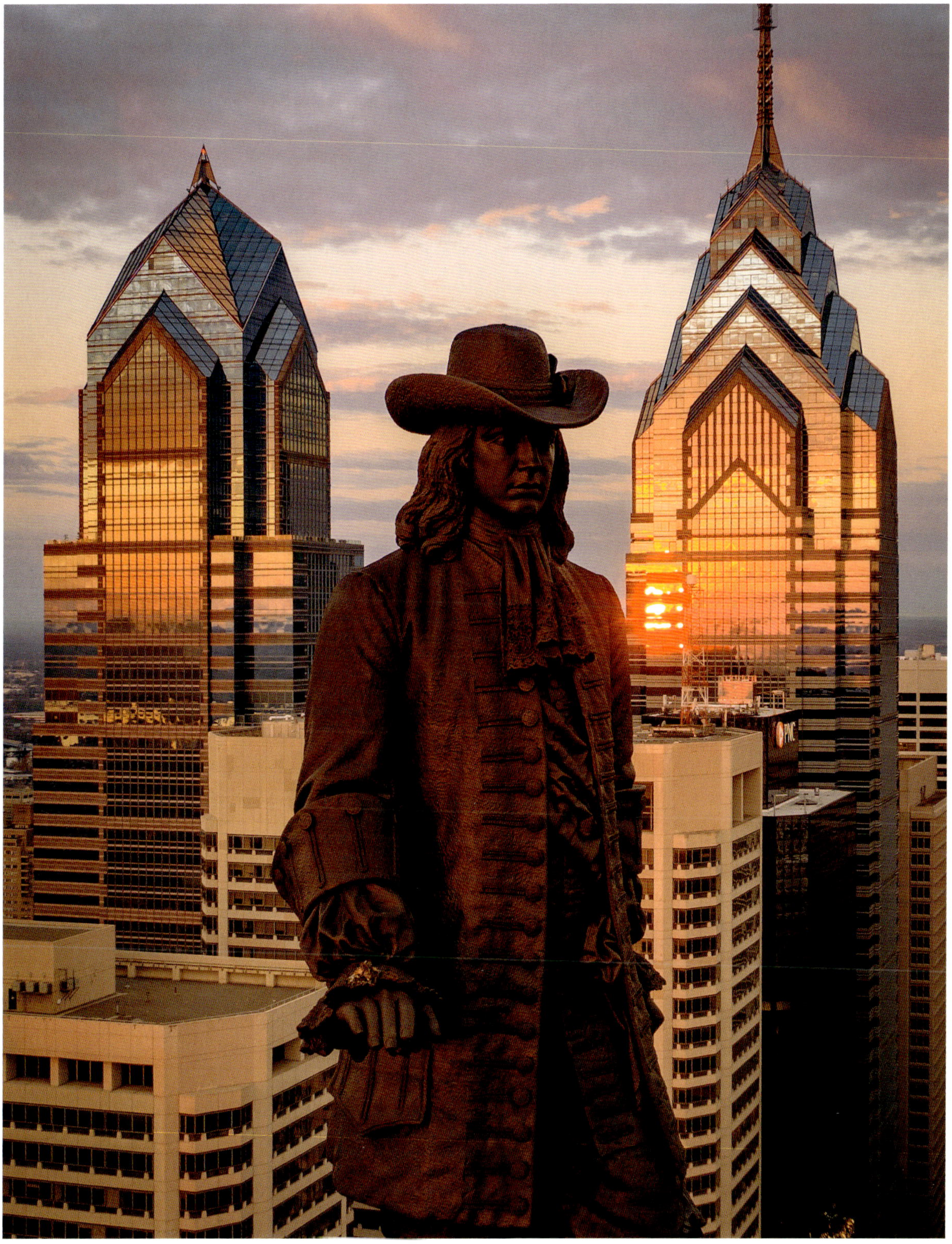
PNC

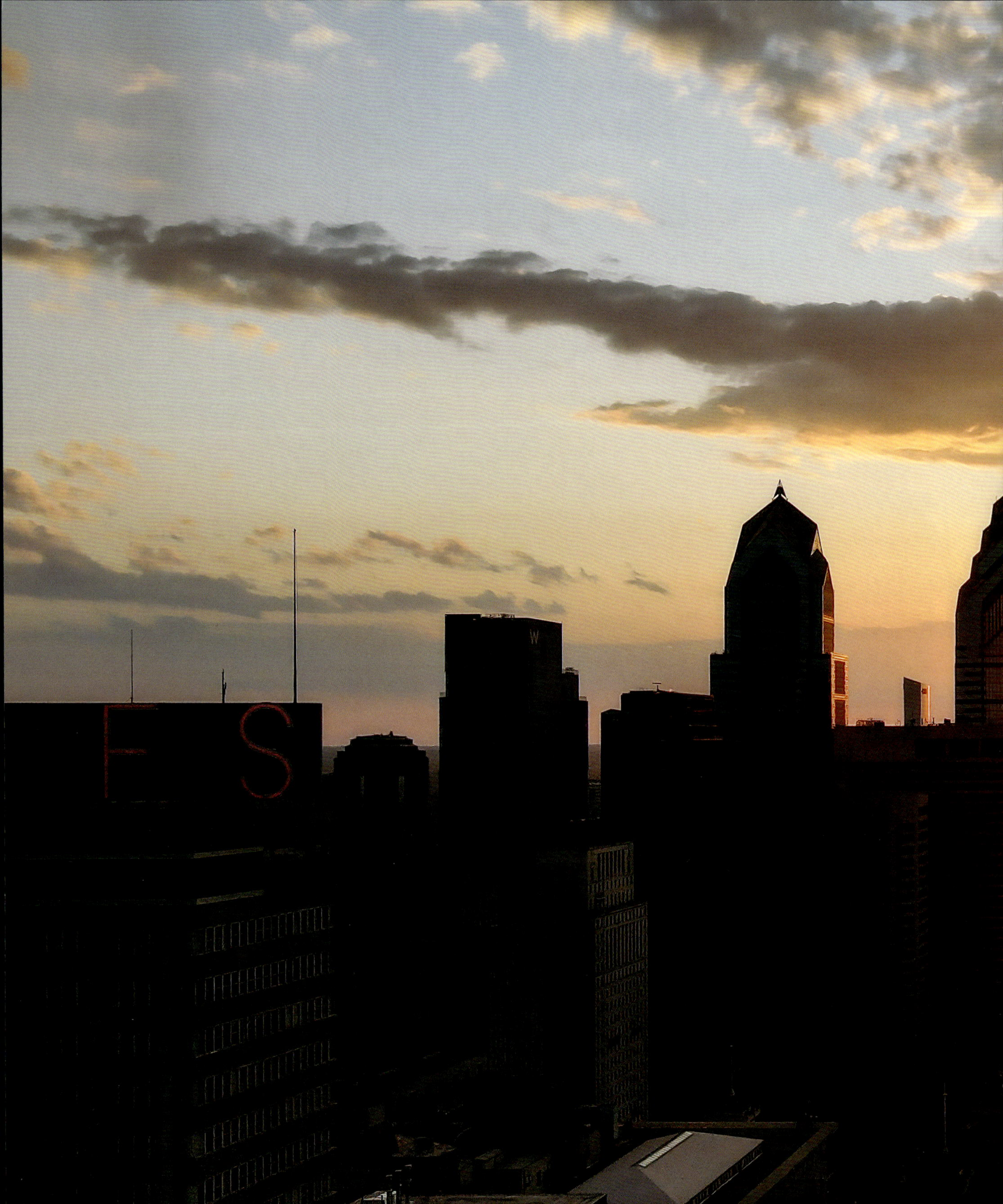

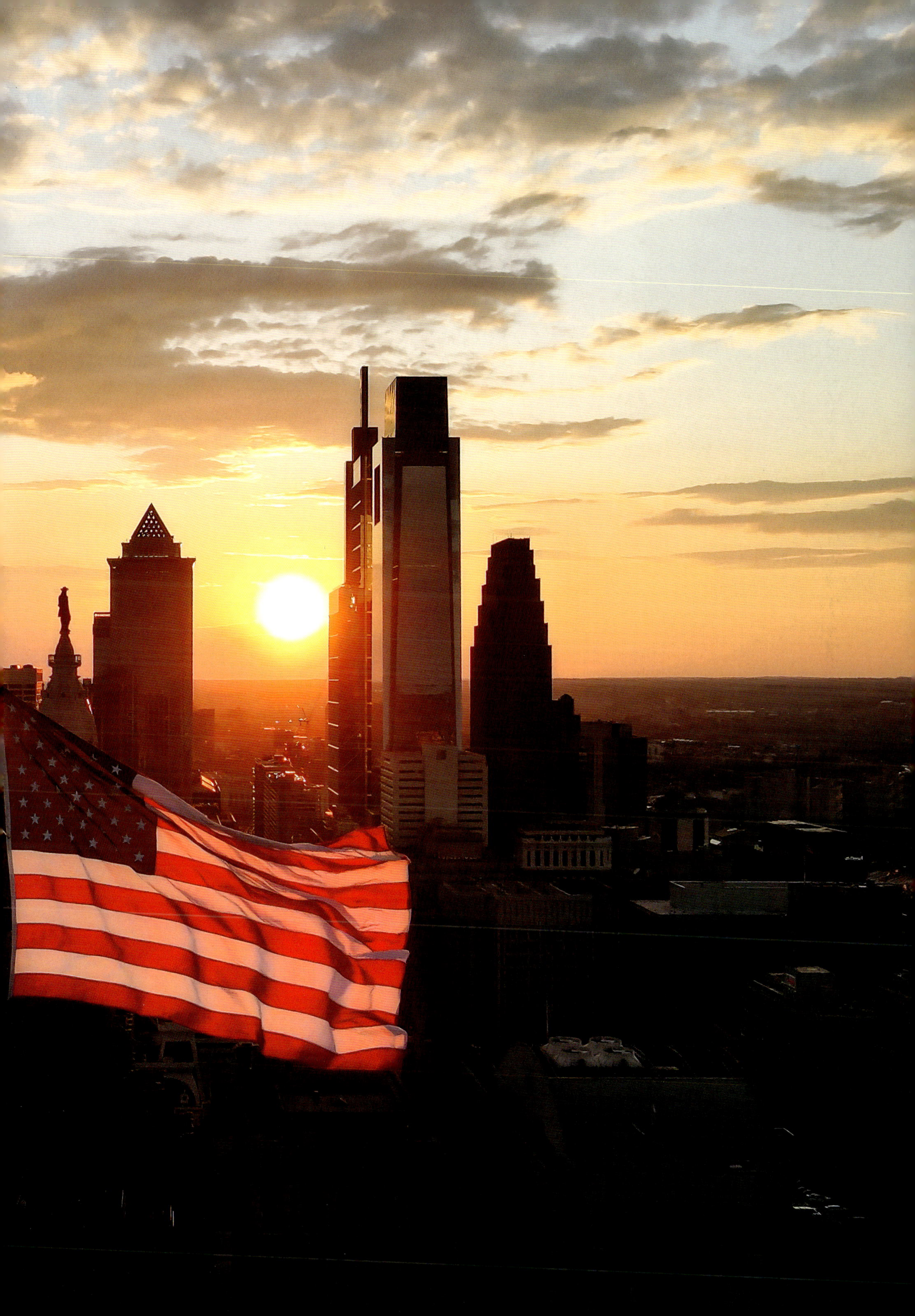

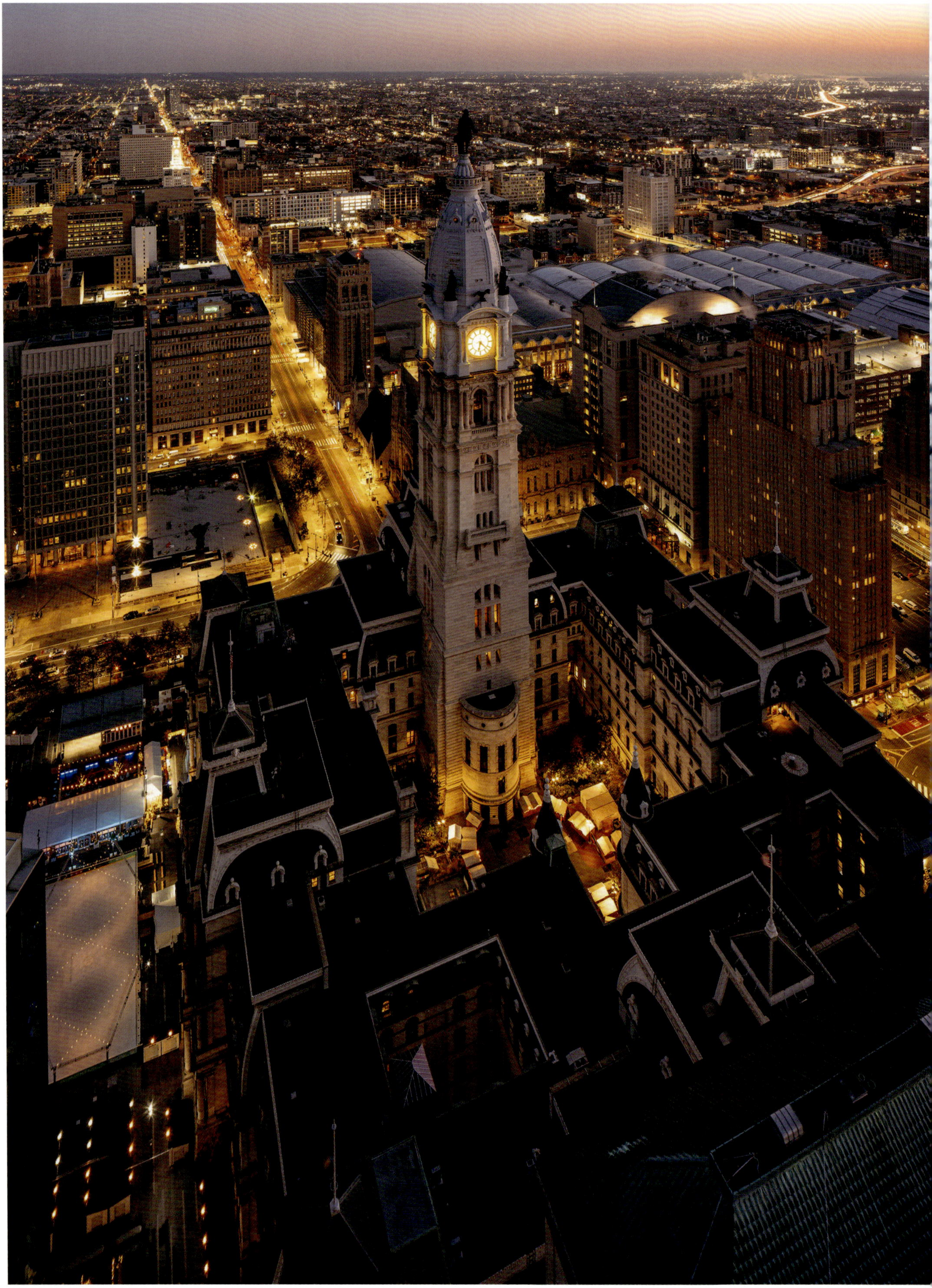

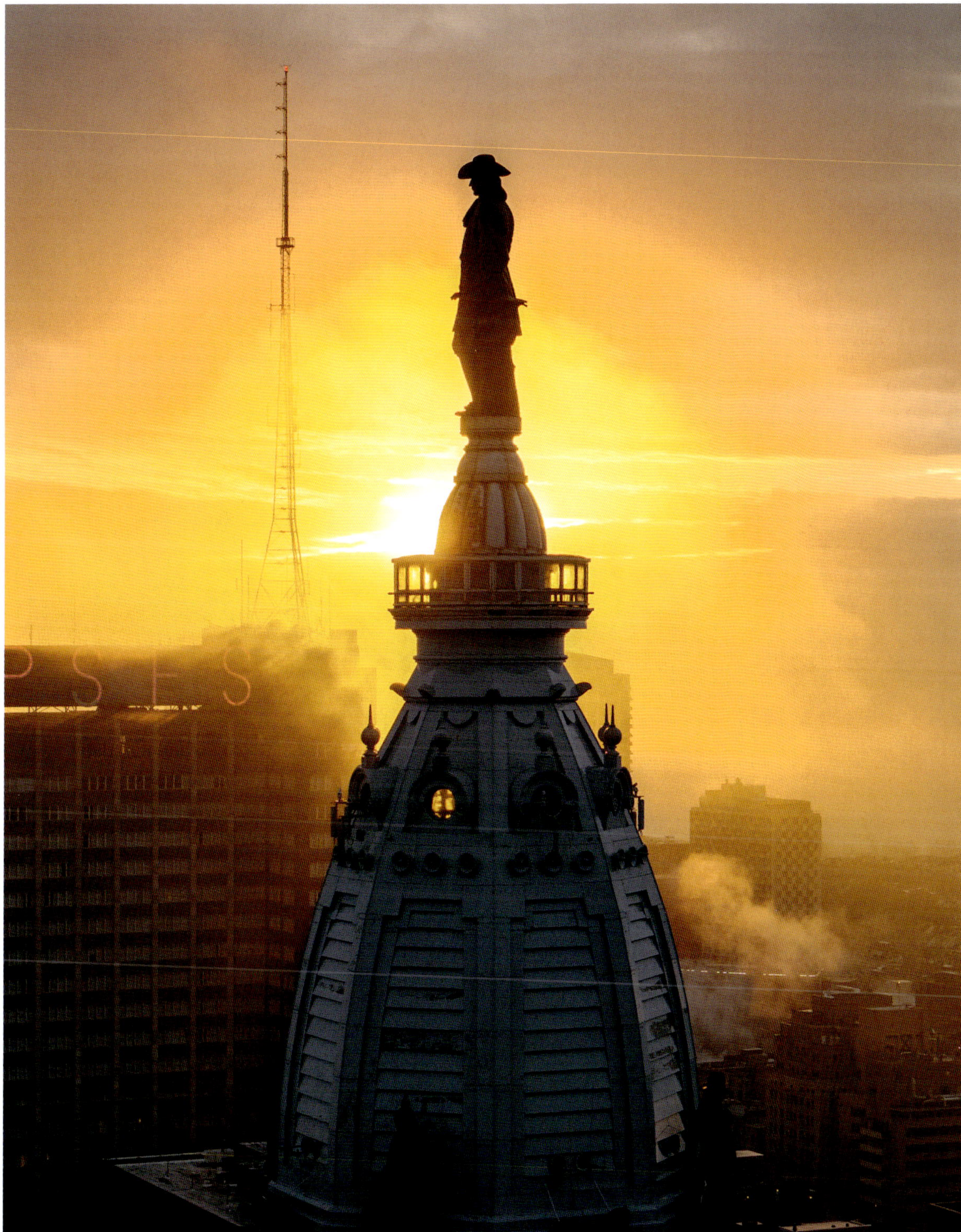

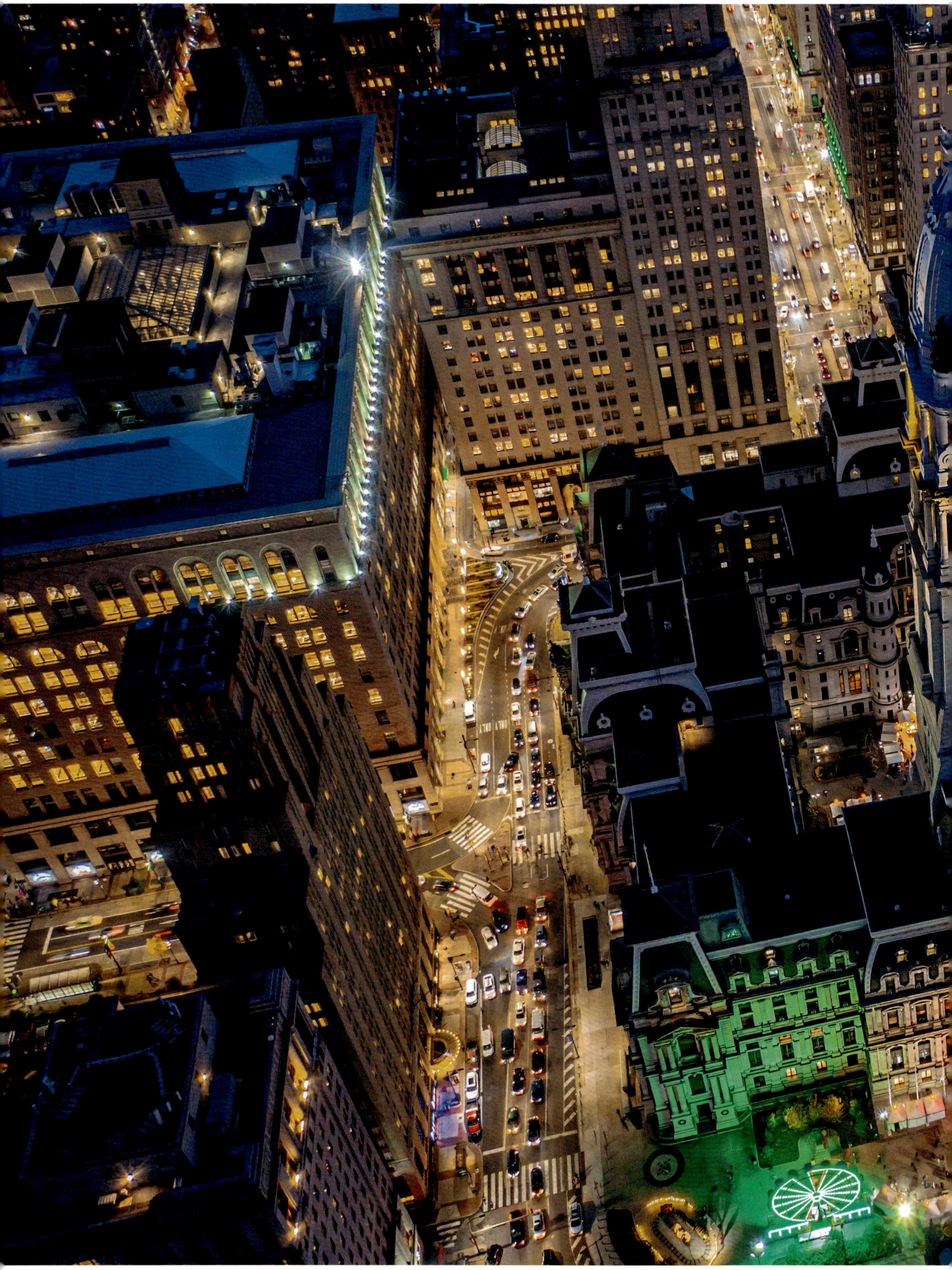

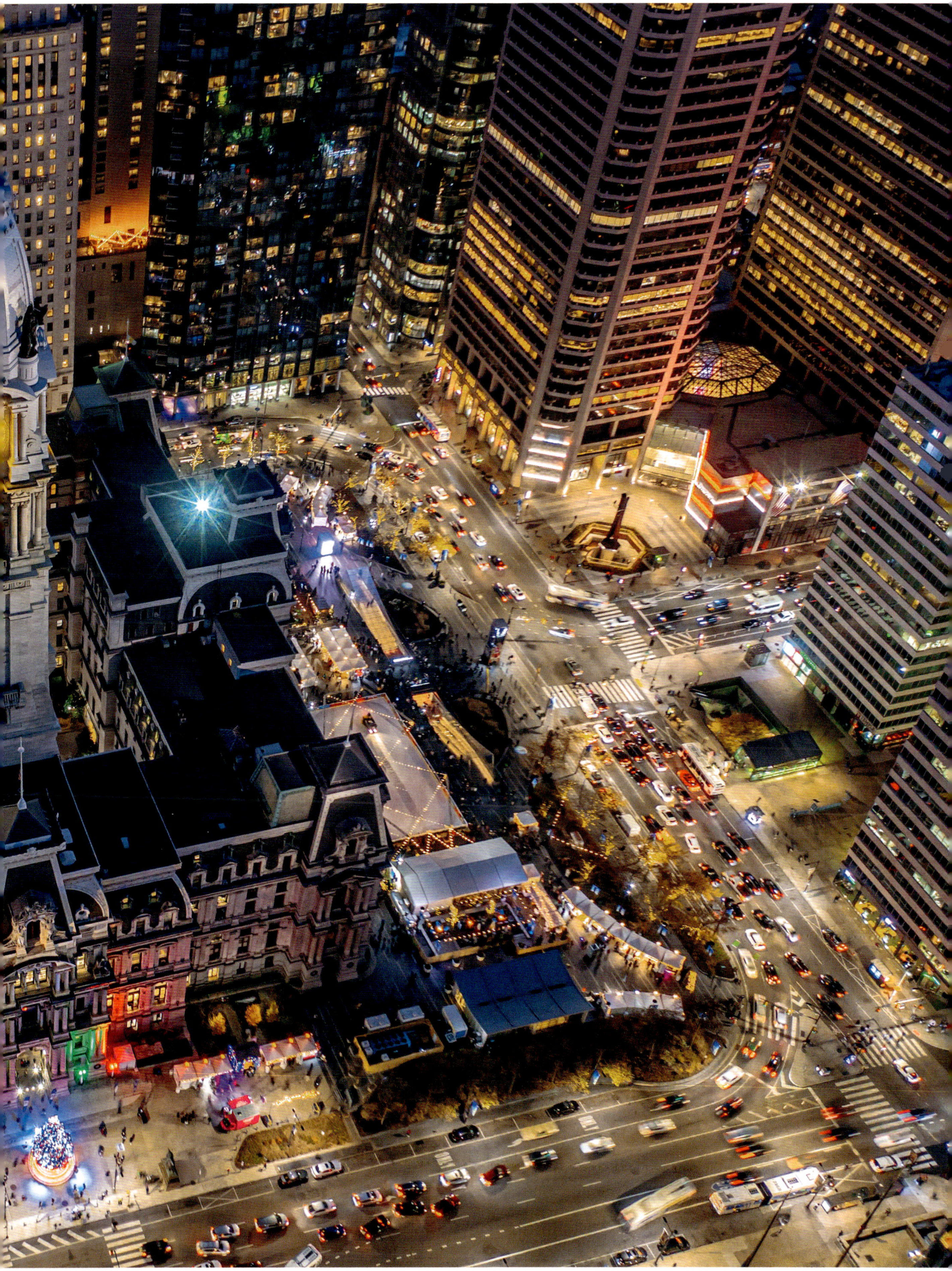

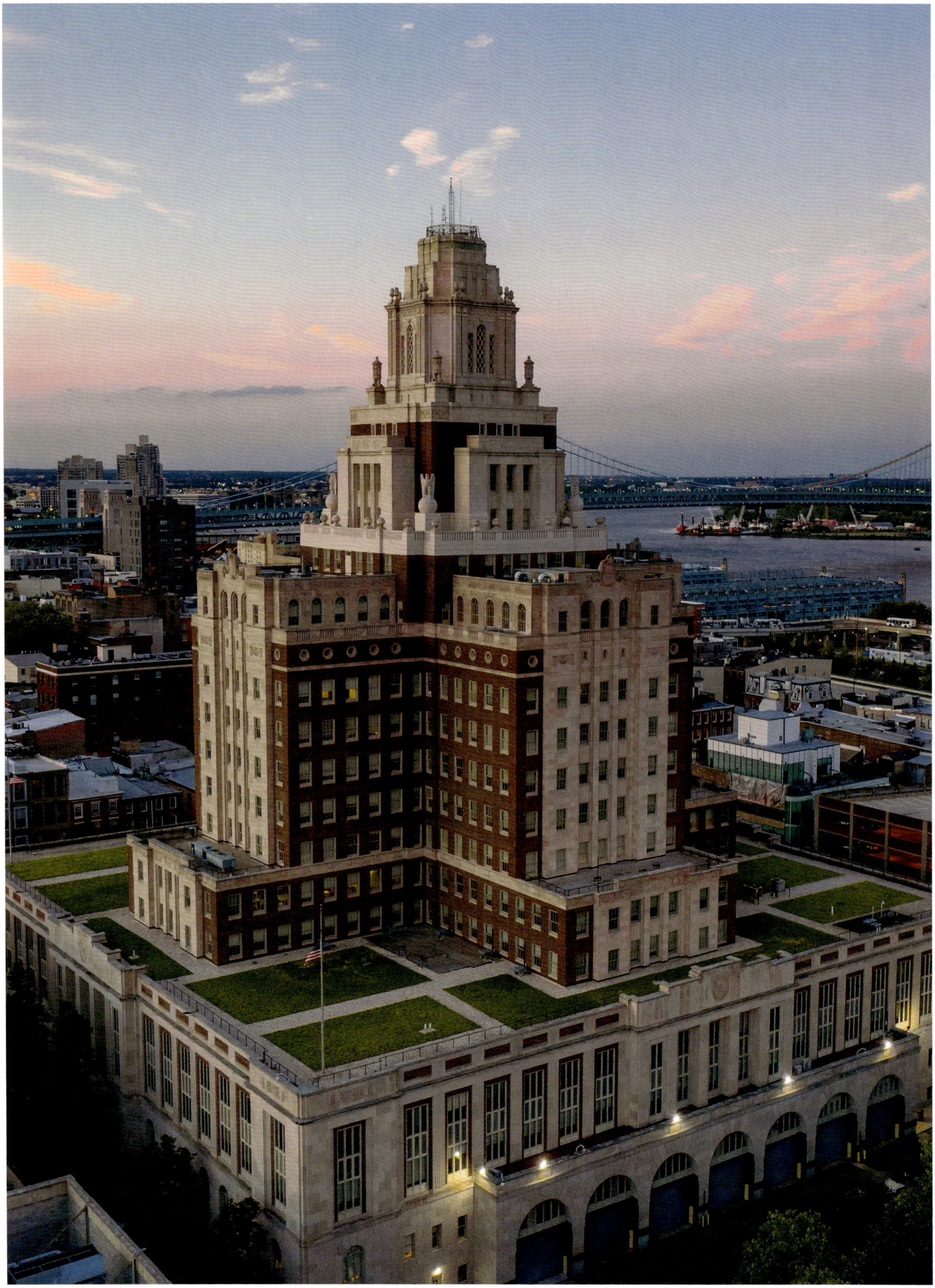

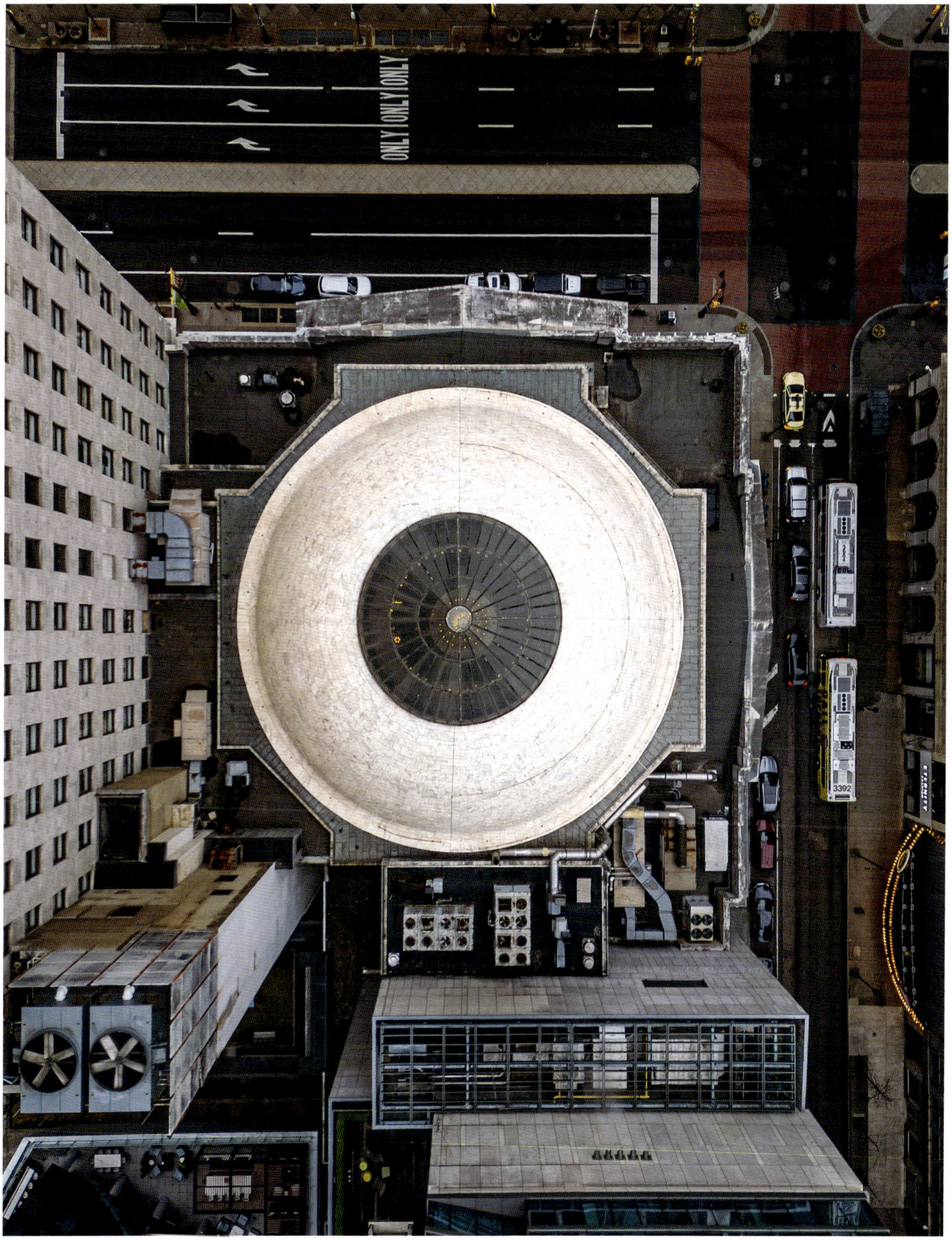
ONLY ONLY ONLY
3392

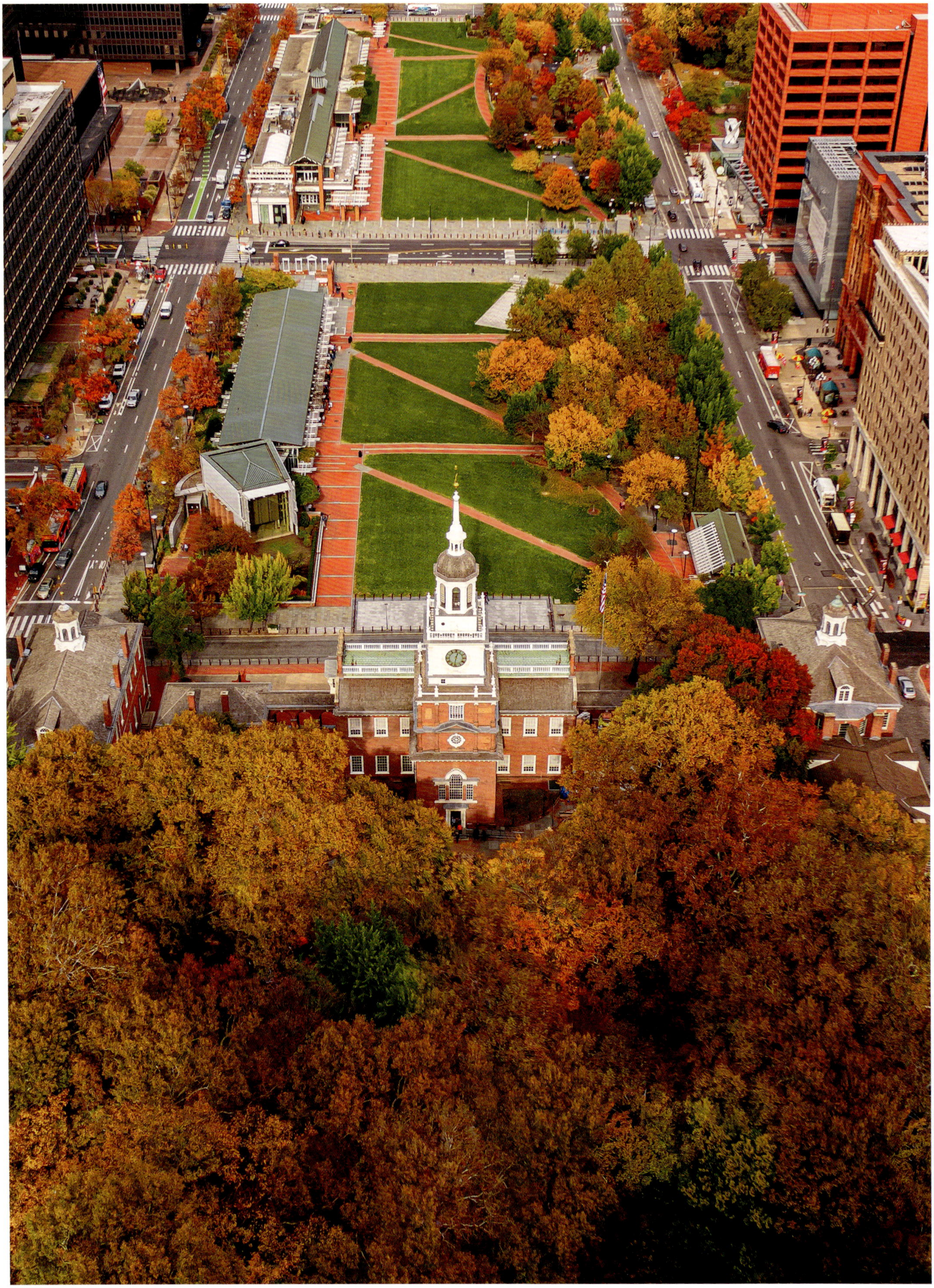

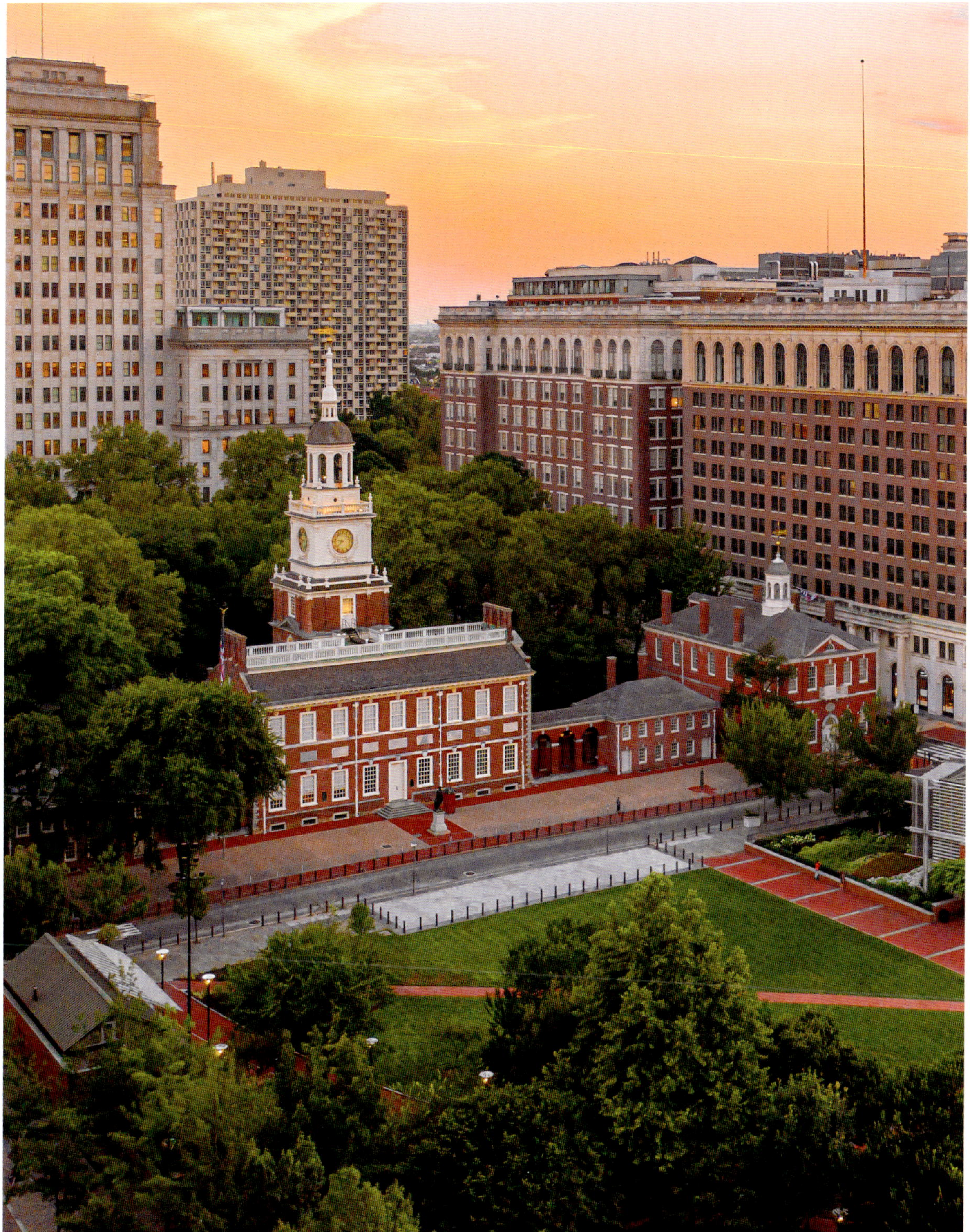

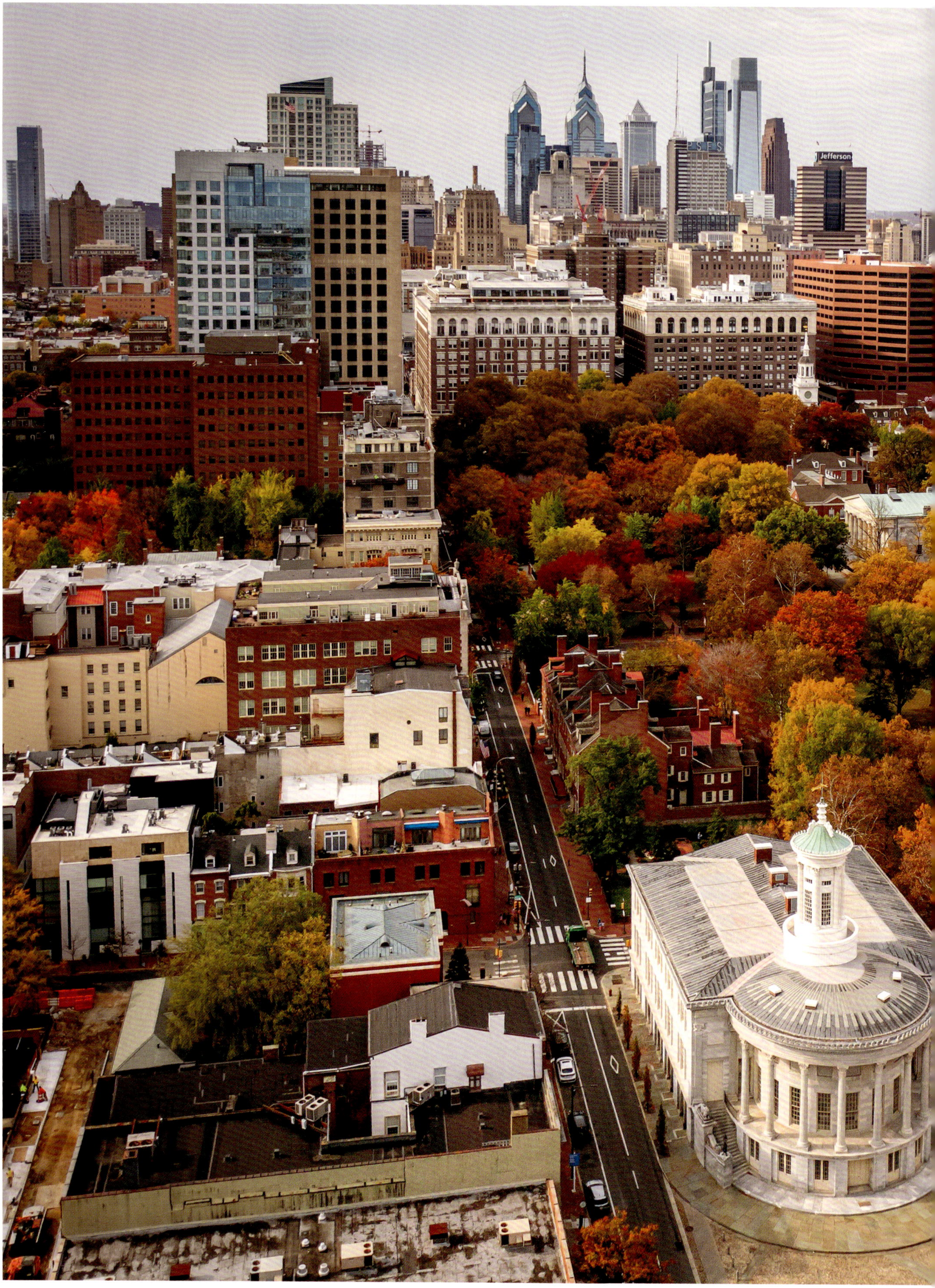

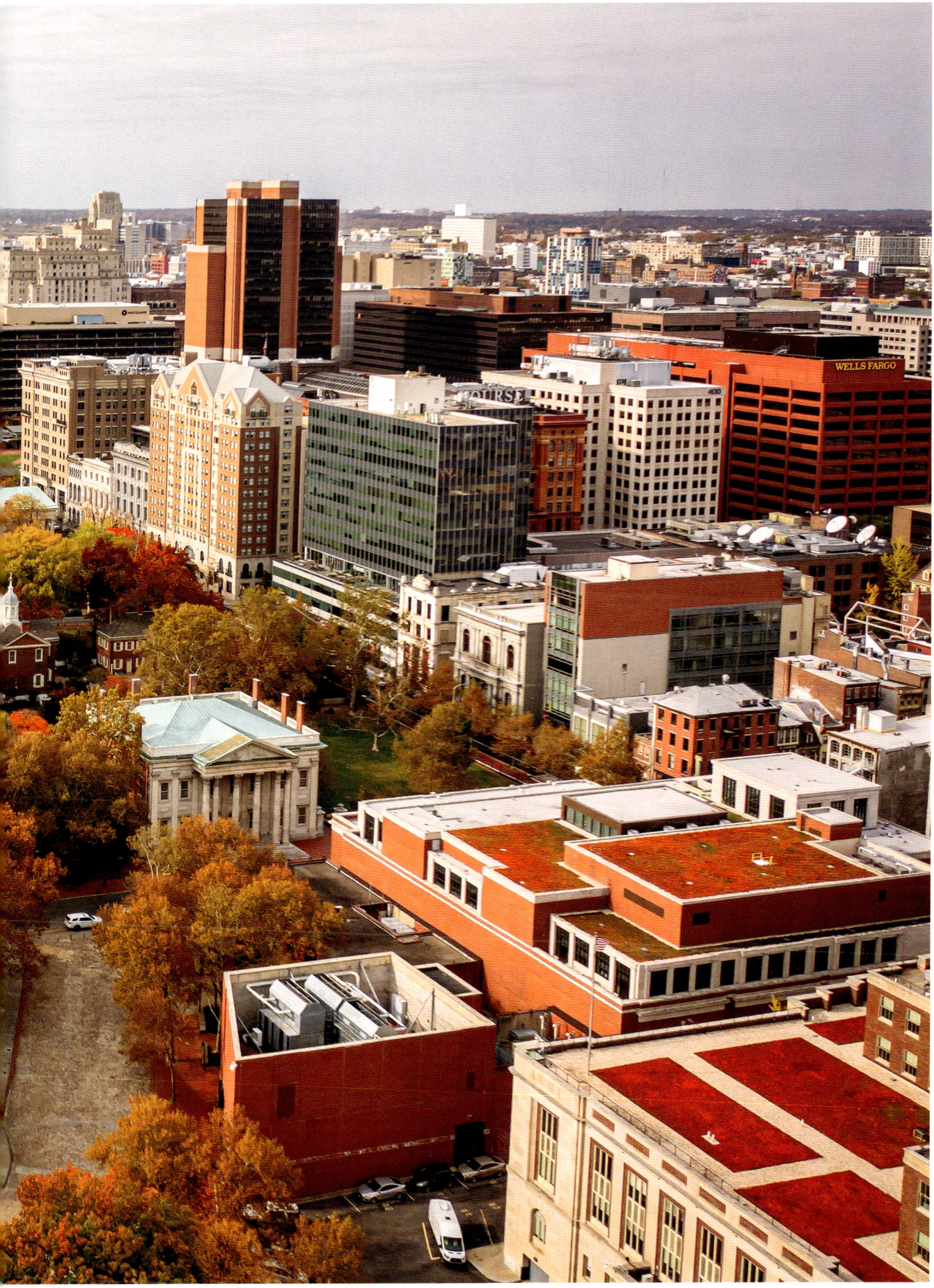
WELLS FARGO

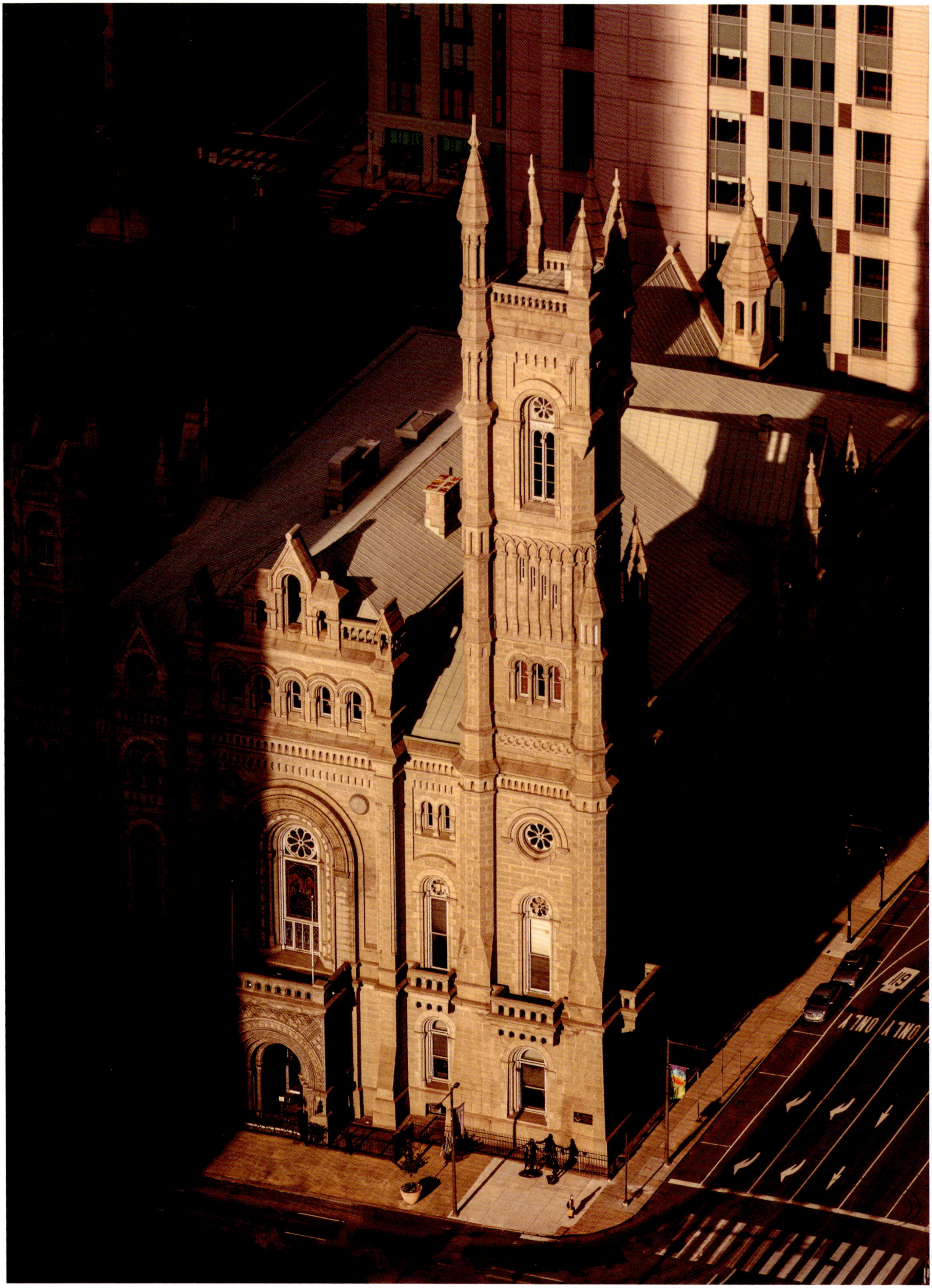

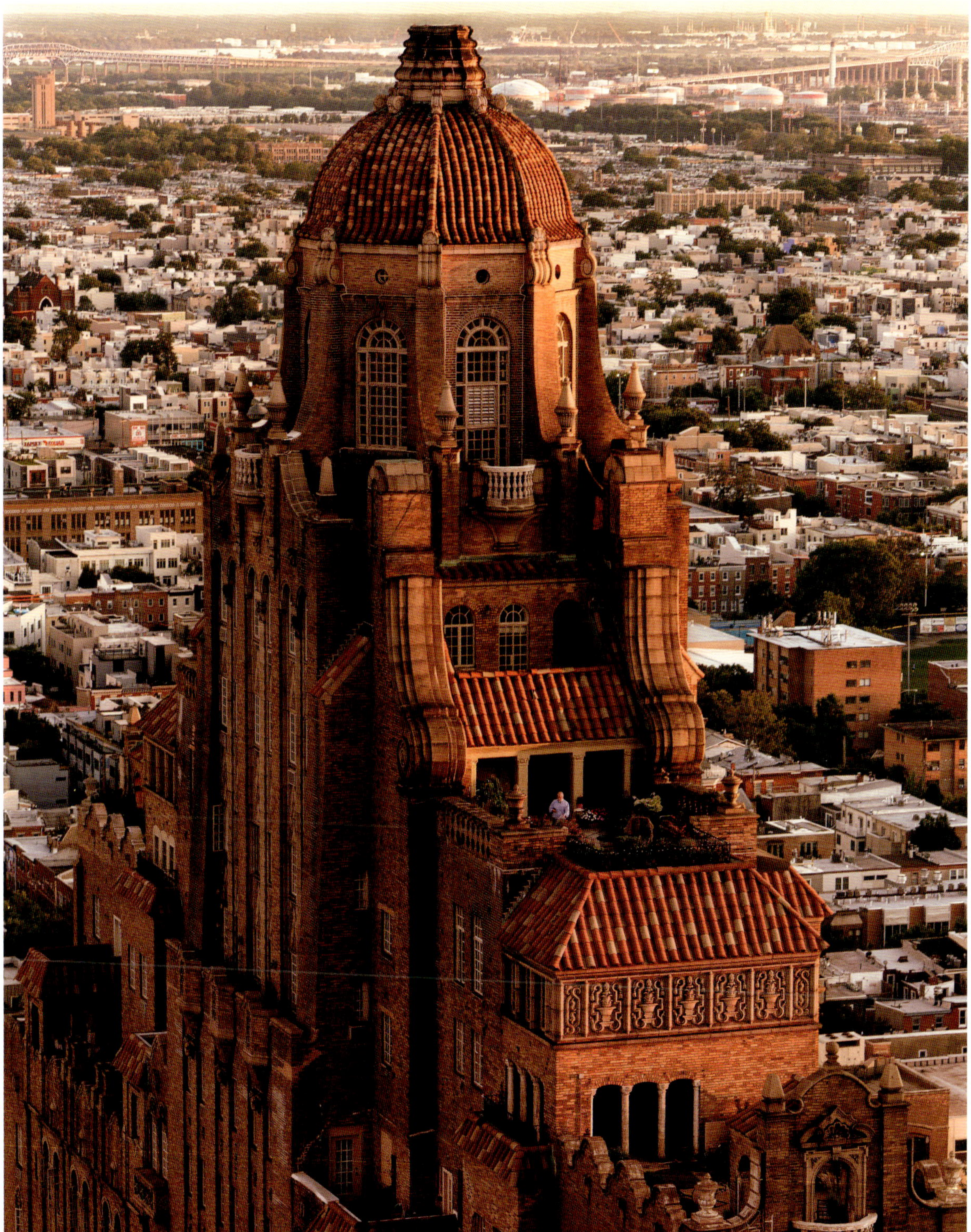

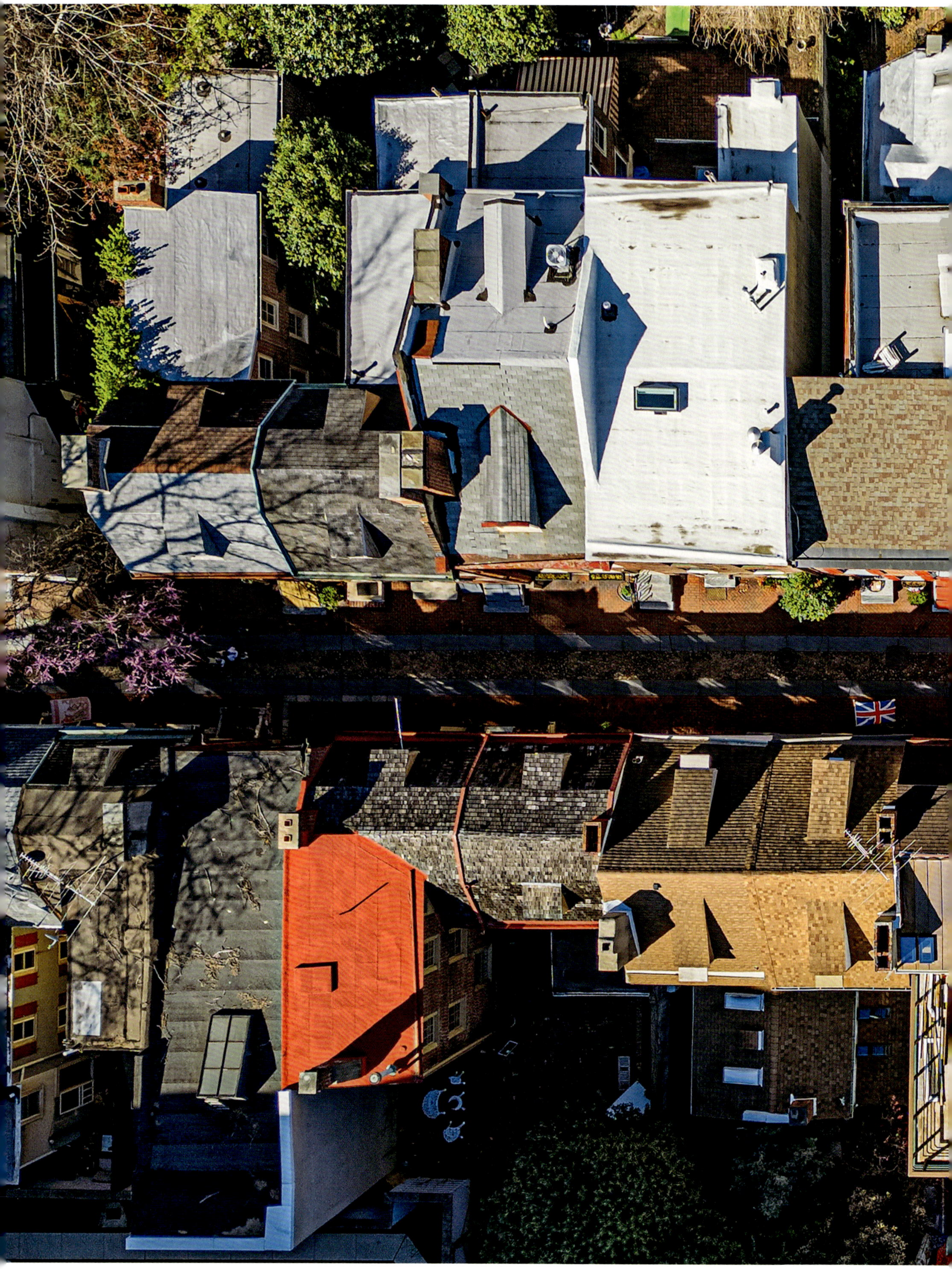

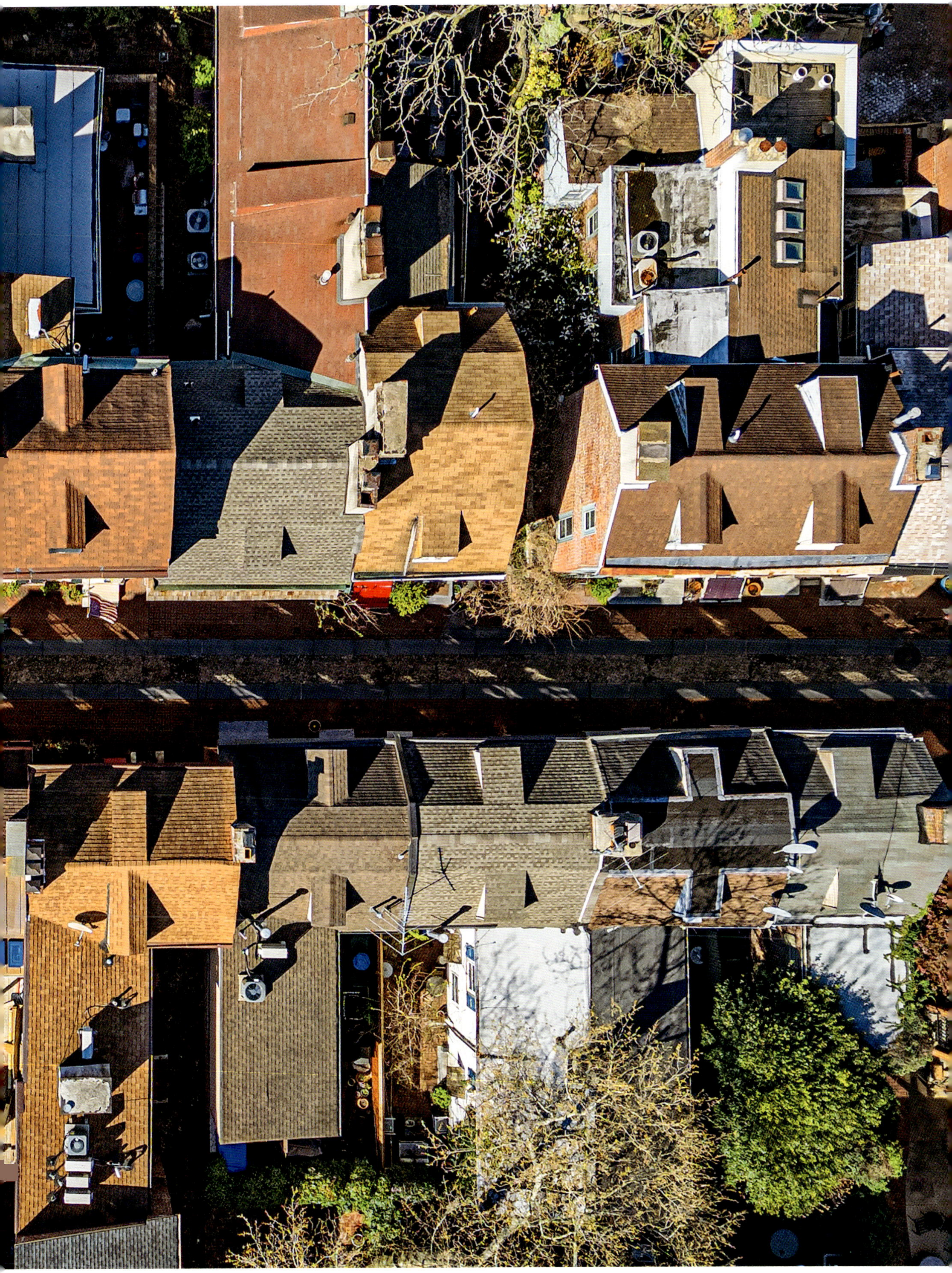

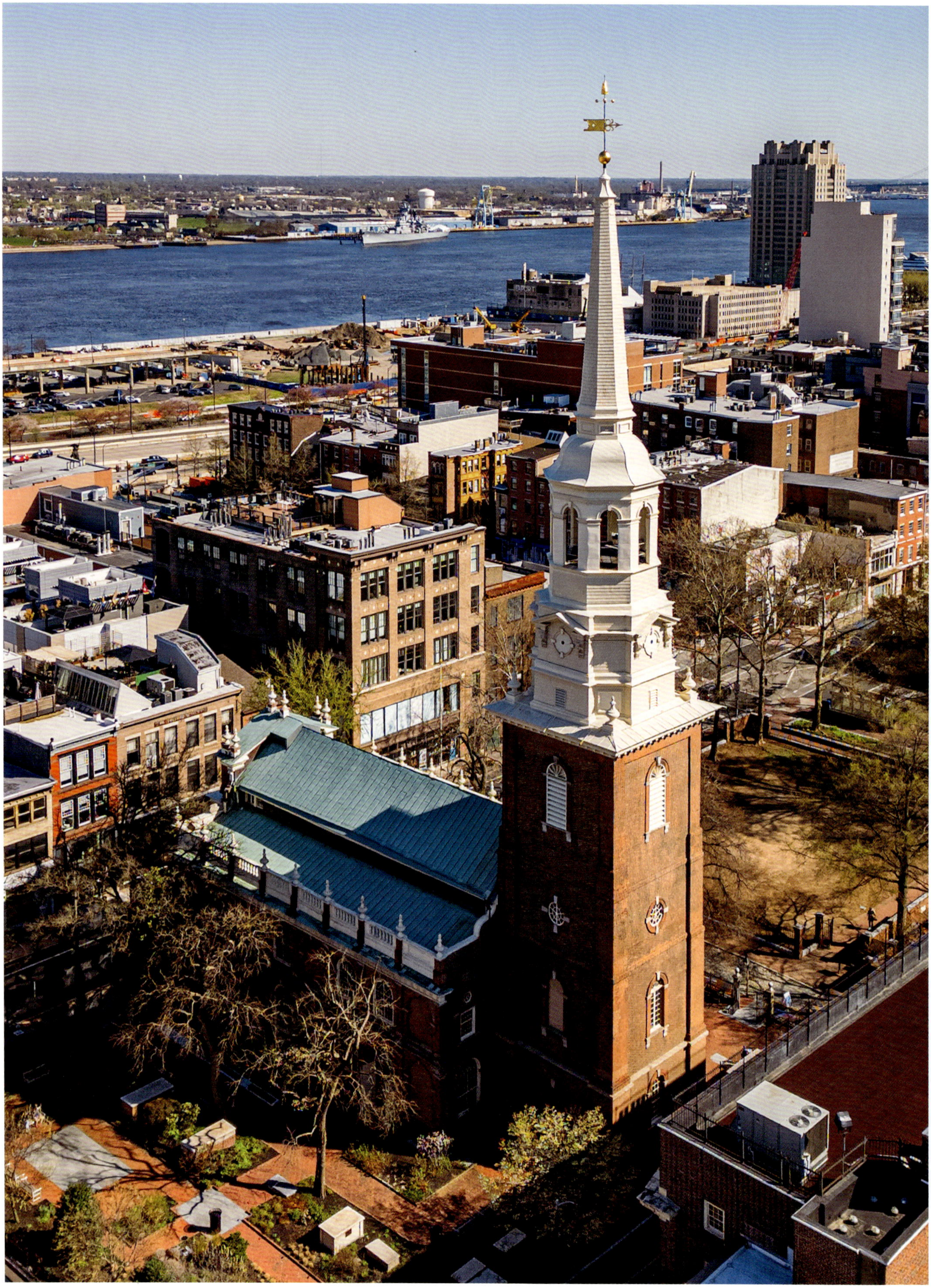

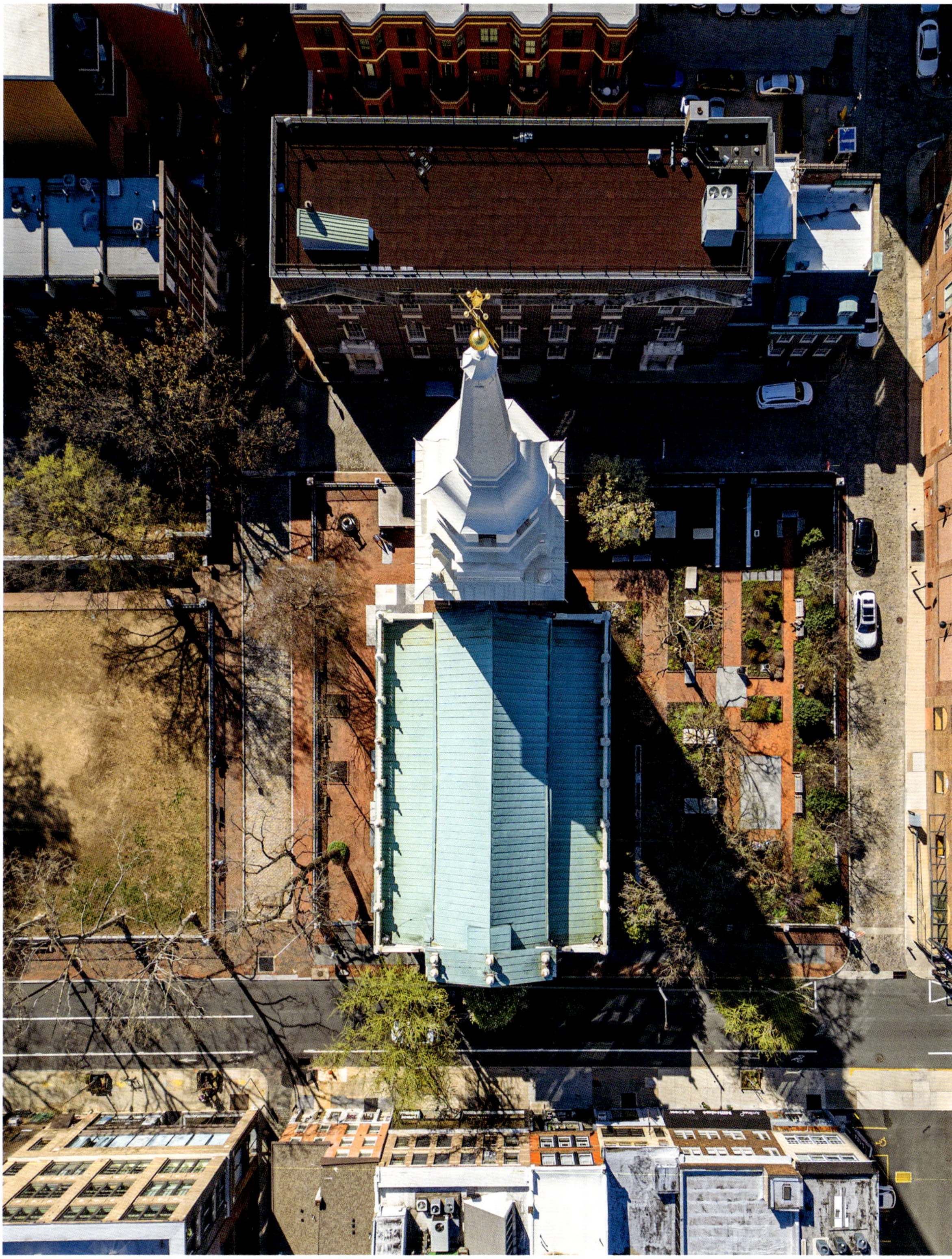

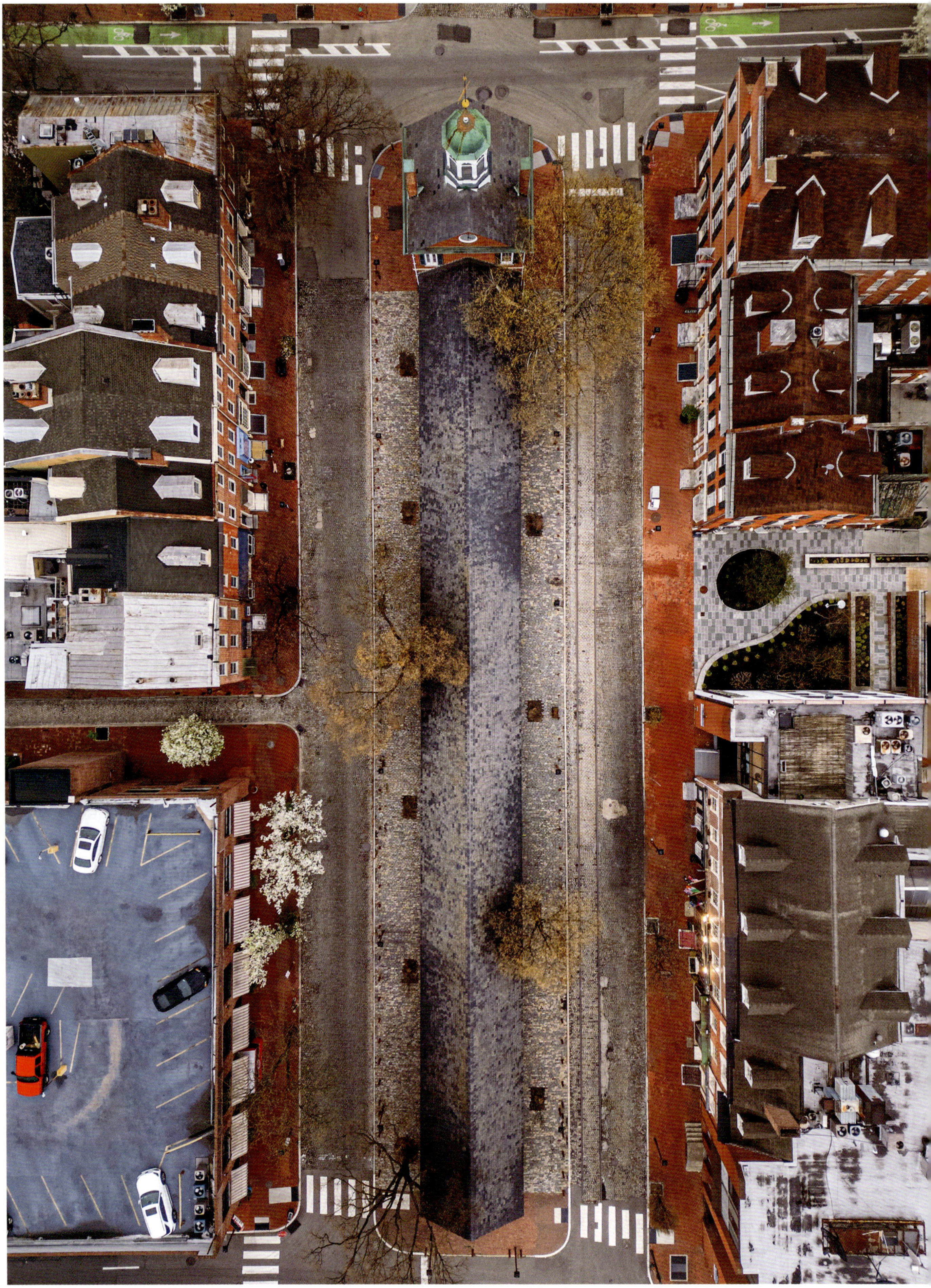

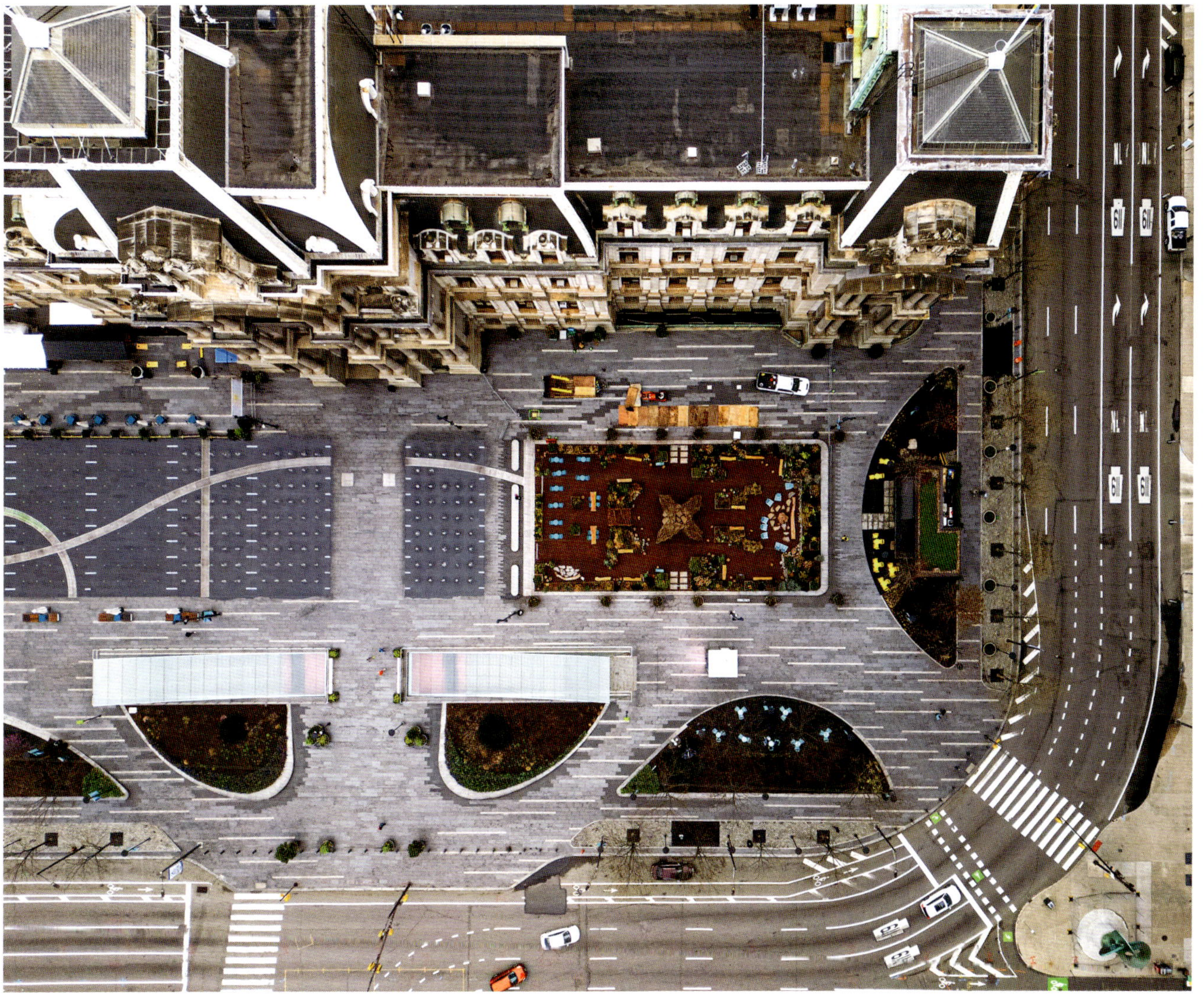

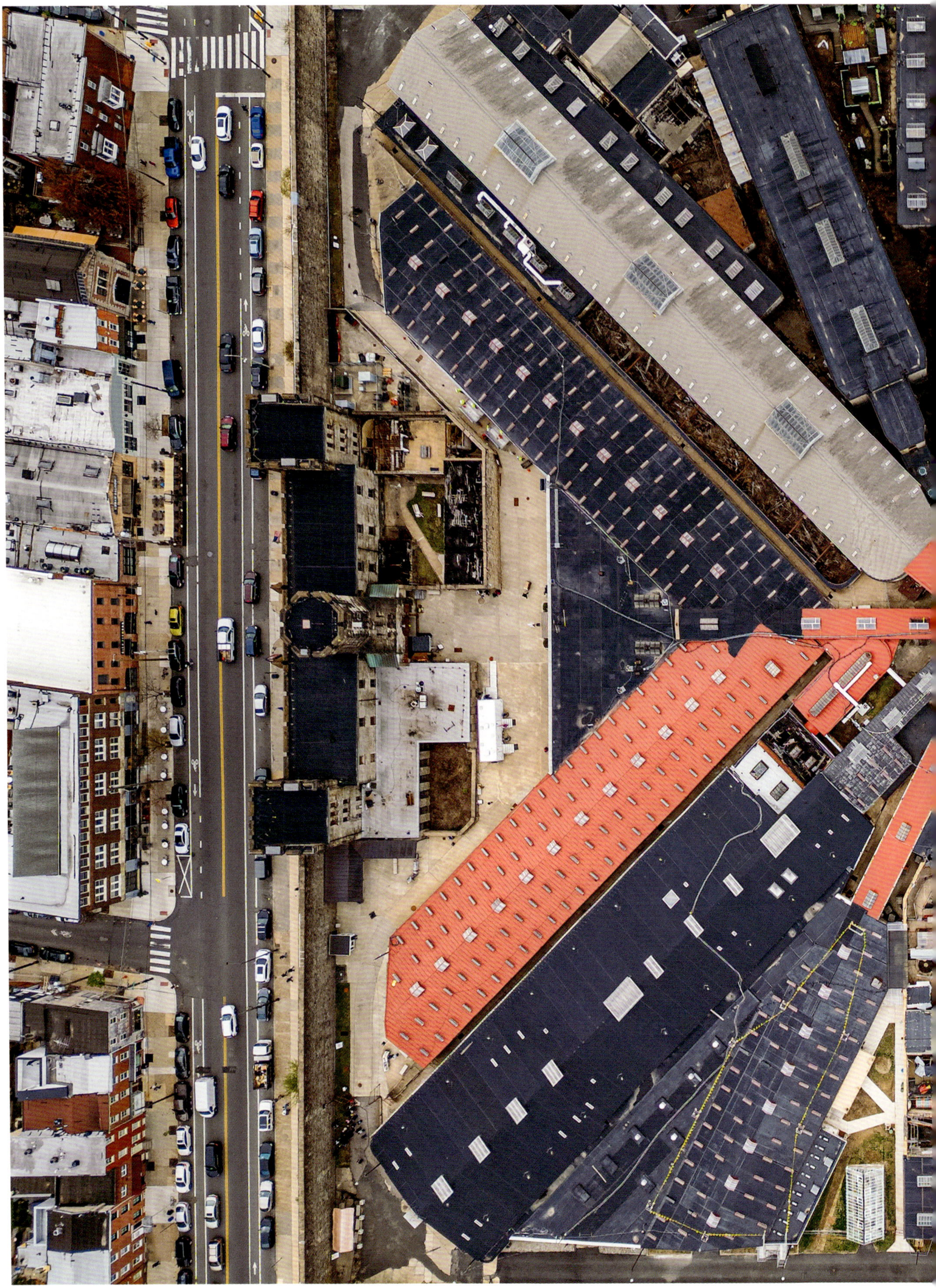

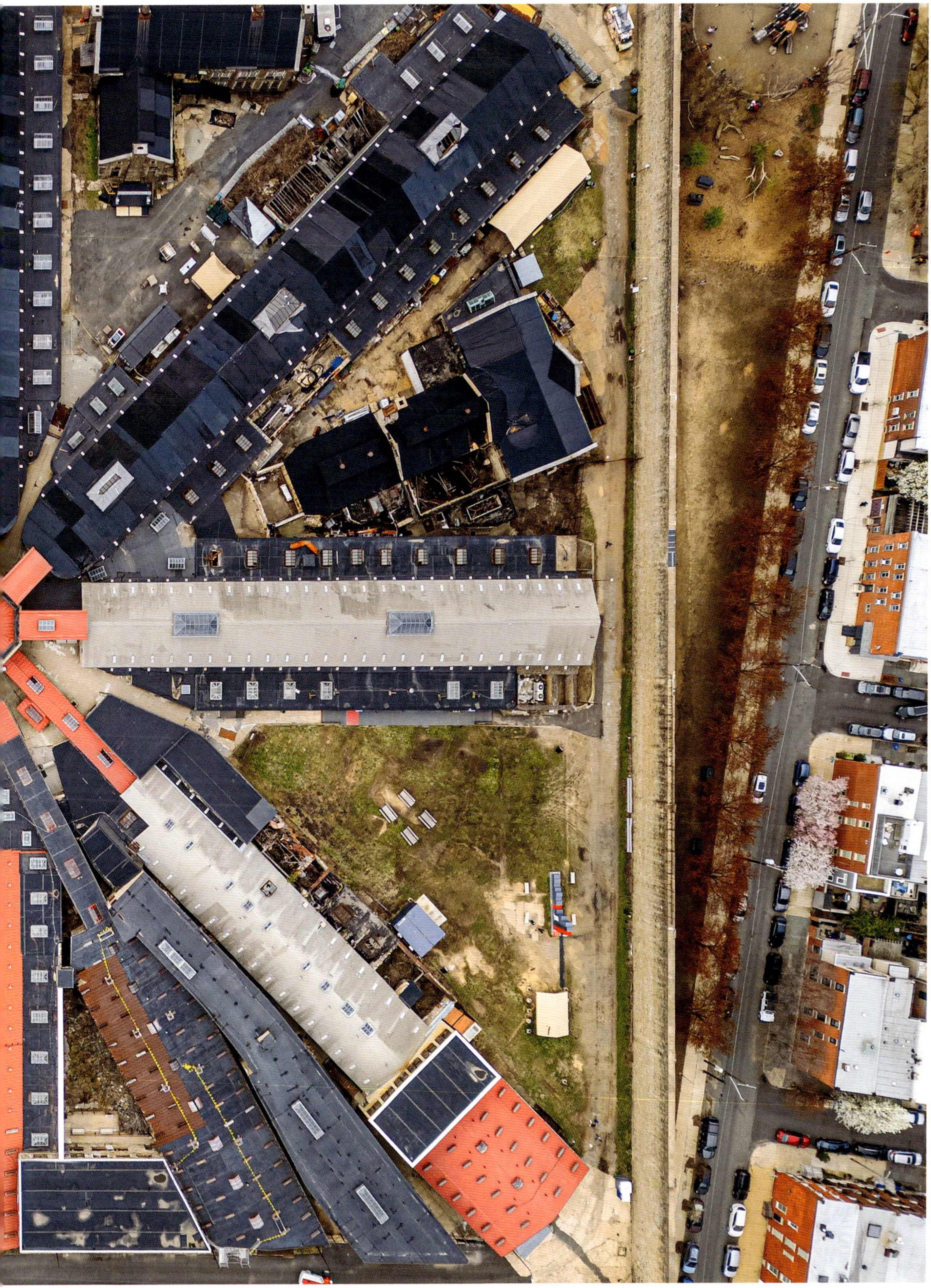

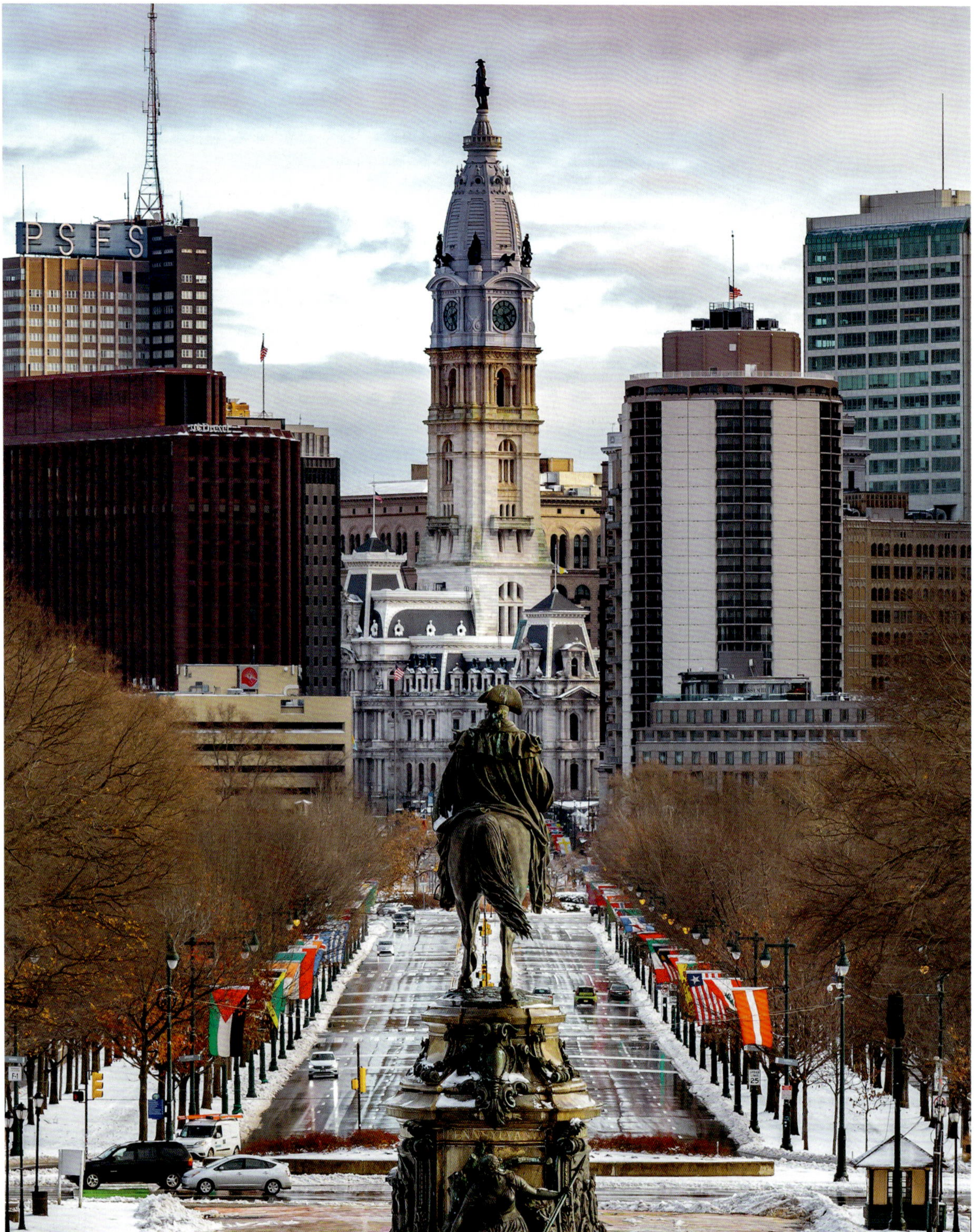
PSFS

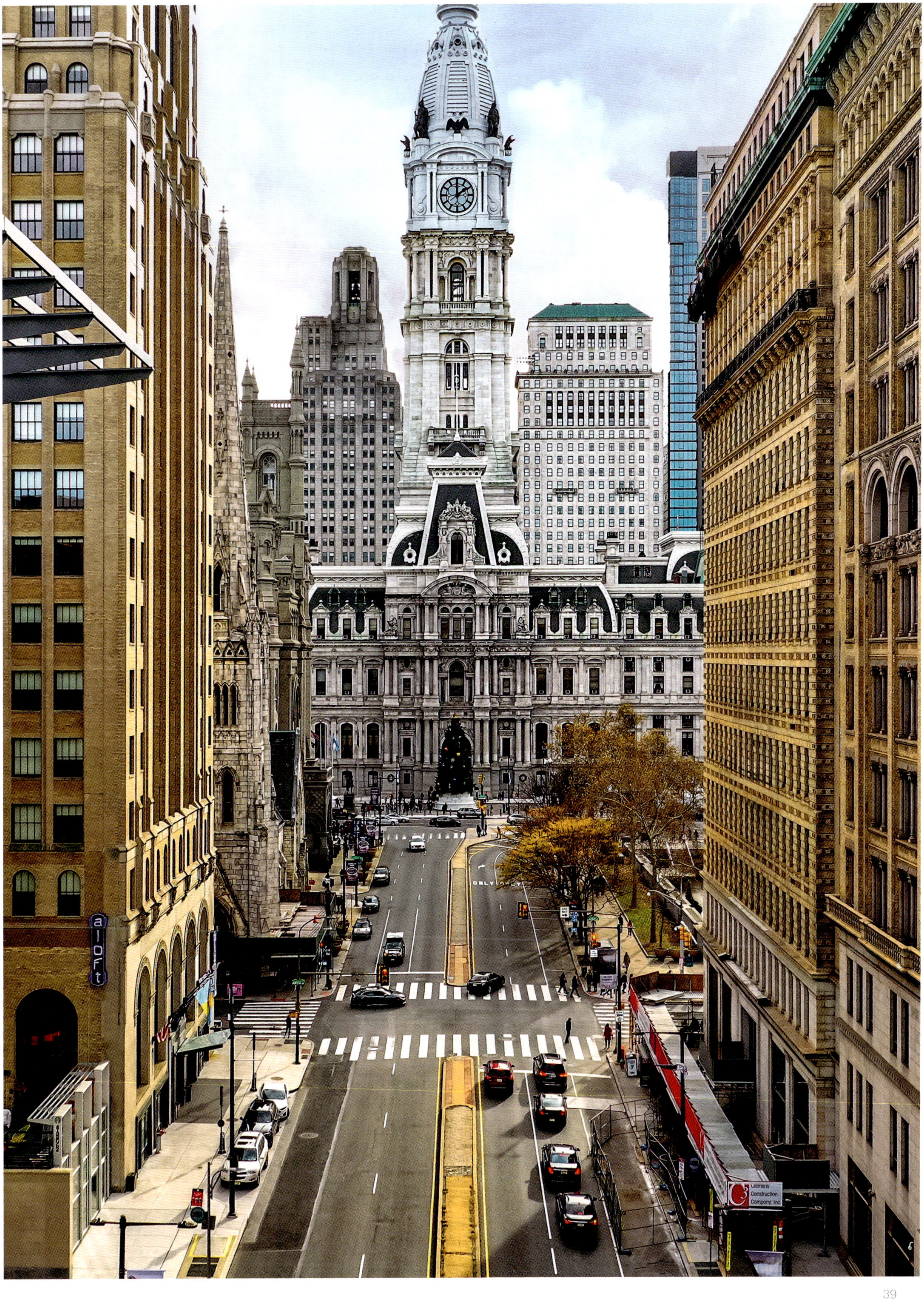
aloft

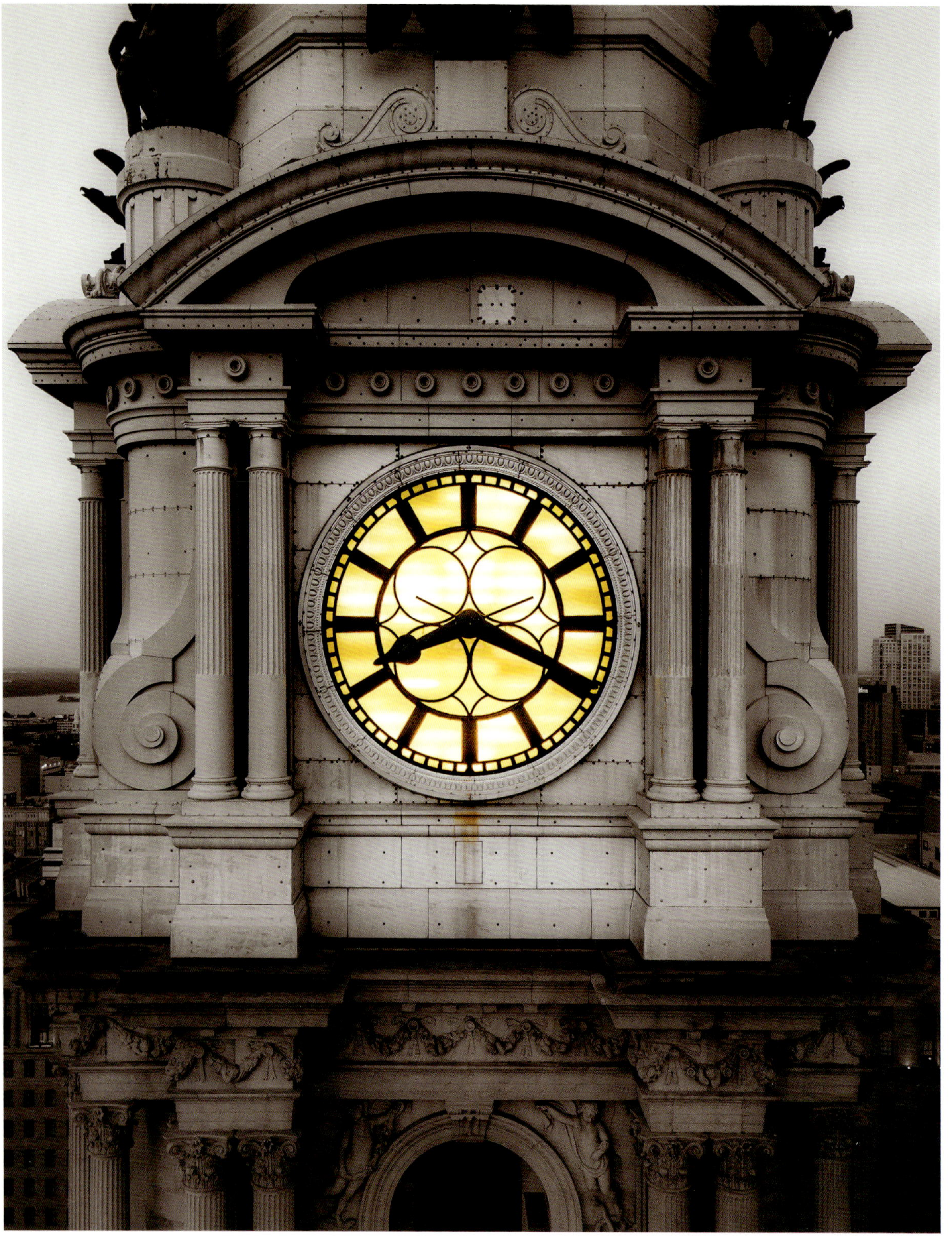

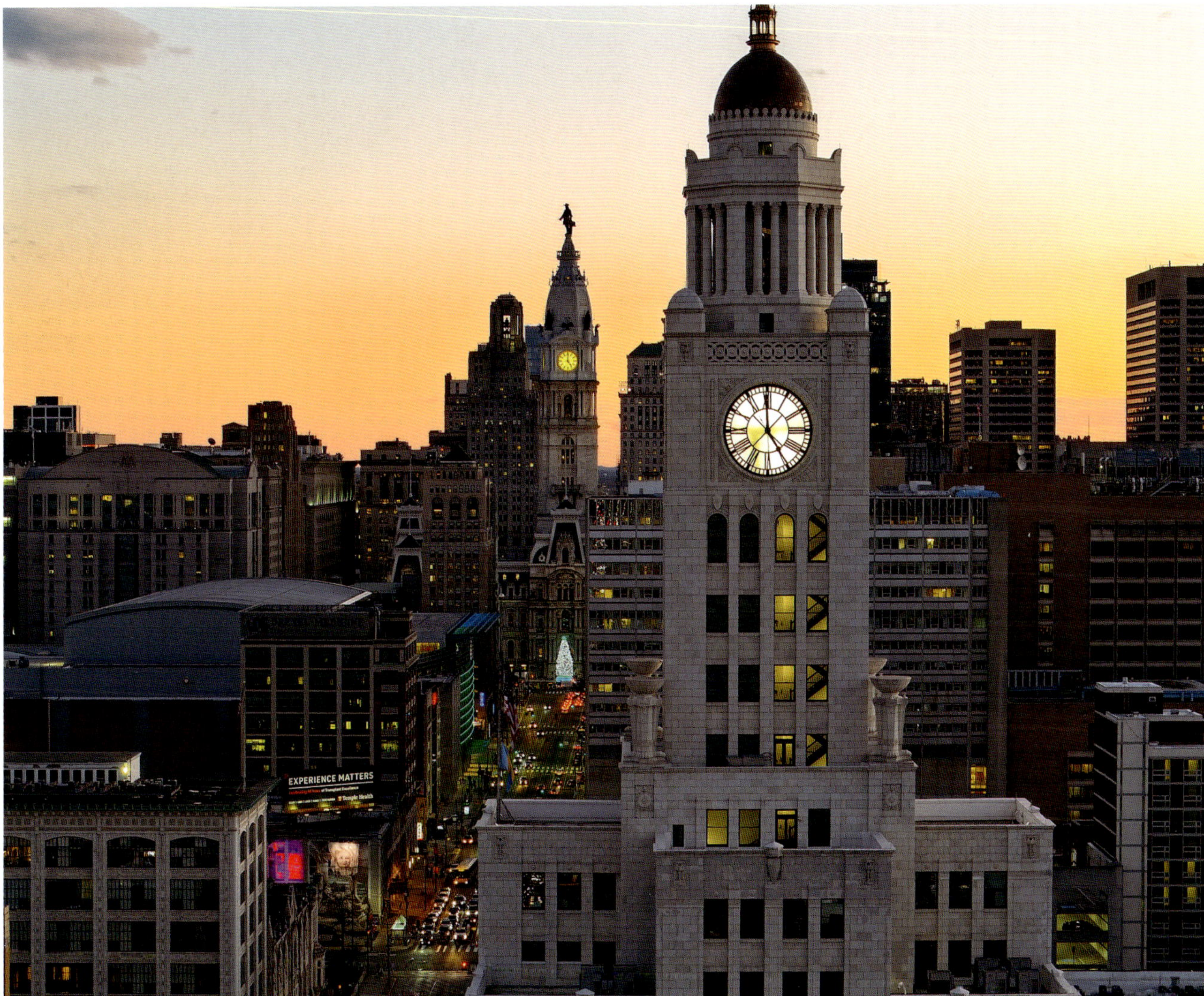
EXPERIENCE MATTERS

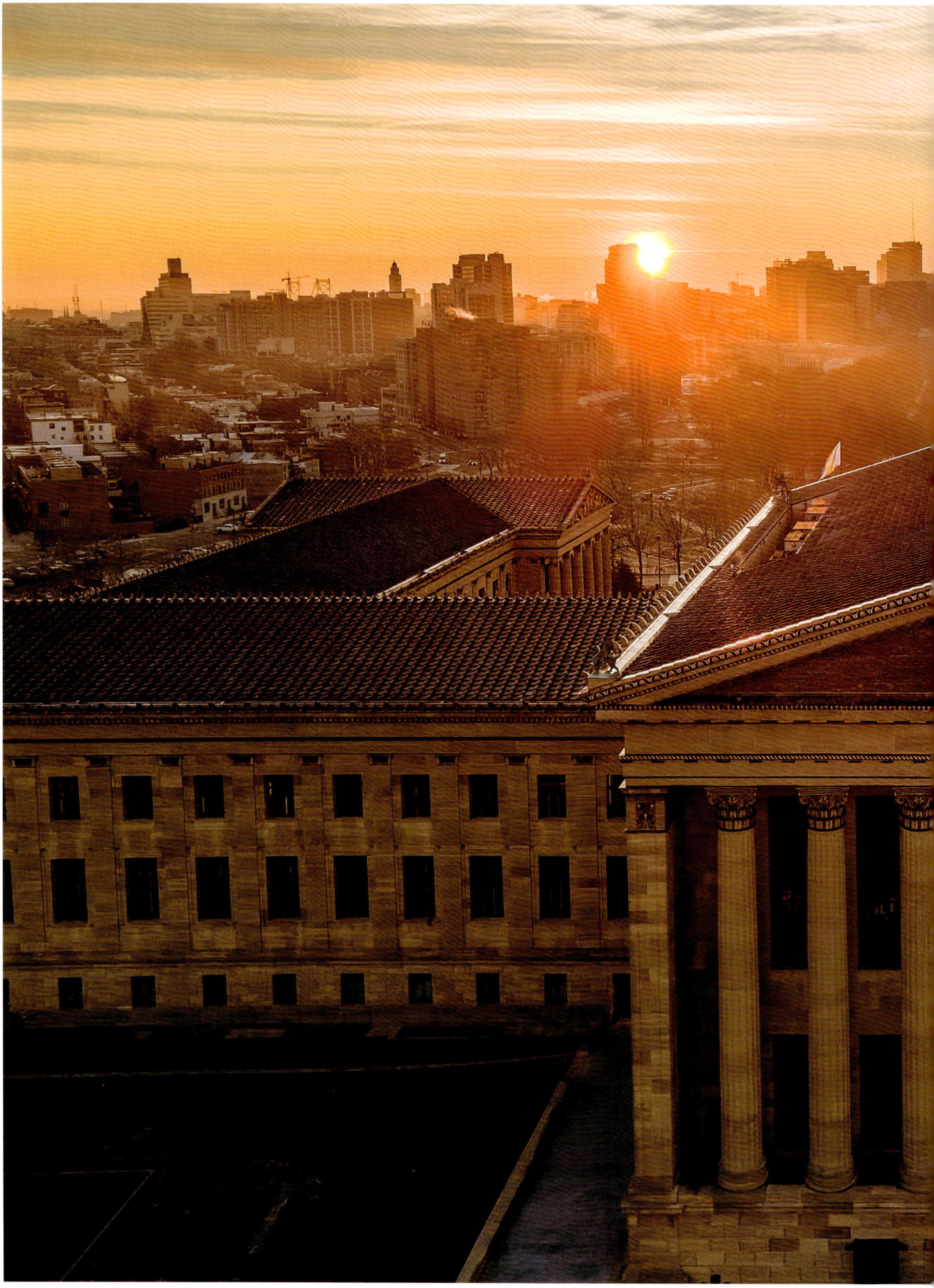

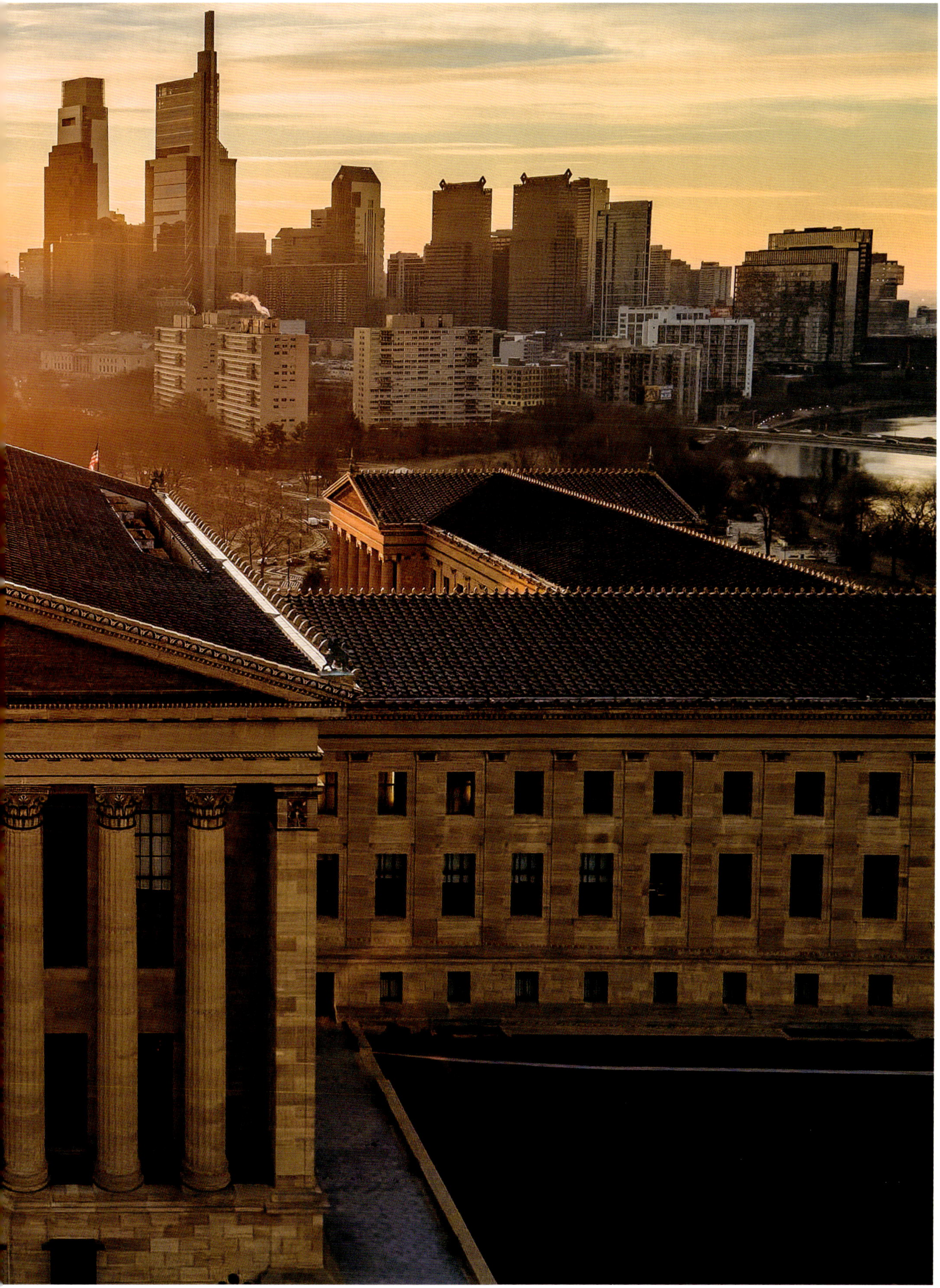

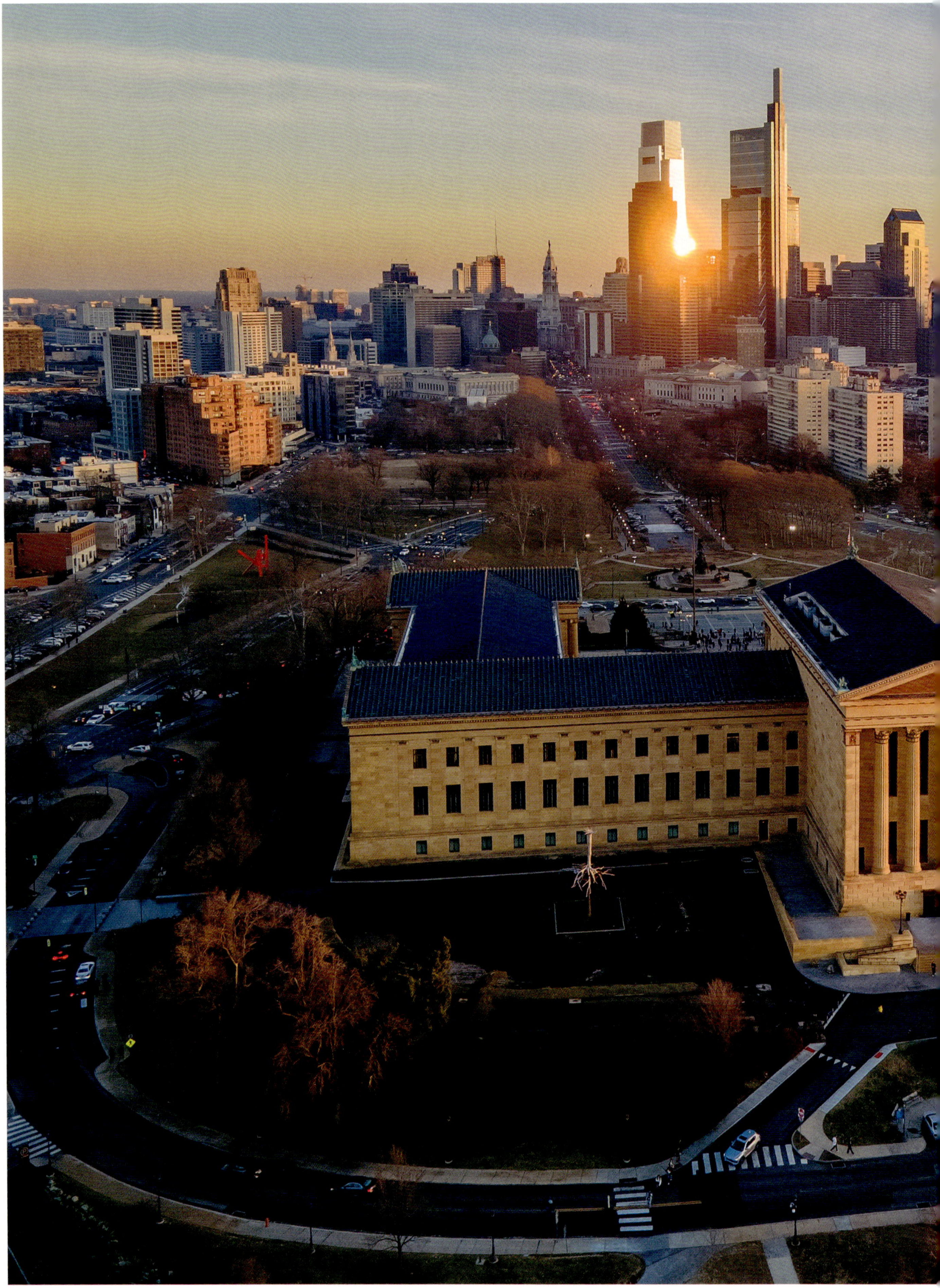

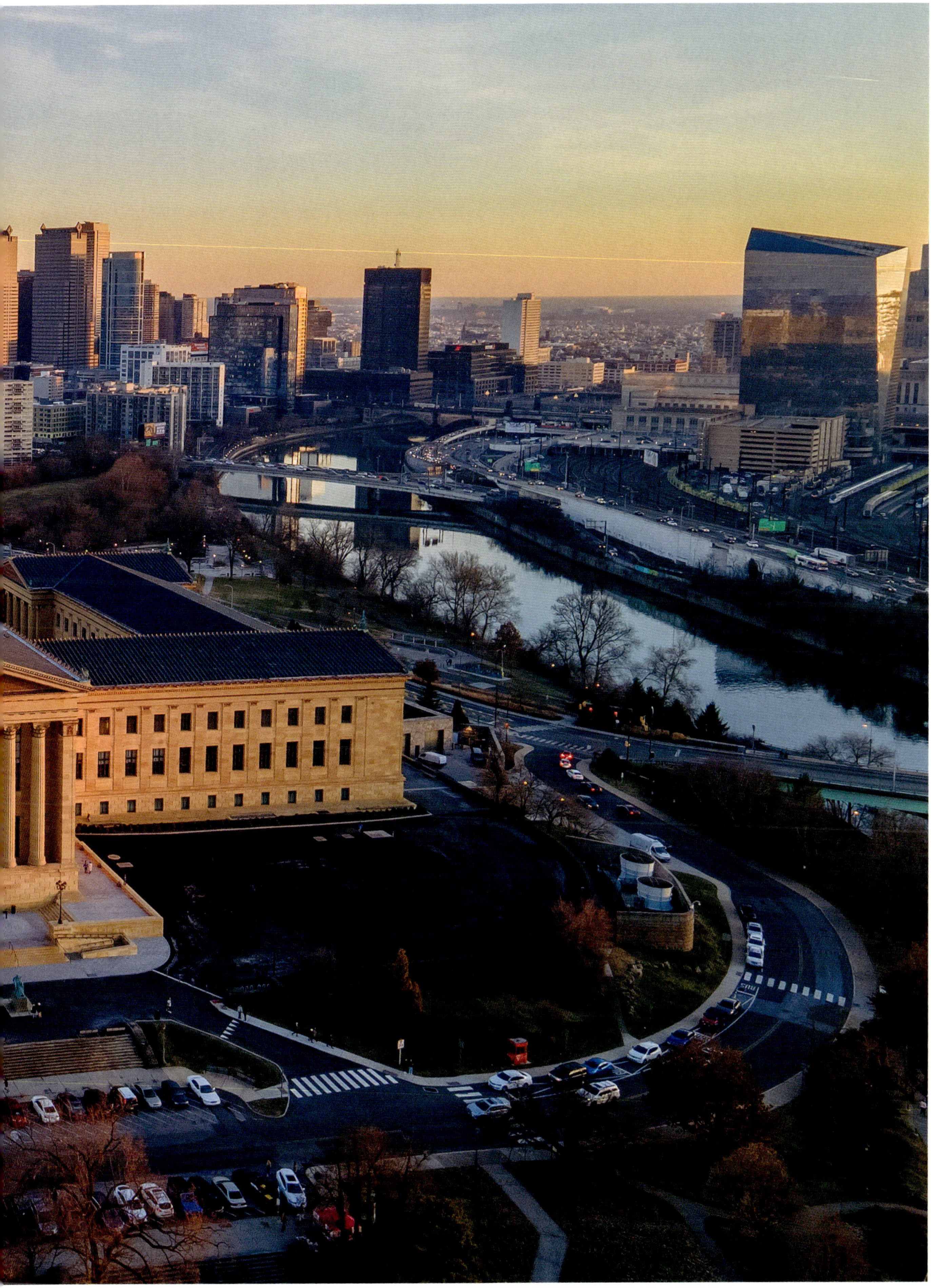

Two Rivers ★ Philadelphia is shaped by two major rivers — the Delaware River and the Schuylkill River. ★ Forming the city's eastern boundary, the Delaware River separates Philadelphia from the neighboring state of New Jersey. The Delaware was long used as a major route for trade and transportation, dating back to colonial times. While still a commercial waterway, today the Delaware River is also a major recreational hub. The revitalized Delaware River Waterfront includes spaces like Spruce Street Harbor Park, a vibrant park with floating gardens, and Penn's Landing, a main hub of waterfront activity that host concerts and festivals and houses the seasonal Blue Cross RiverRink. ★ The Benjamin Franklin Bridge is a suspension bridge that spans across the Delaware River, connecting Philadelphia with Camden, New Jersey. Construction on the bridge began in 1922 and was officially opened to traffic in 1926. When it opened, the bridge was the longest suspension bridge in the world, surpassing the Brooklyn Bridge with a main span of 1,750 feet. Originally called the Delaware River Bridge, it was renamed in 1955 to honor Benjamin Franklin, one of Philadelphia's founding fathers. ★ The Schuylkill River runs through the heart of Philadelphia from northwest to southeast, eventually joining the Delaware River near South Philadelphia. Popular with runners, cyclists, and commuters, the Schuylkill River Trail is a multi-use path that stretches over 82 miles, offering scenic views and access to various parks and historical sites. ★ Boathouse Row lies along the eastern bank of the Schuylkill River. A picturesque collection of 15 boathouses, Boathouse Row is a center for competitive rowing and recreational boating. At night, the boathouses are illuminated with outline lighting, creating a glowing effect that reflects in the water and has become a beloved landmark in the city.

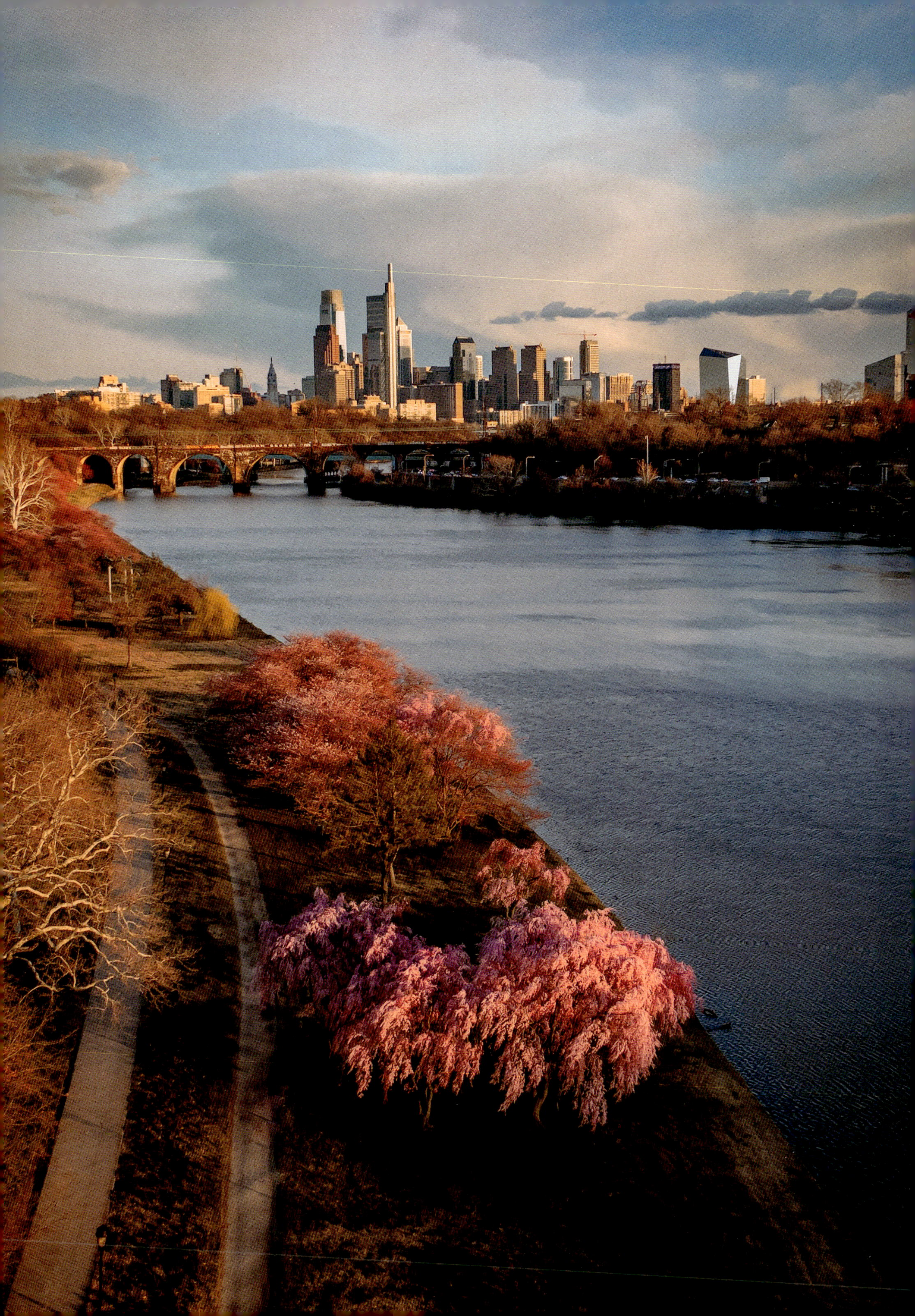

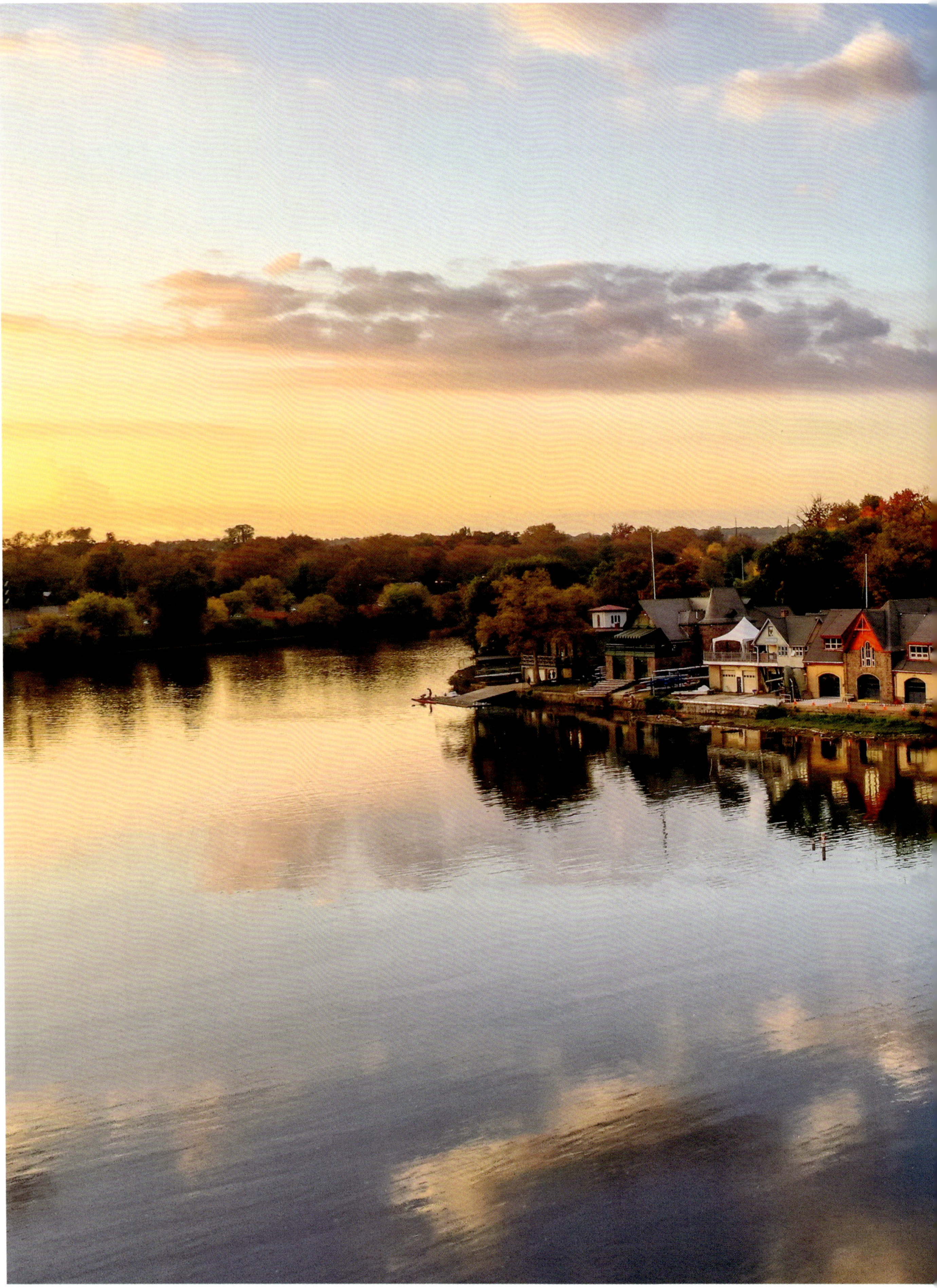

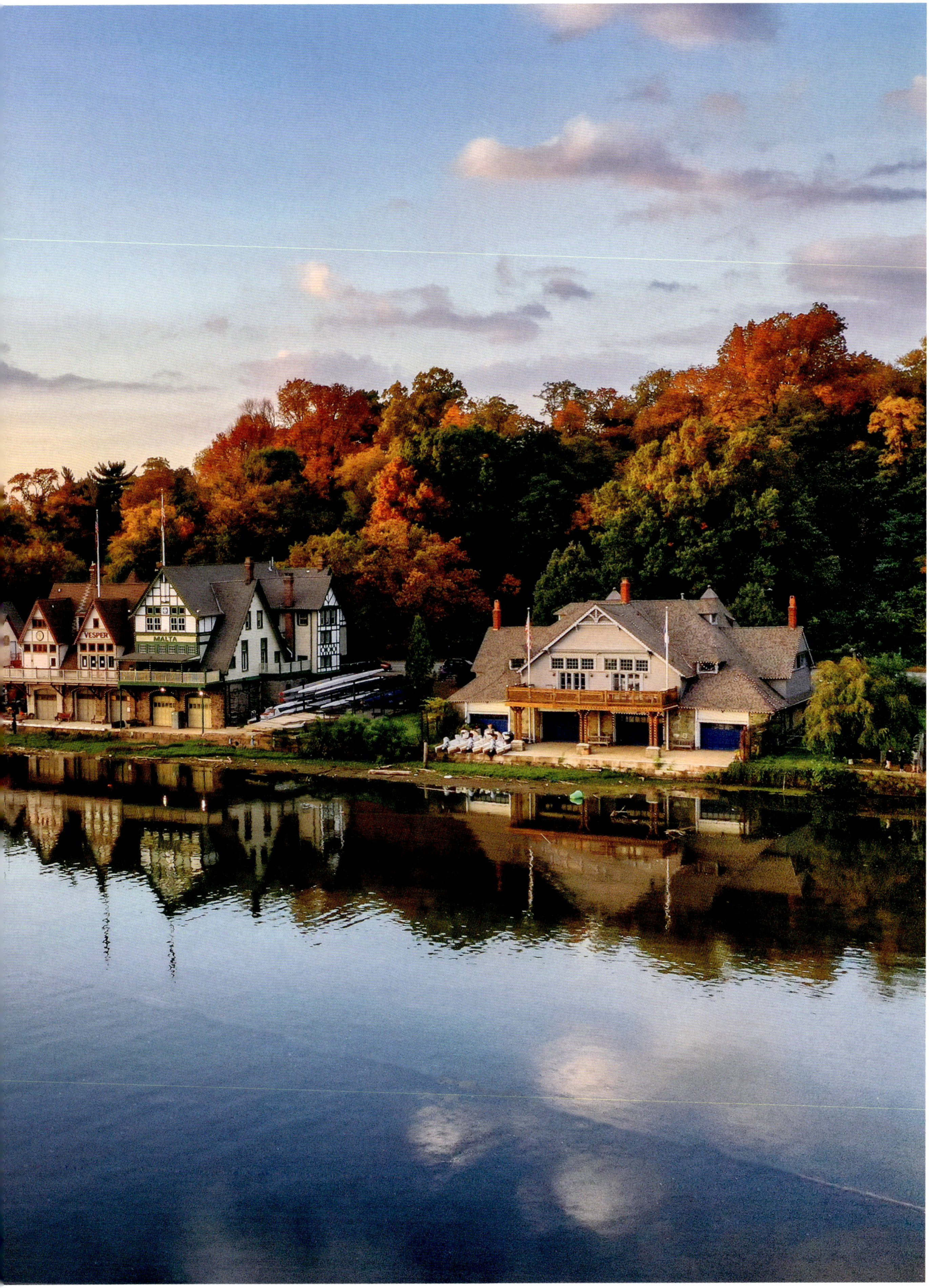
VESPER
MALTA

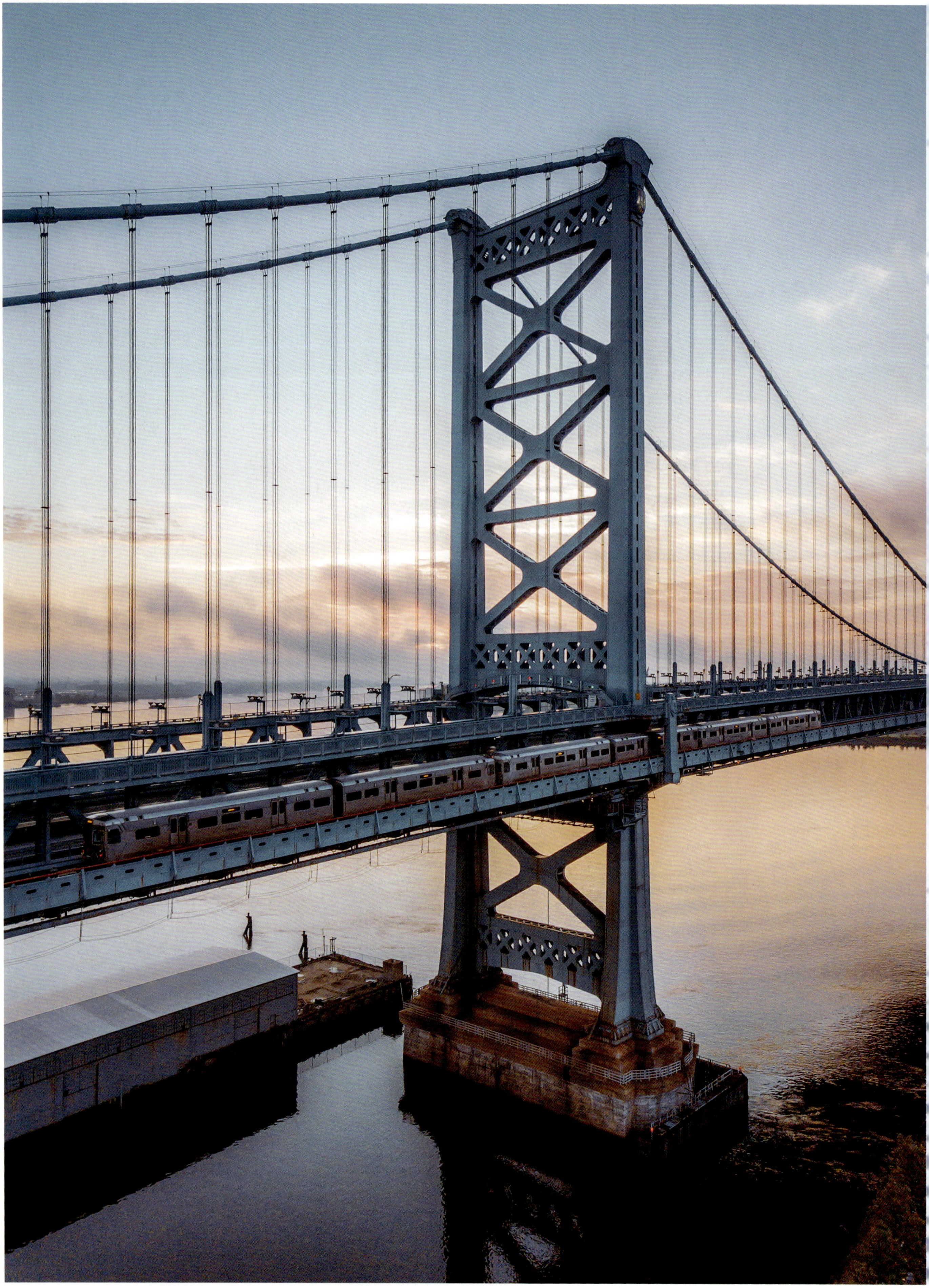

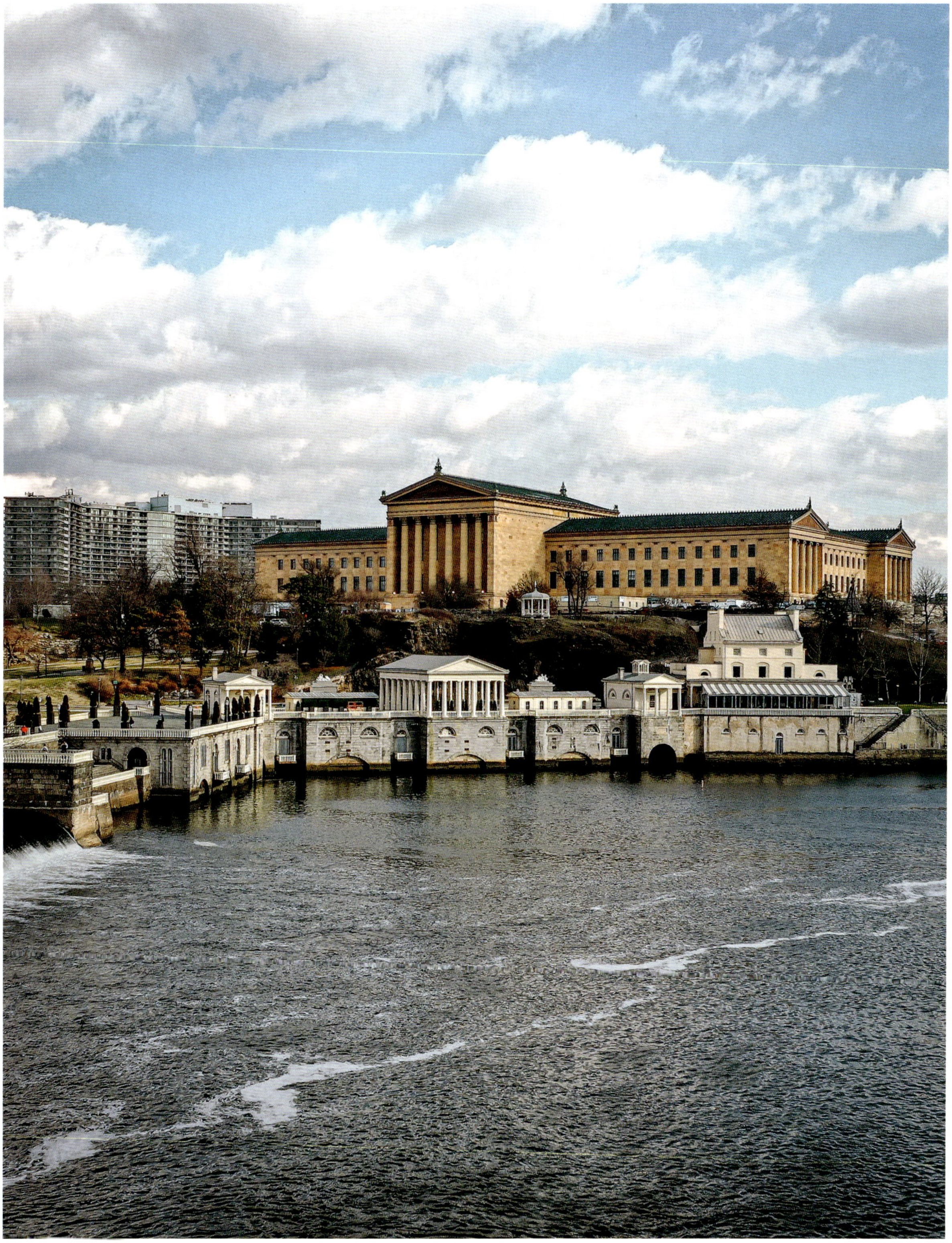

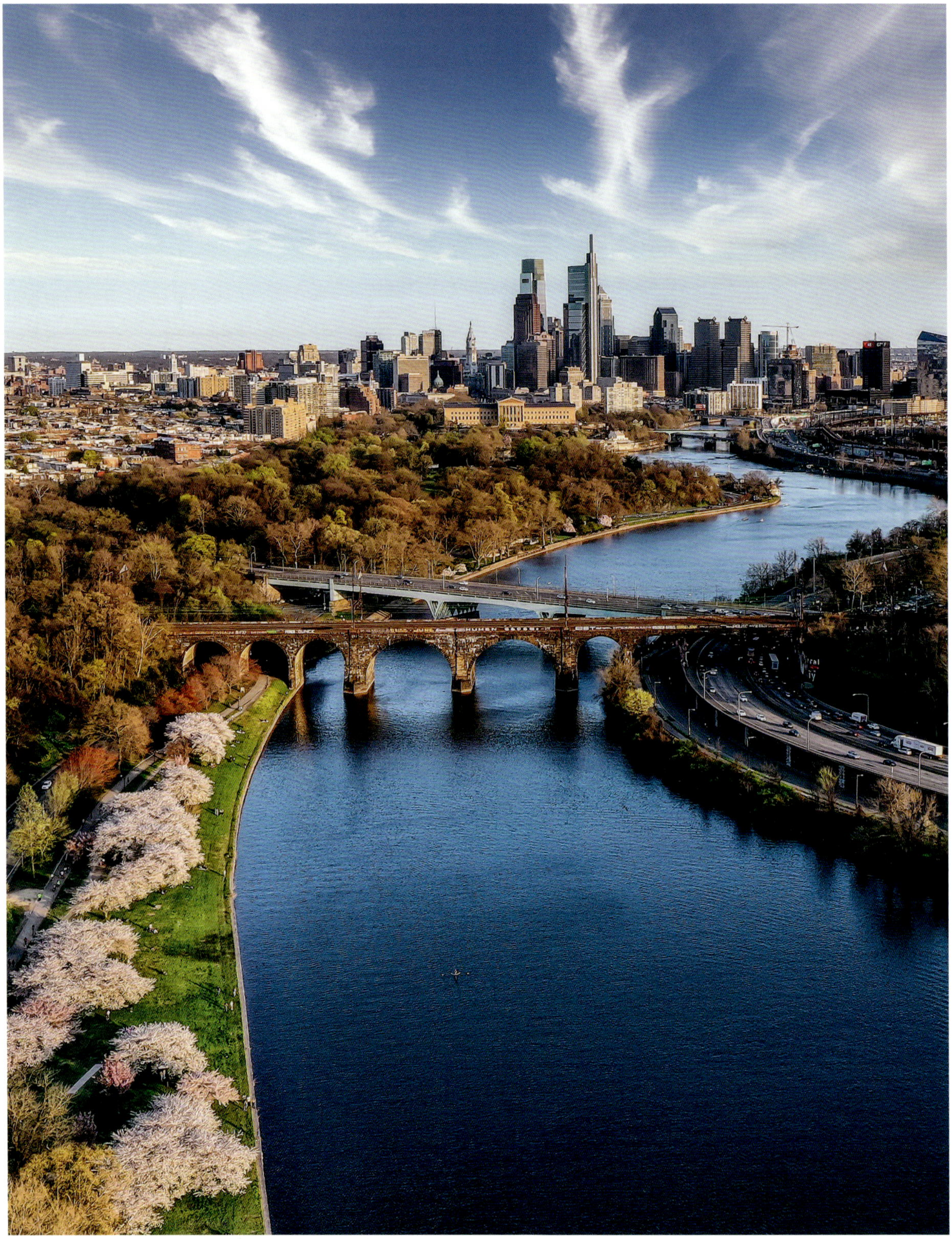

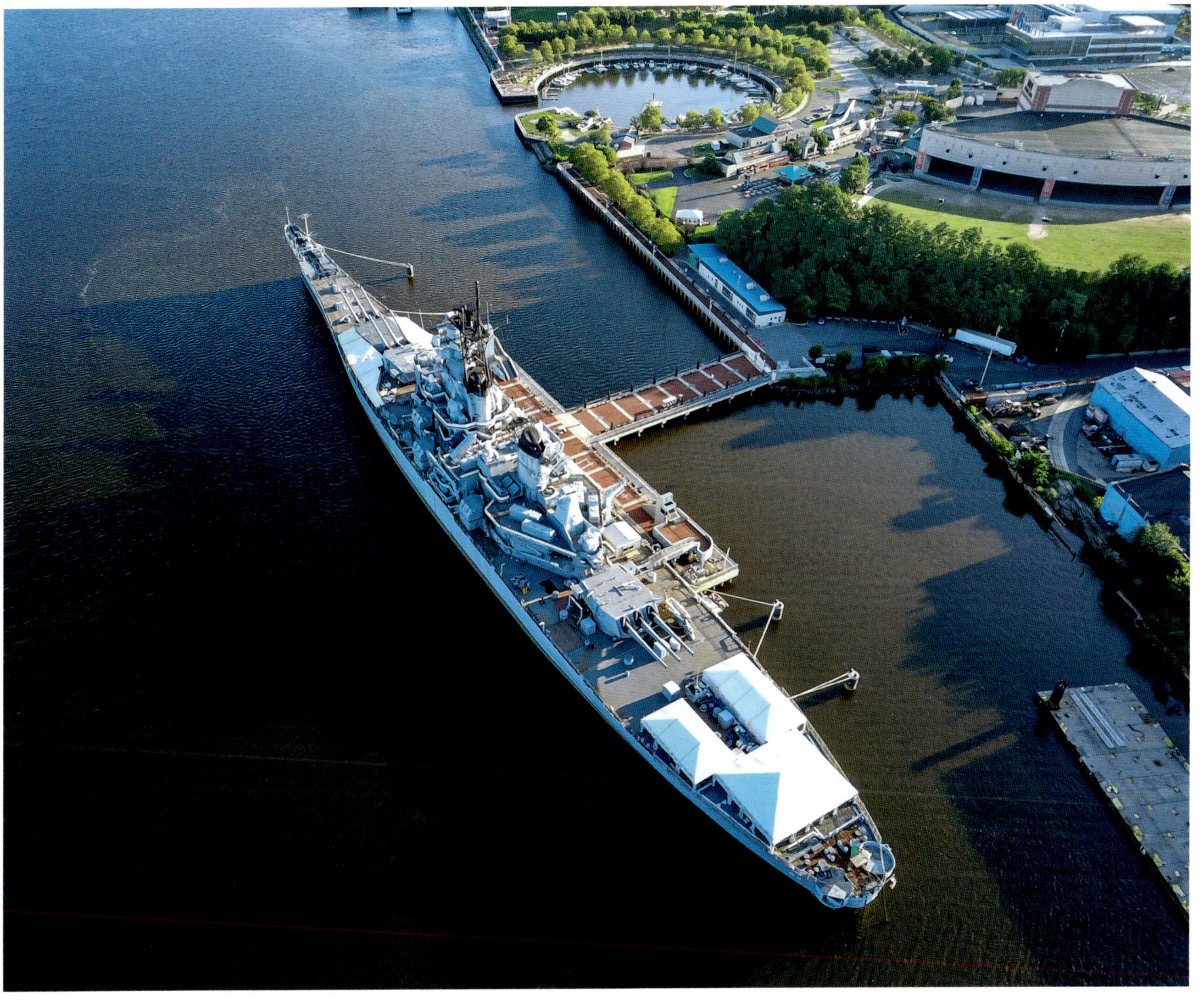

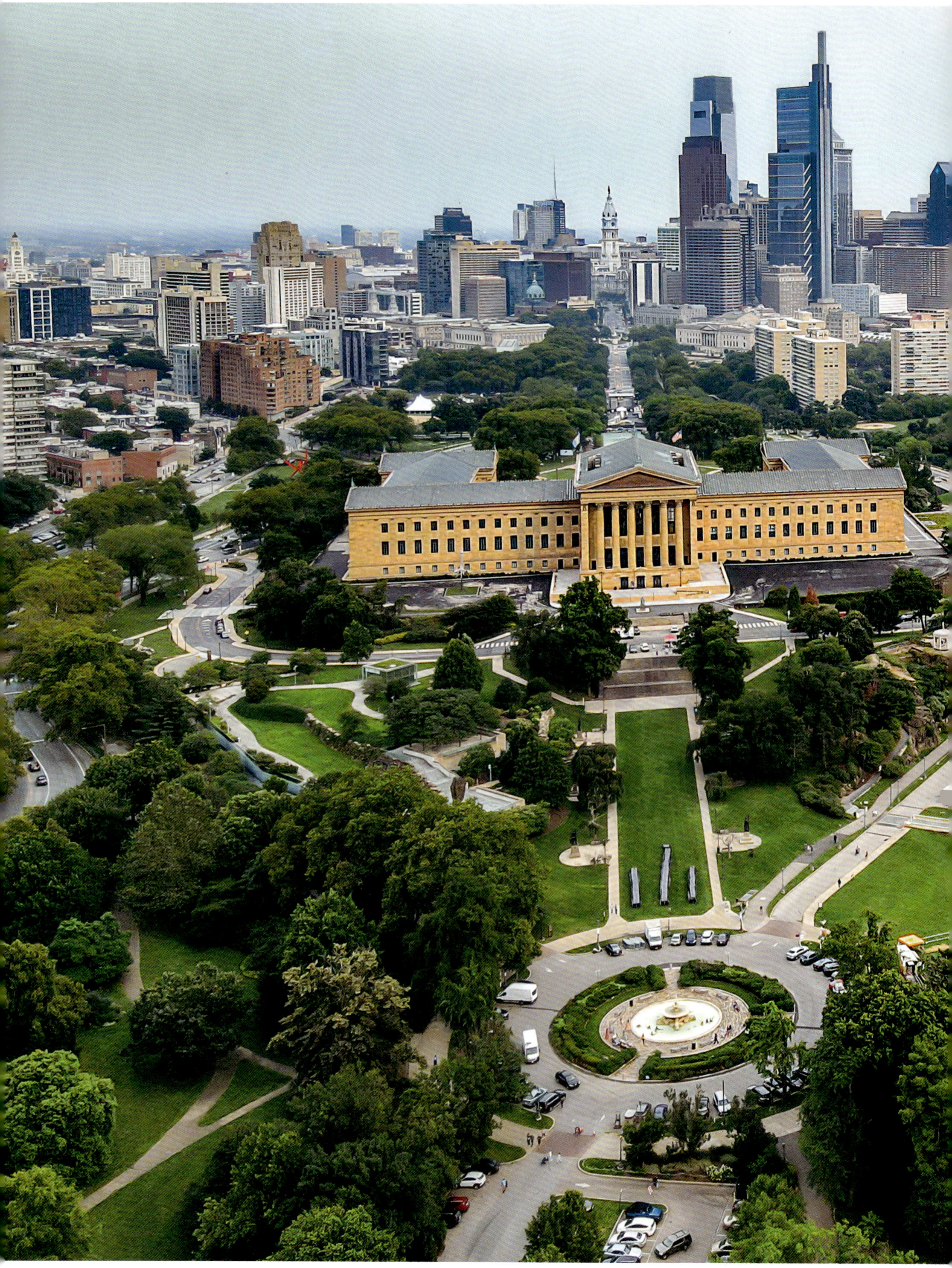

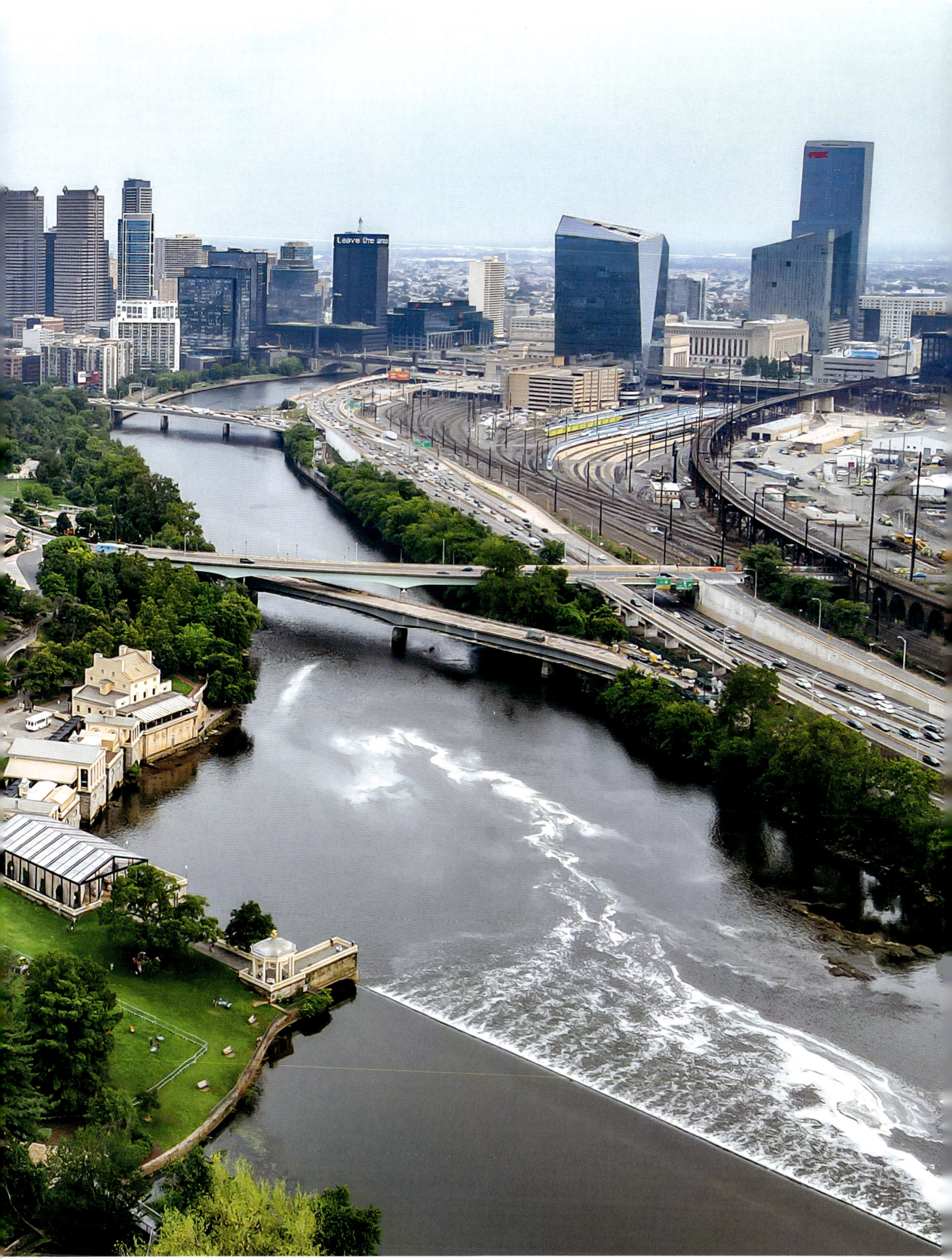

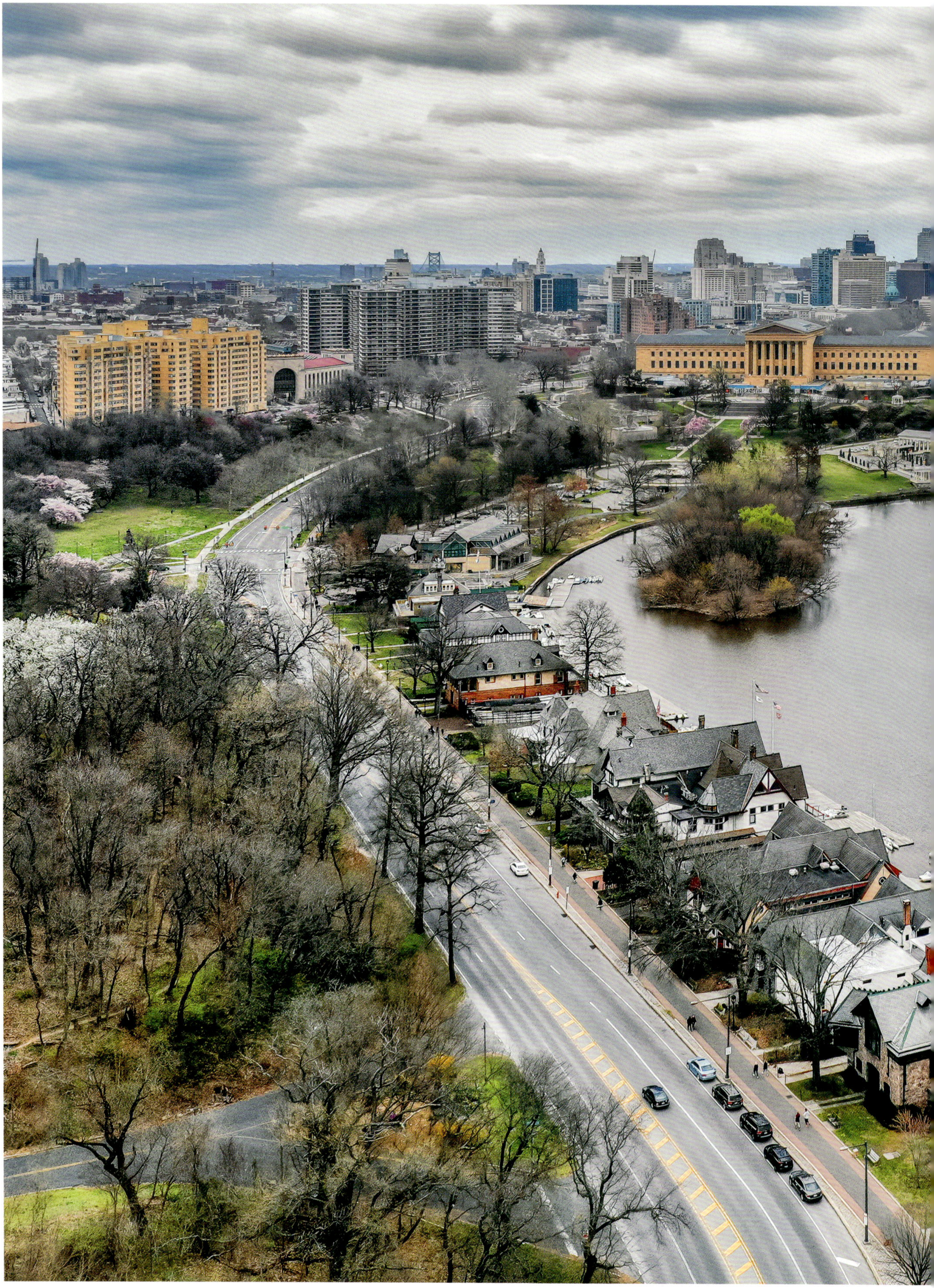

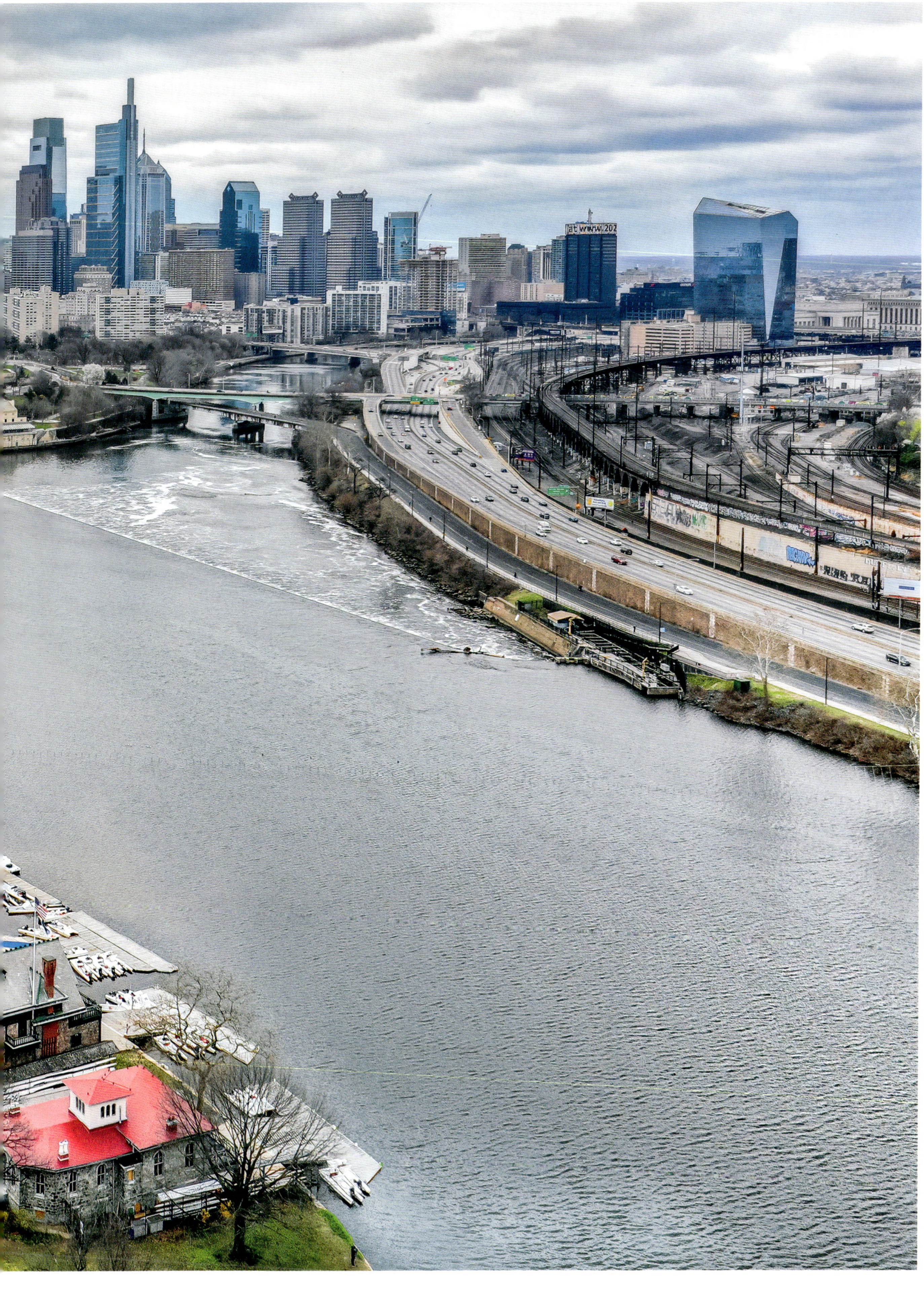

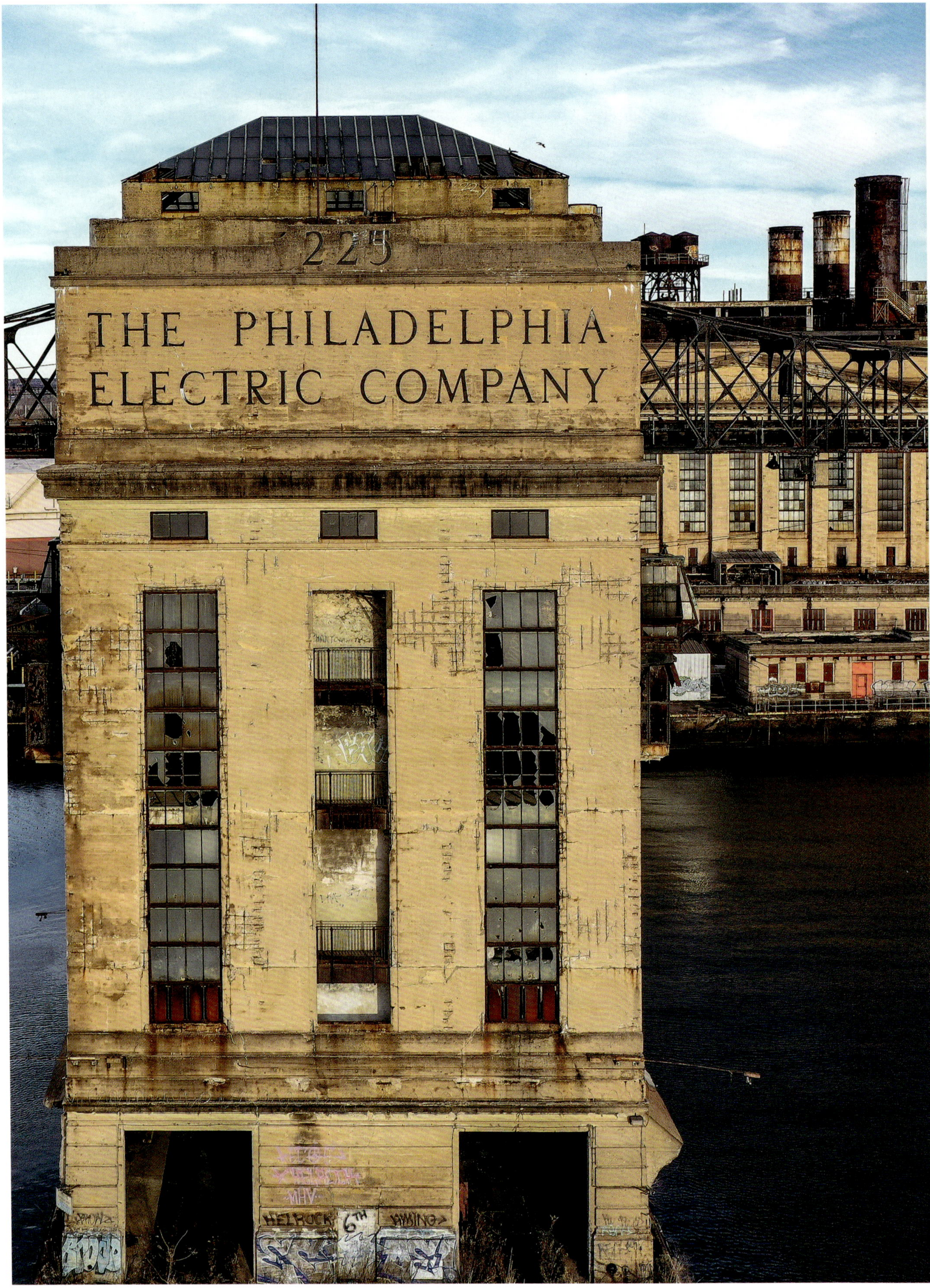
225
THE PHILADELPHIA
ELECTRIC COMPANY

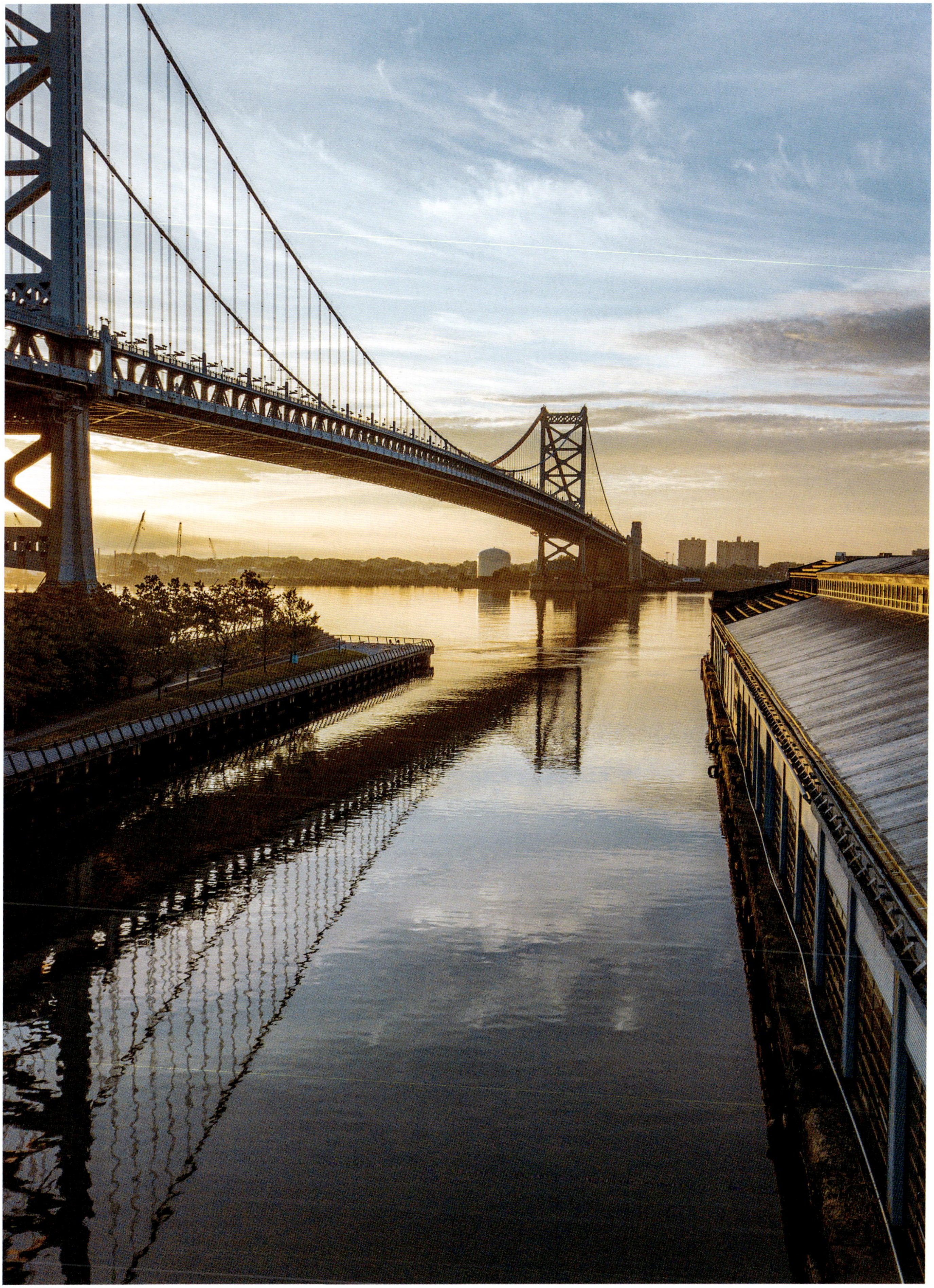

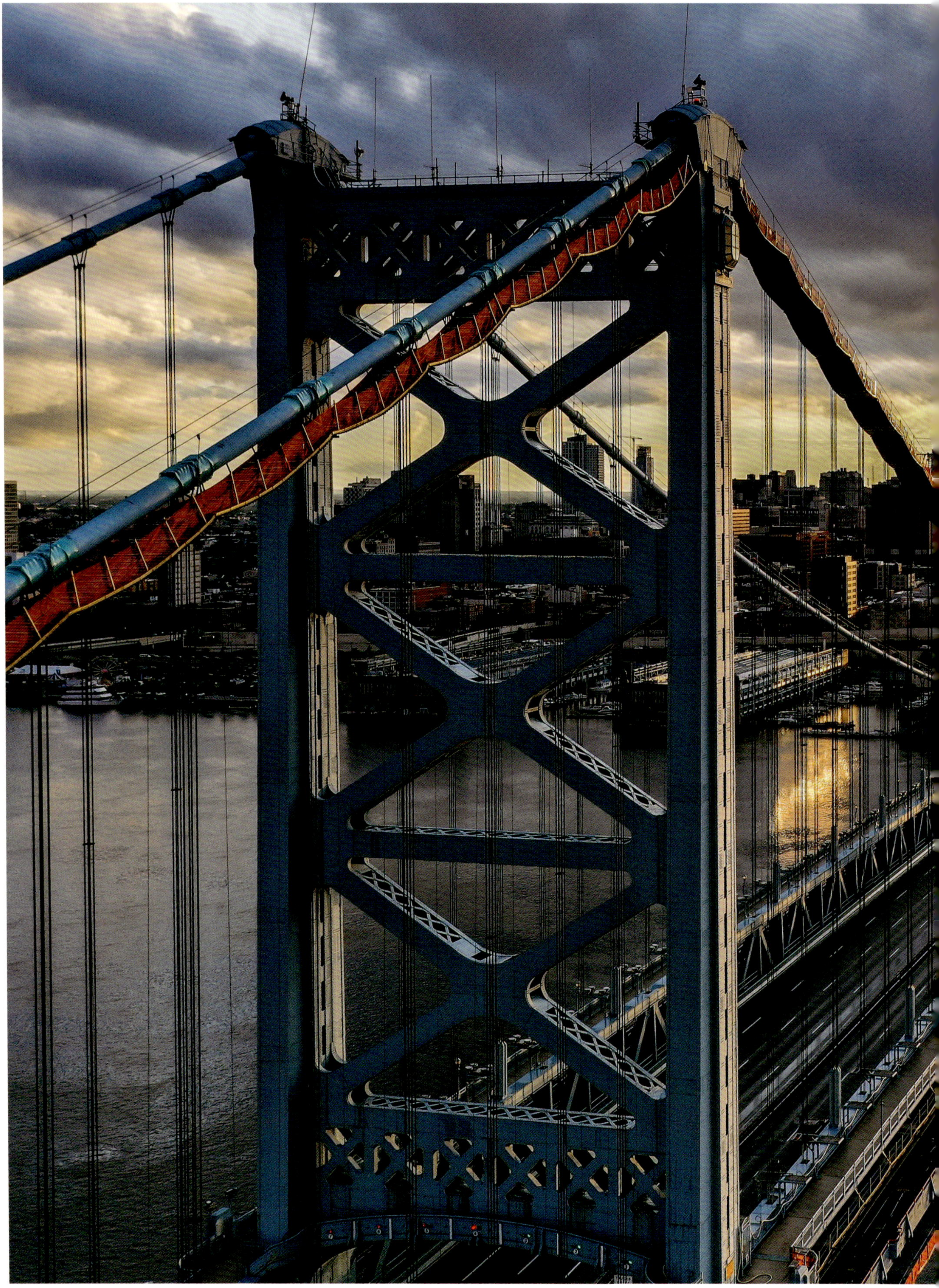

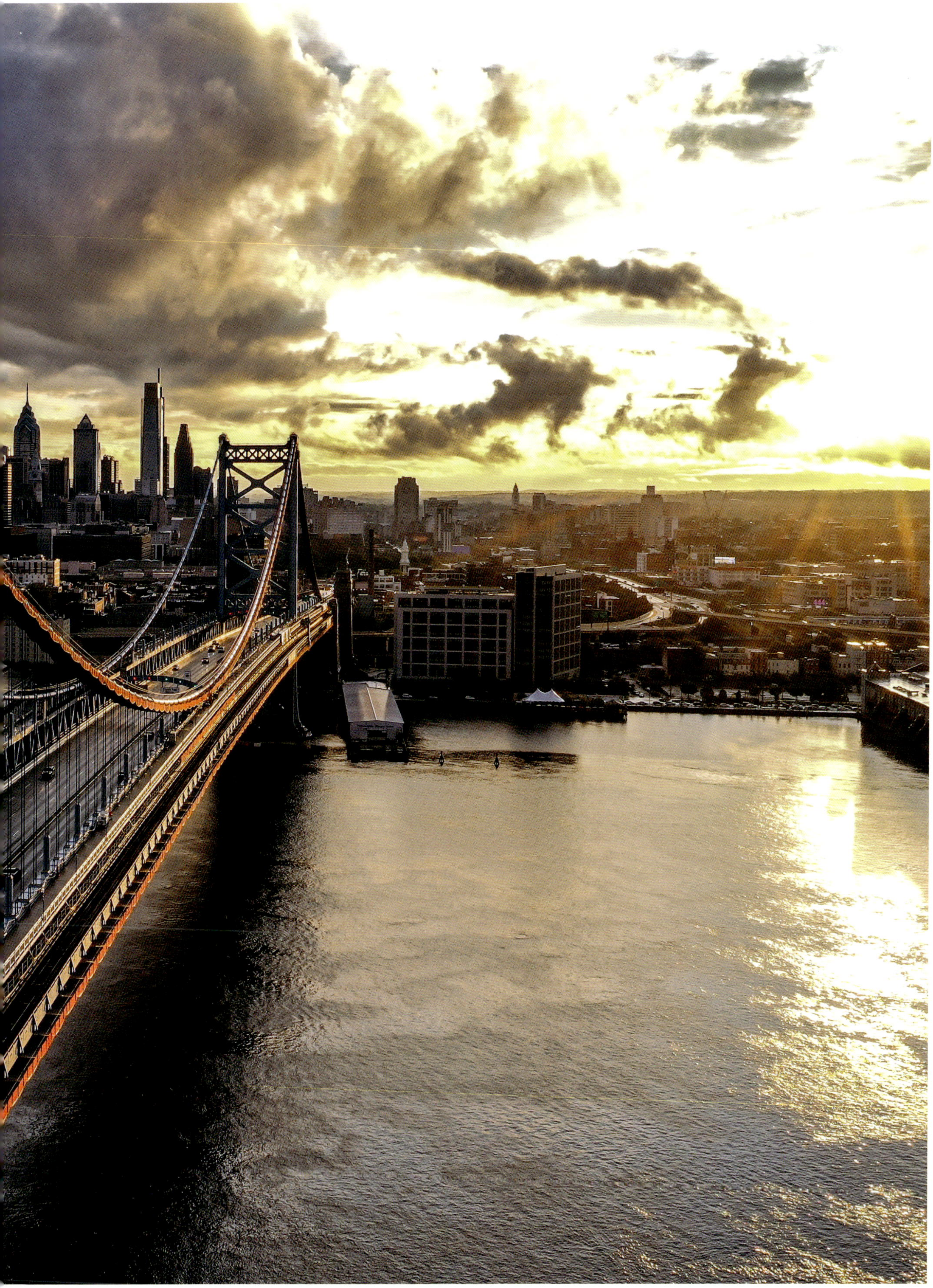

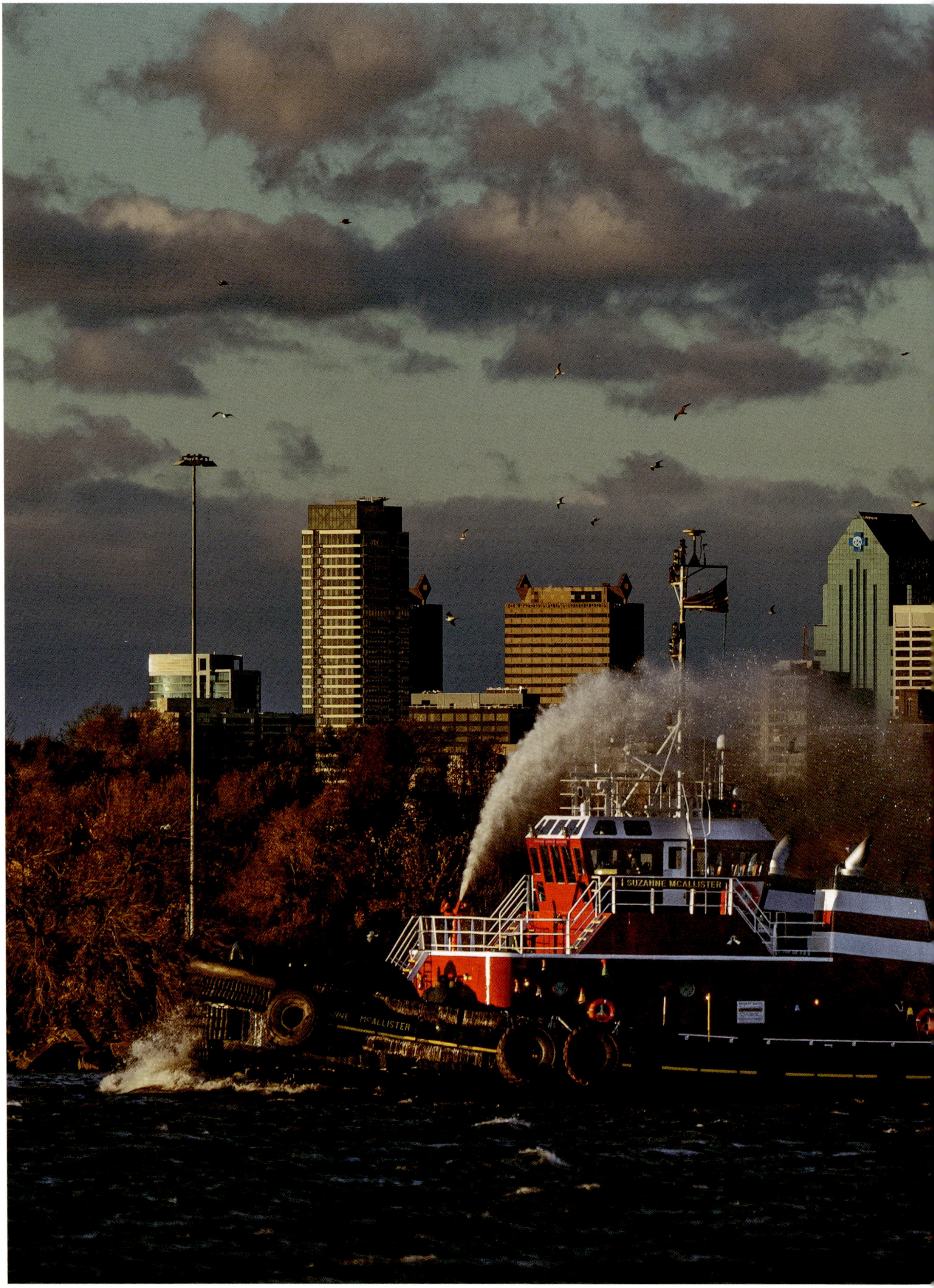
SUZANNE McALLISTER

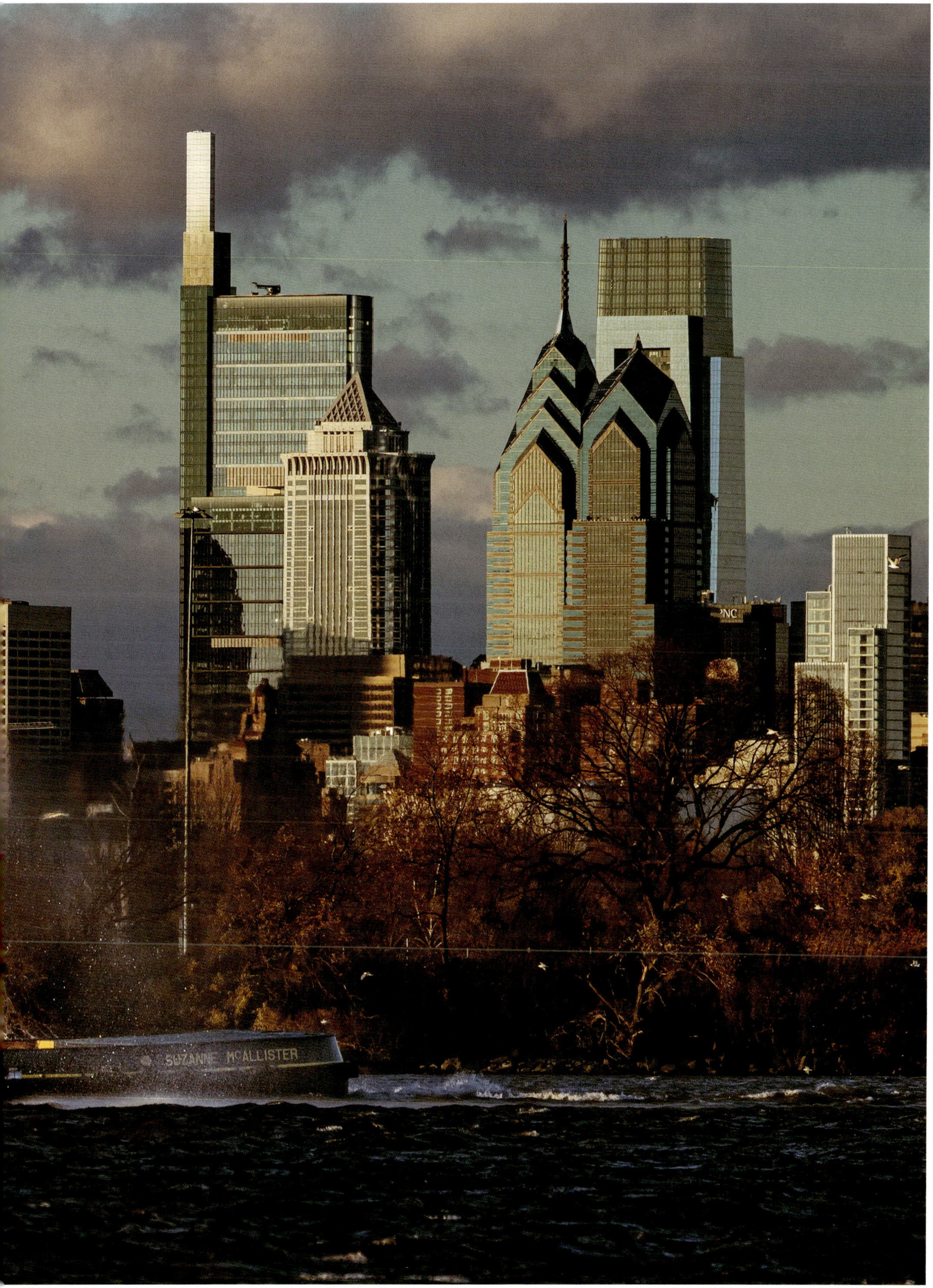
SUZANNE McALLISTER

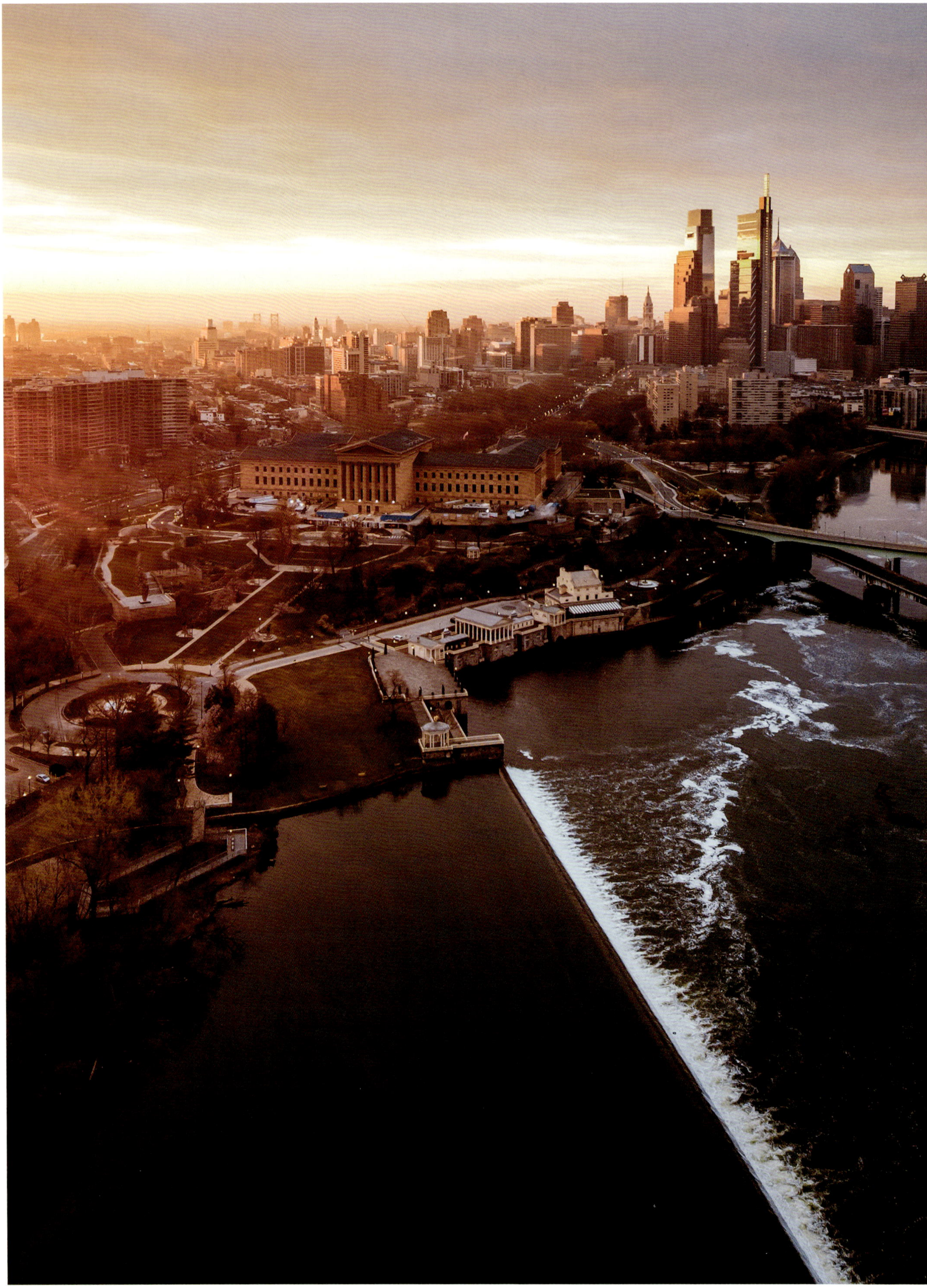

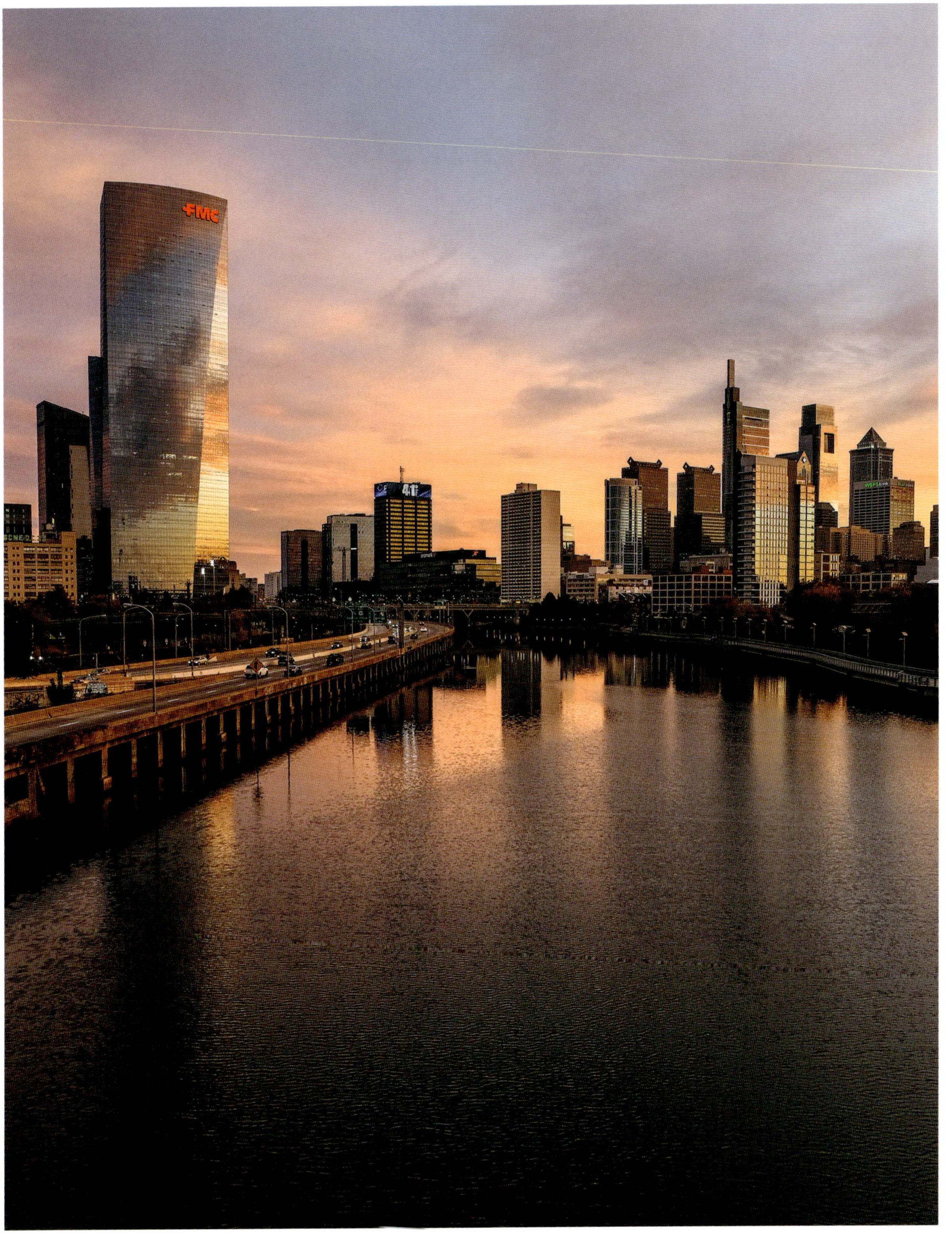
FMC

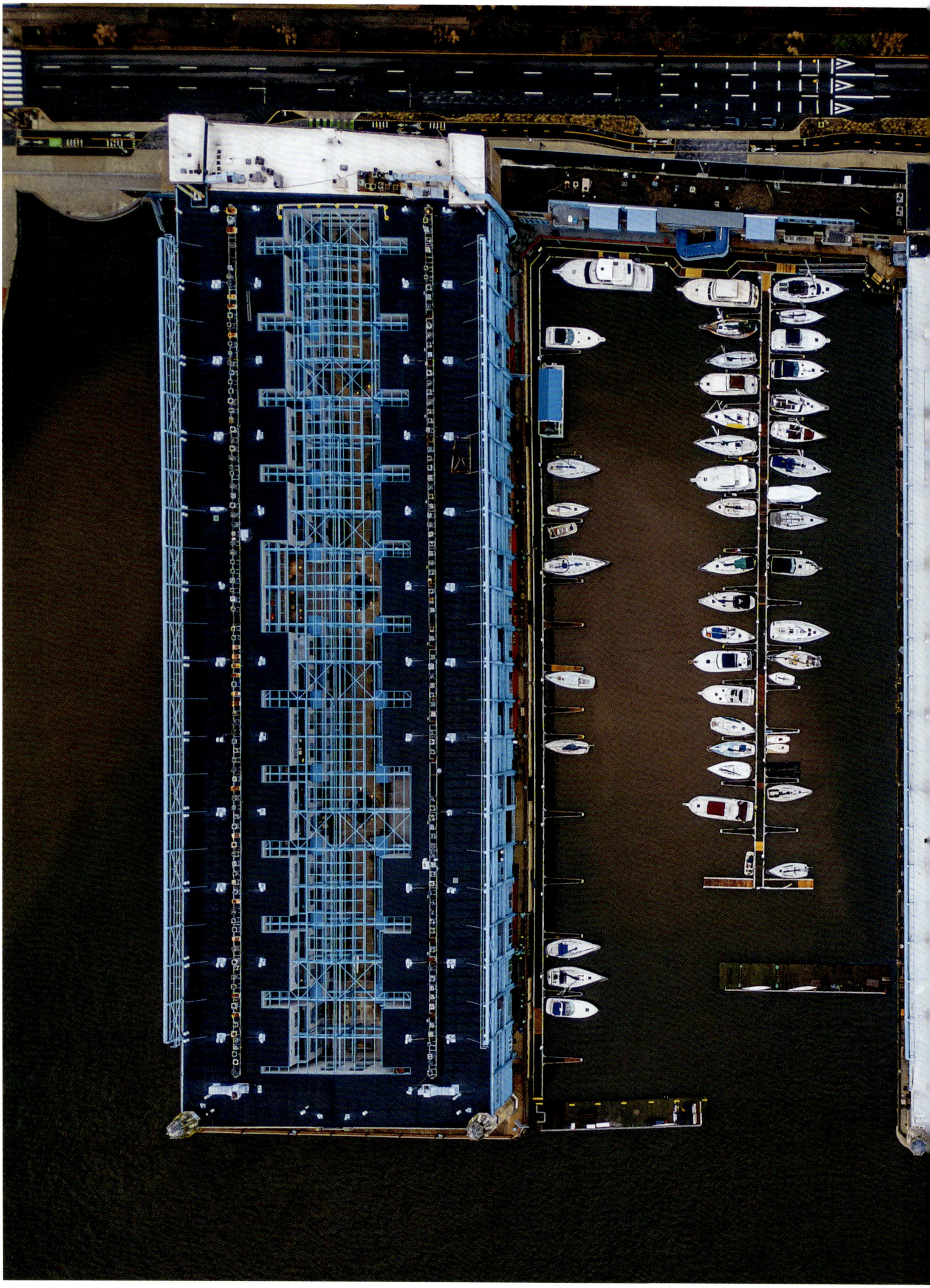

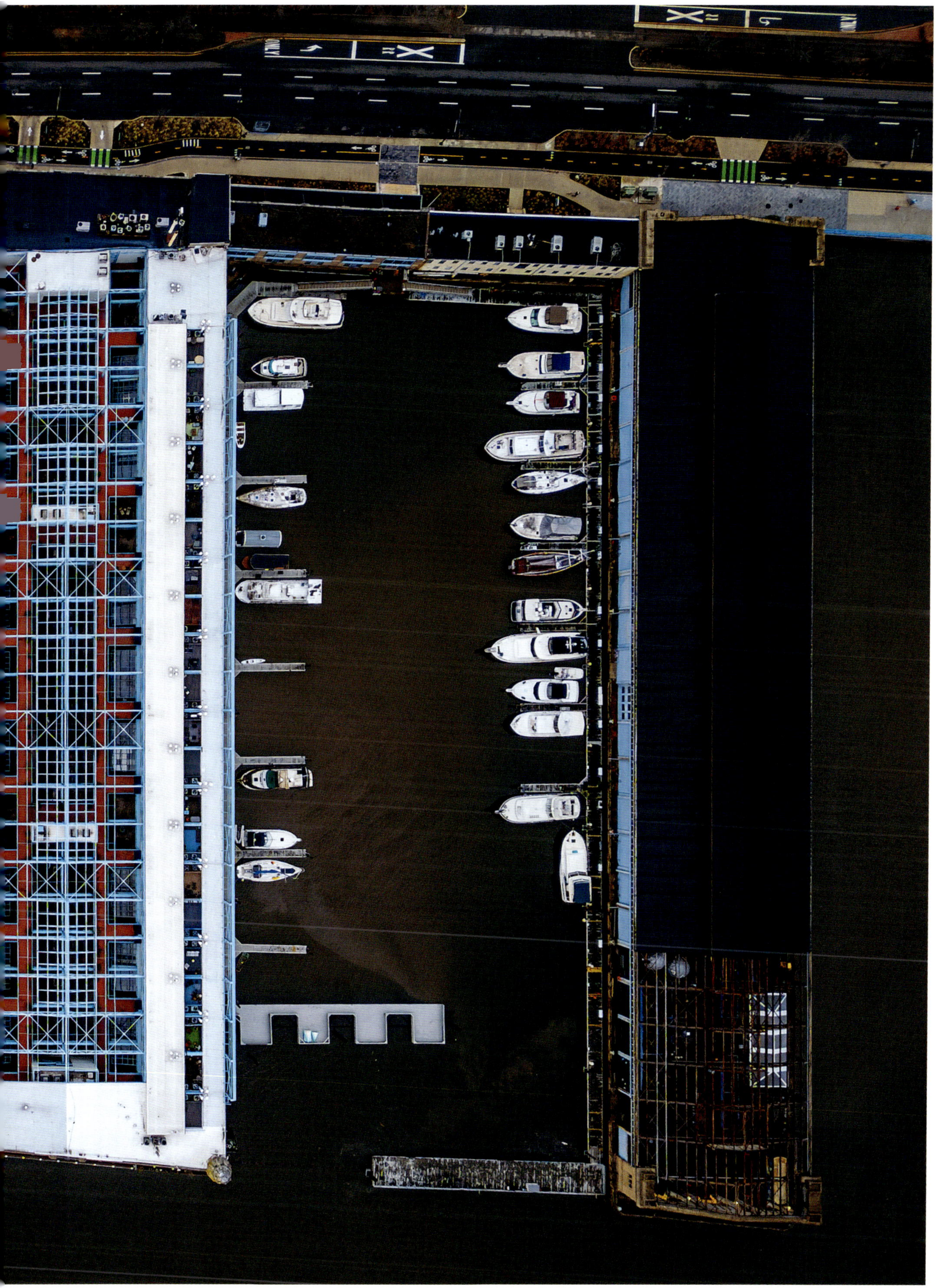

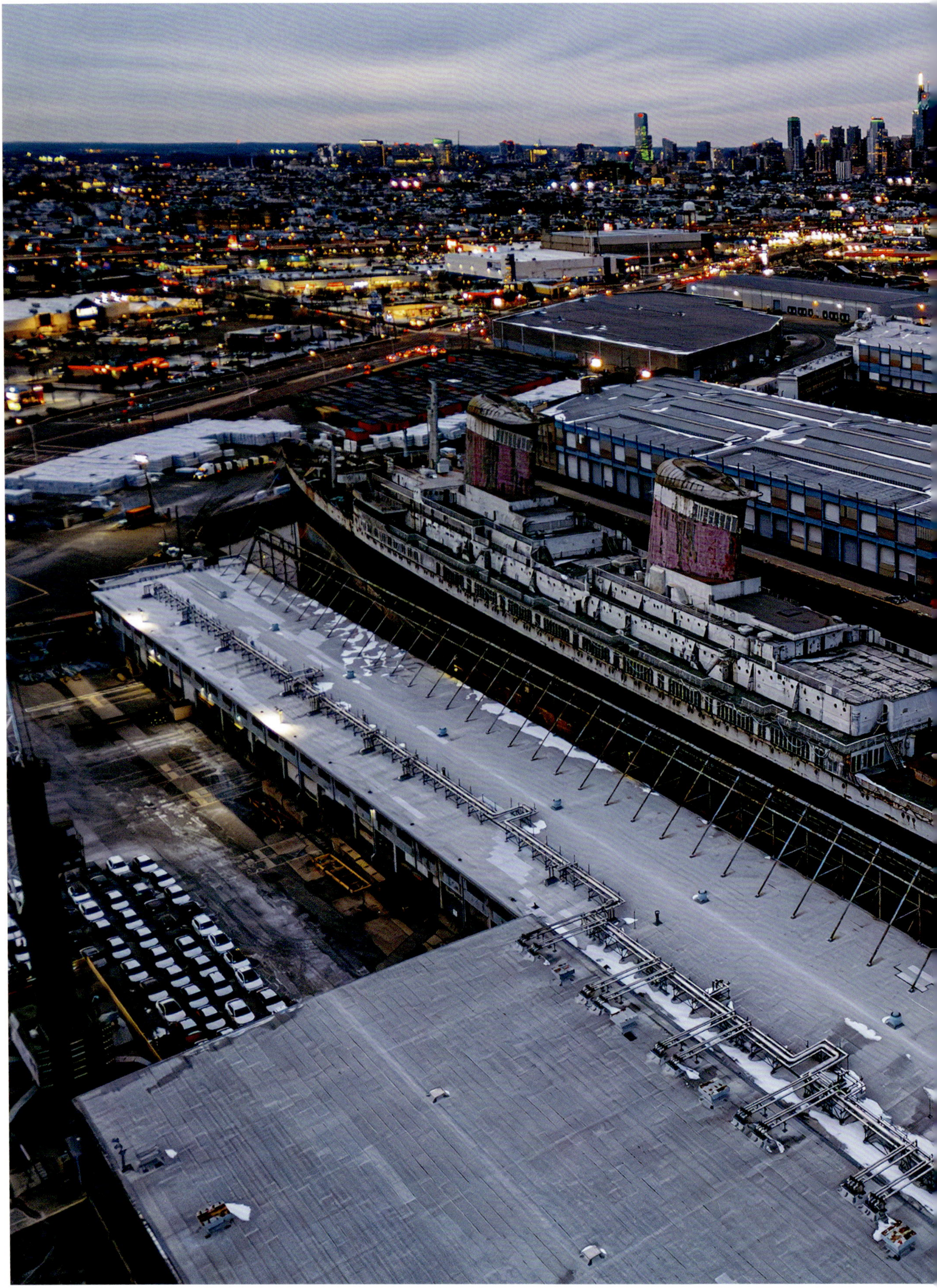

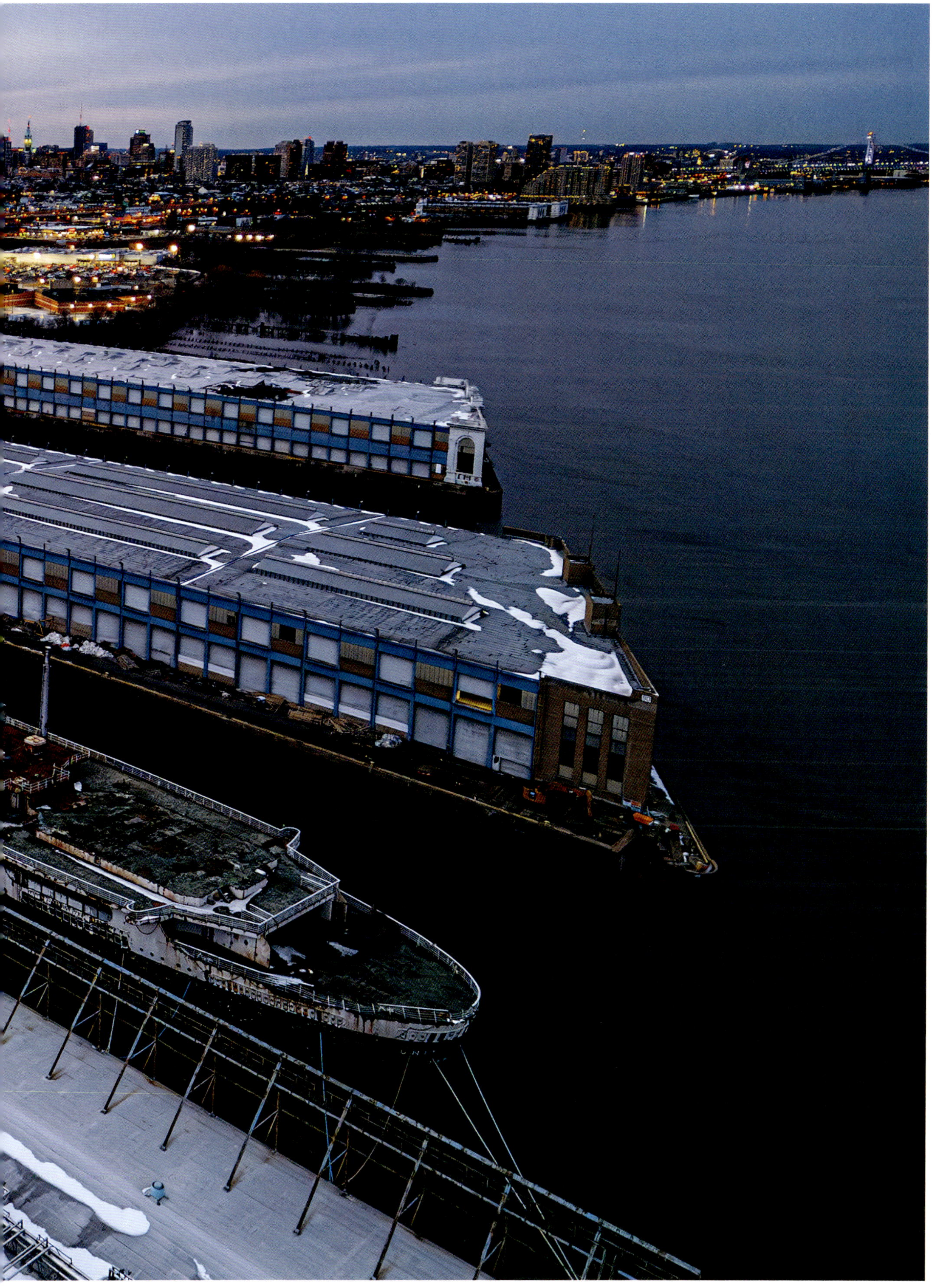

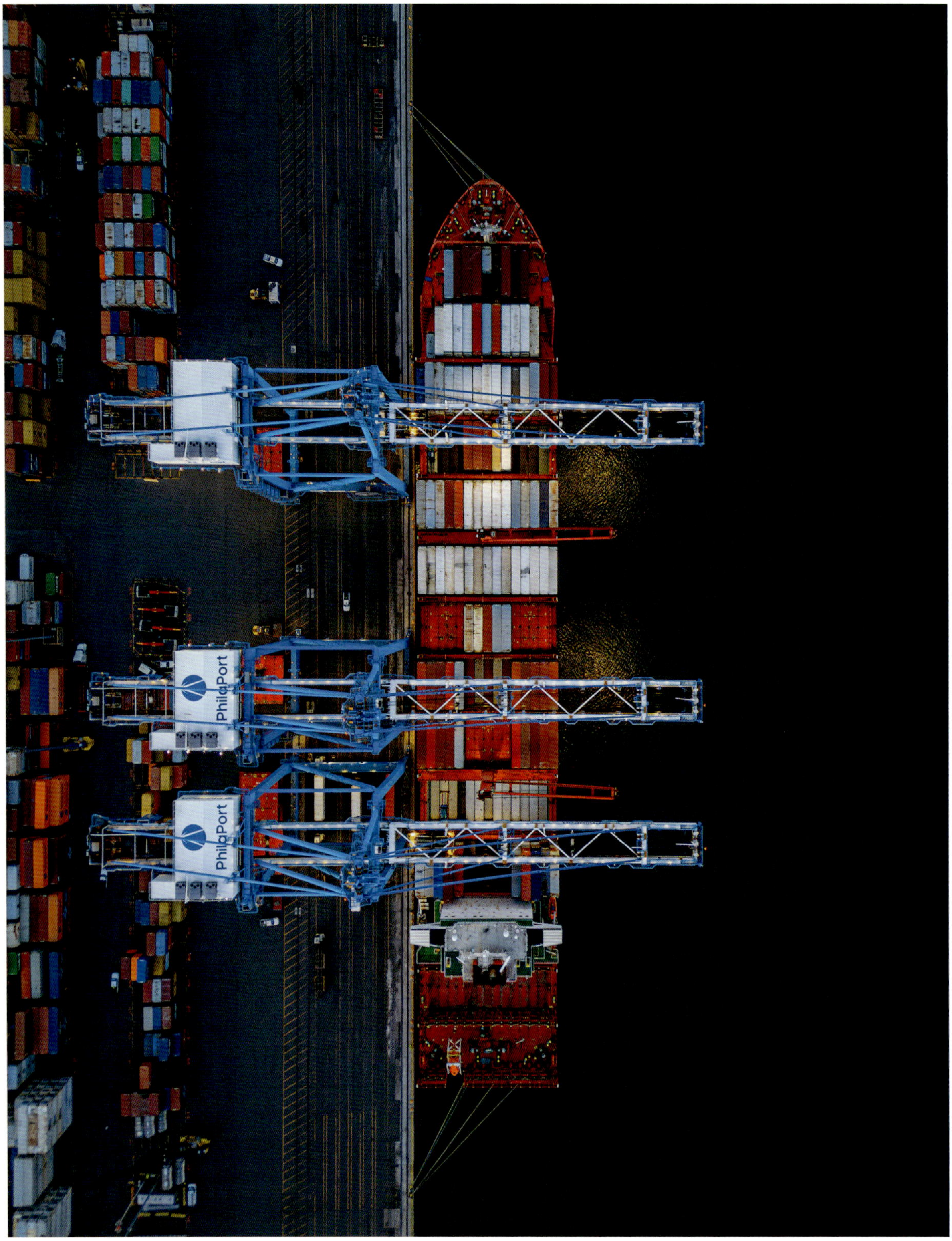
PhilaPort
PhilaPort

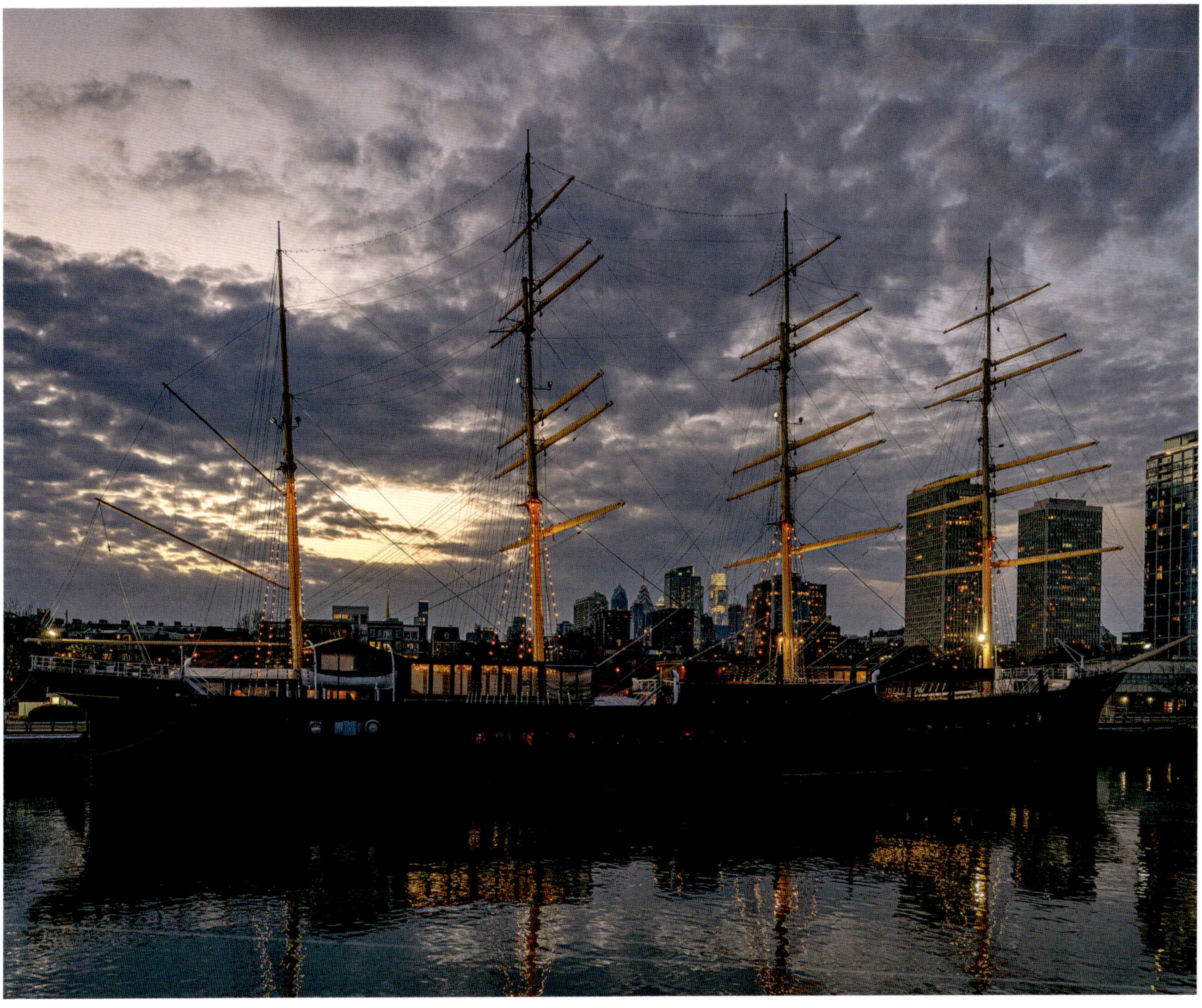

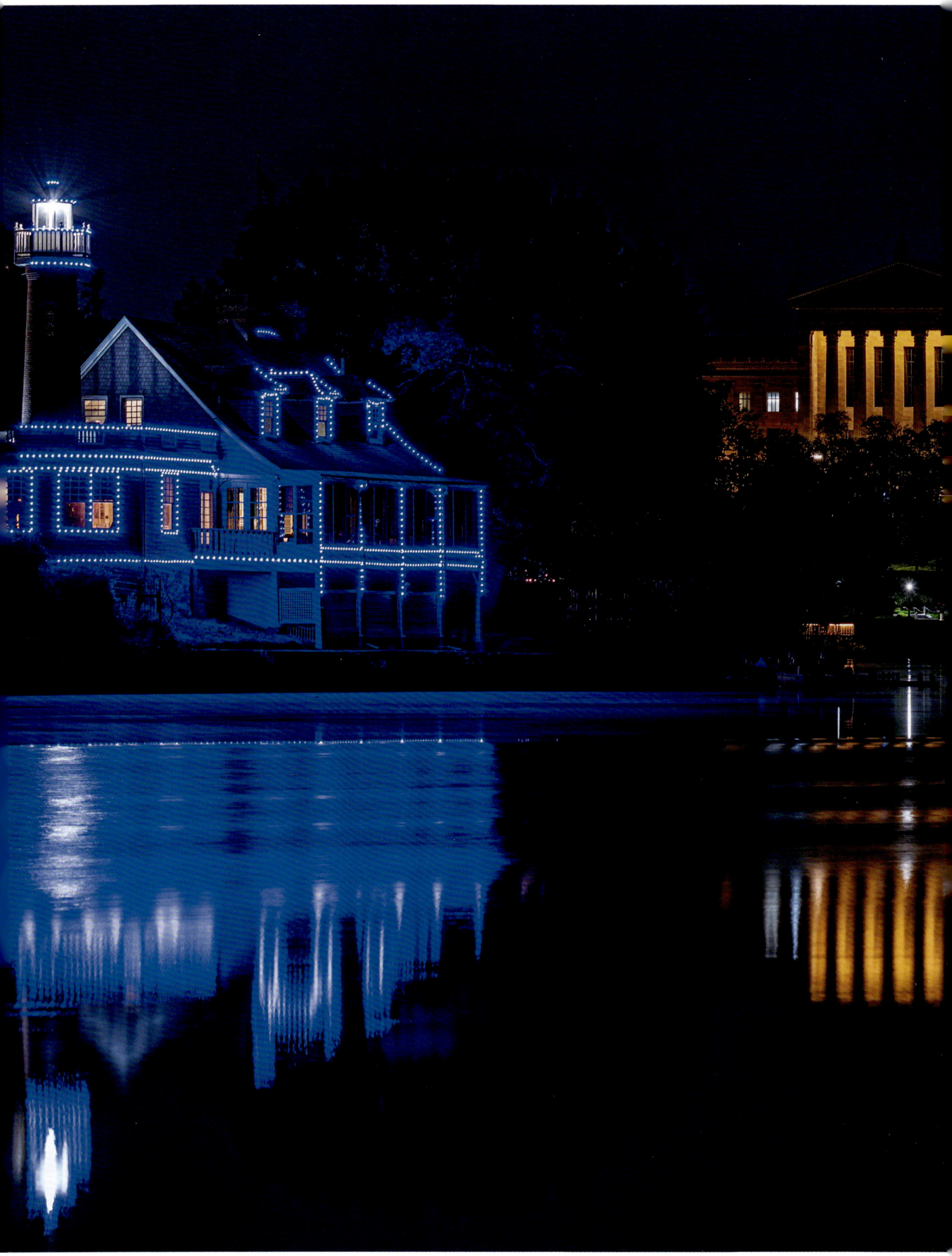

Jefferson
PSFS

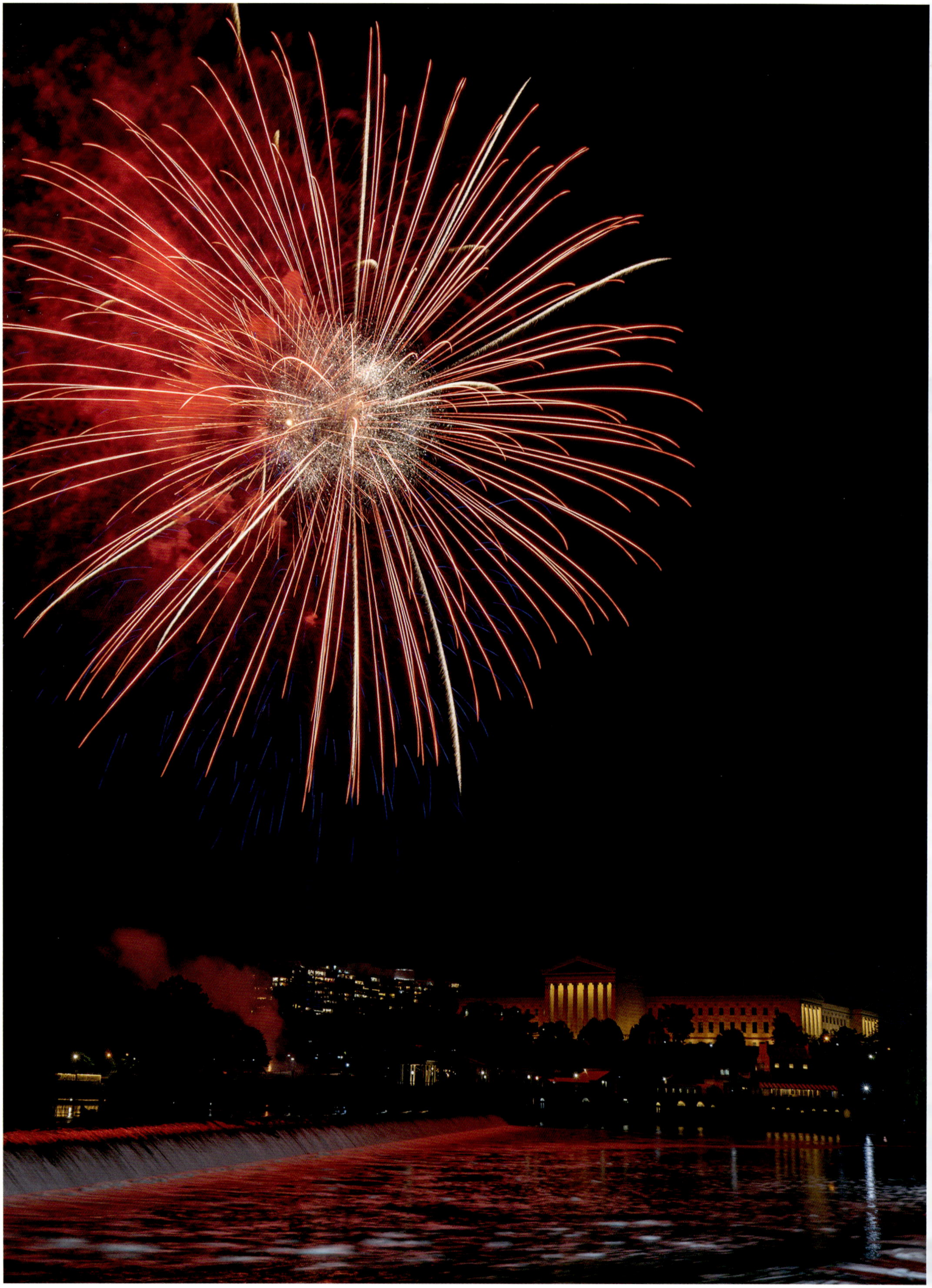

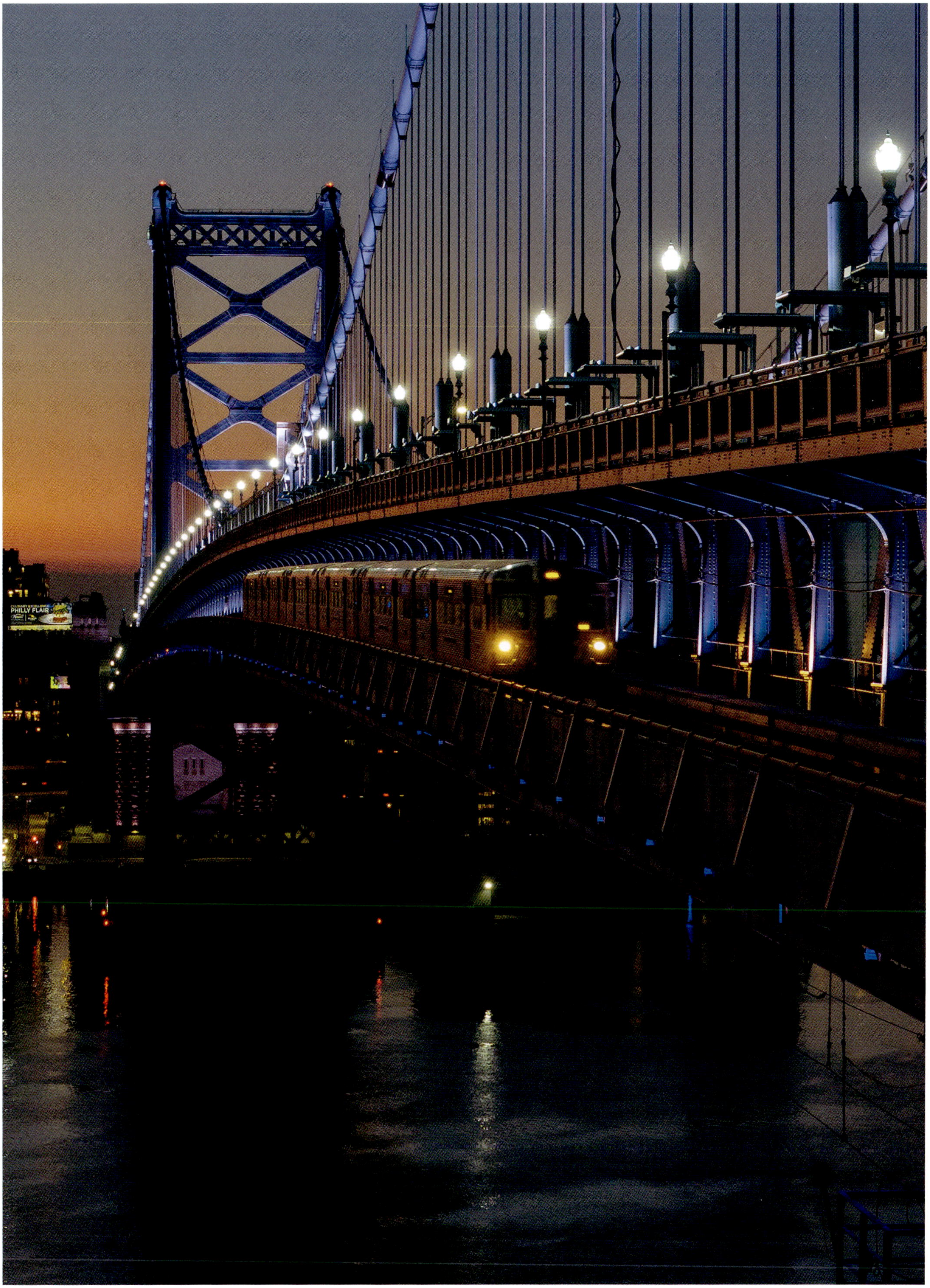
PHILLY FLAIR

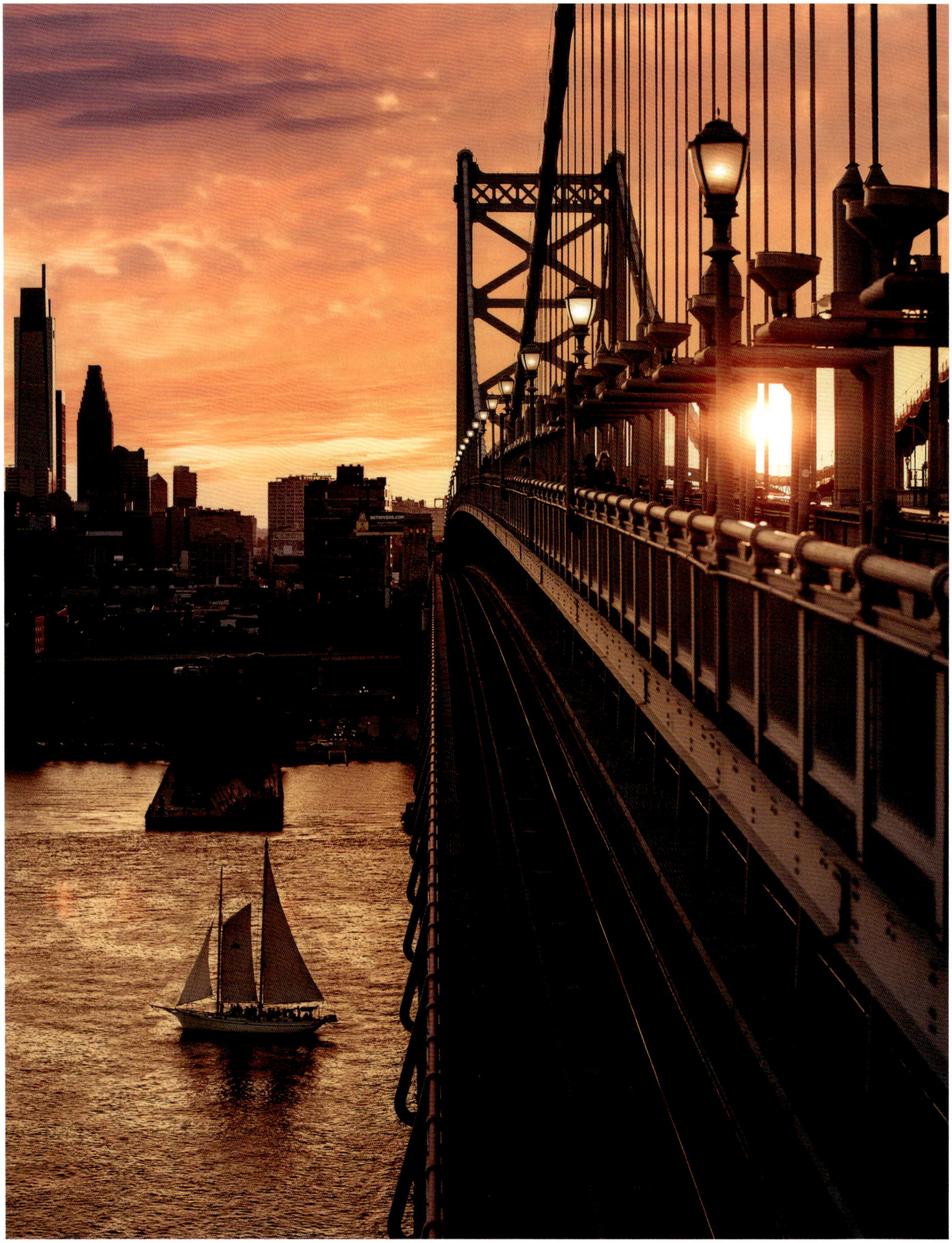

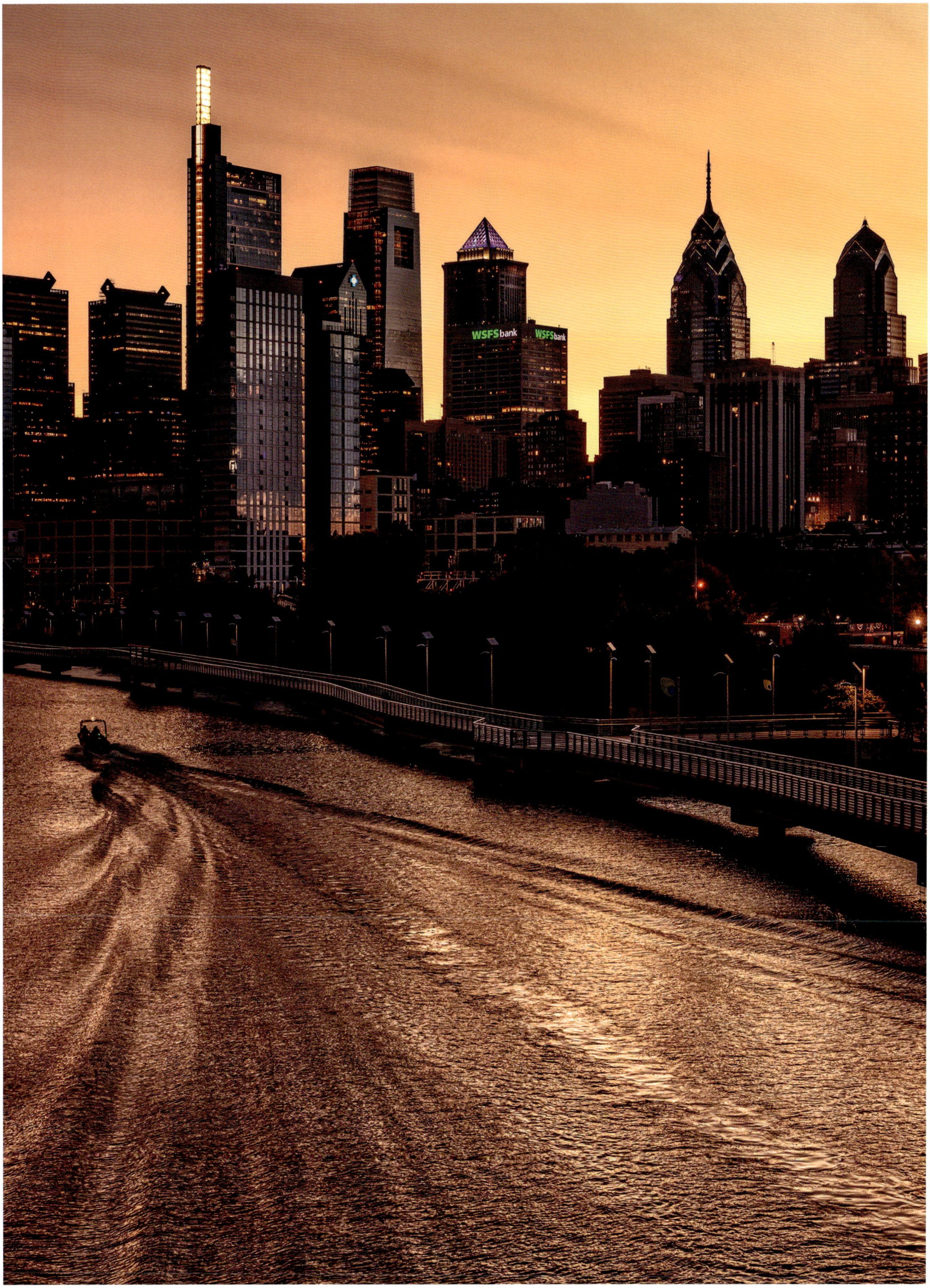
WSFS bank
WSFS bank

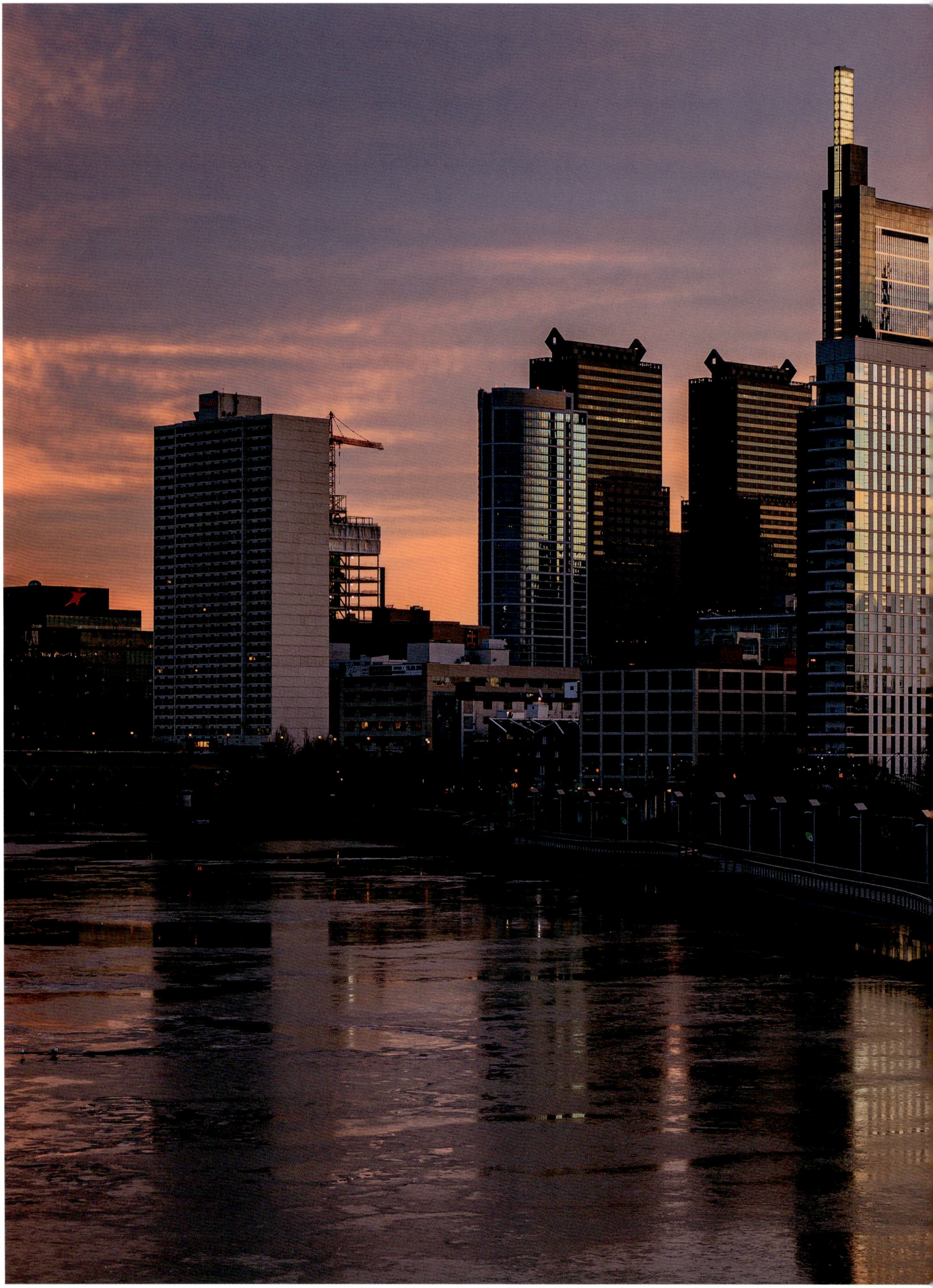

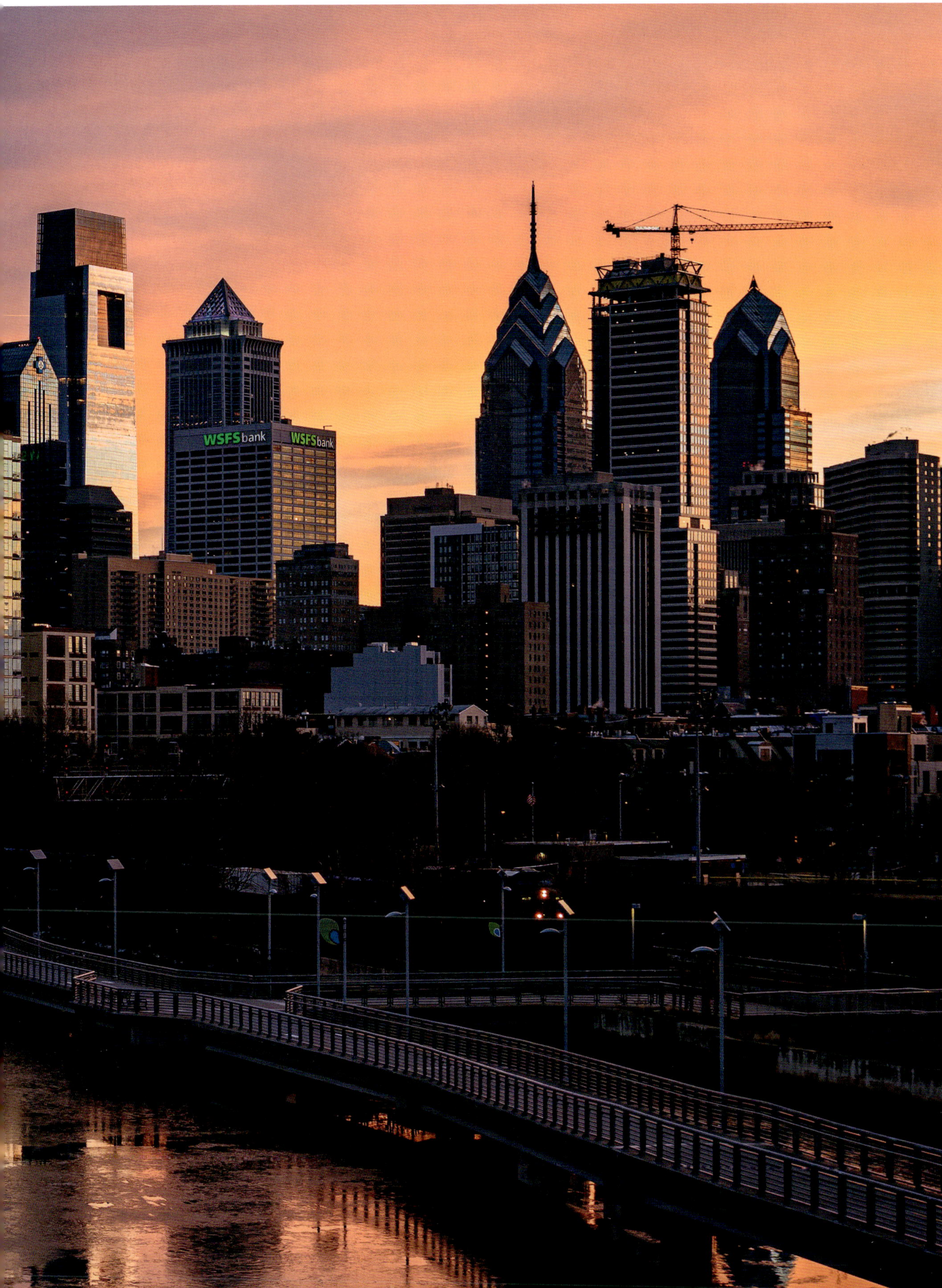
WSFS bank
WSFSbank

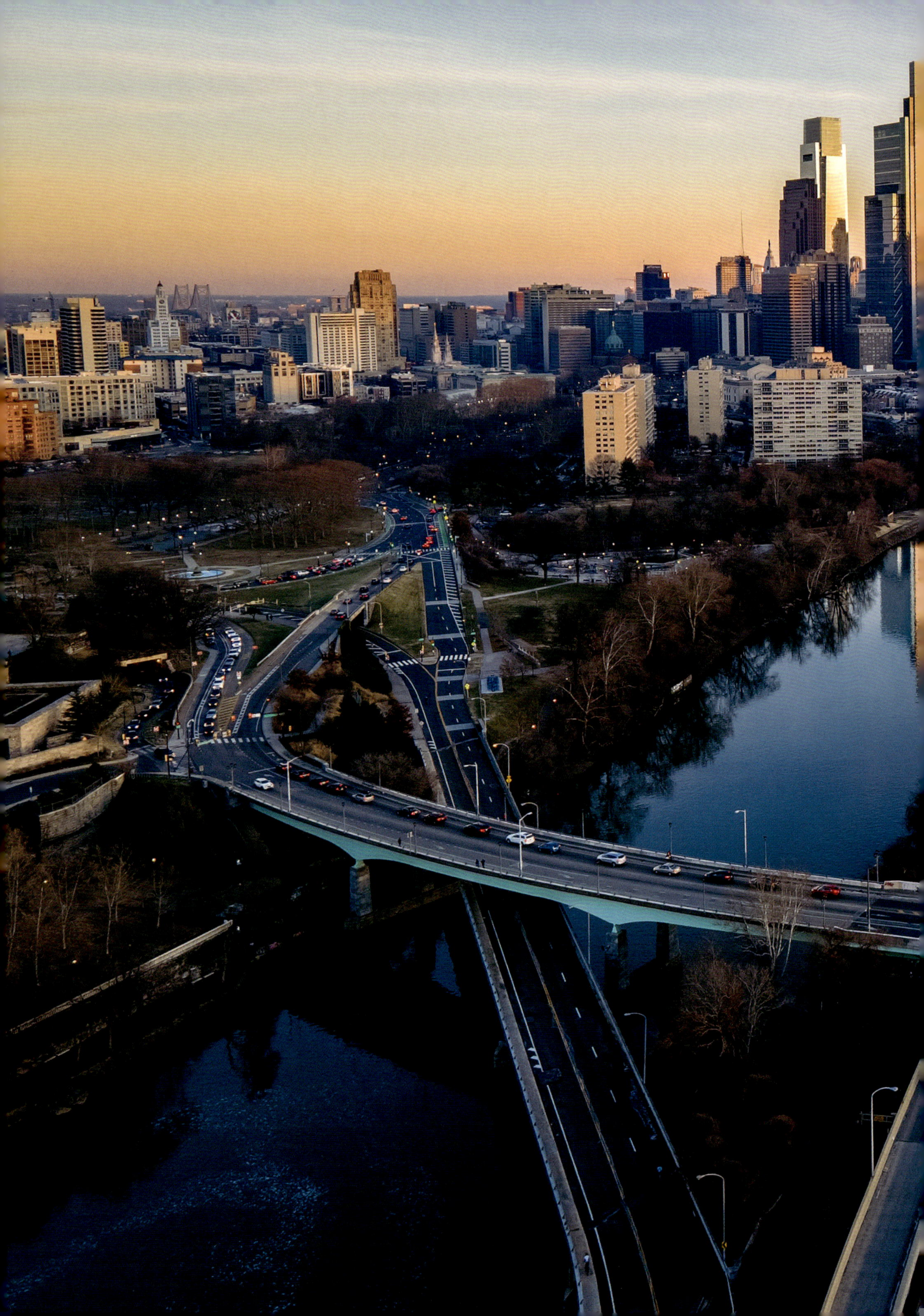

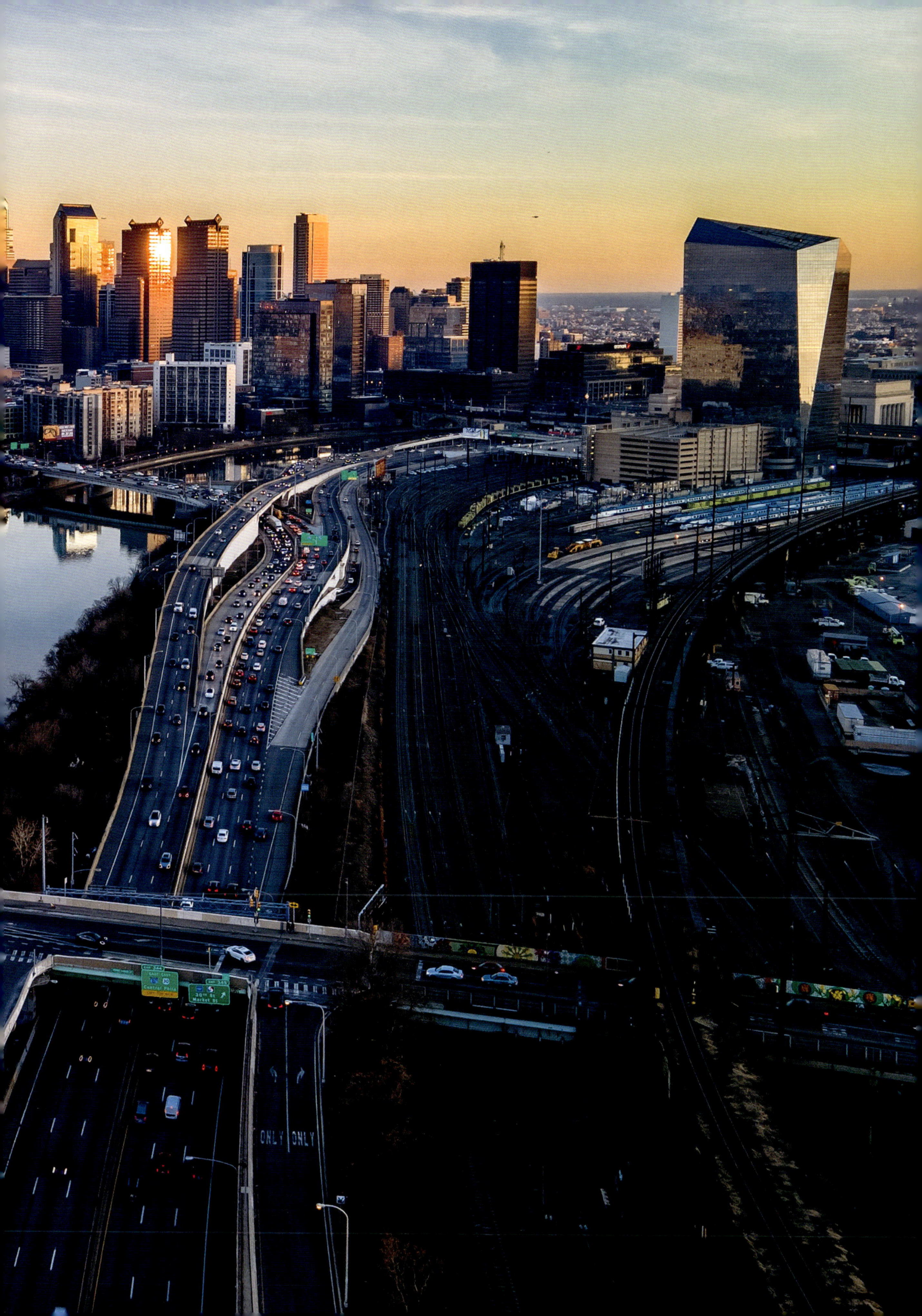
ONLY ONLY

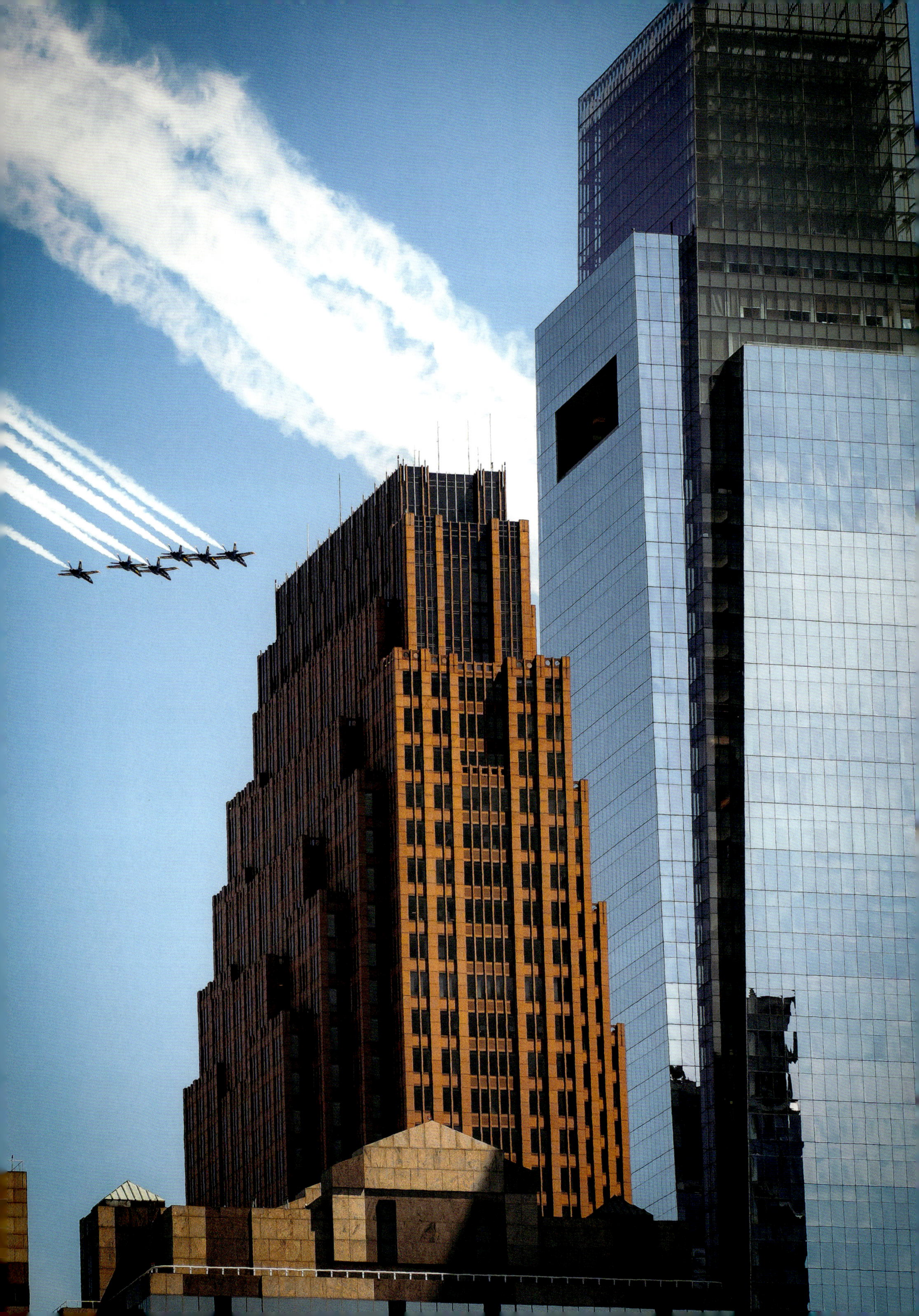

Center City ★ Philadelphia features a unique mix of historic and modern architecture. The city's skyline remained relatively low for much of the 20th century due to a longstanding "gentlemen's agreement" that no building should surpass the statue of William Penn atop City Hall, then the tallest habitable building in the world at 548 feet. This informal rule preserved Philadelphia's historic character but also constrained its vertical growth. As other cities embraced the modern skyscraper, Philadelphia maintained a modest silhouette dominated by the architecture of City Hall. ★ Completed in 1898 and designed by architect Daniel H. Burnham, the Land Title Building is one of the earliest examples of a steel-framed skyscraper in Philadelphia. Located at 1400 Chestnut Street, the original building rose 10 stories, and its steel-frame construction allowed for greater height and fireproofing than was typical at the time. A 27-story tower was added to the site just a few years later. Designed by Horace Trumbauer and featuring Beaux-Arts style elements, the expanded complex reached a height of 331 feet but still stood below the height of William Penn. ★ This tradition lasted until 1984 when plans were announced to build an office complex with two towers taller than City Hall. 1987 marked the completion of One Liberty Place, a 945-foot postmodern skyscraper designed by Helmut Jahn that shattered the city's height barrier and redefined Philadelphia's architectural ambitions. One Liberty Place became the city's first skyscraper, and its iconic design and spire make the complex a recognizable part of the Philadelphia skyline. Construction on Two Liberty Place and BNY Mellon Center followed soon after. 21st-century skyscrapers including the Comcast Center and Comcast Technology Center brought sleek, modern designs to the Philadelphia skyline, further transforming the city from colonial capital to the modern metropolis it is today.

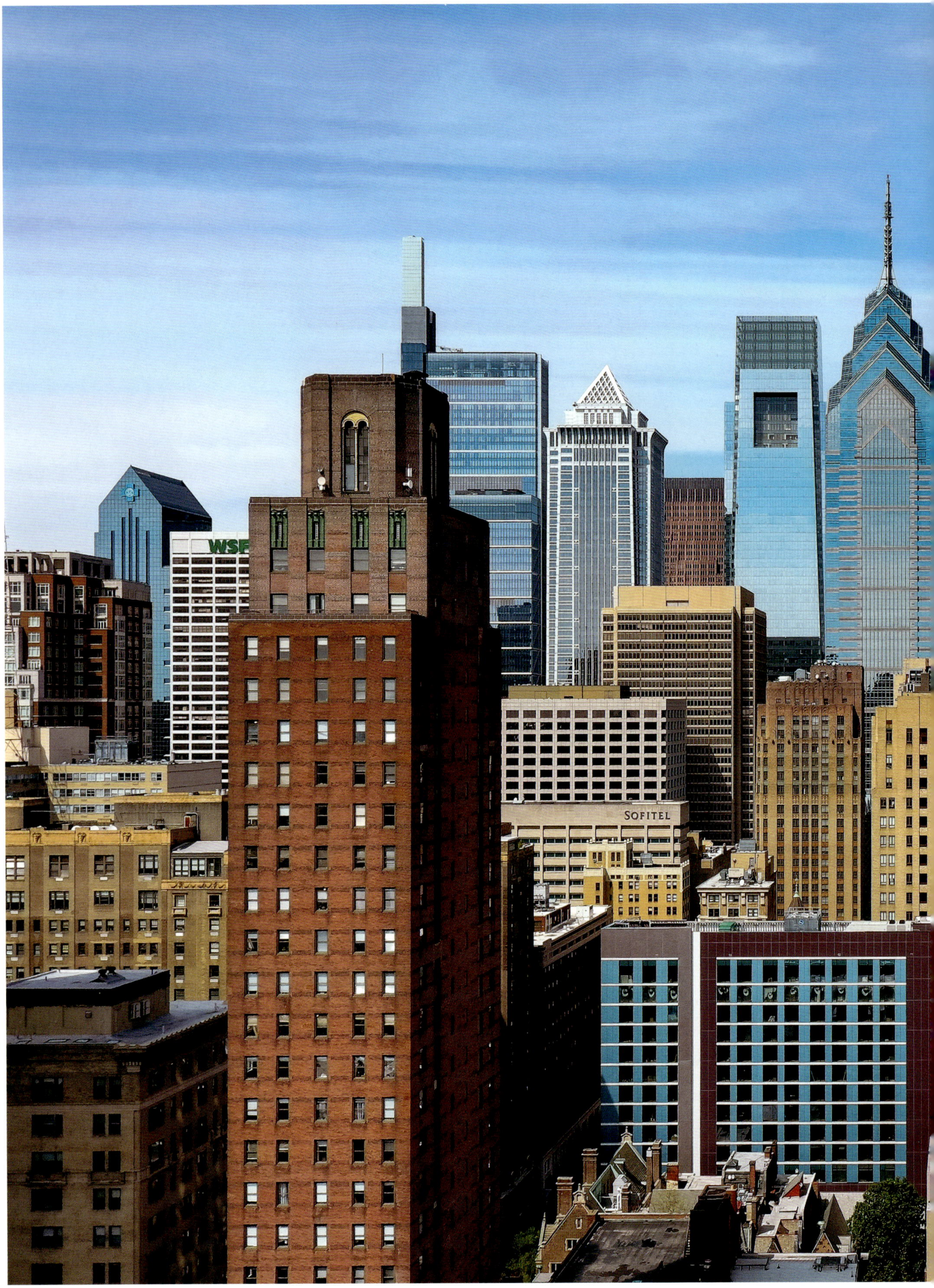
WSF
SOFITEL

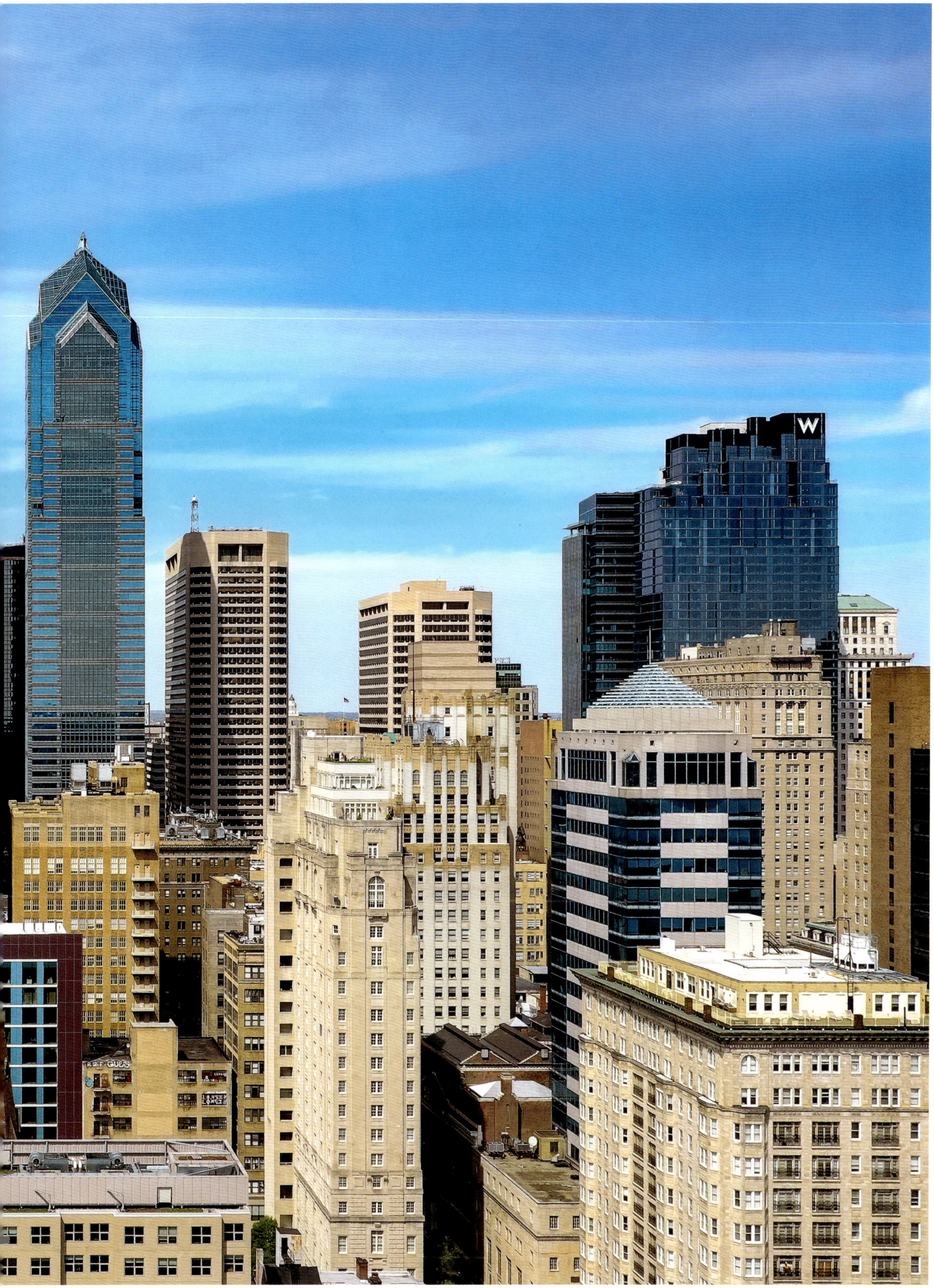
W

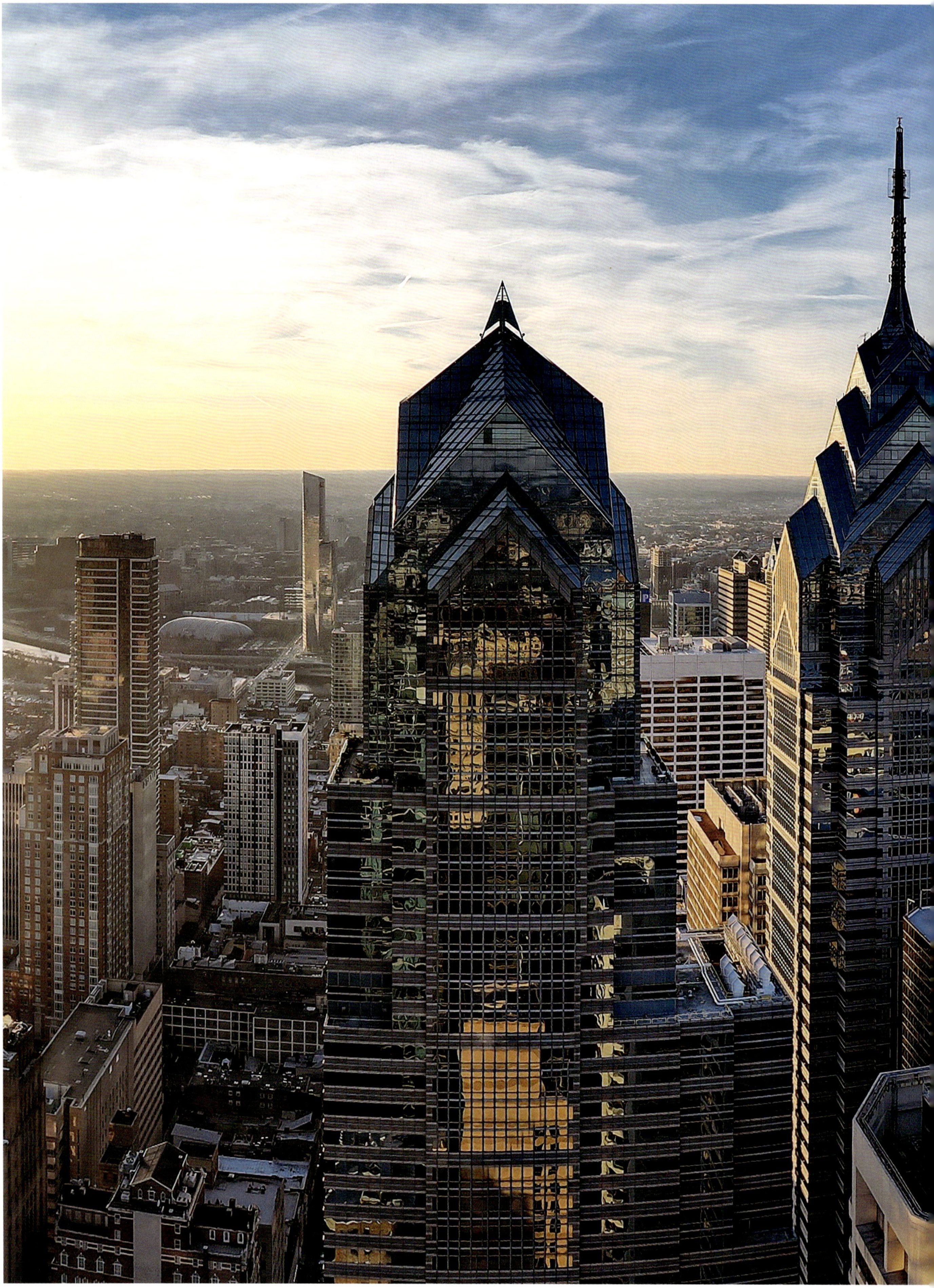

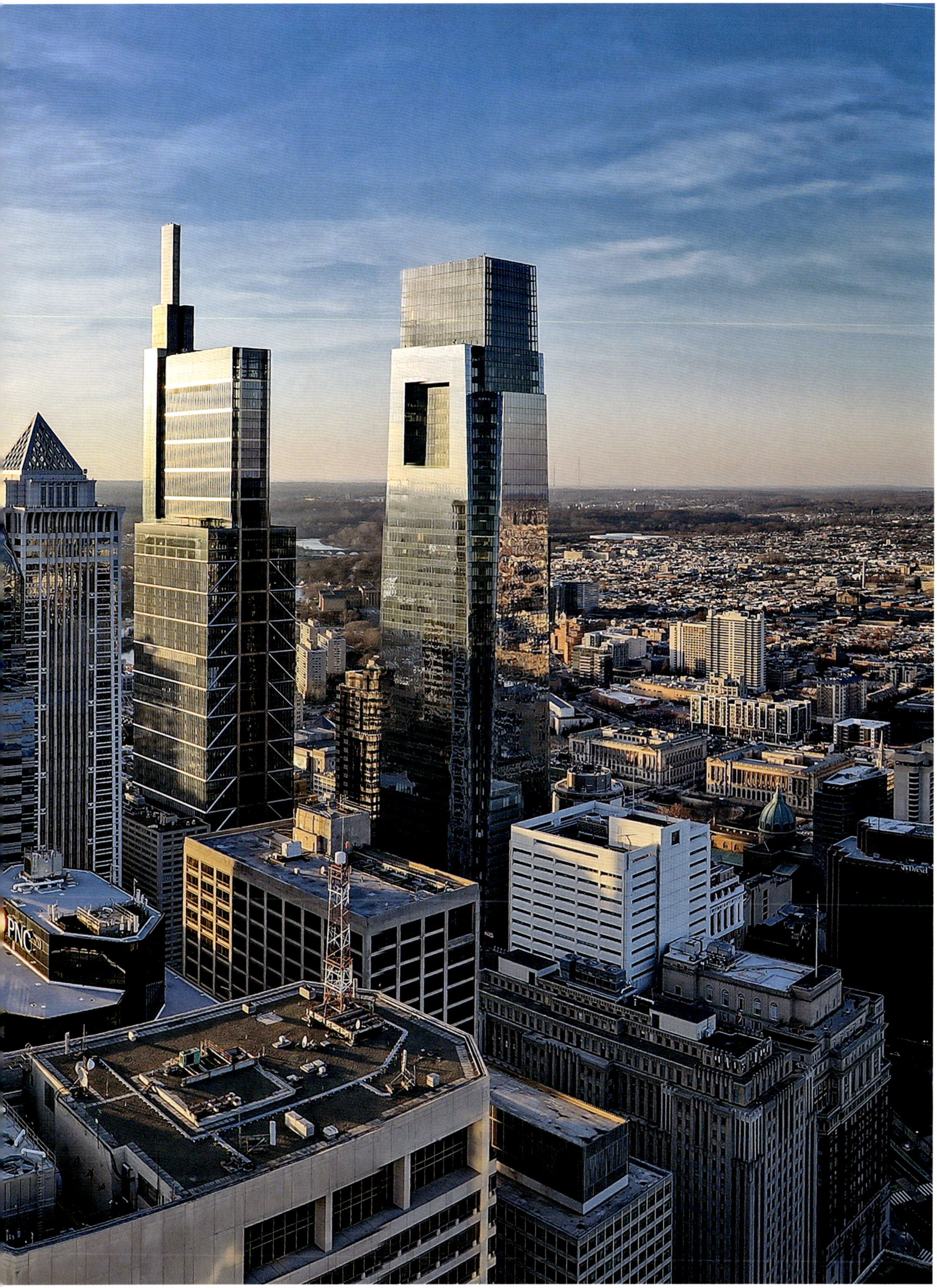

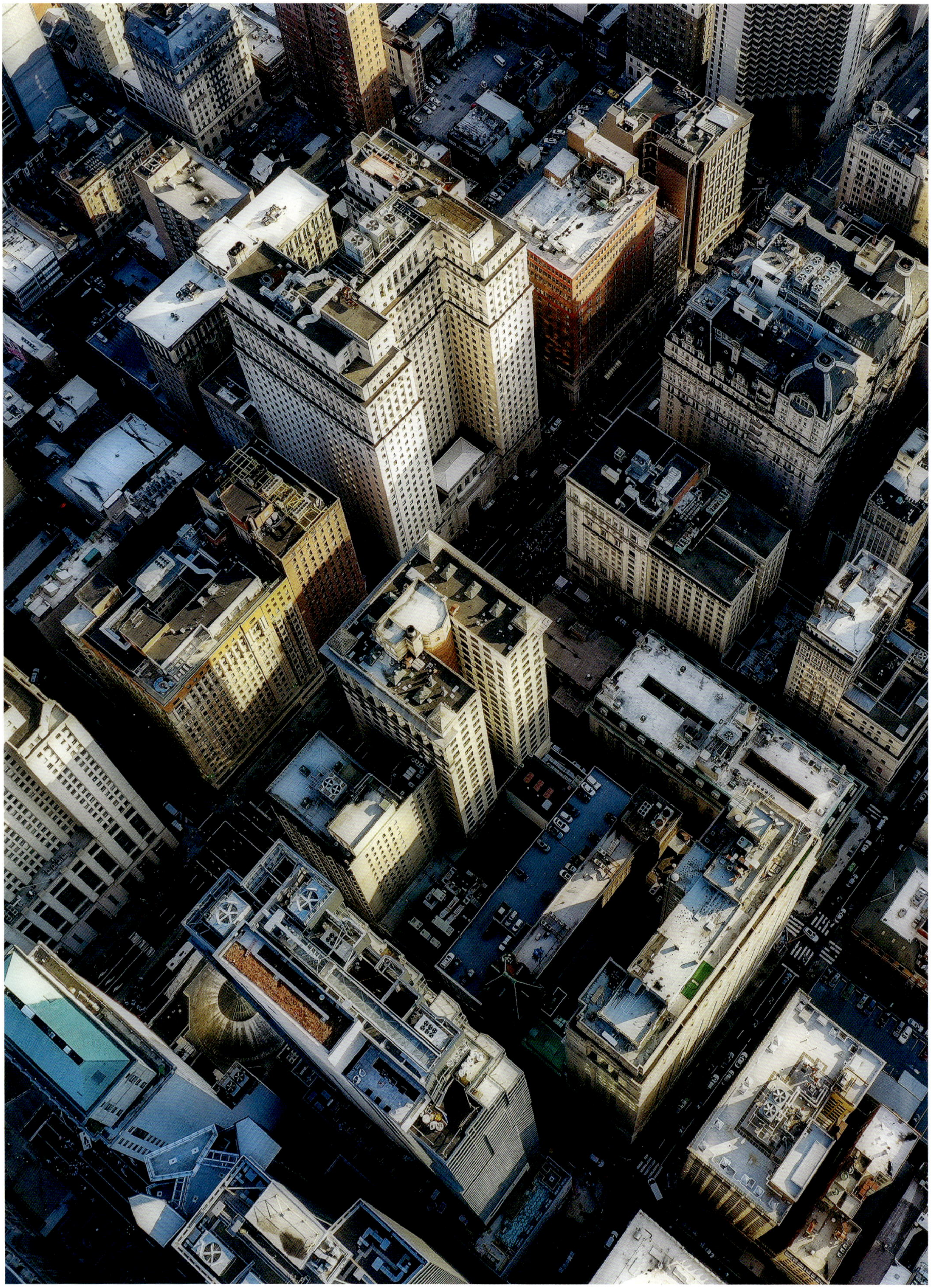

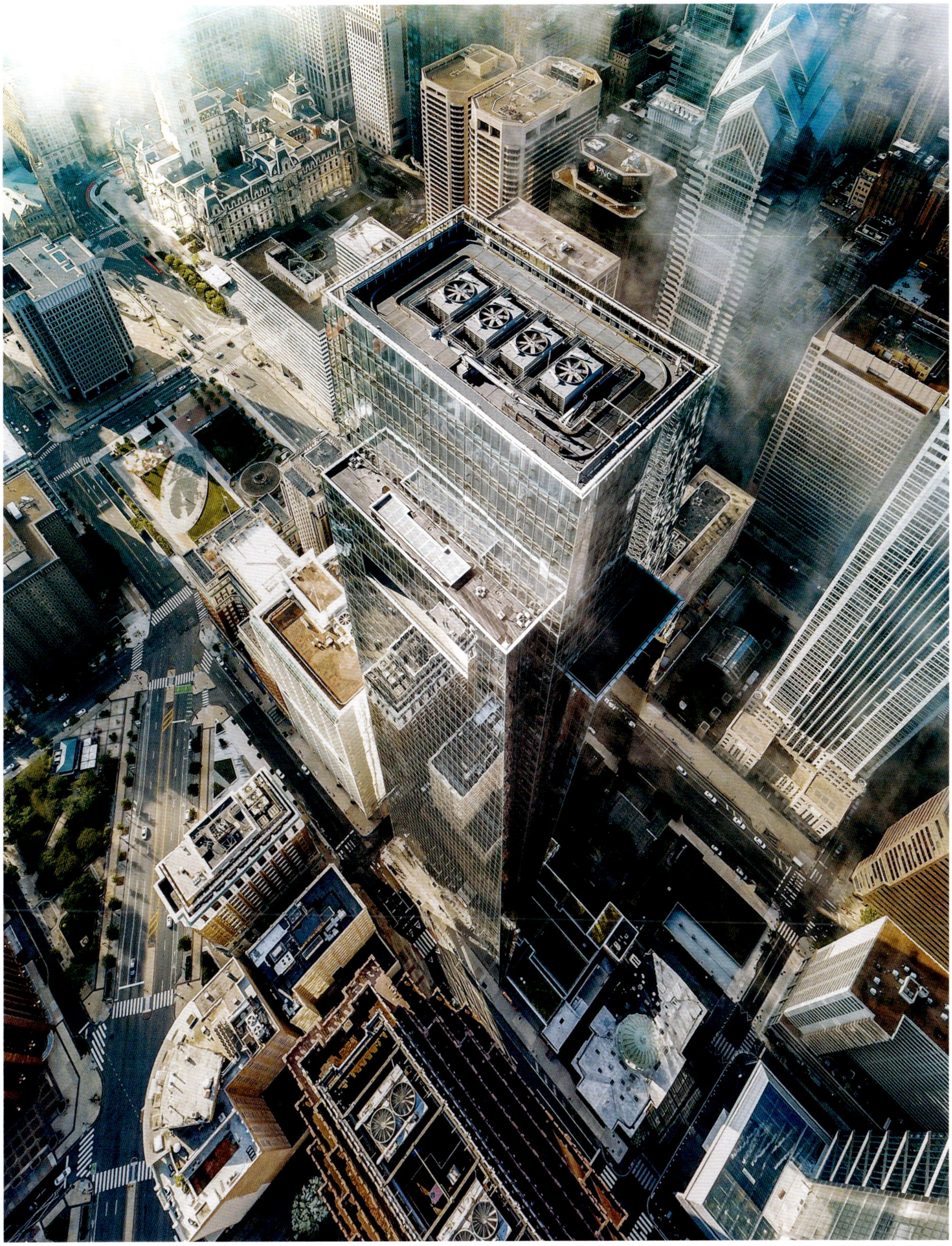
PNC

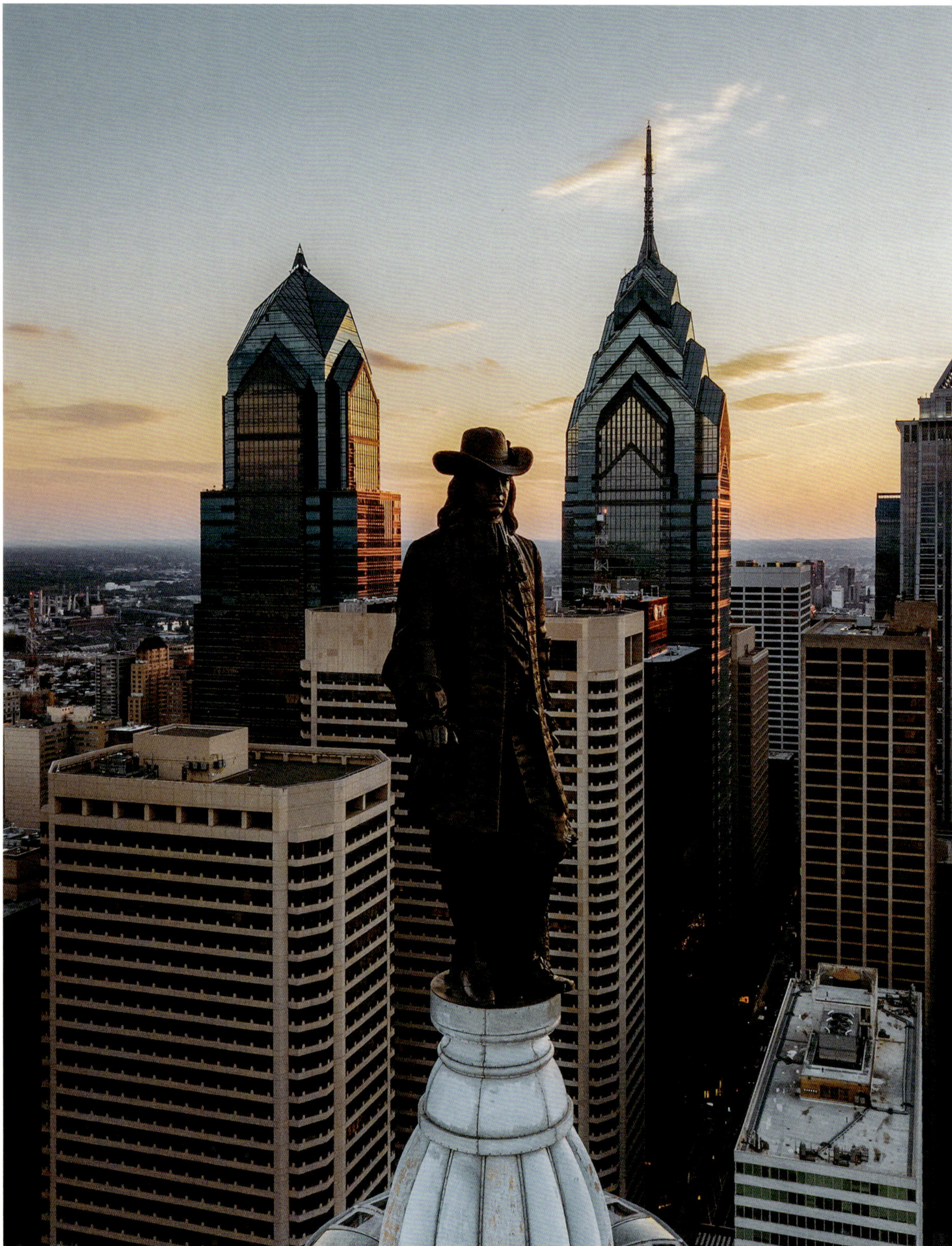

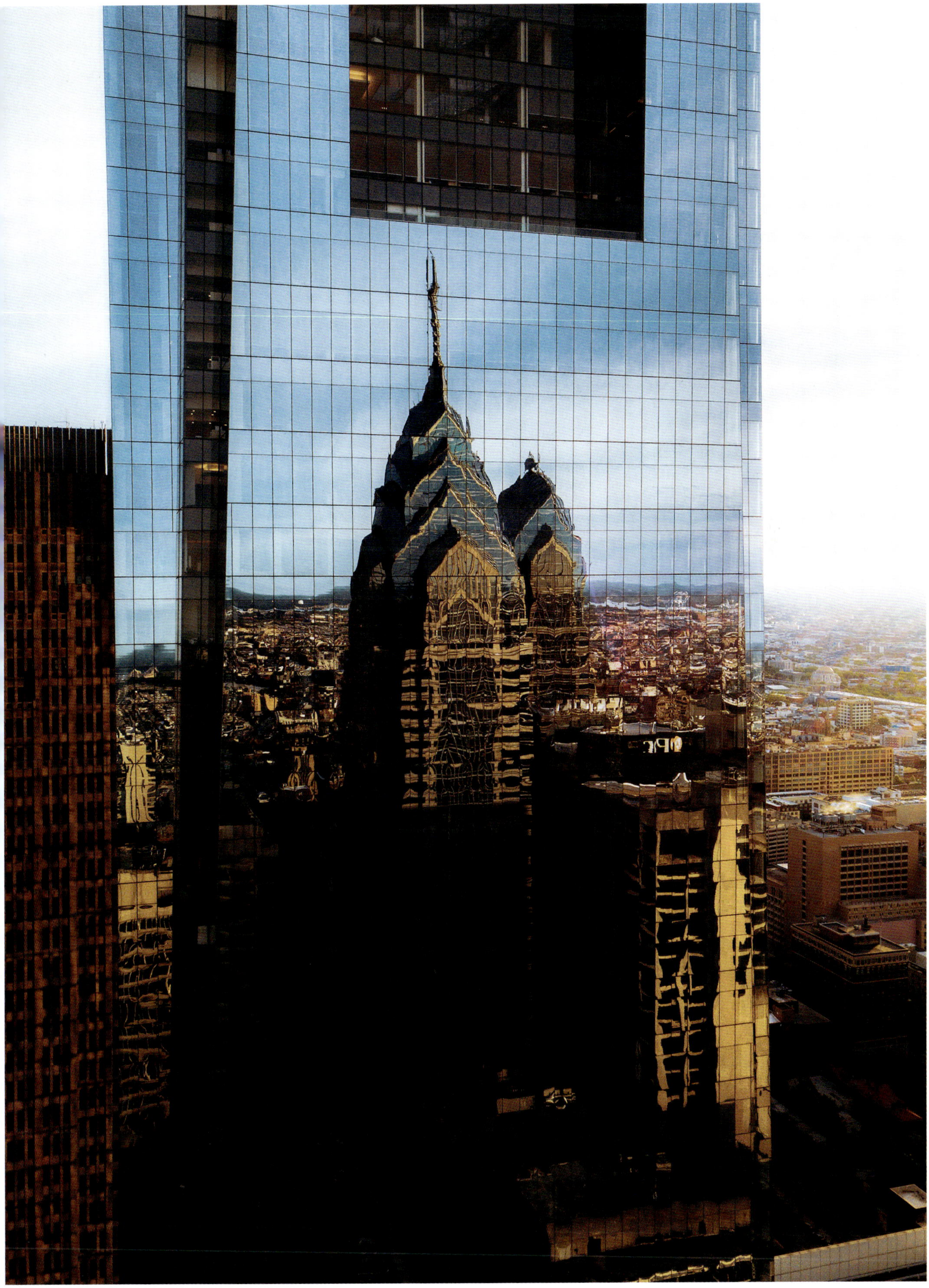

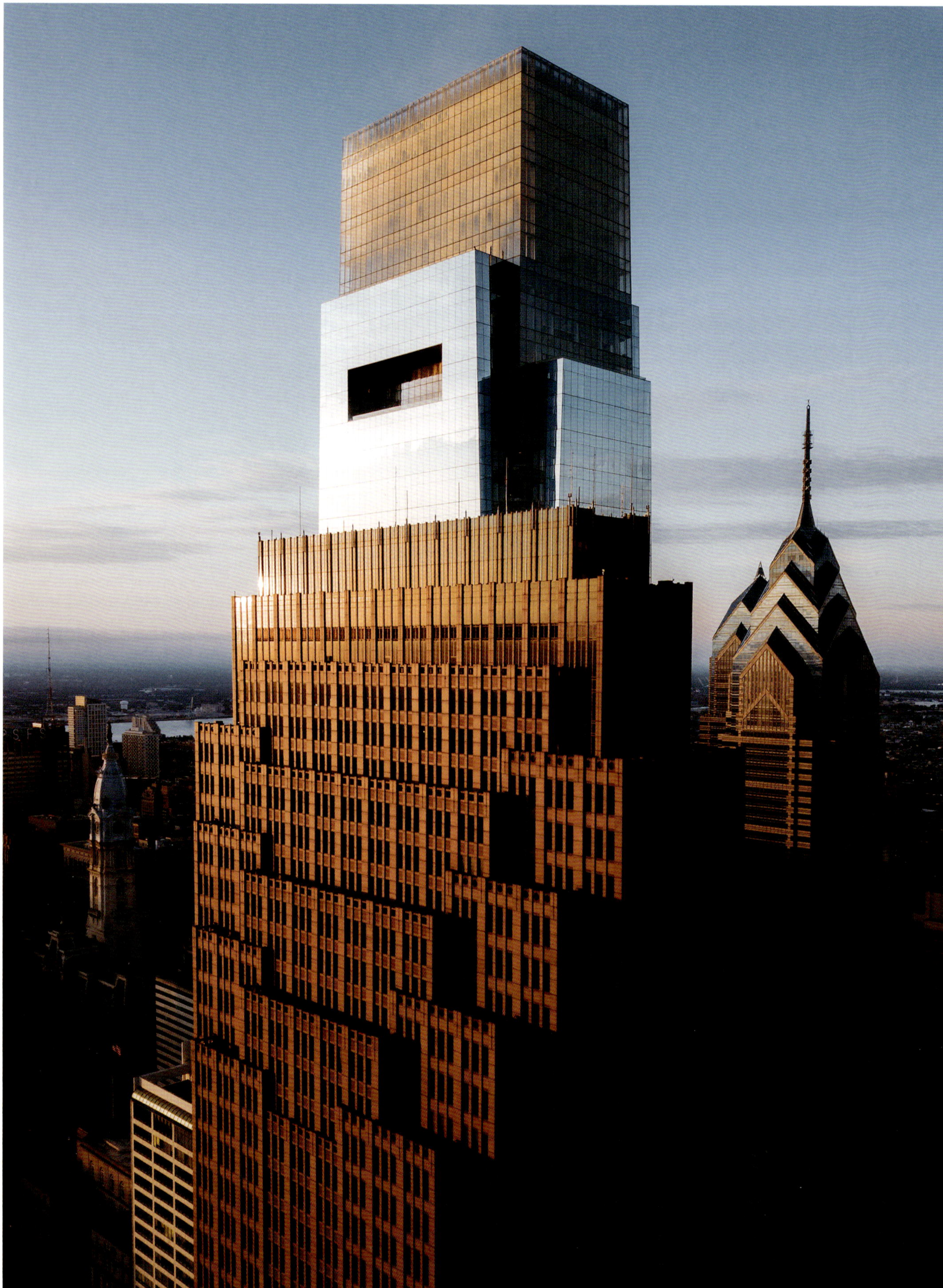

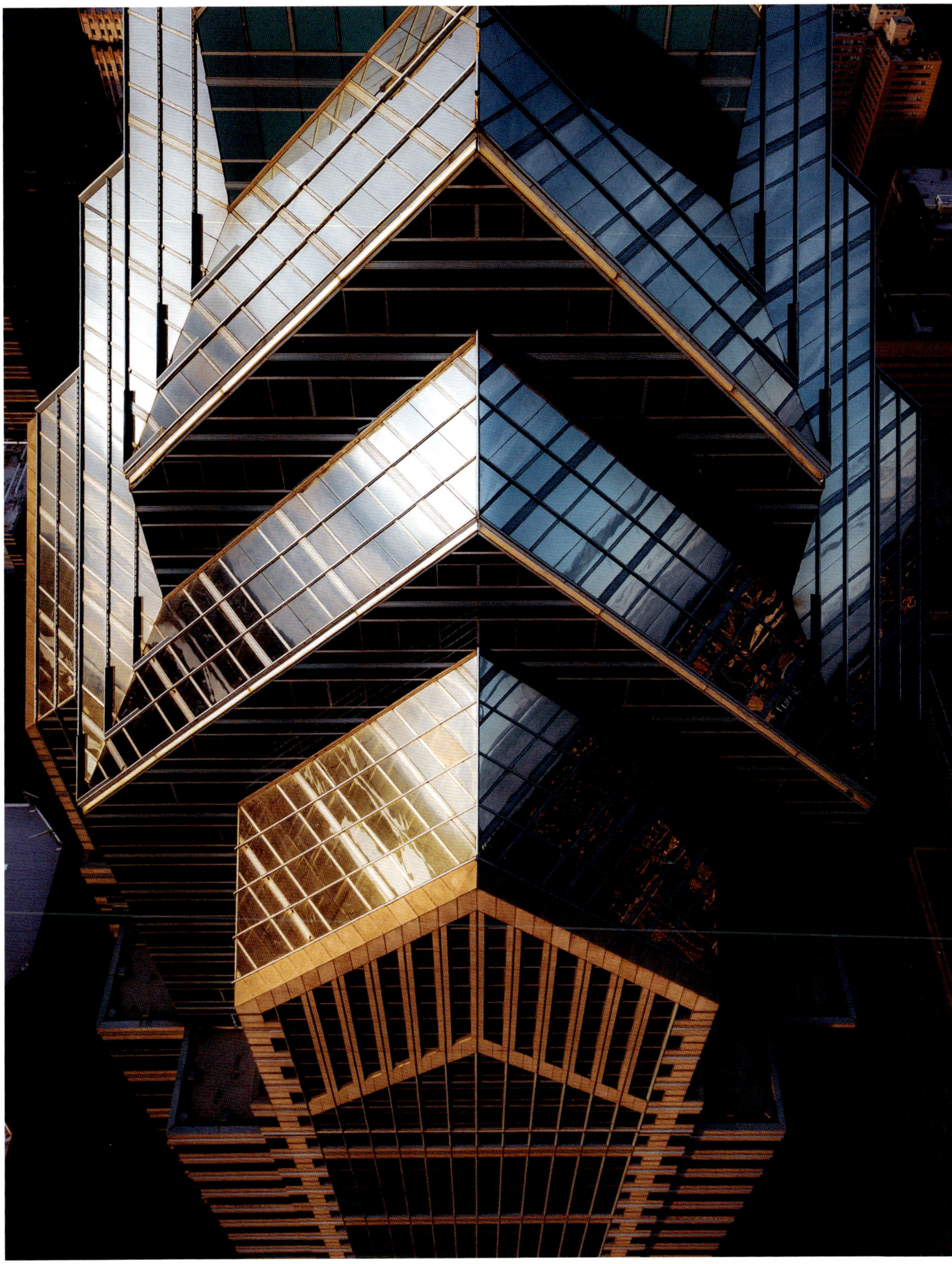

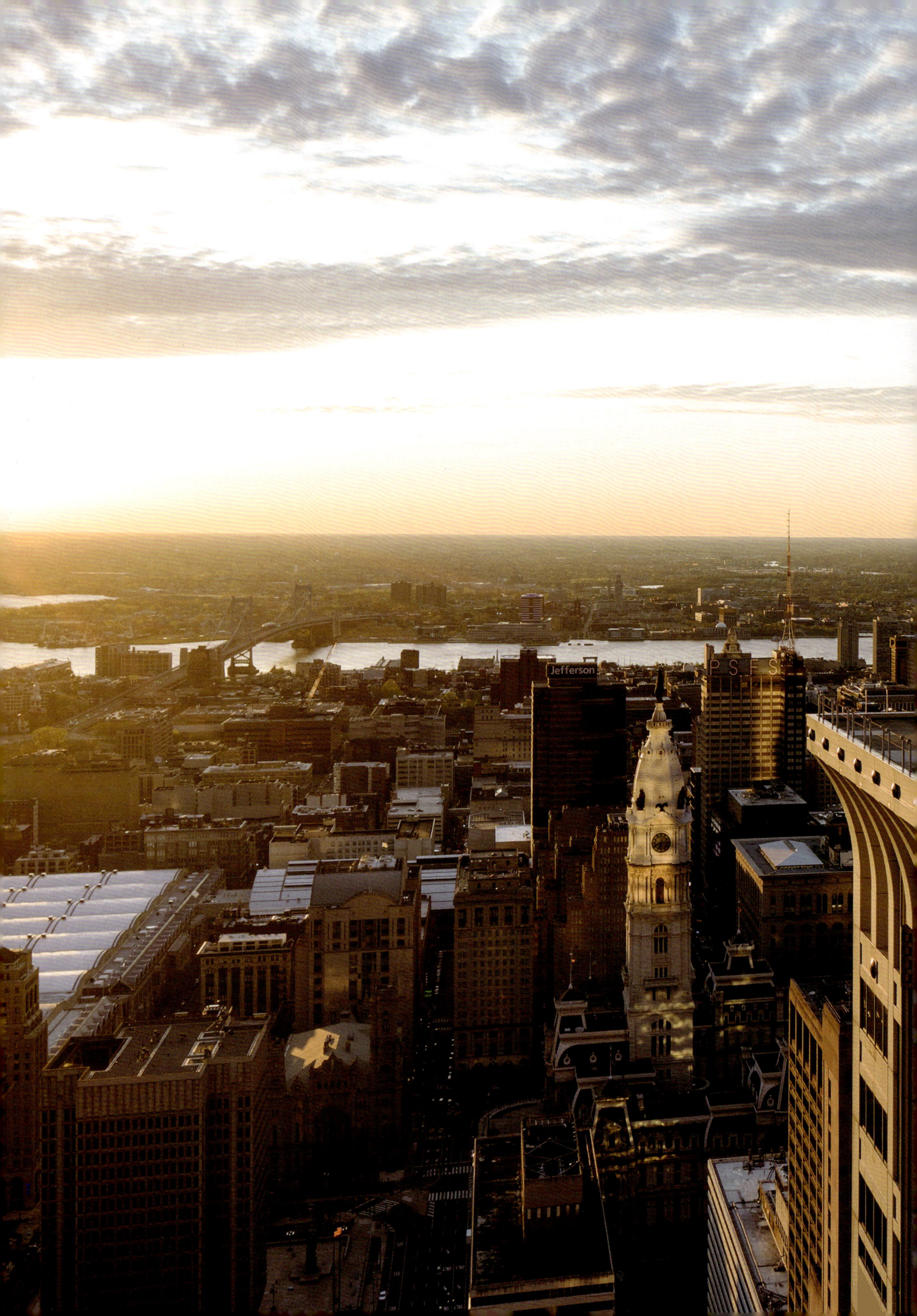
Jefferson
PSFS

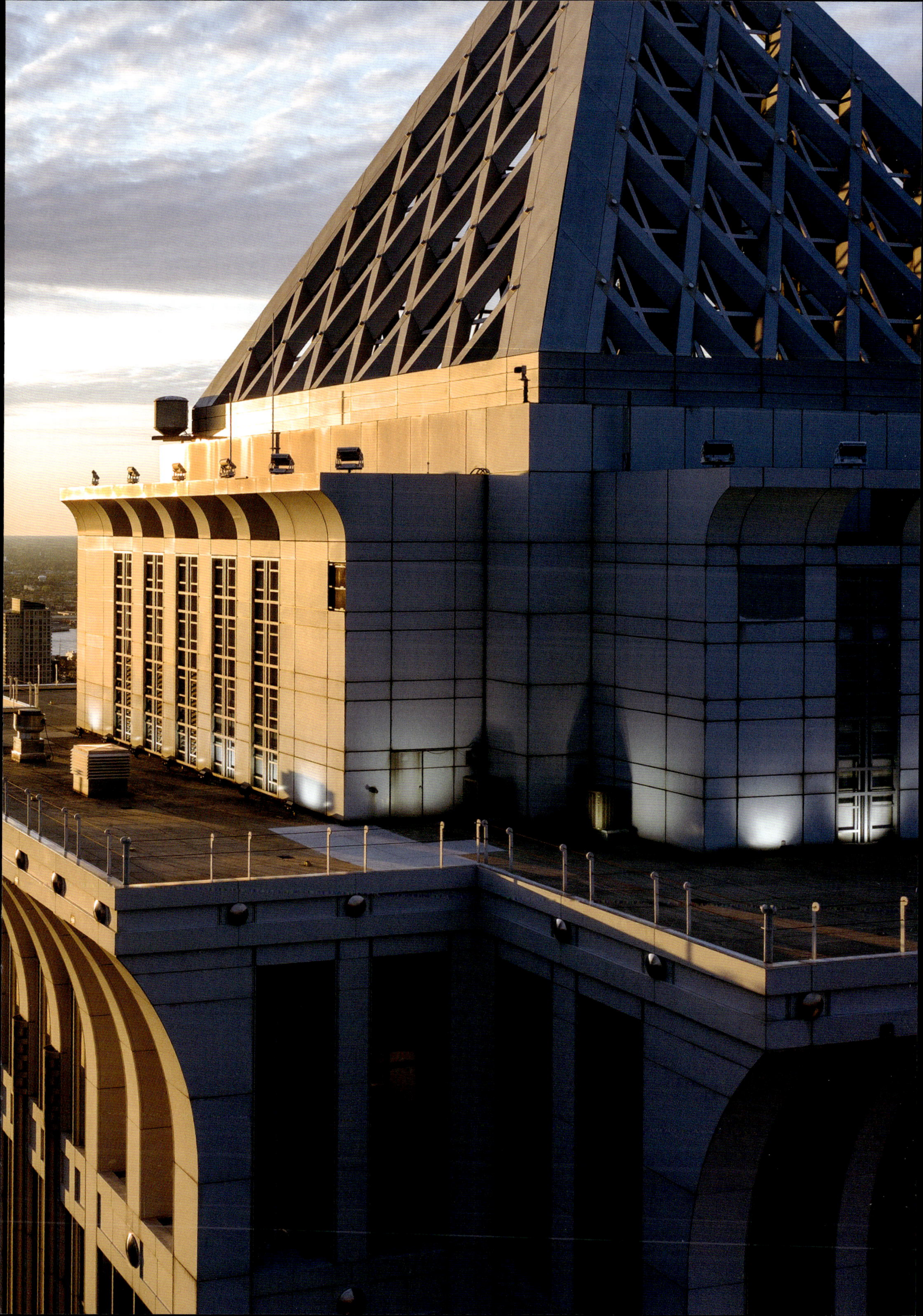

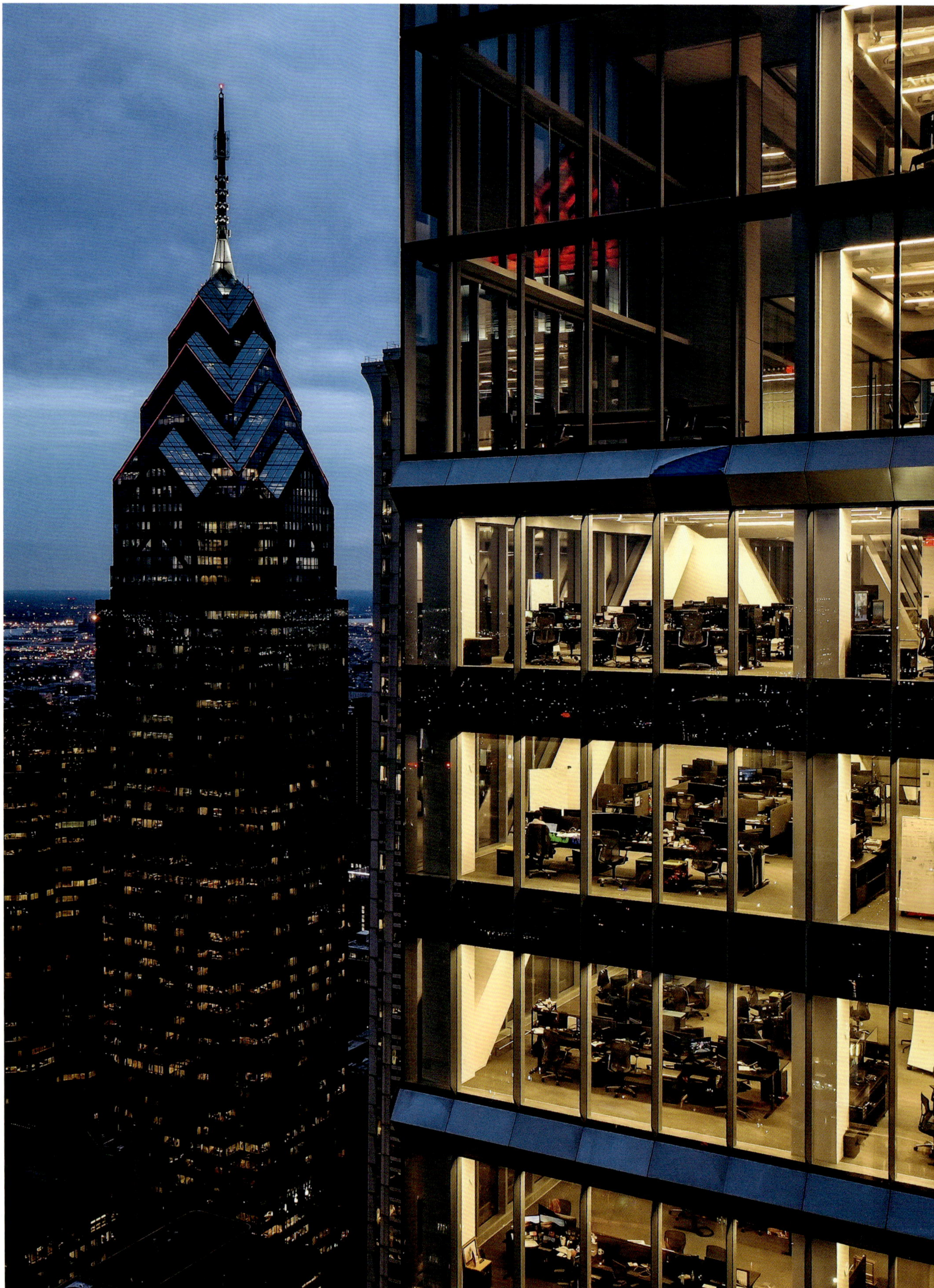

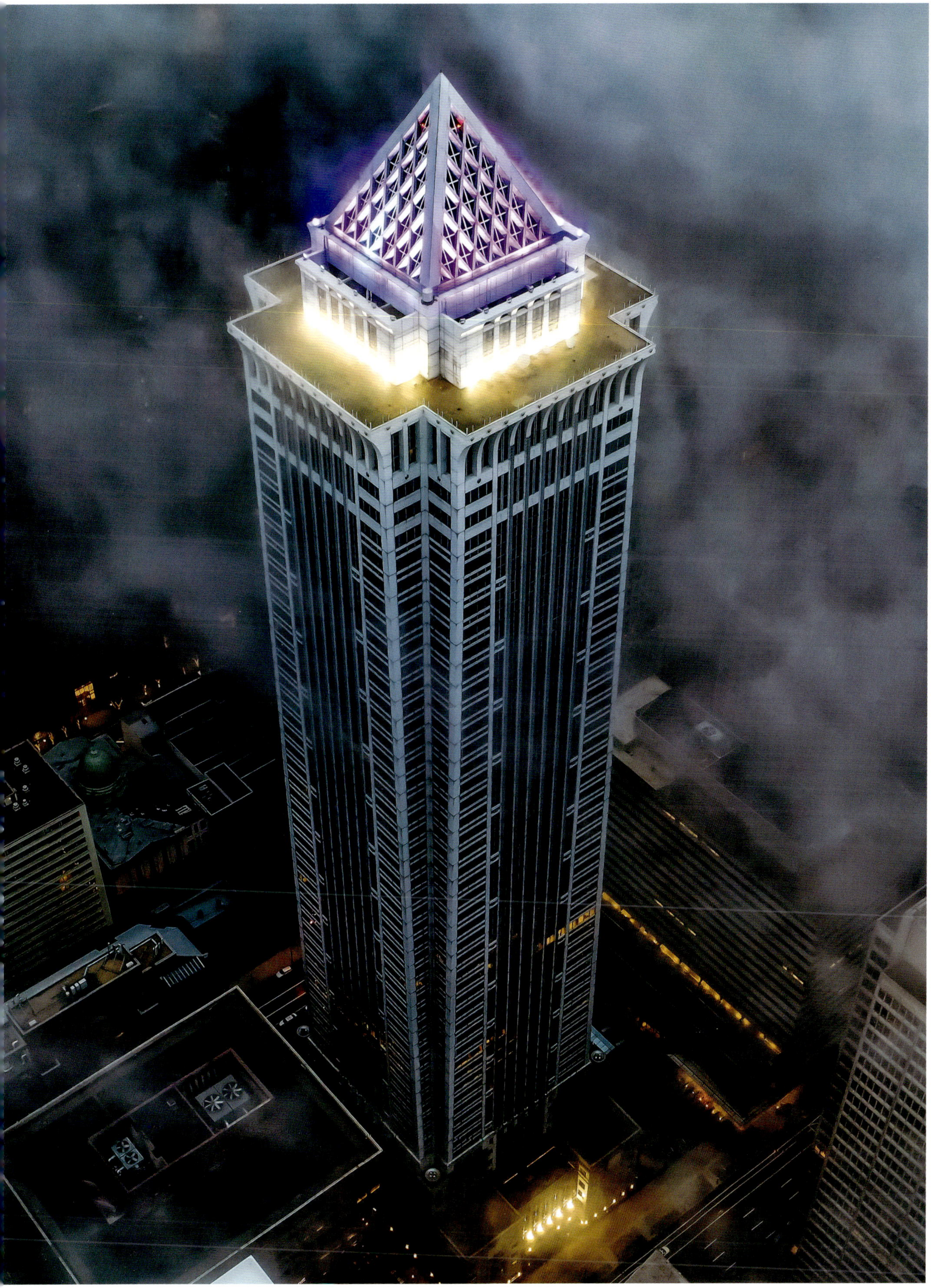

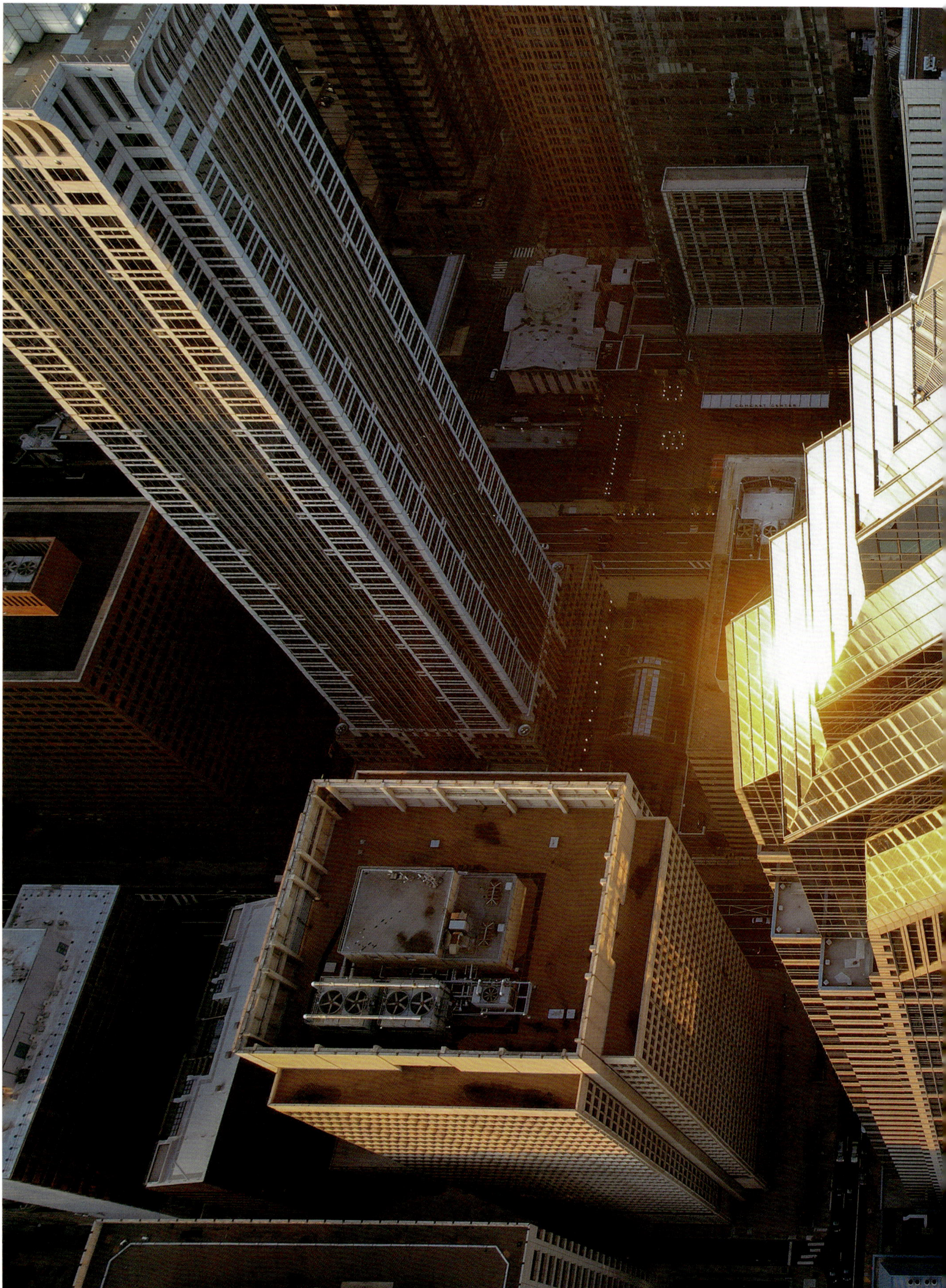

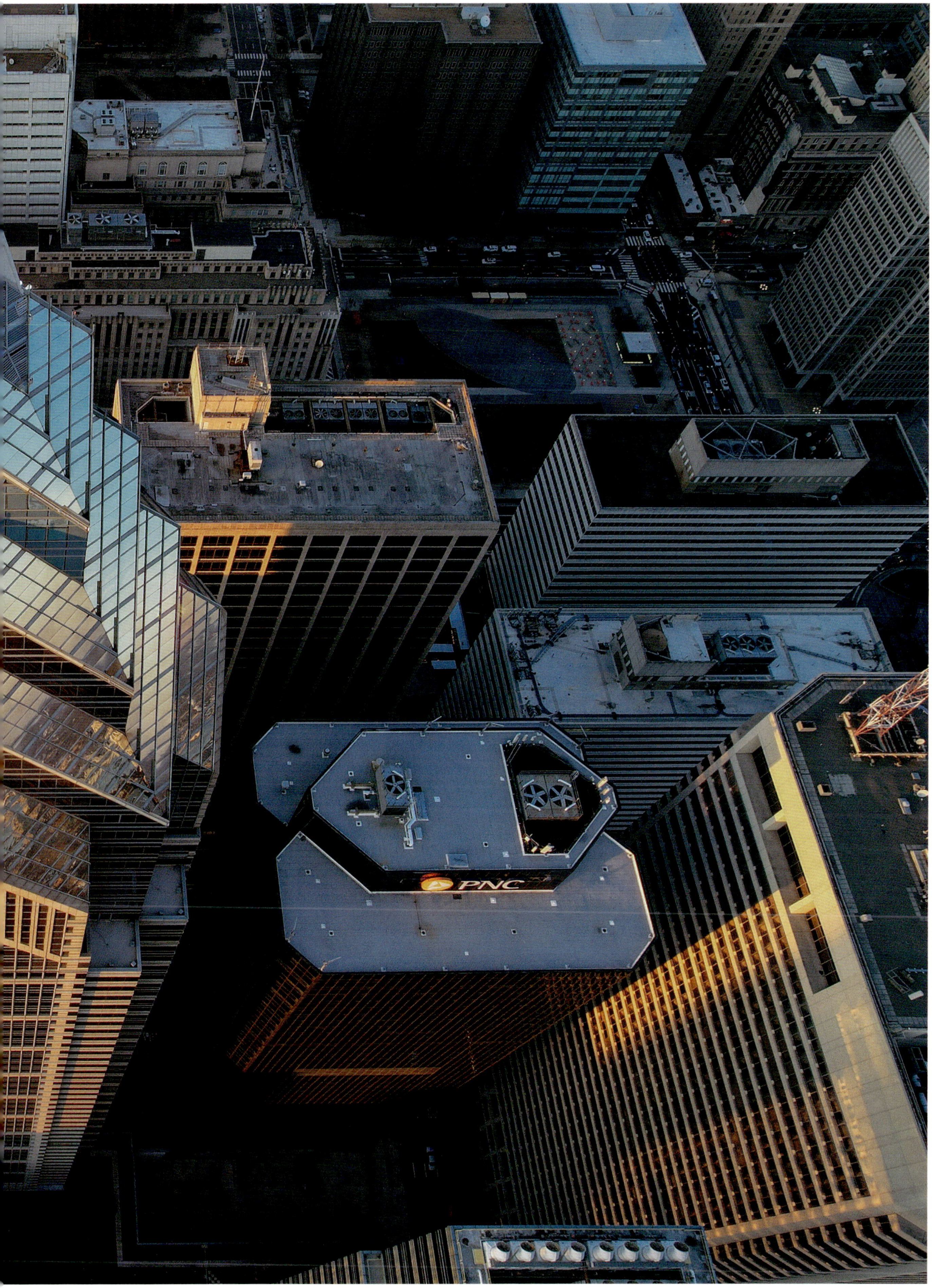
PNC

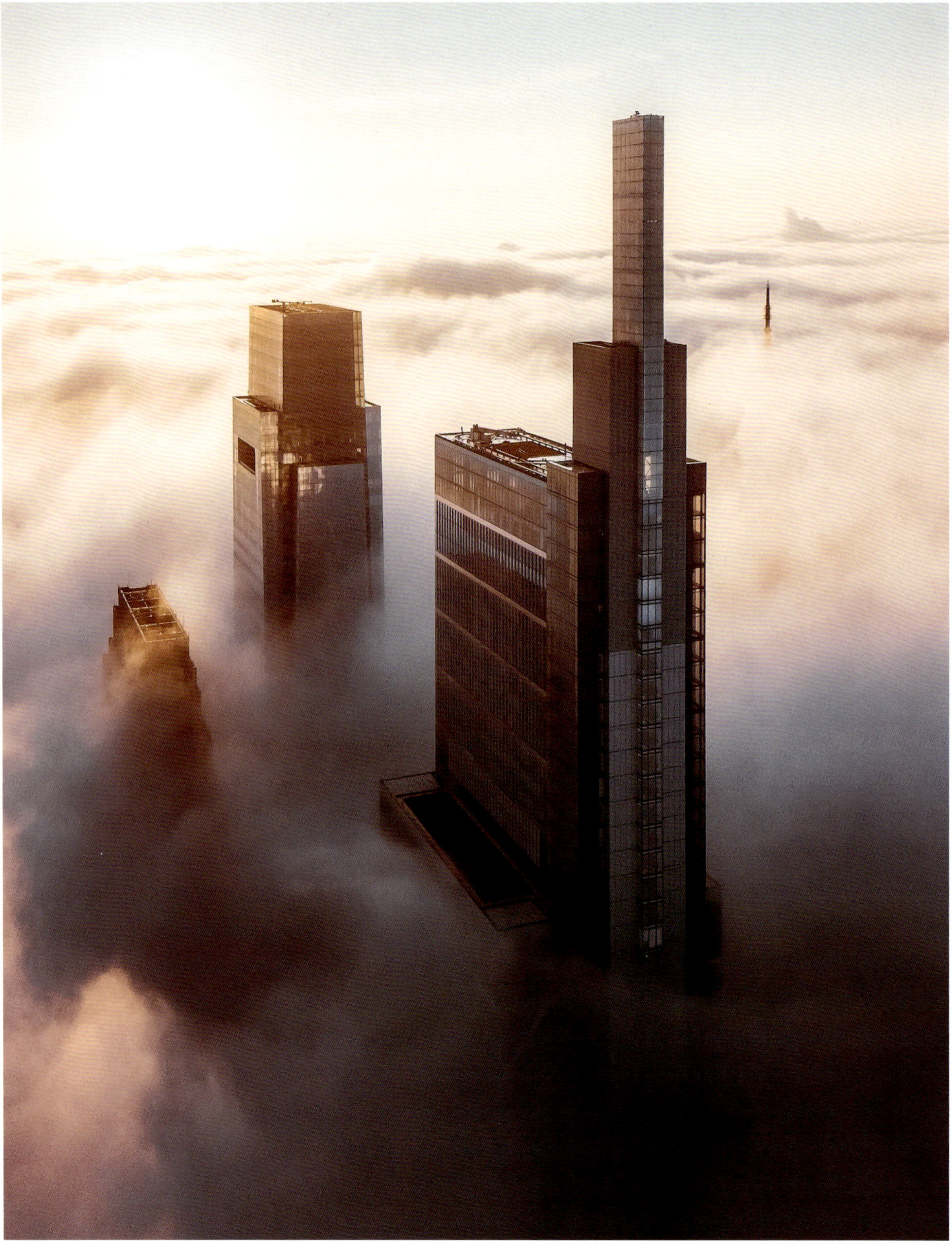

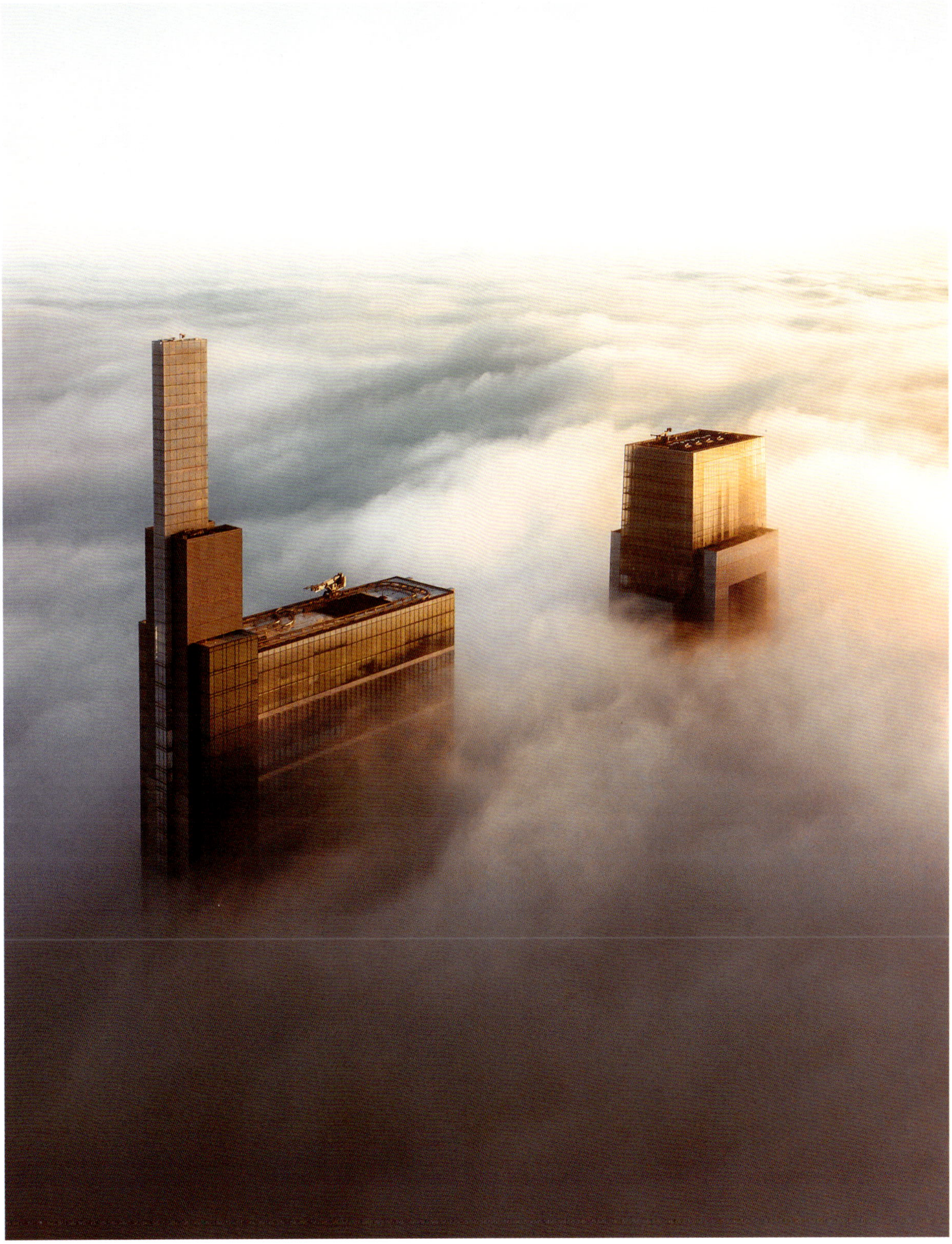

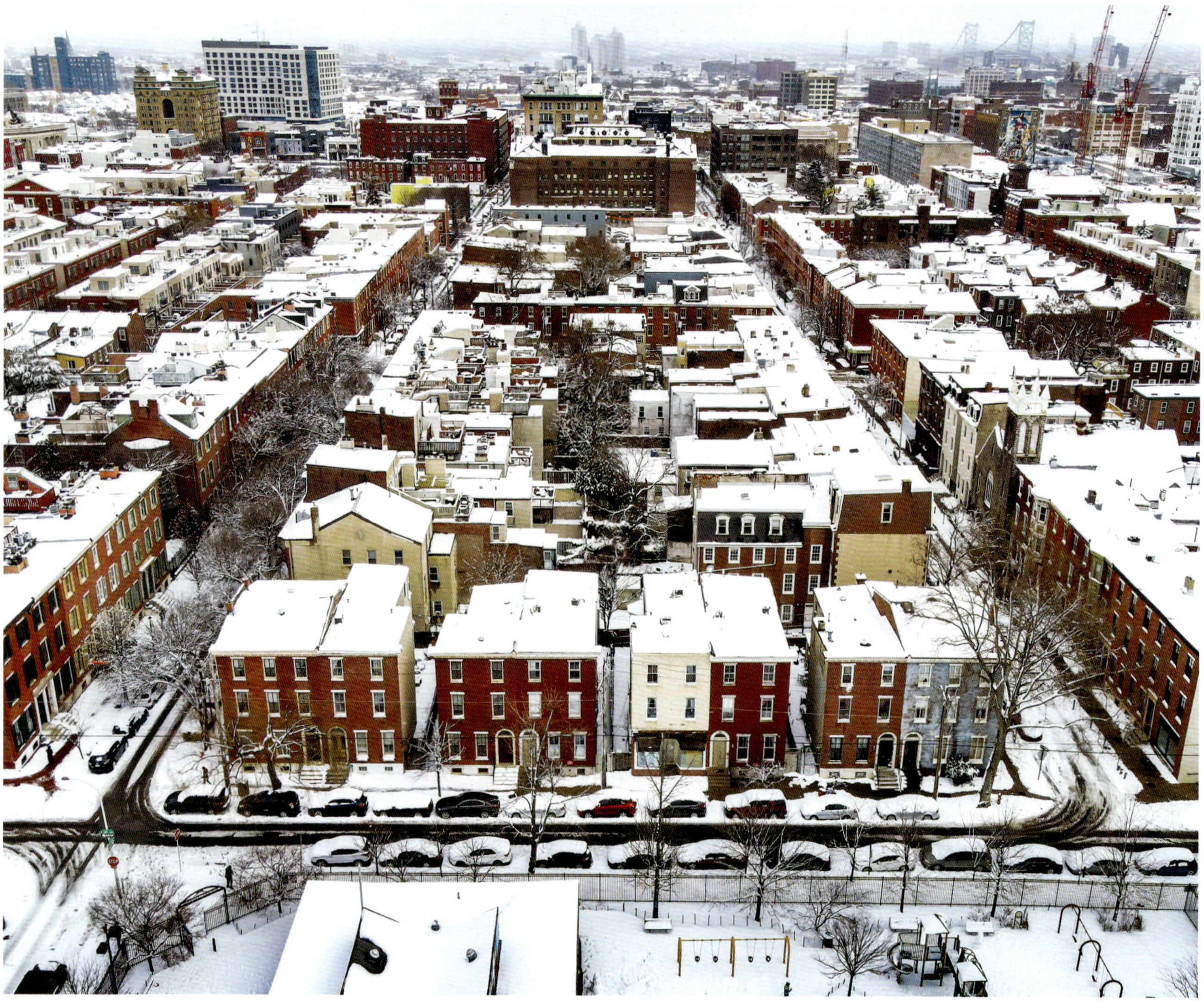

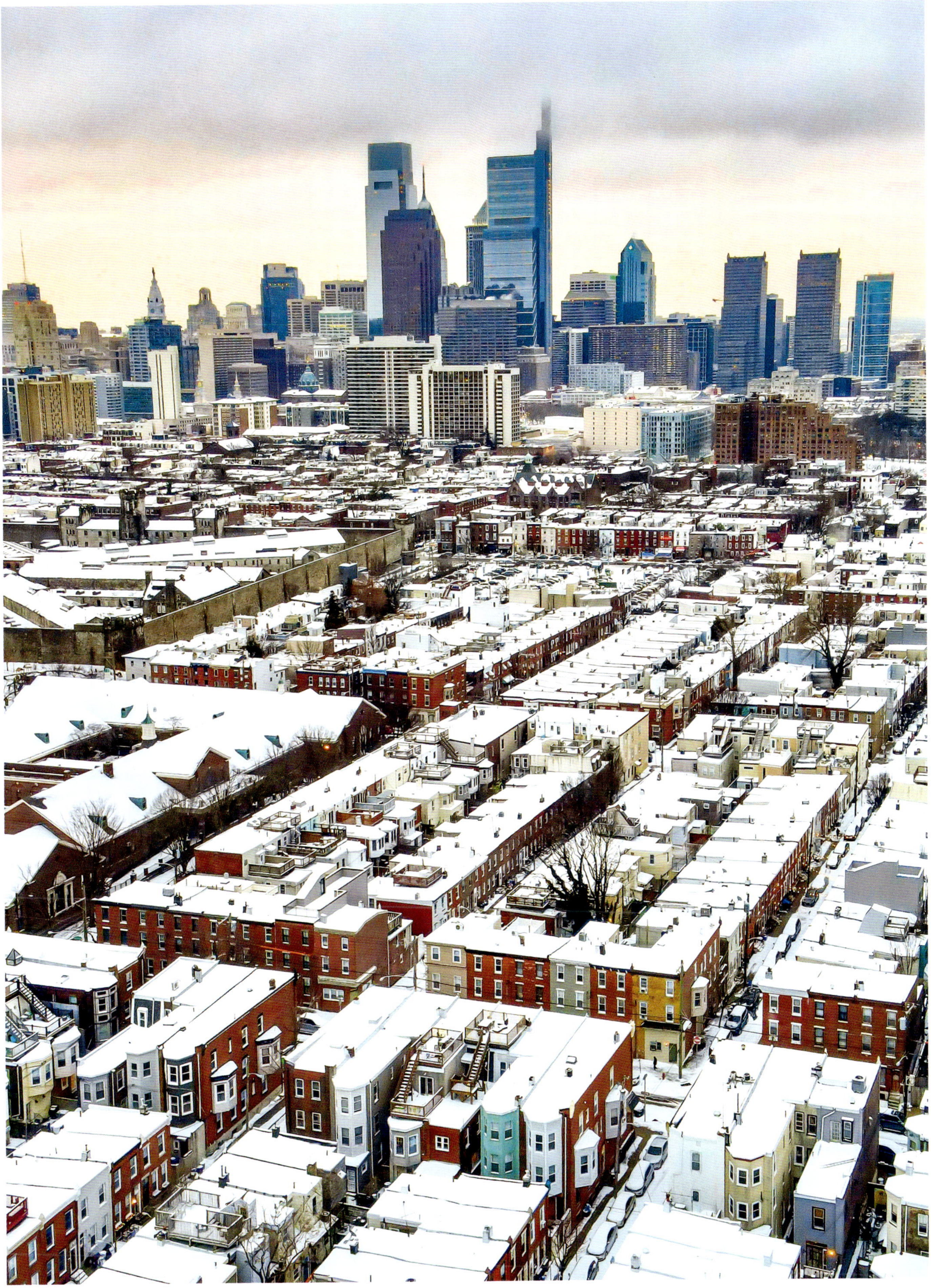

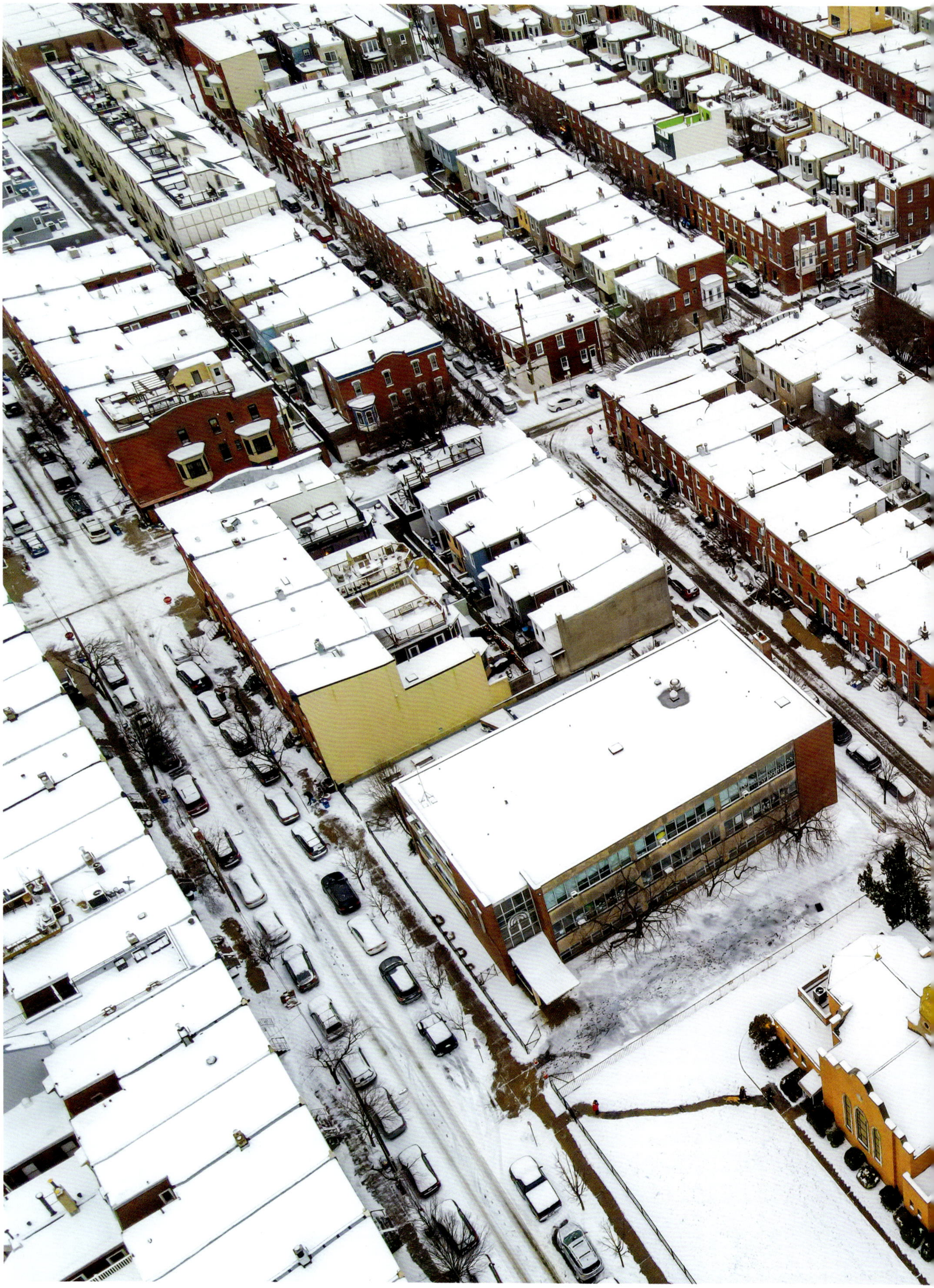

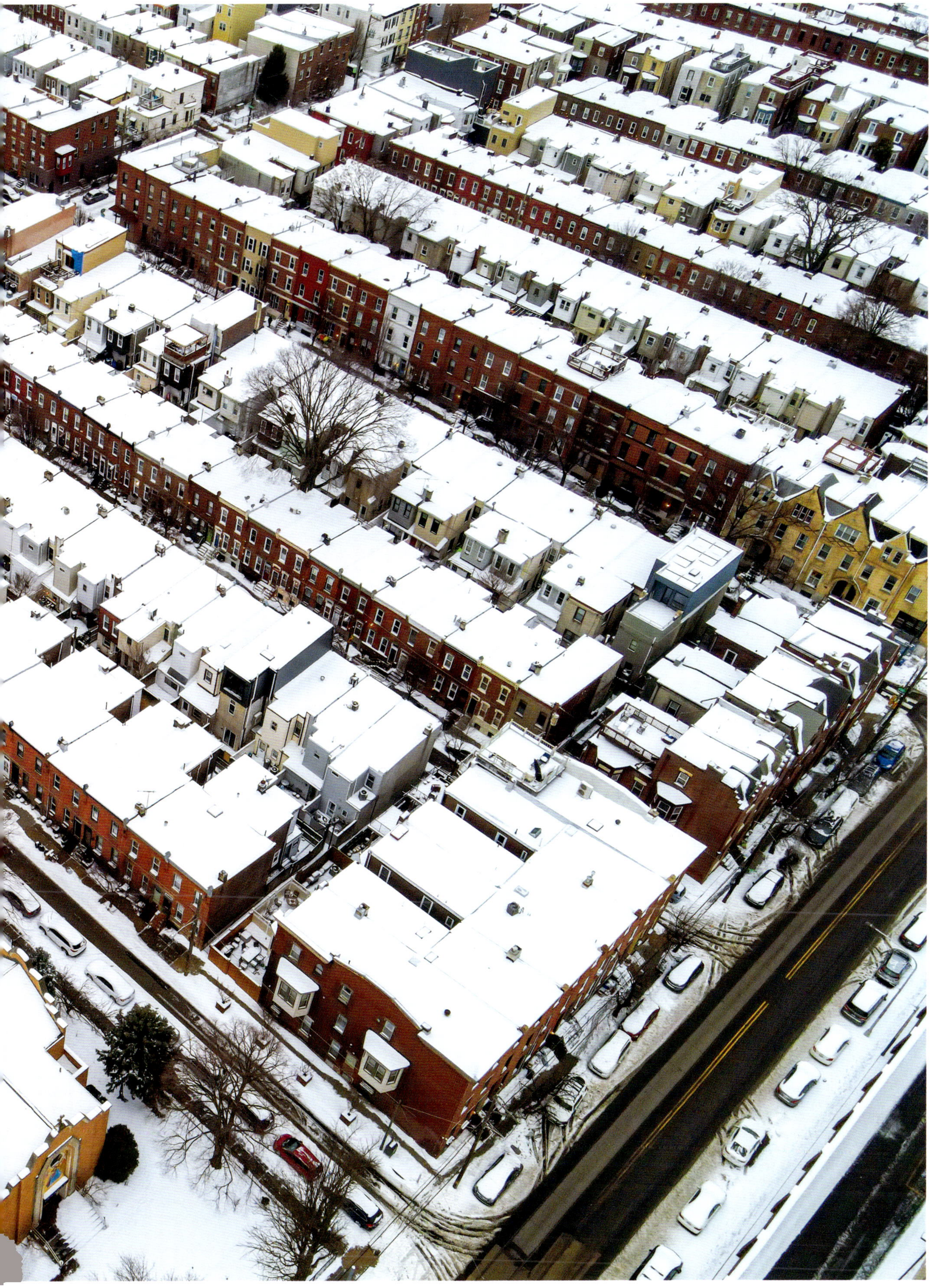

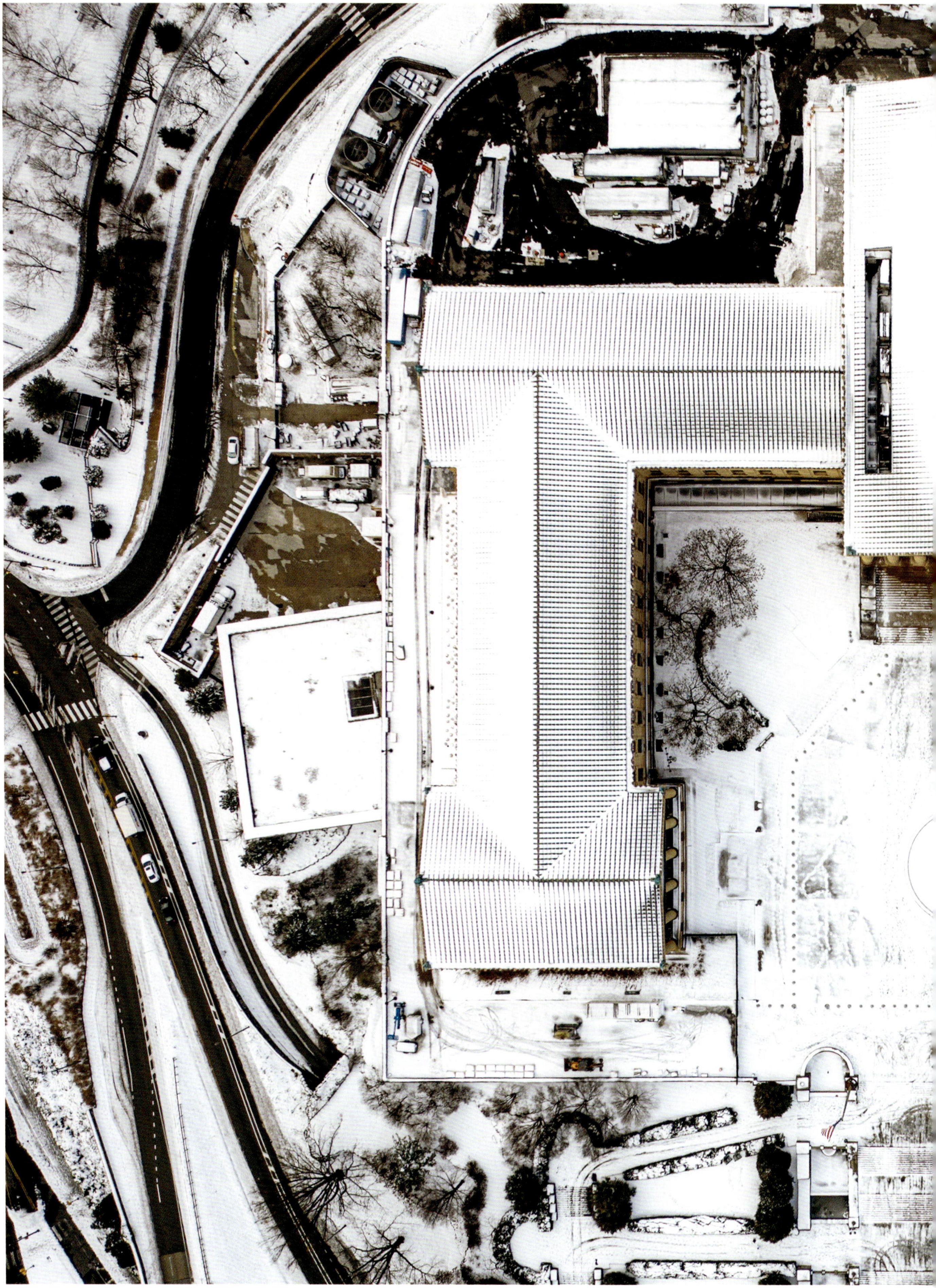

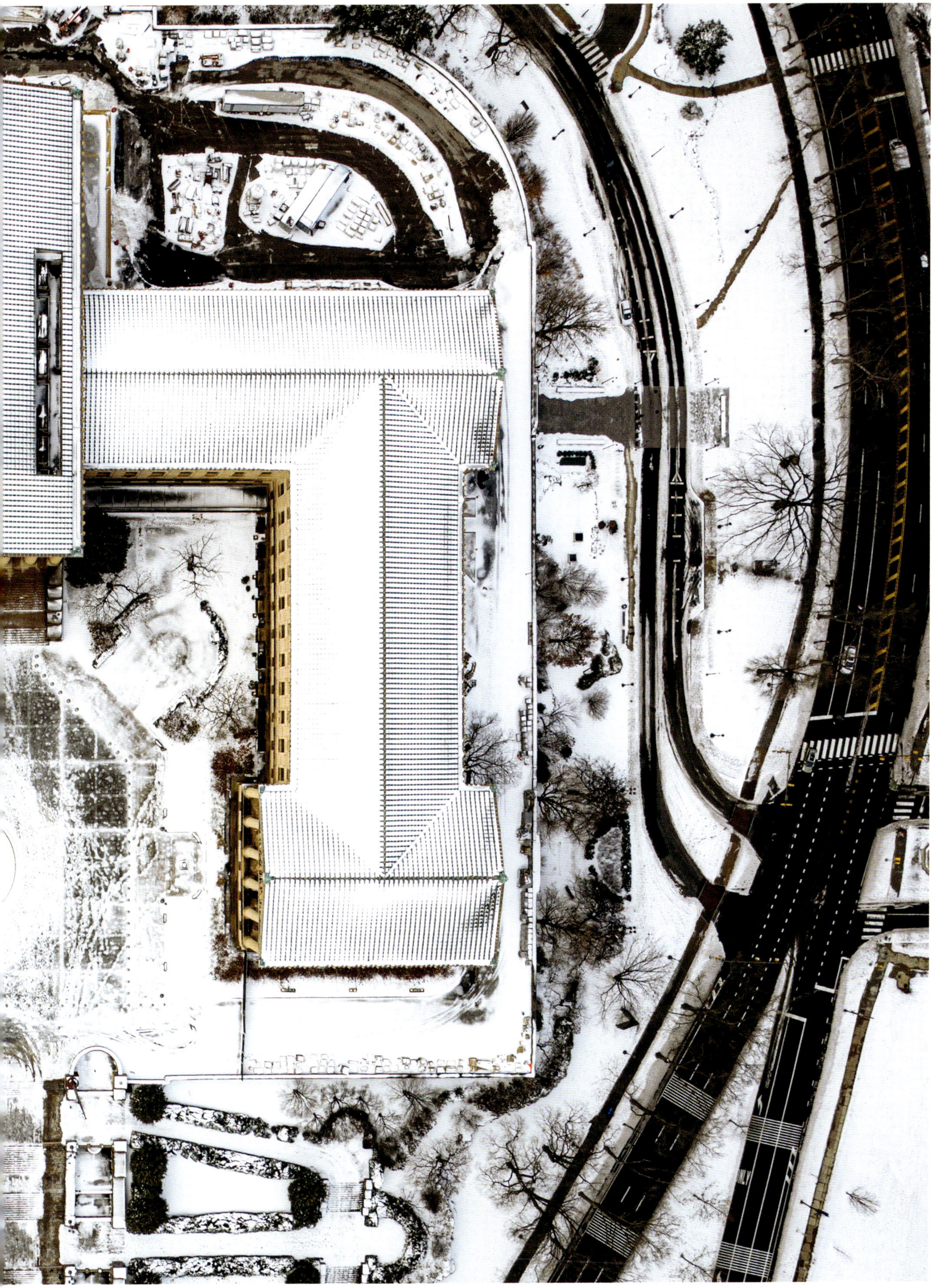

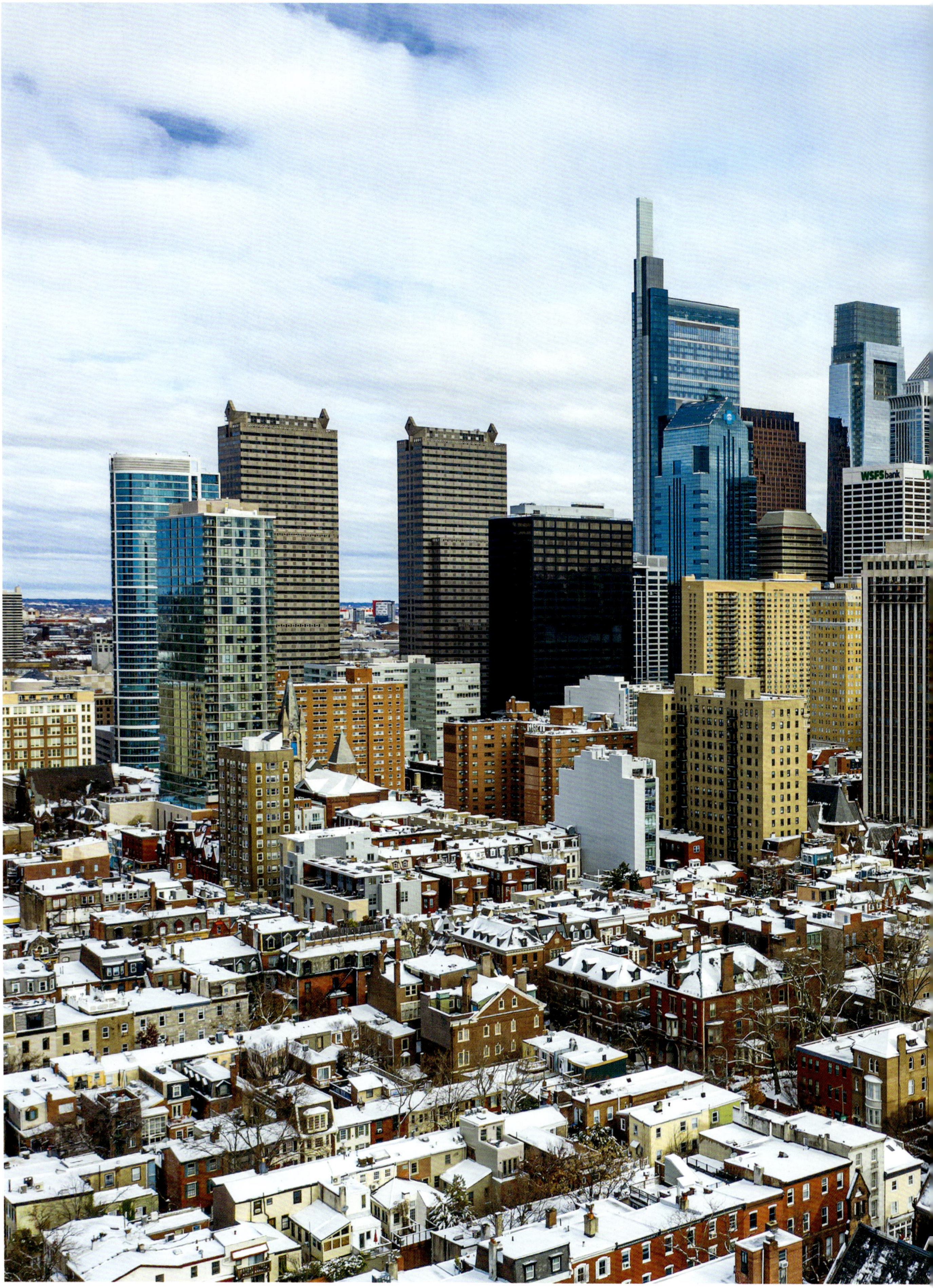
WSFS bank

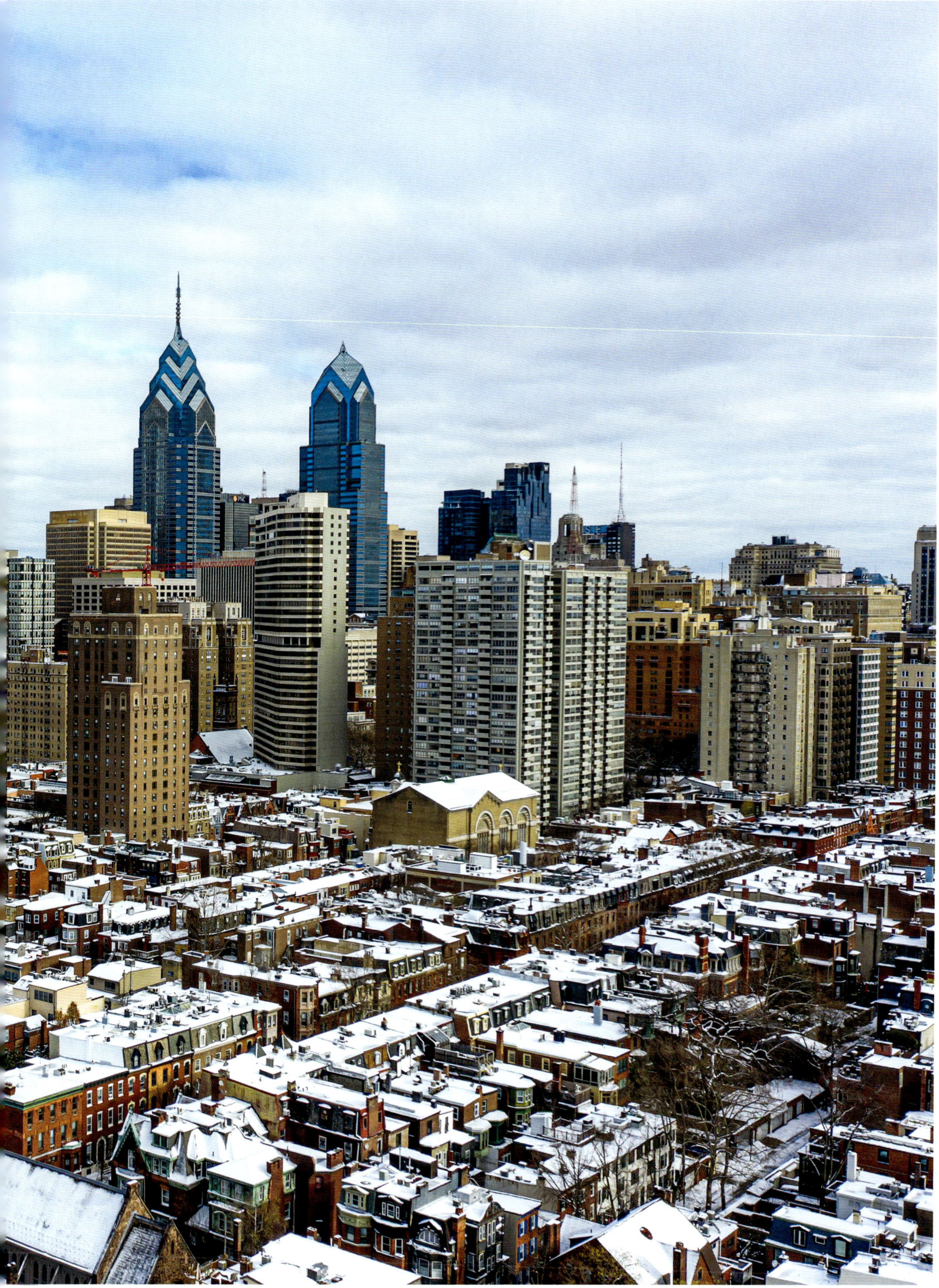

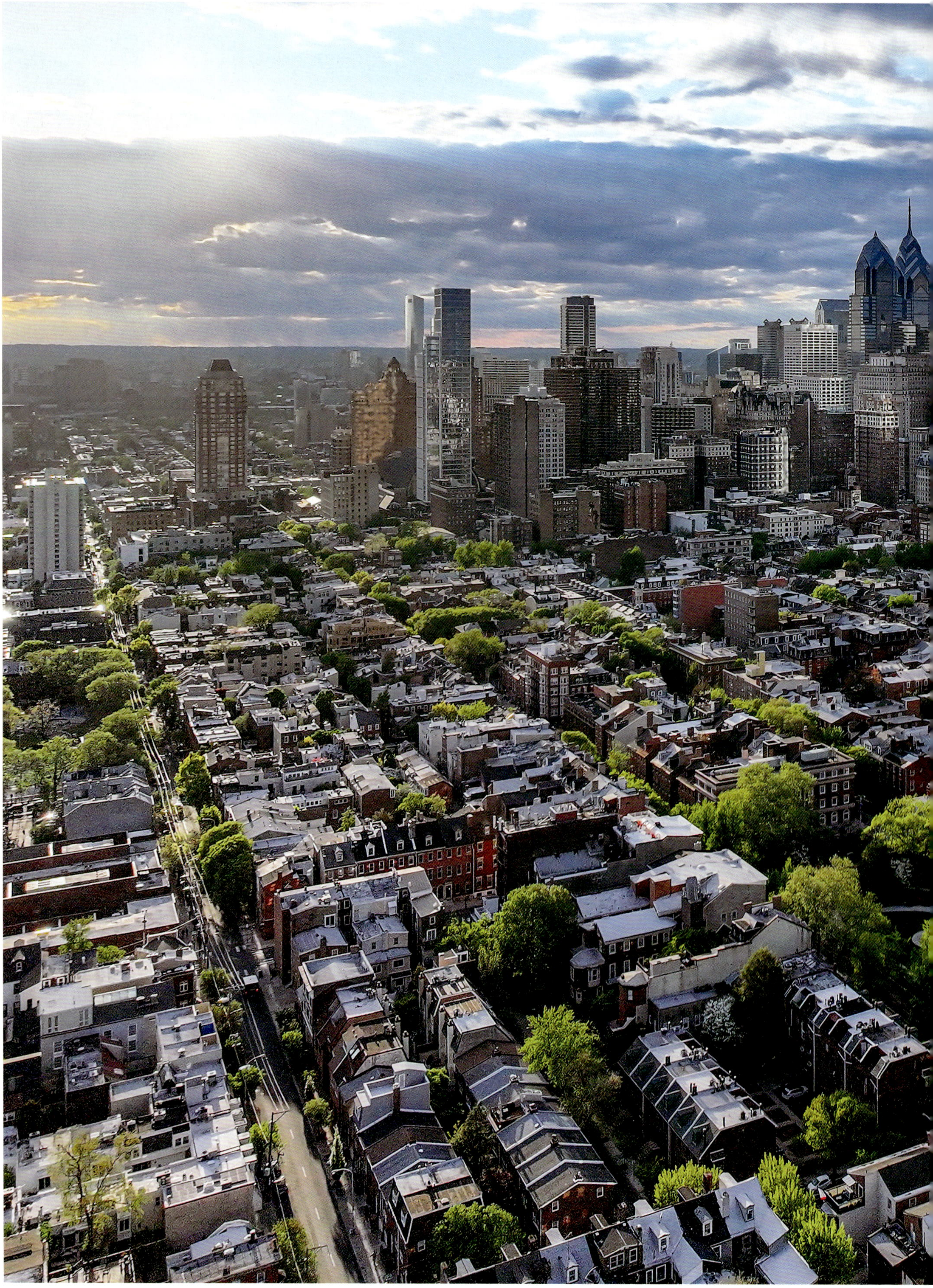

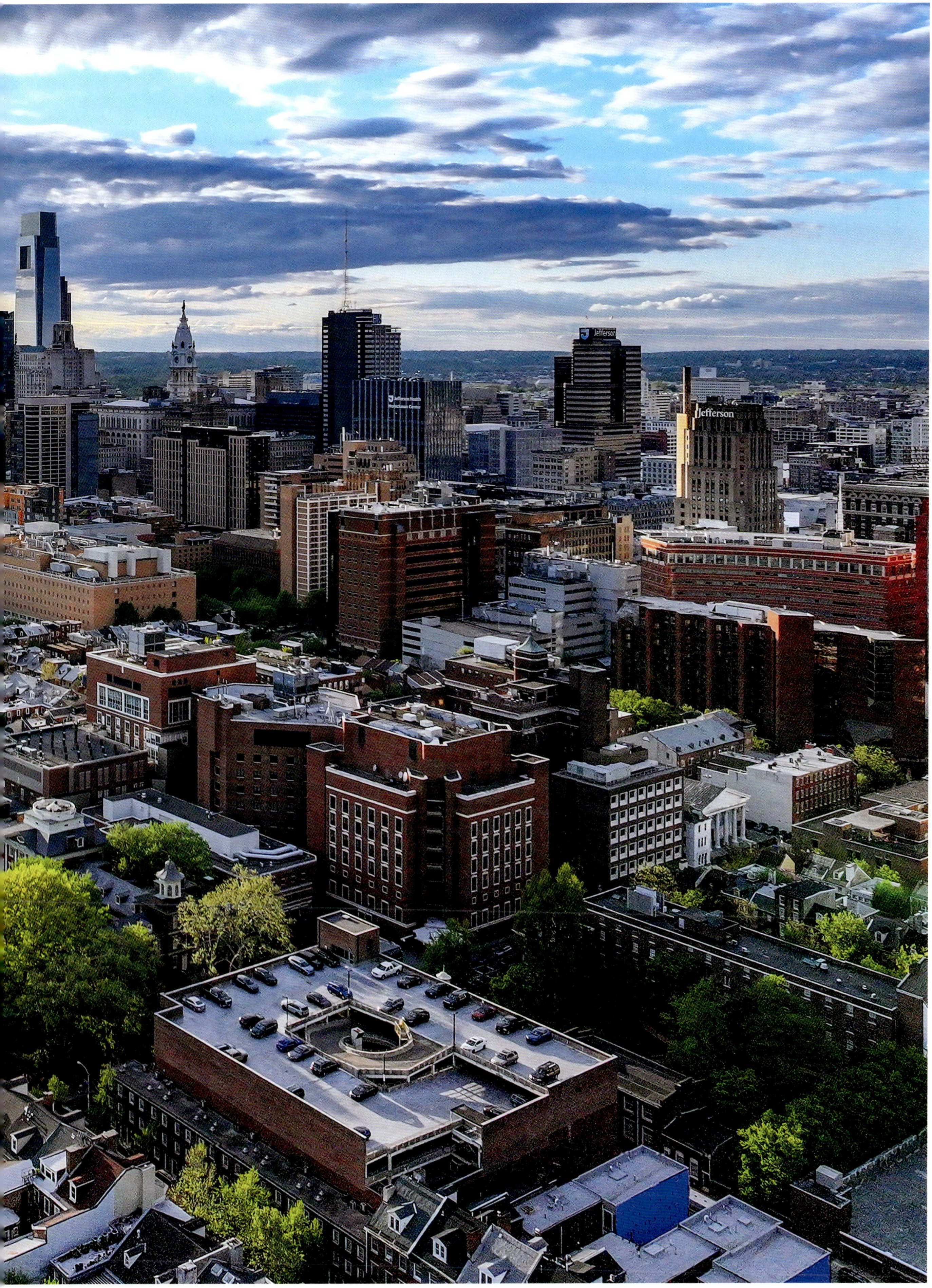
Jefferson
Jefferson

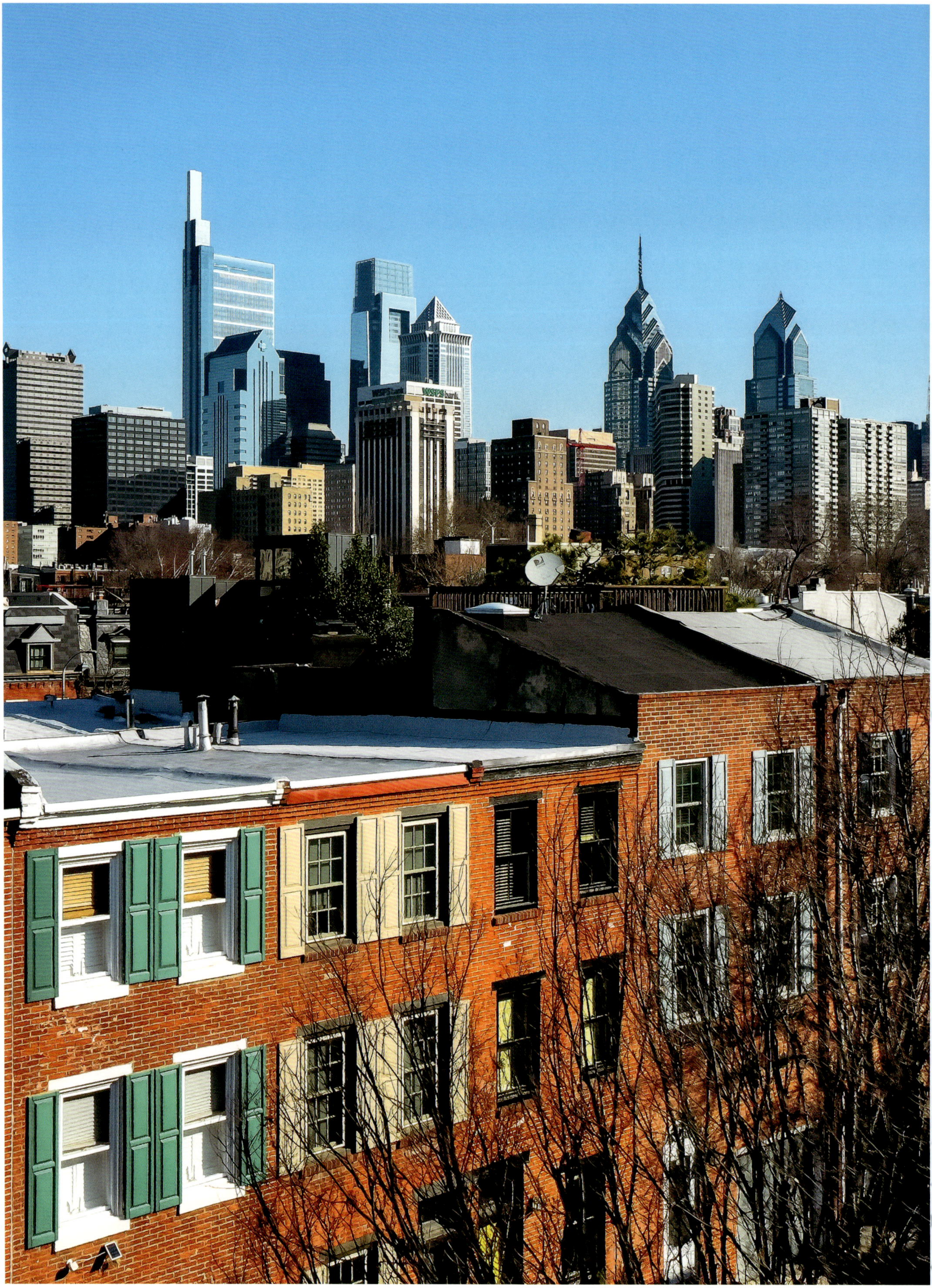

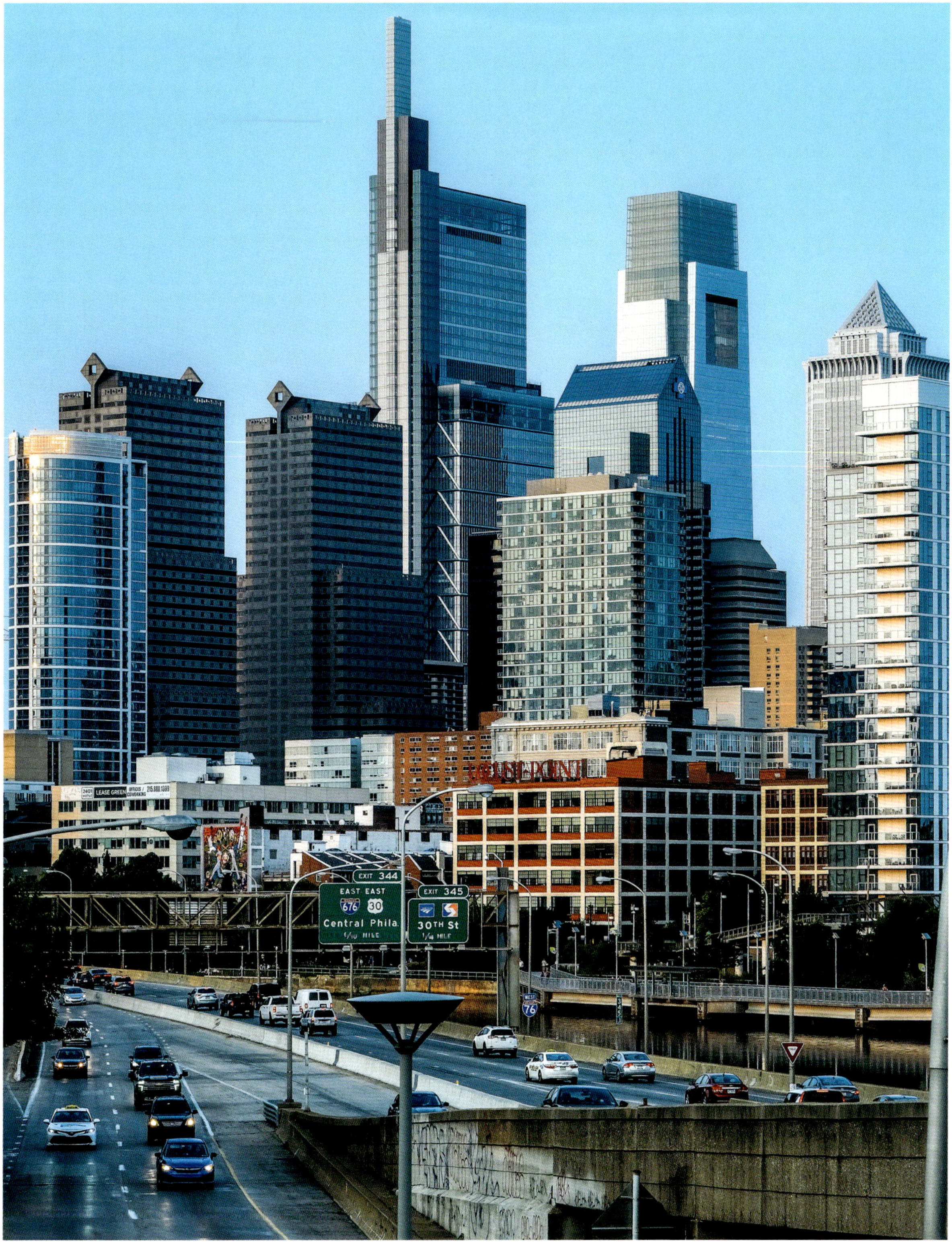
EXIT 344
EAST EAST
676
30
Central Phila
EXIT 345
30TH St

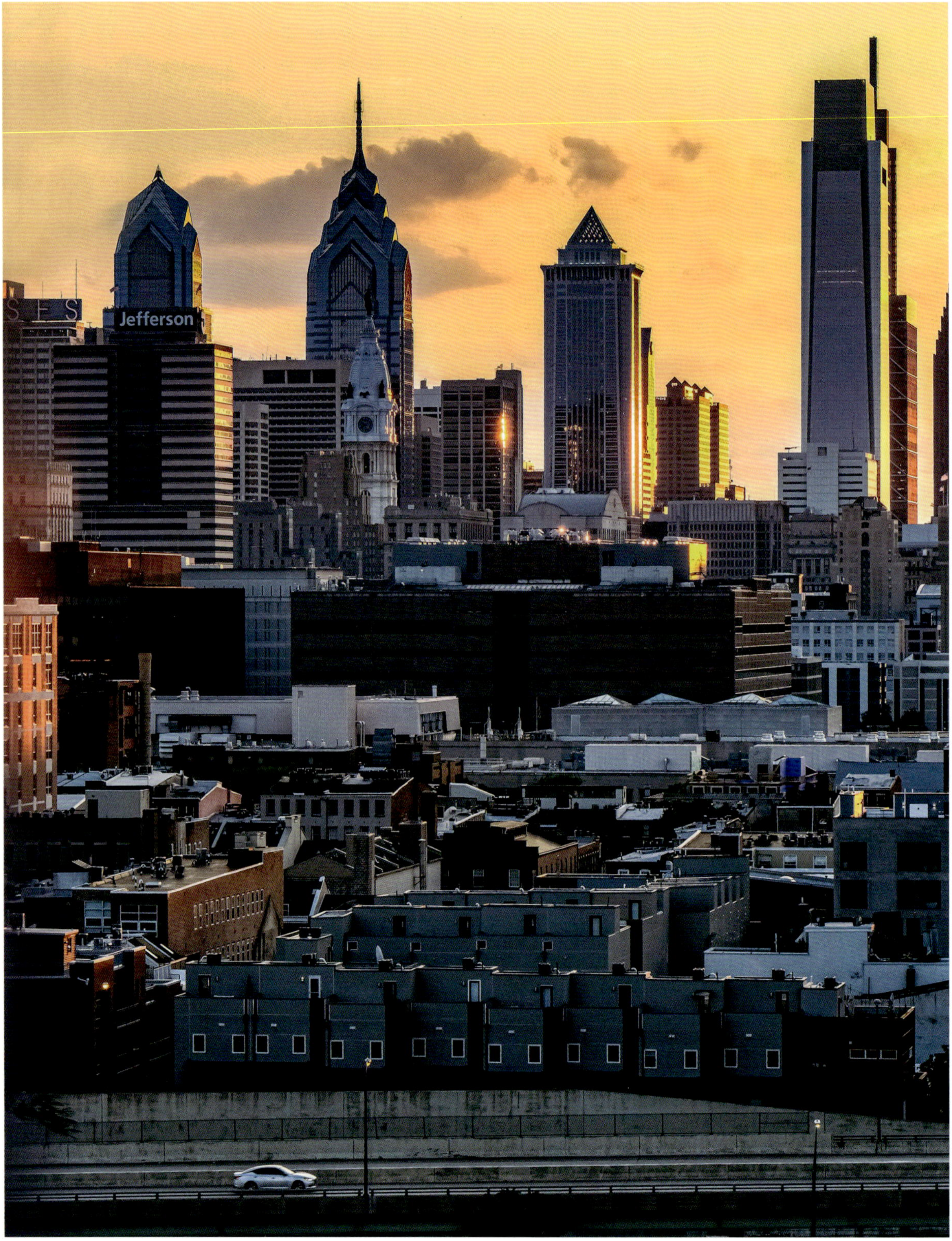
Jefferson

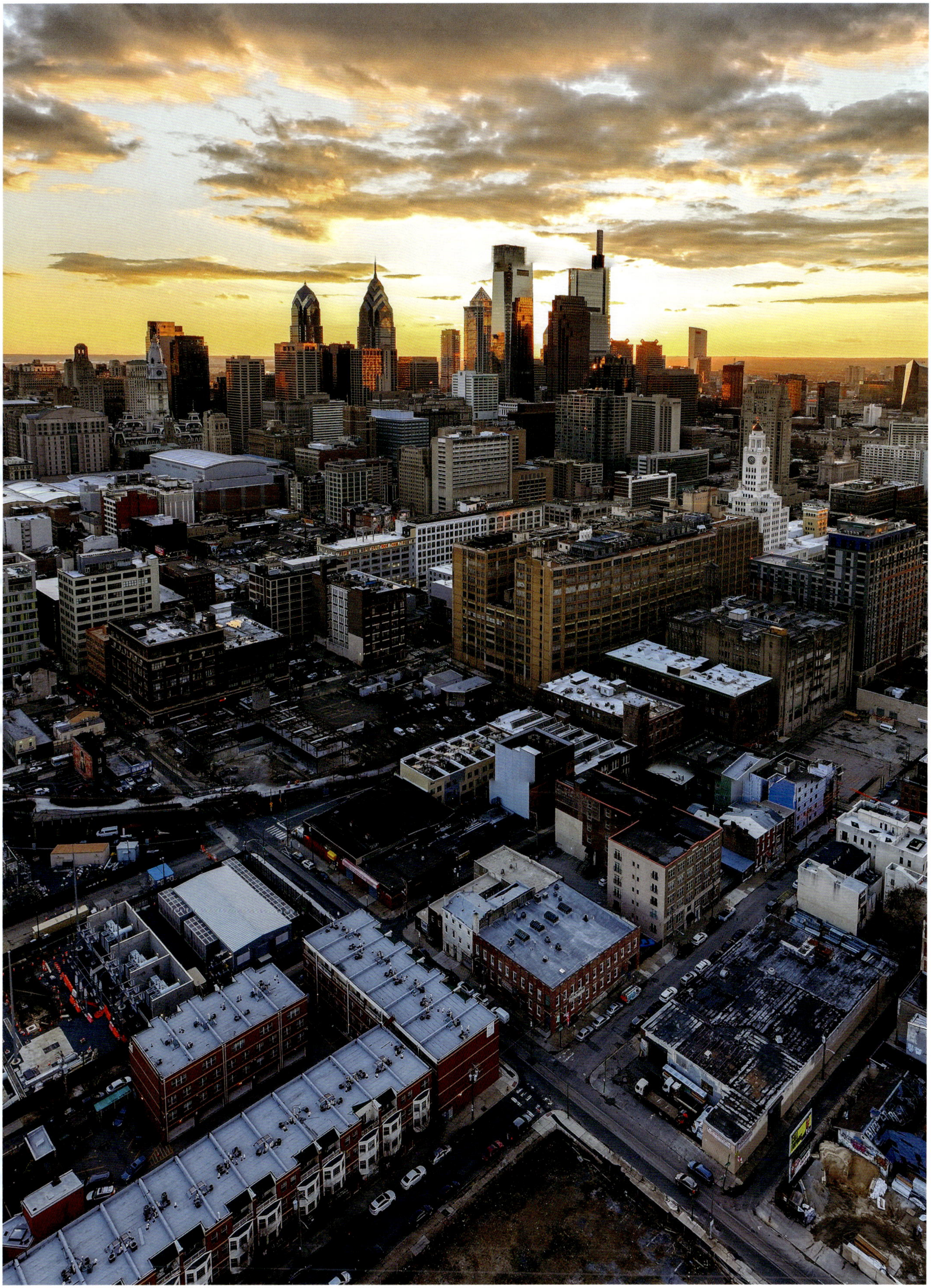

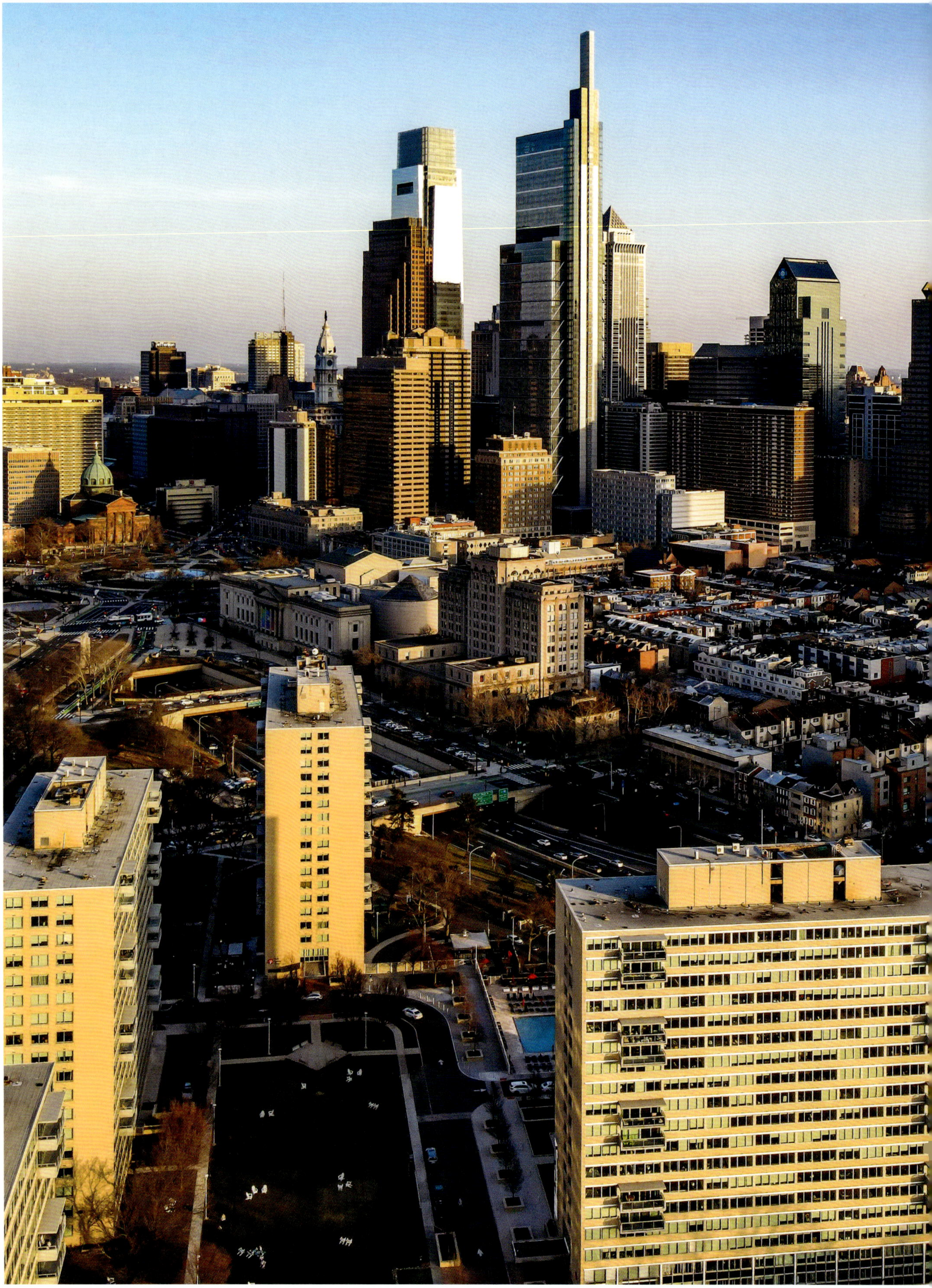

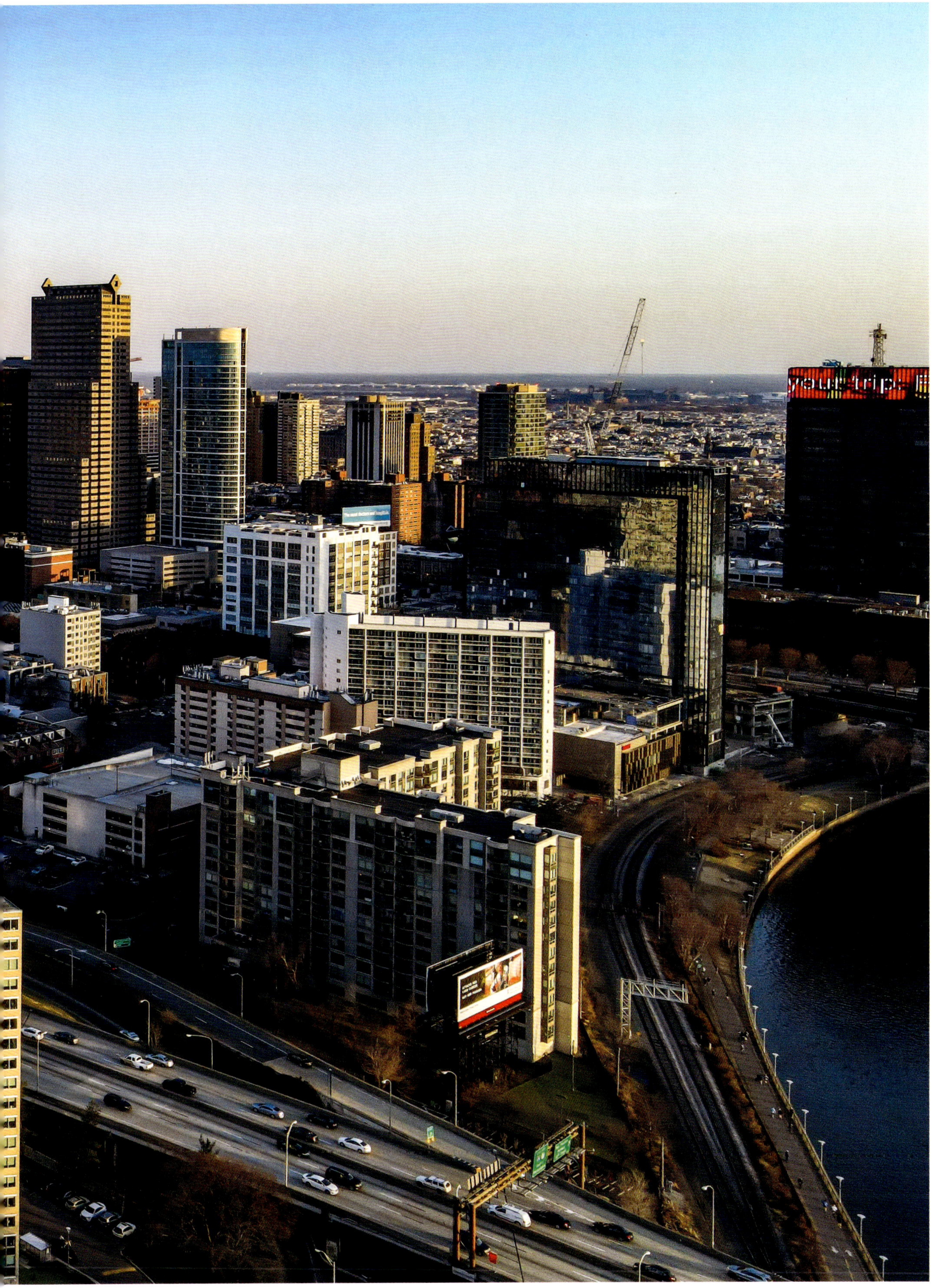

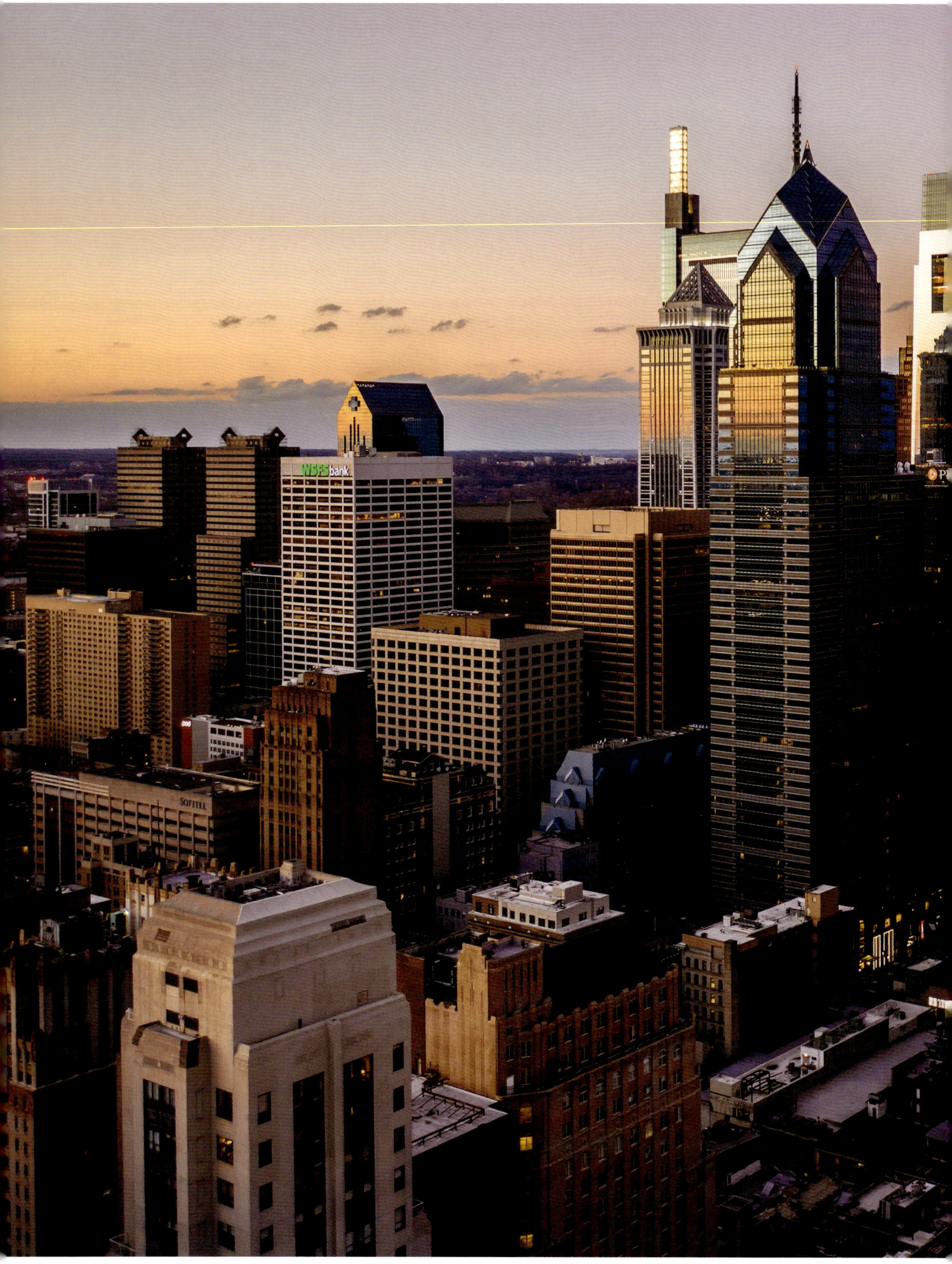
WSFS bank
SOFITEL

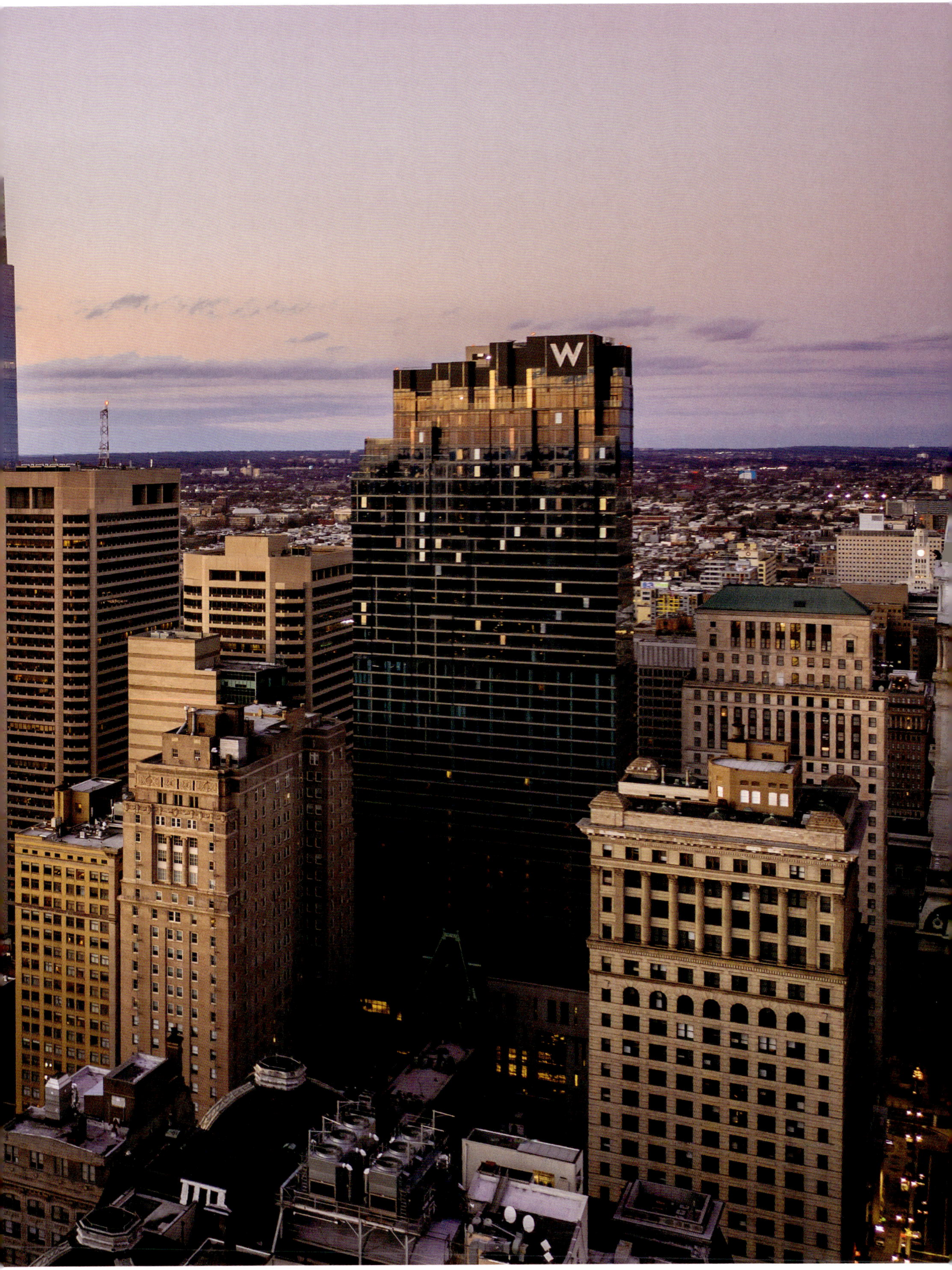

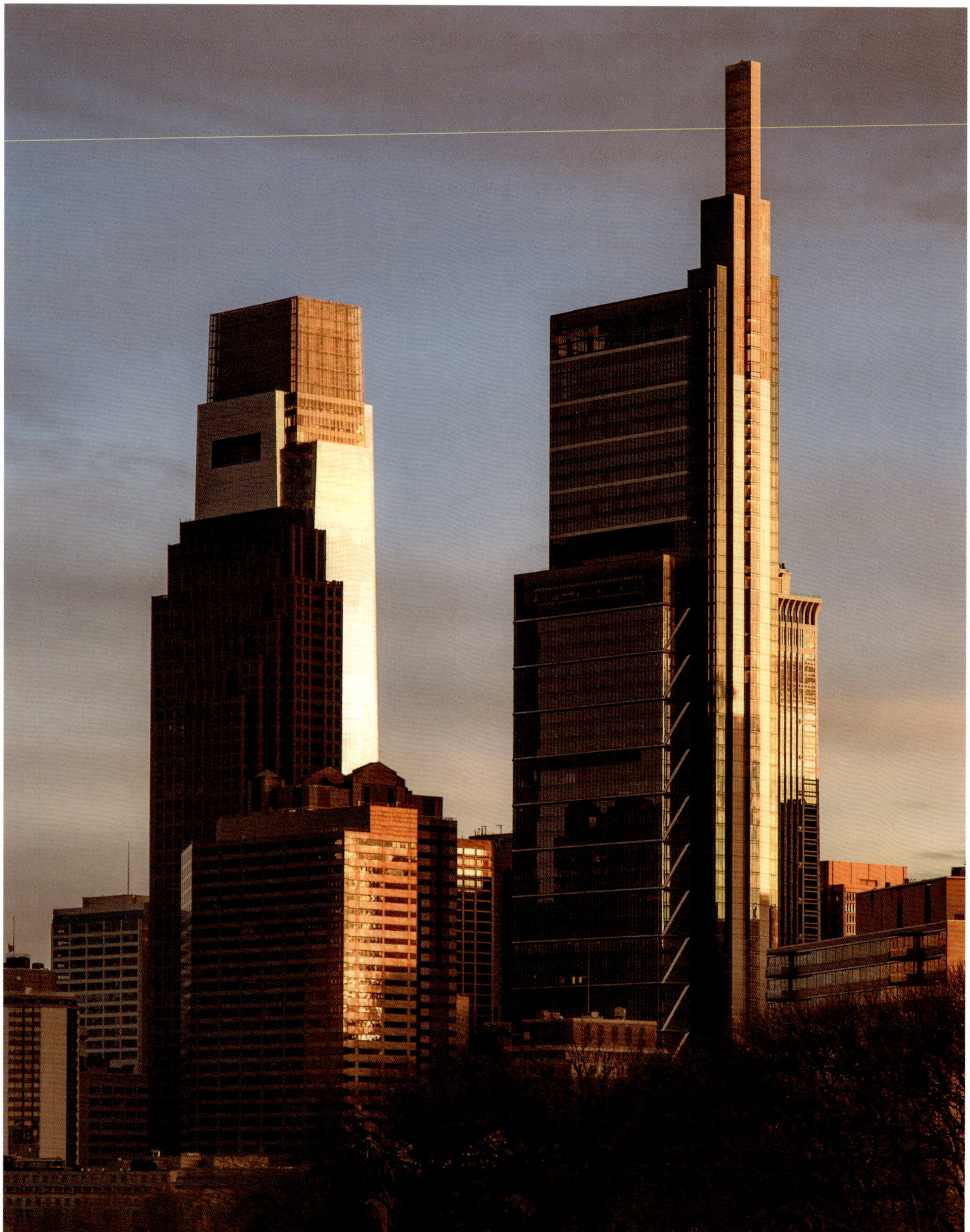

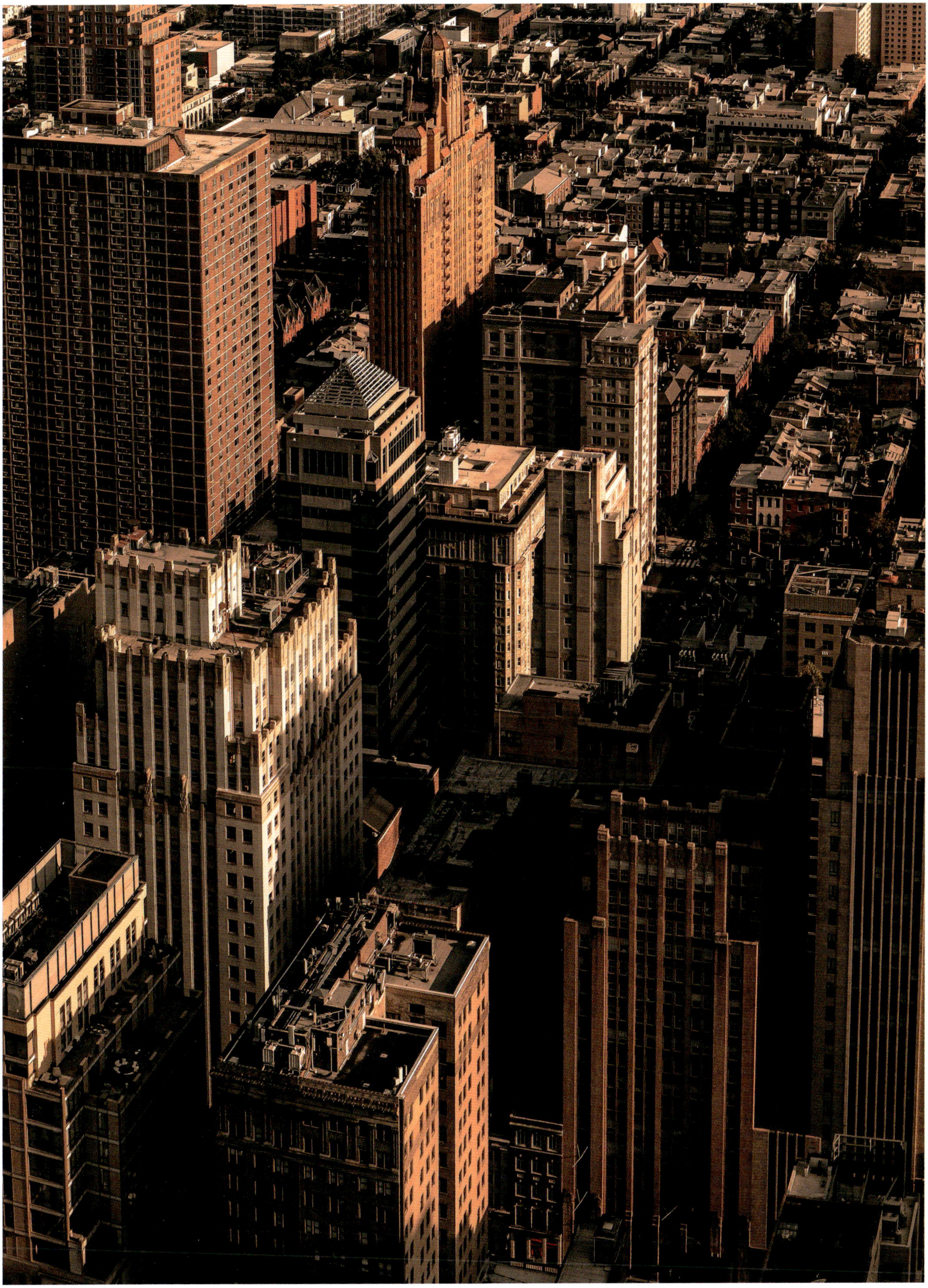

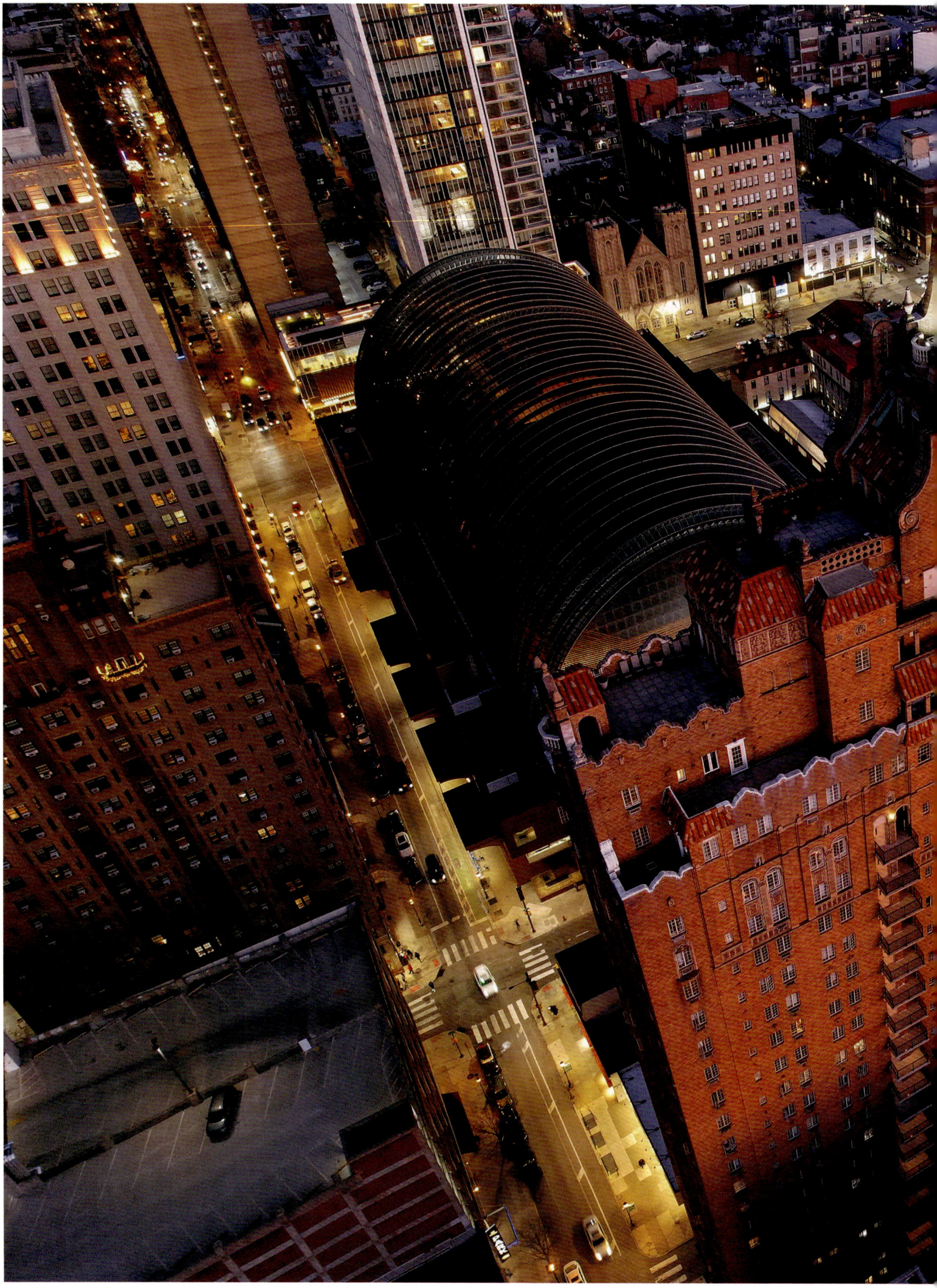

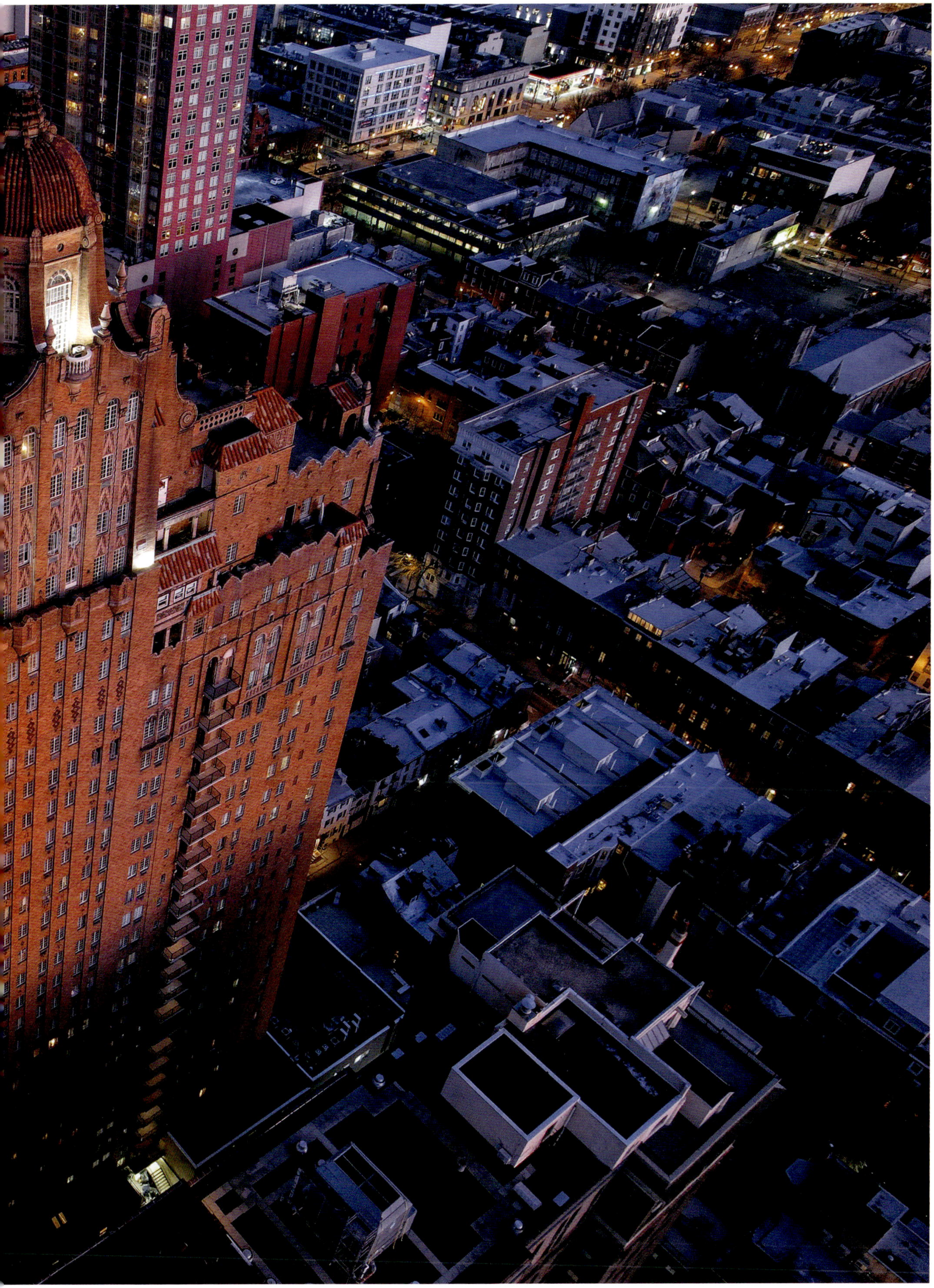

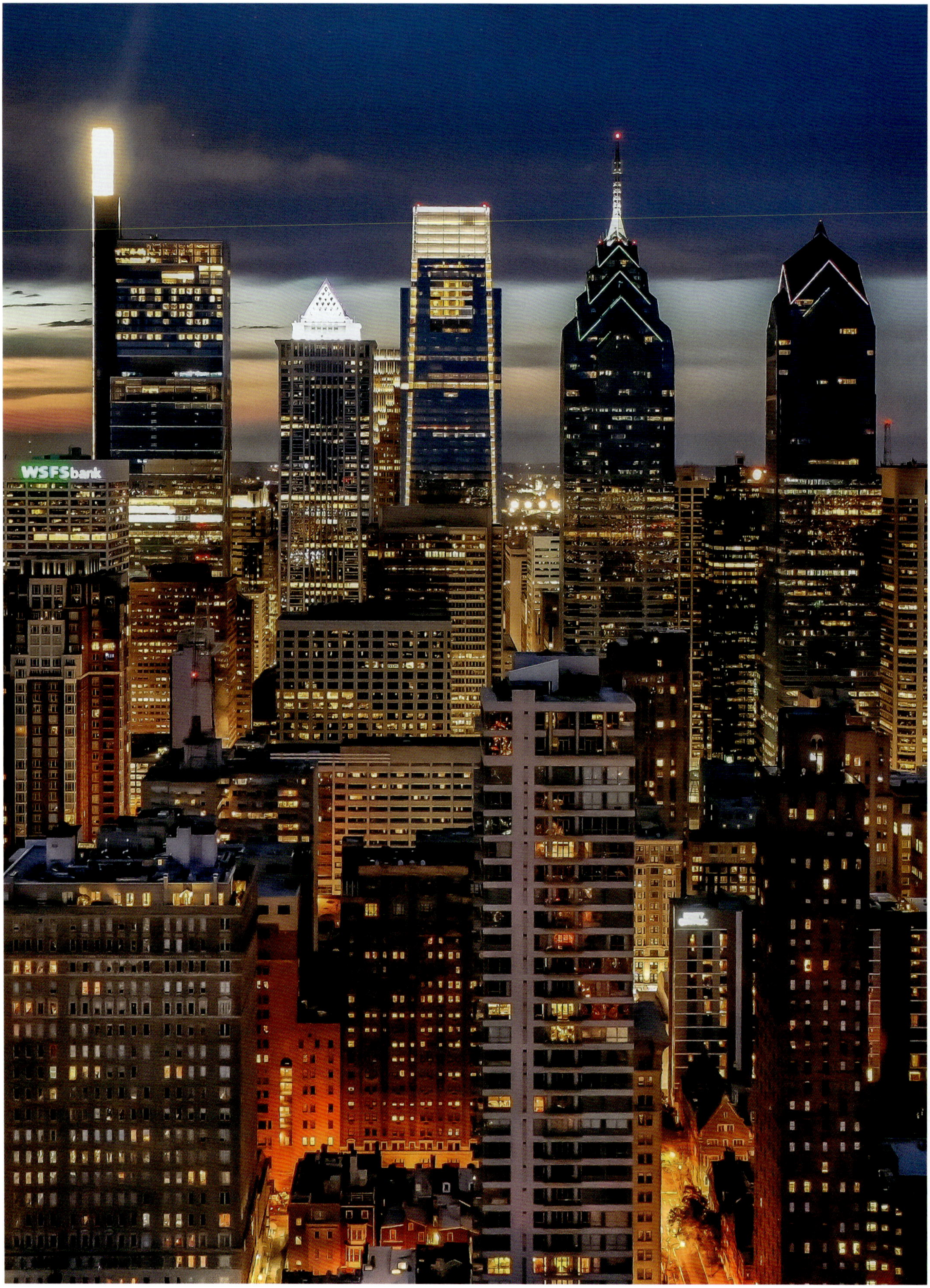
WSFSbank

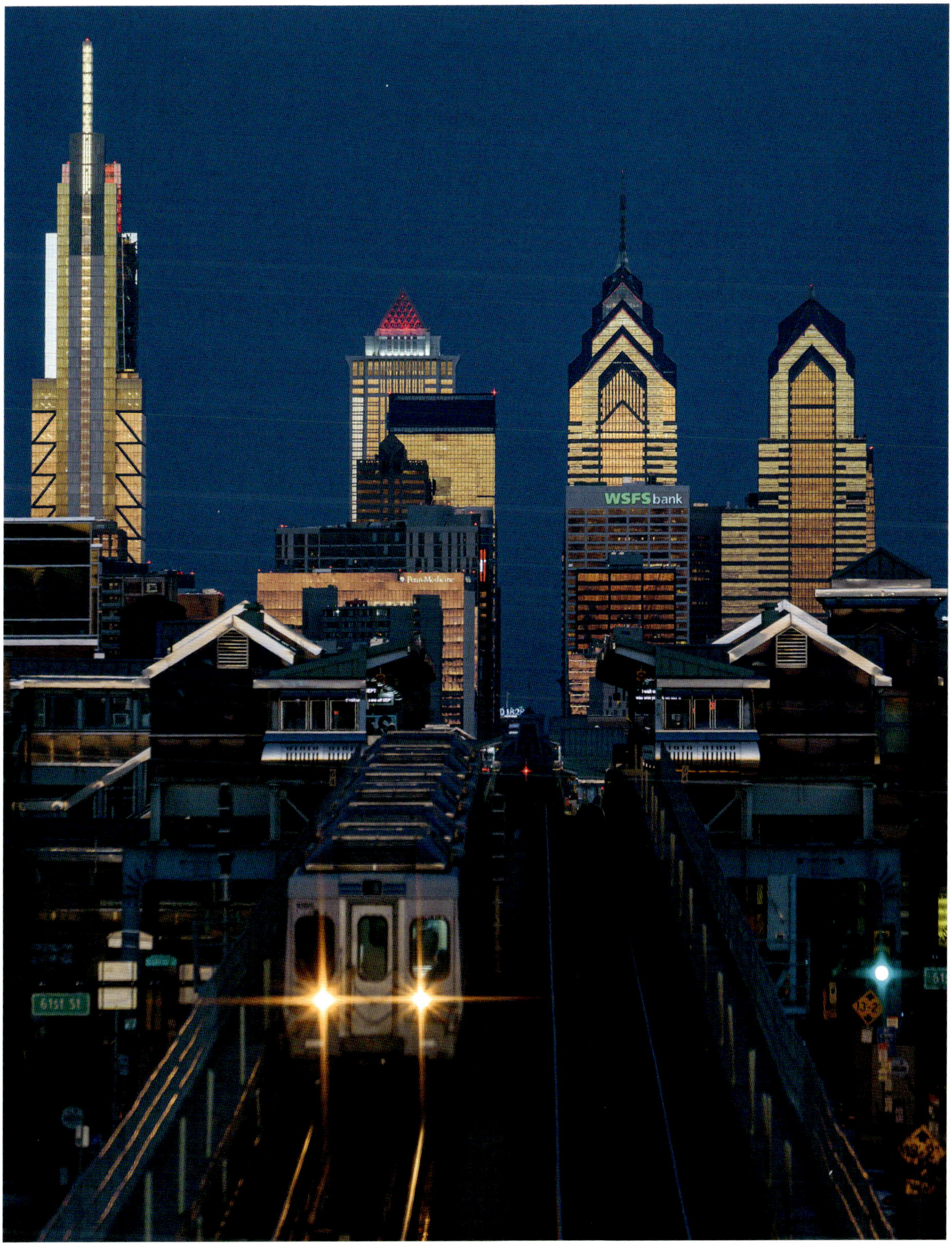
WSFS bank
61st St

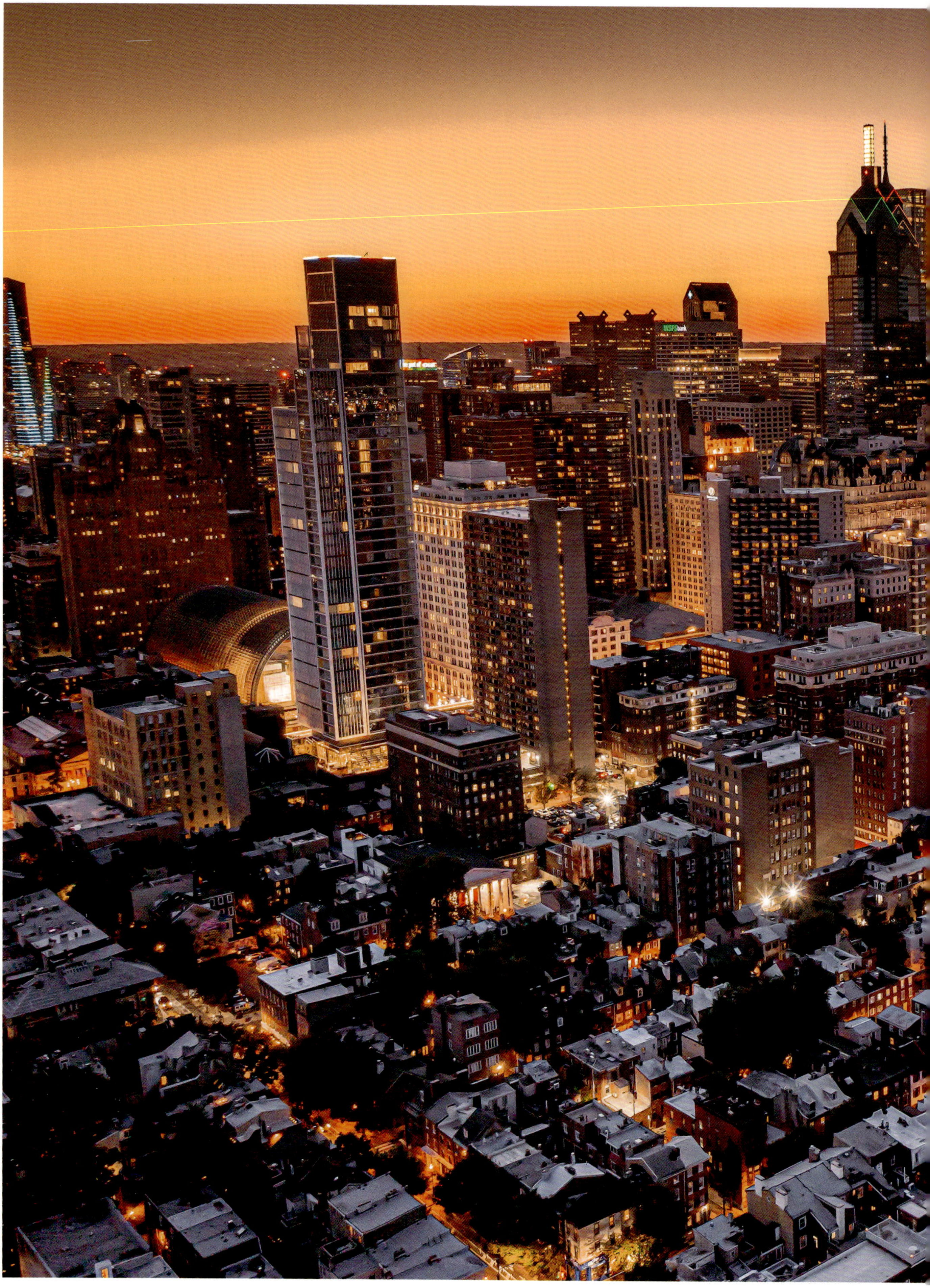

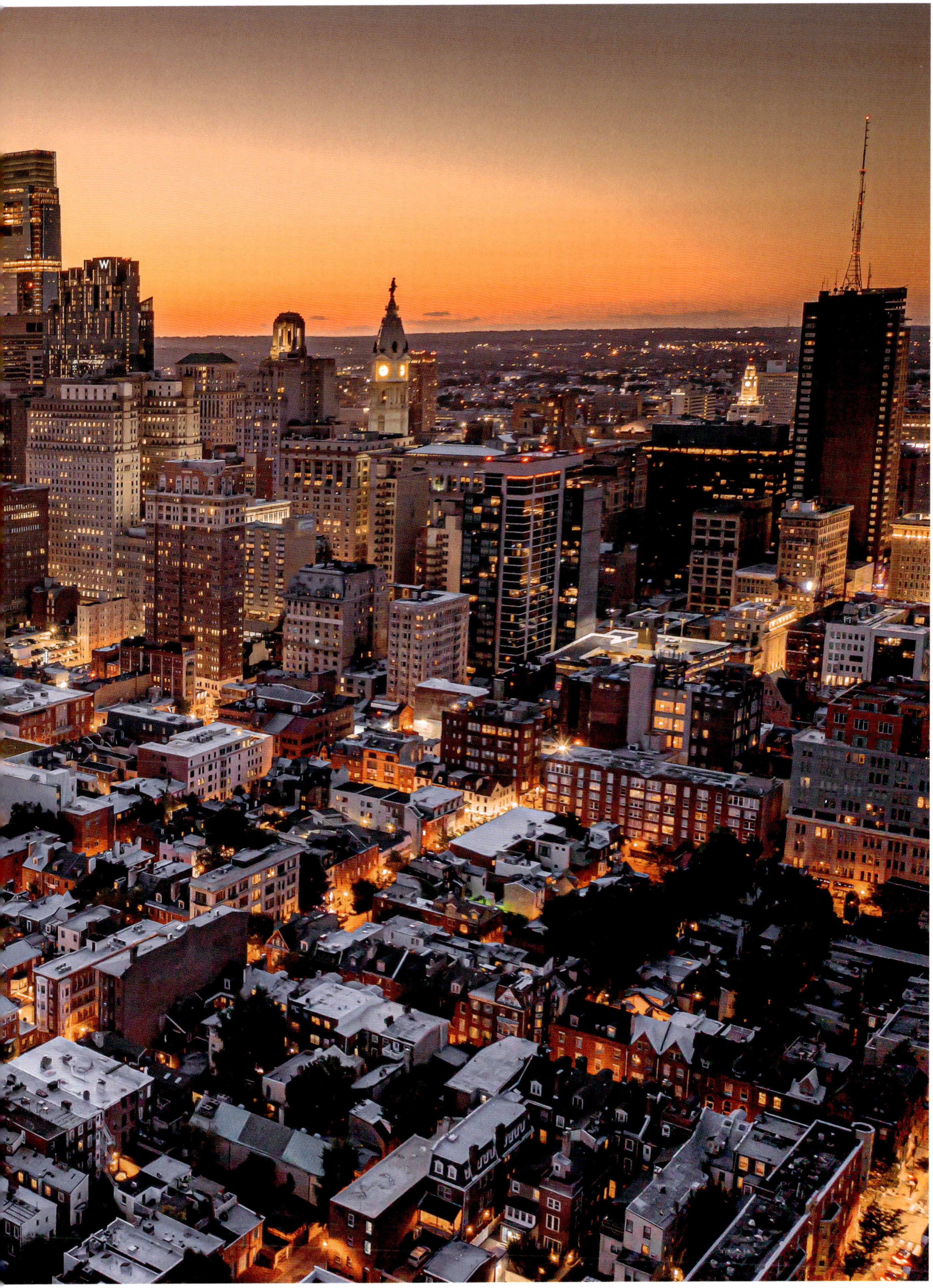

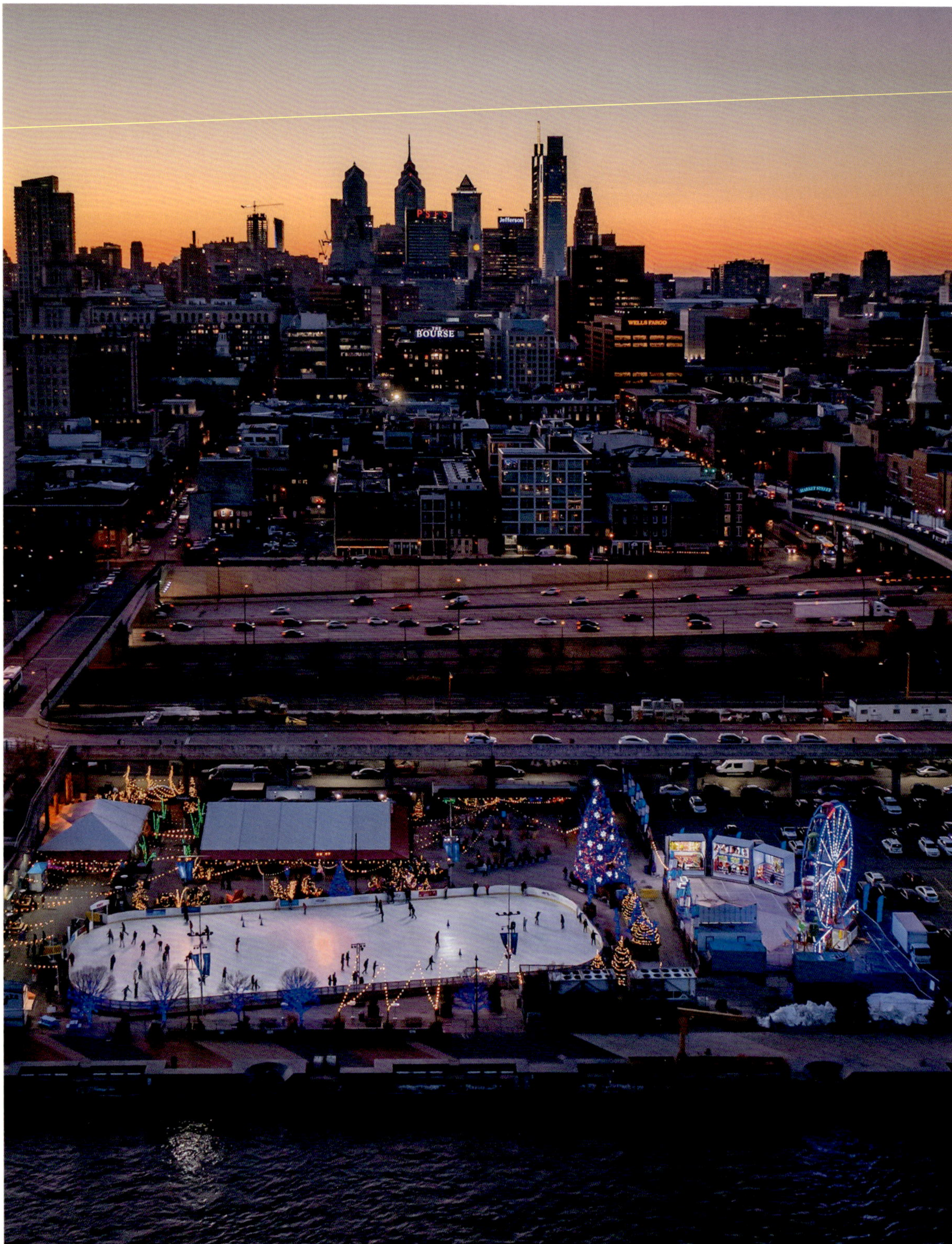

PSFS
Jefferson
THE BOURSE
WELLS FARGO

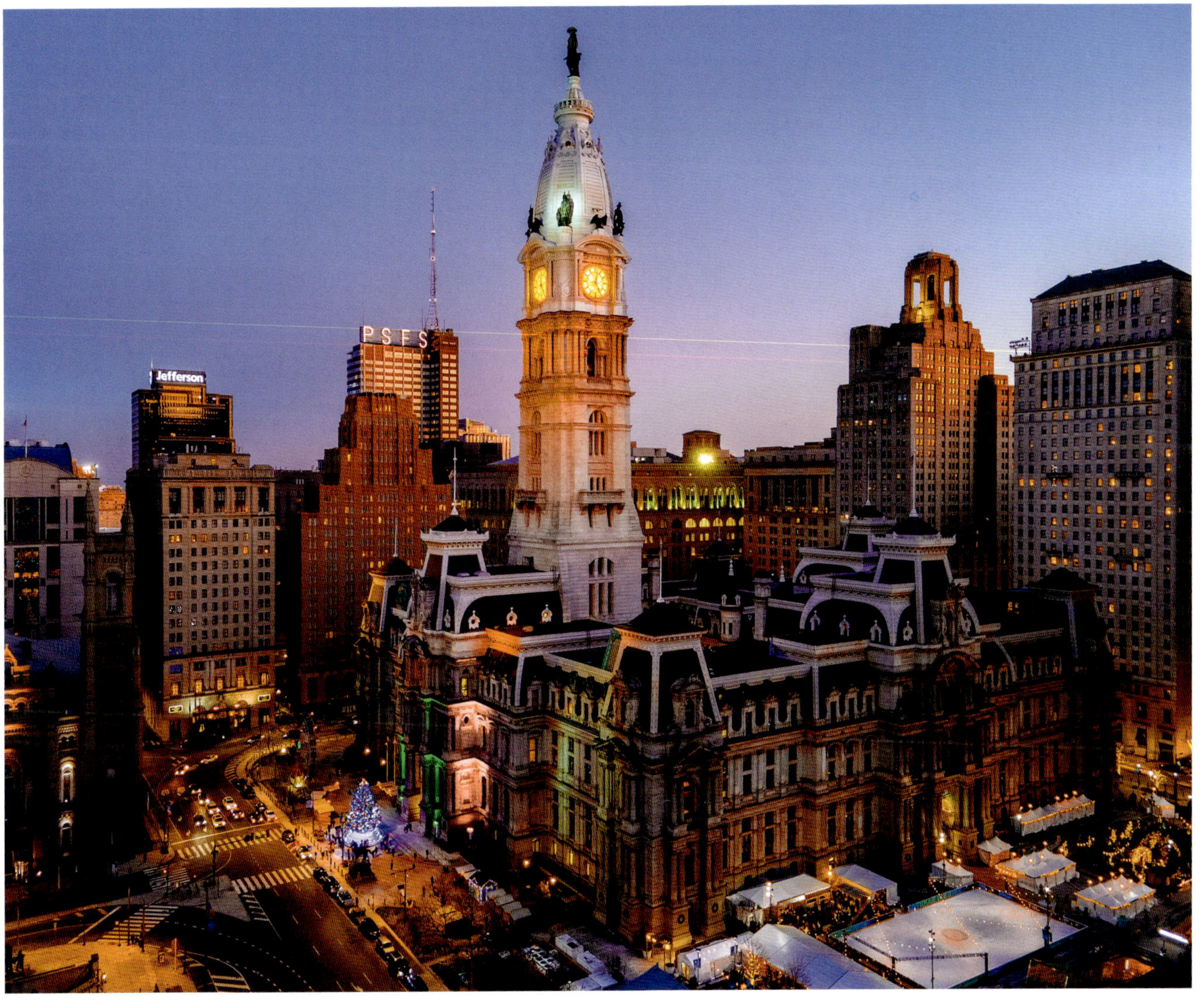
Jefferson
PSFS

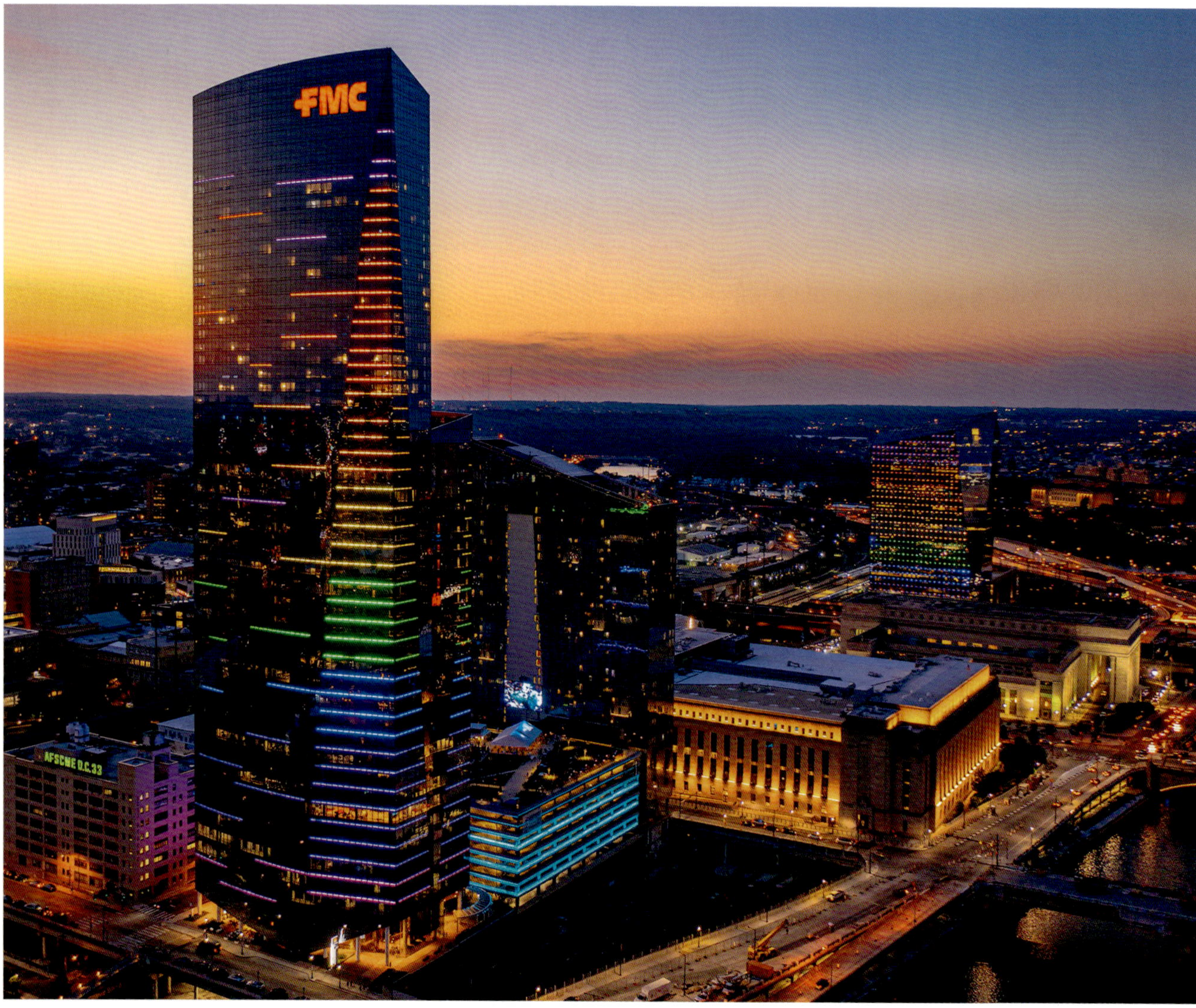
FMC
AFSCME D.C.33

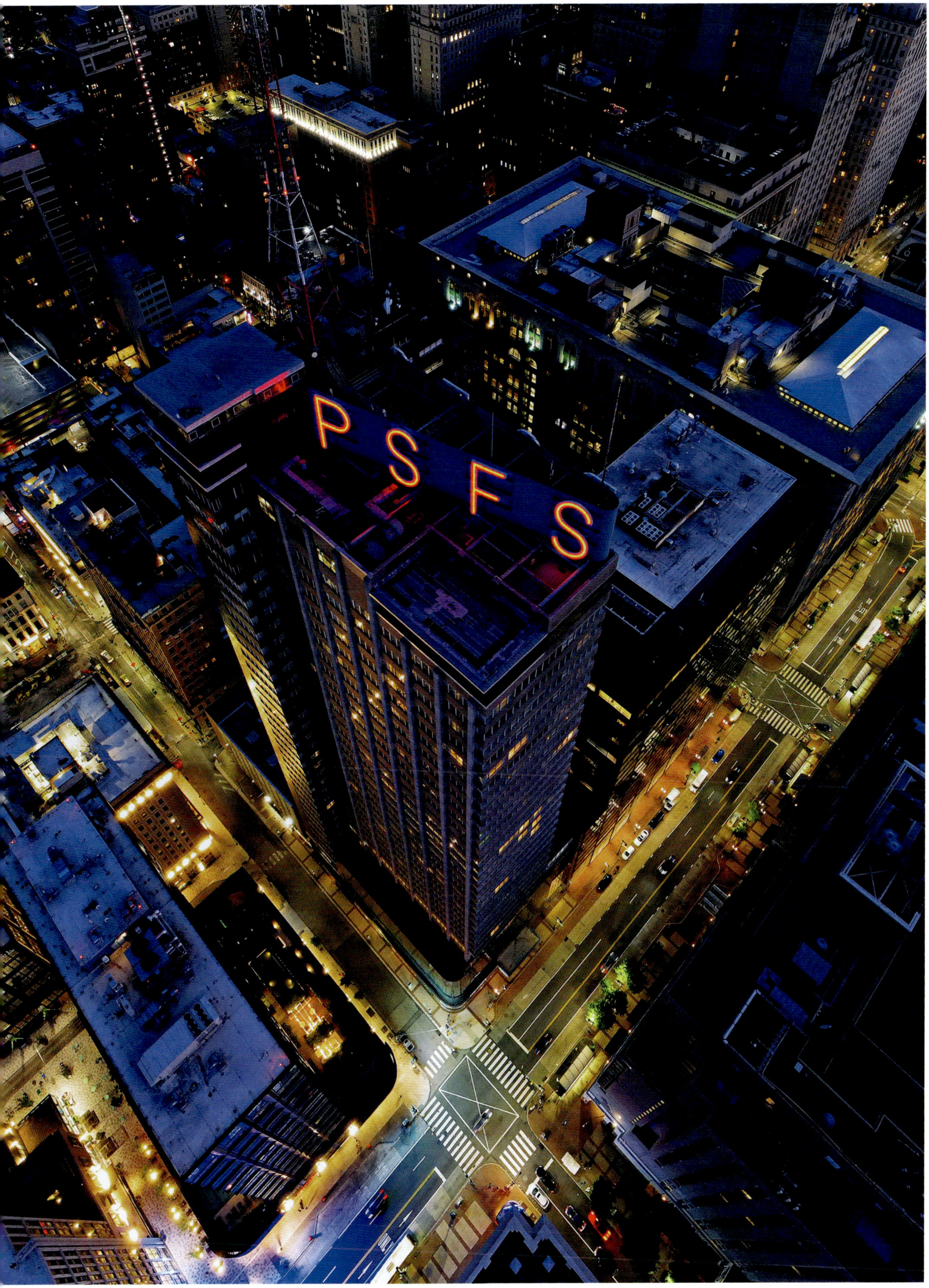
PSFS

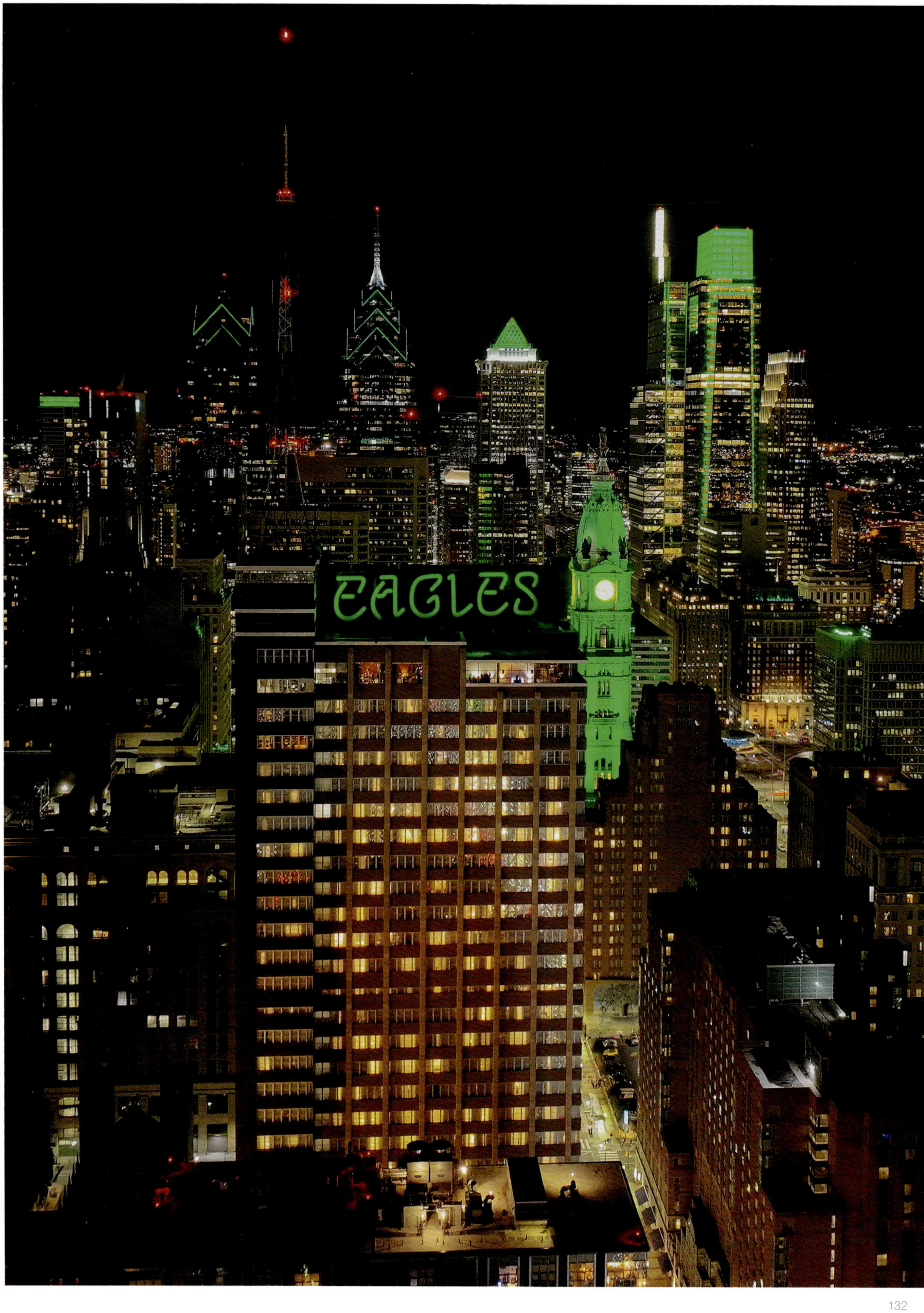
EAGLES

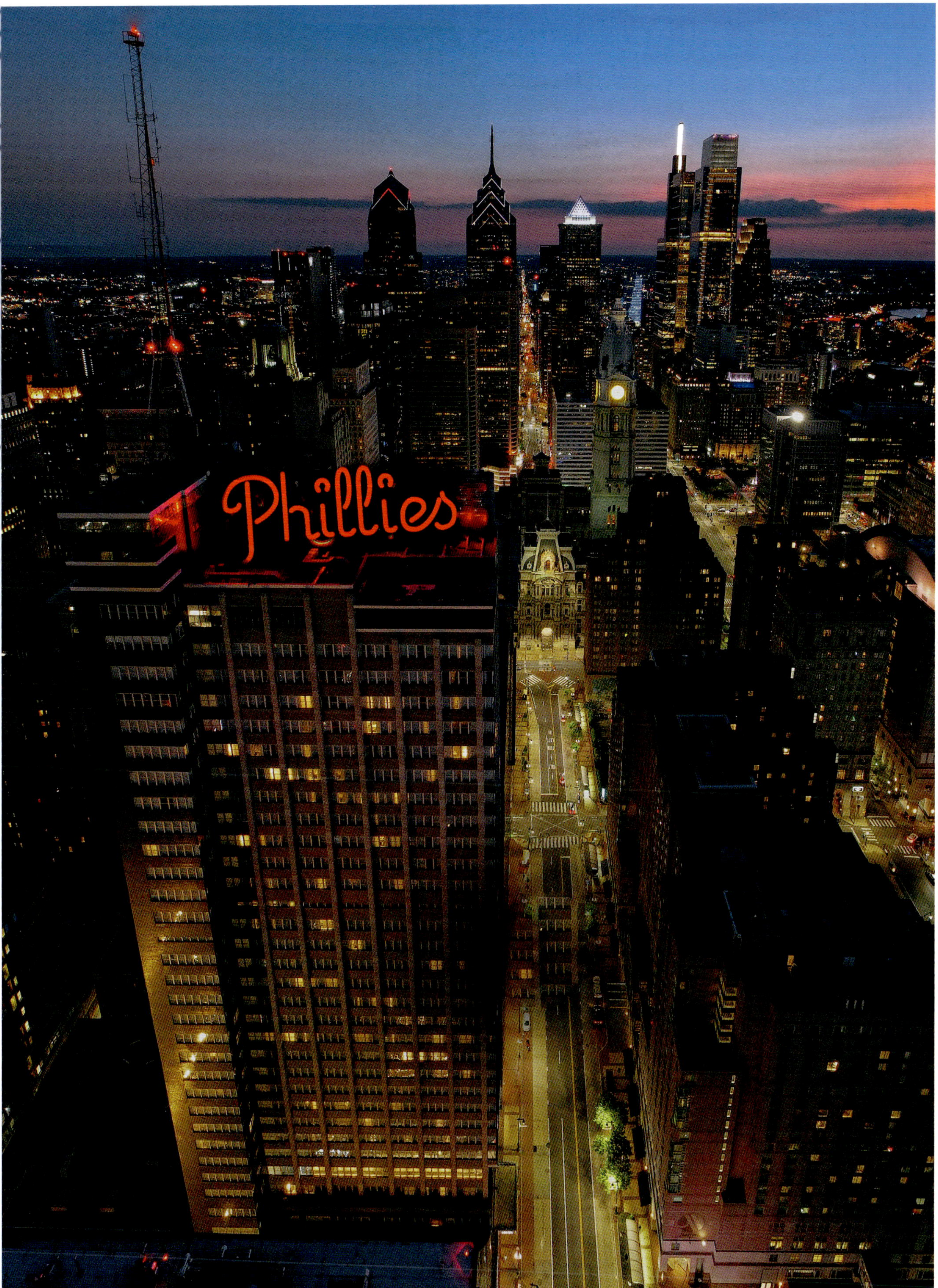
Phillies

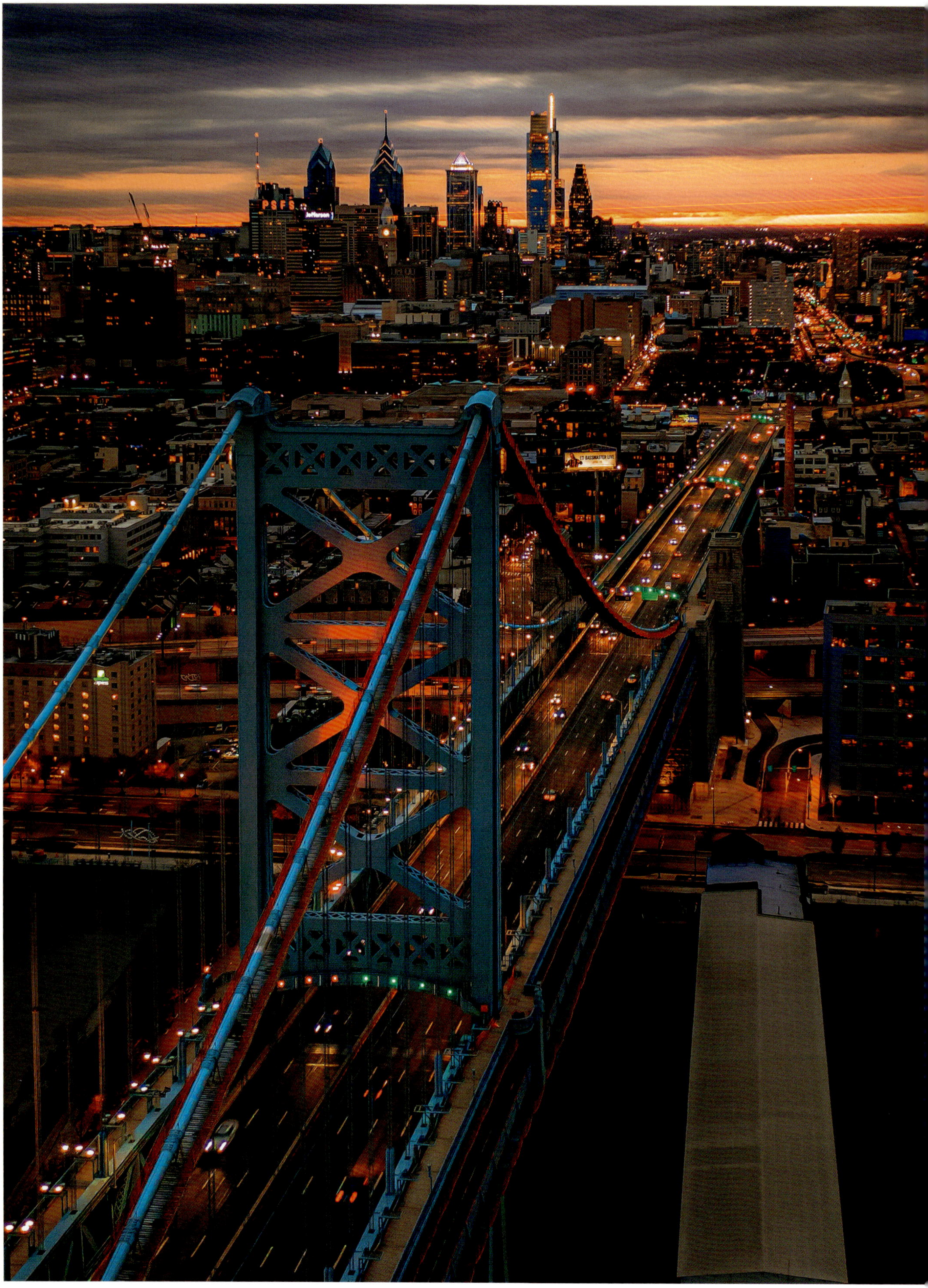

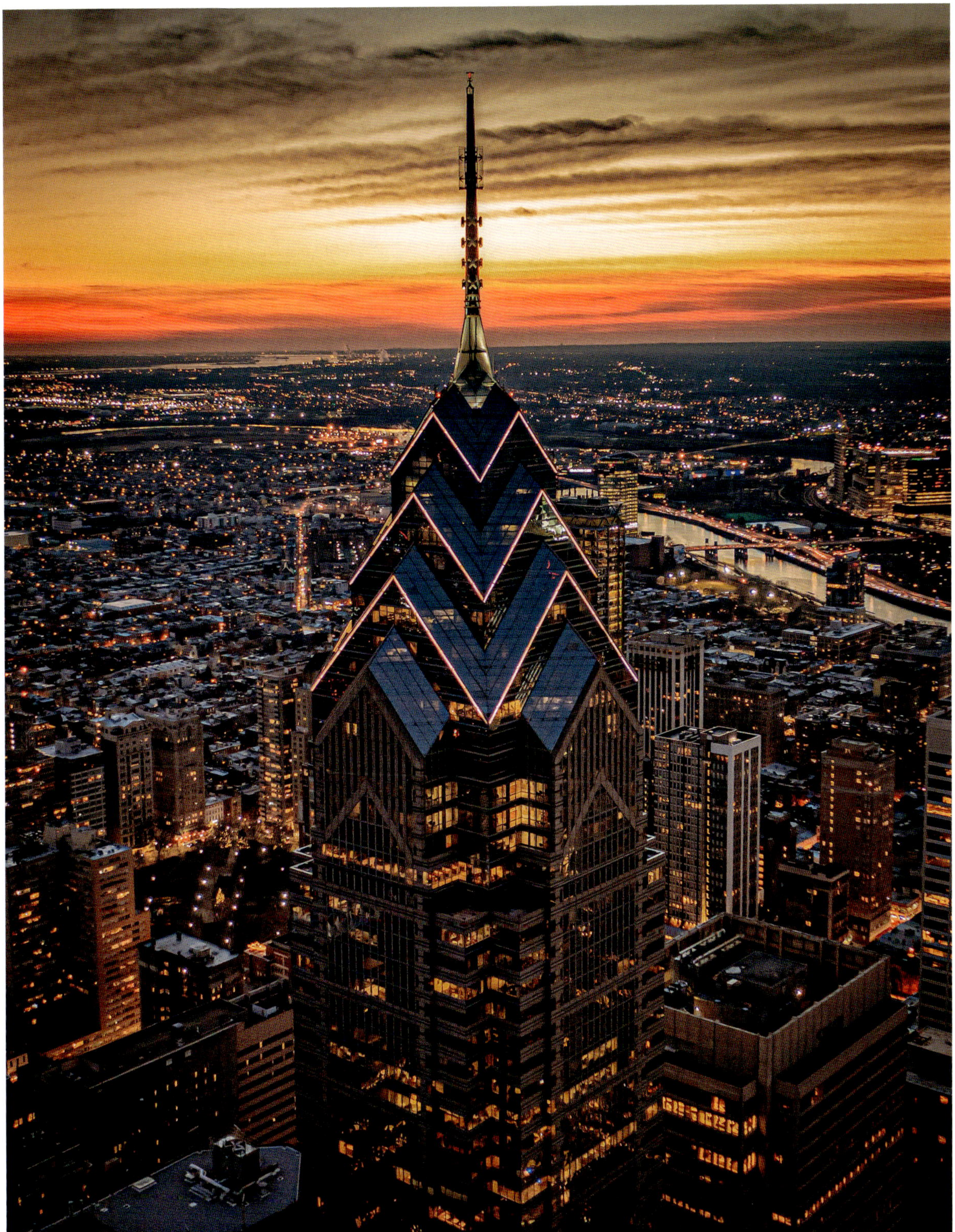

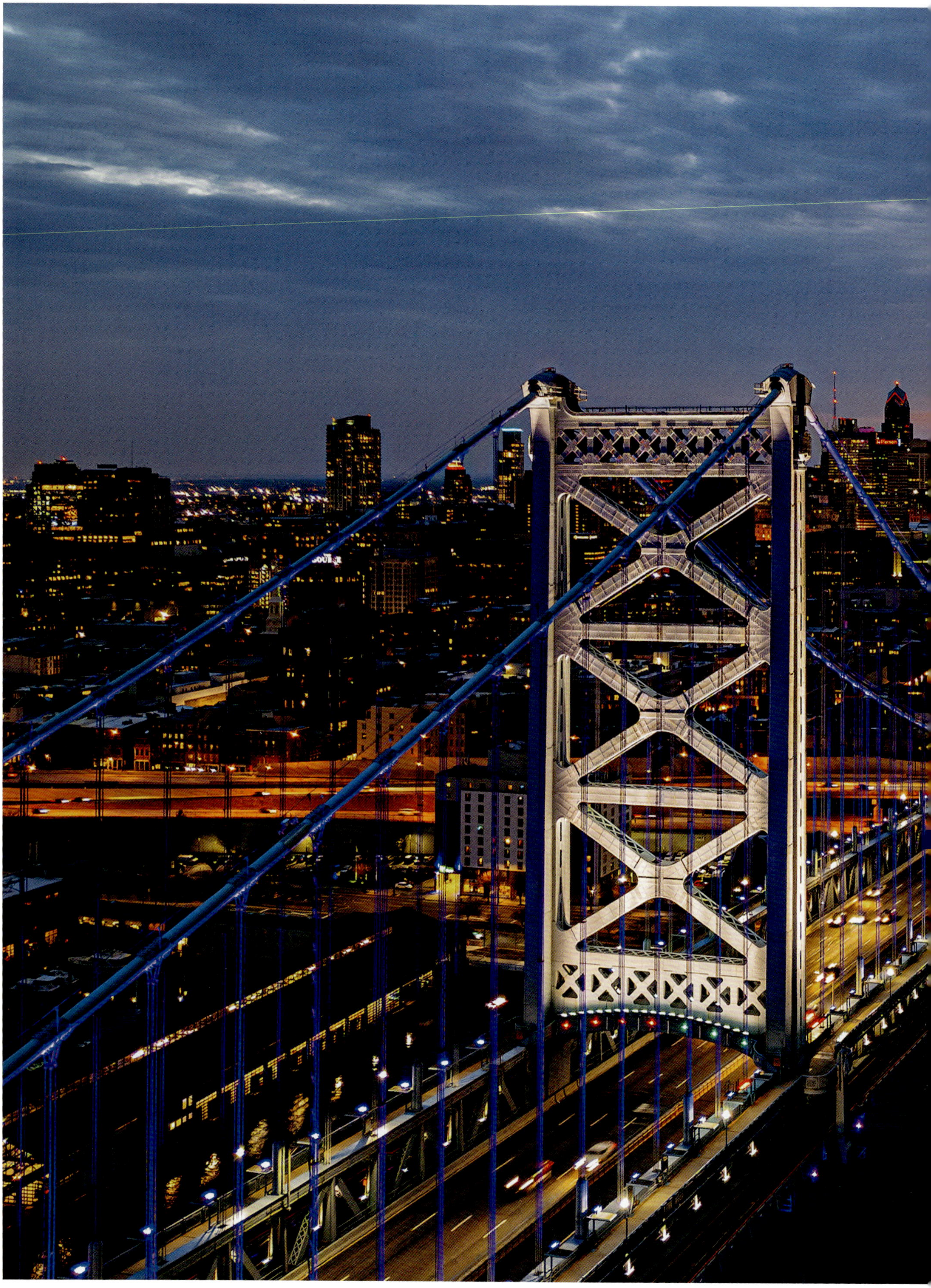

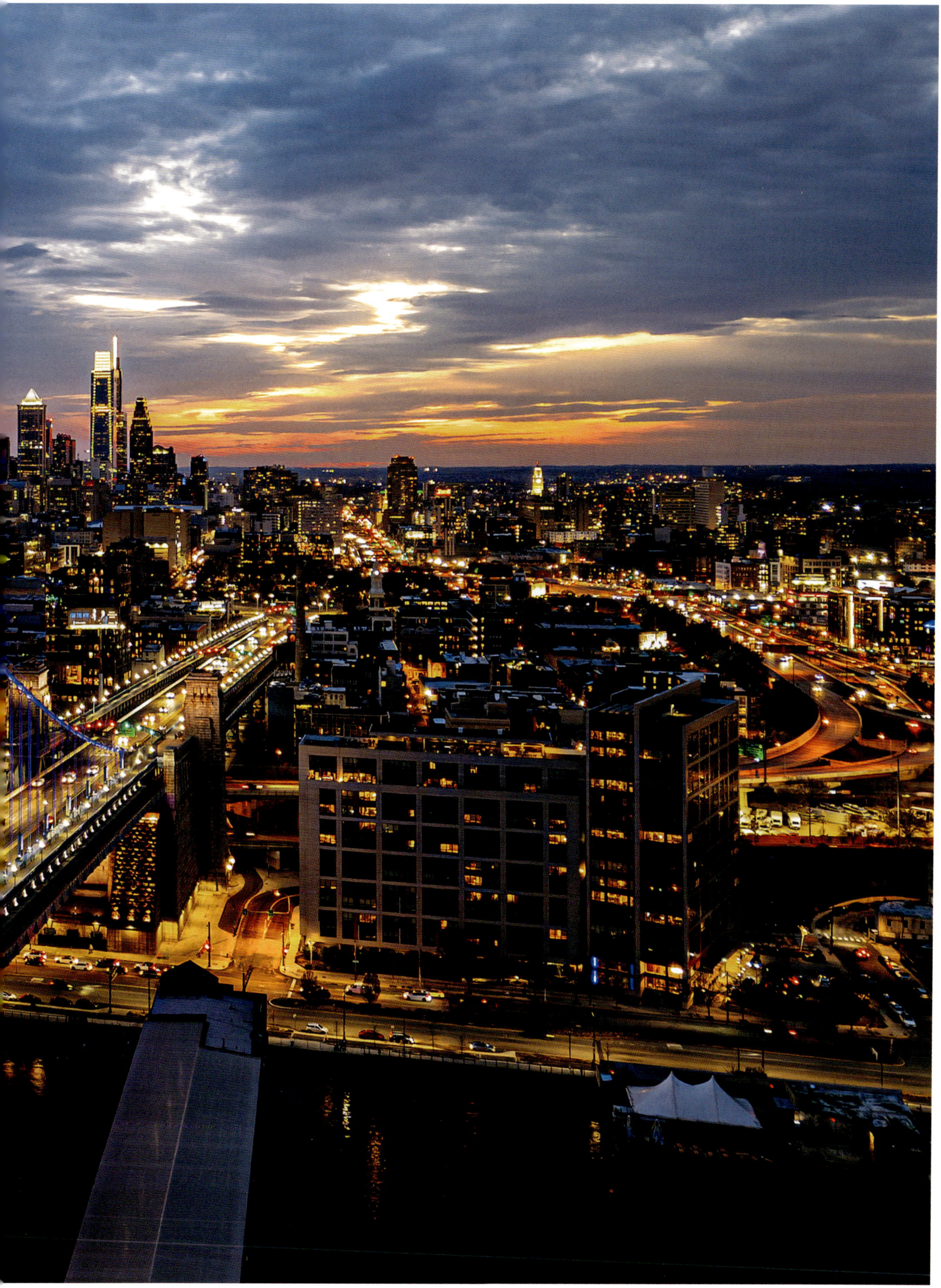

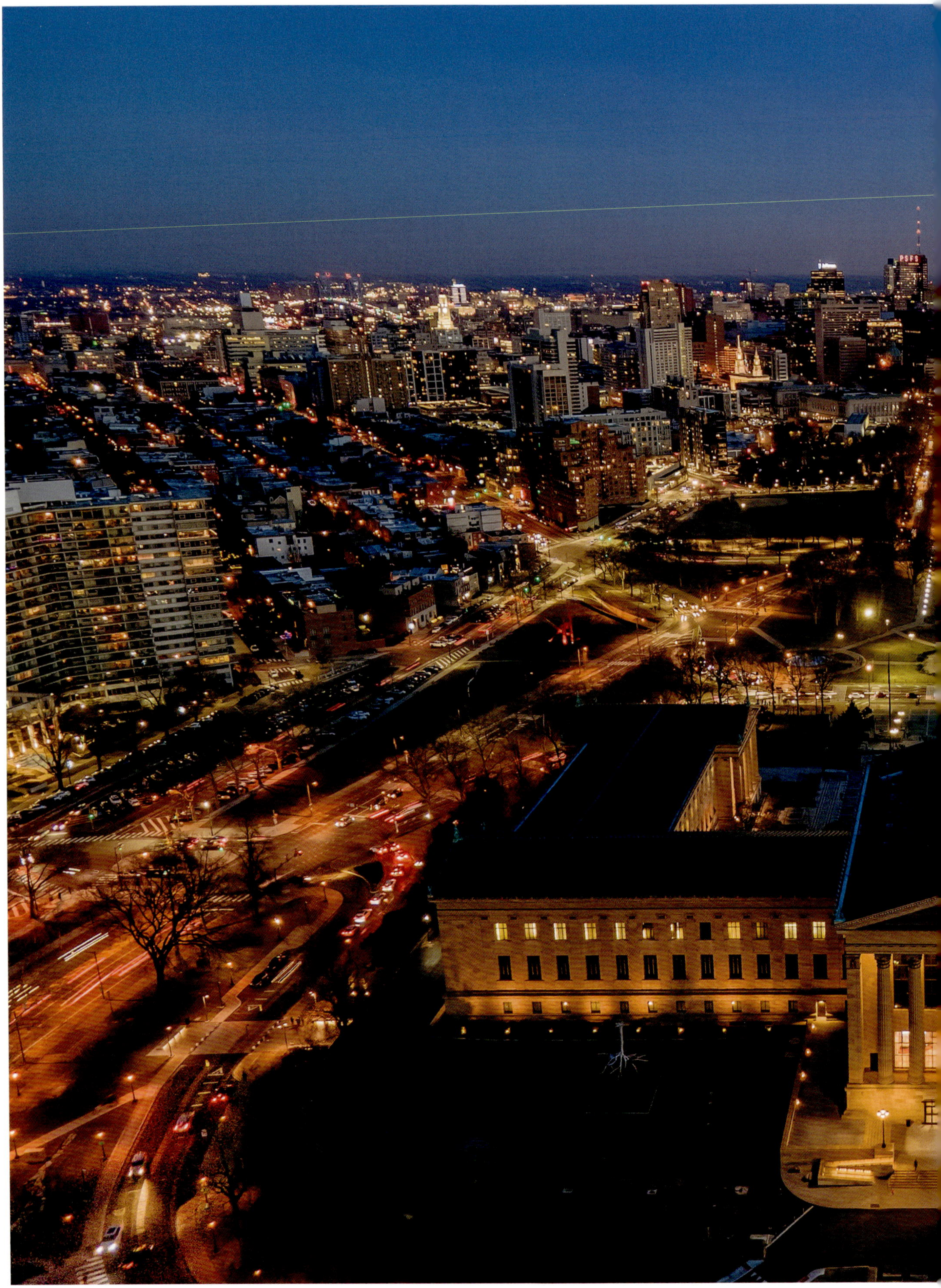

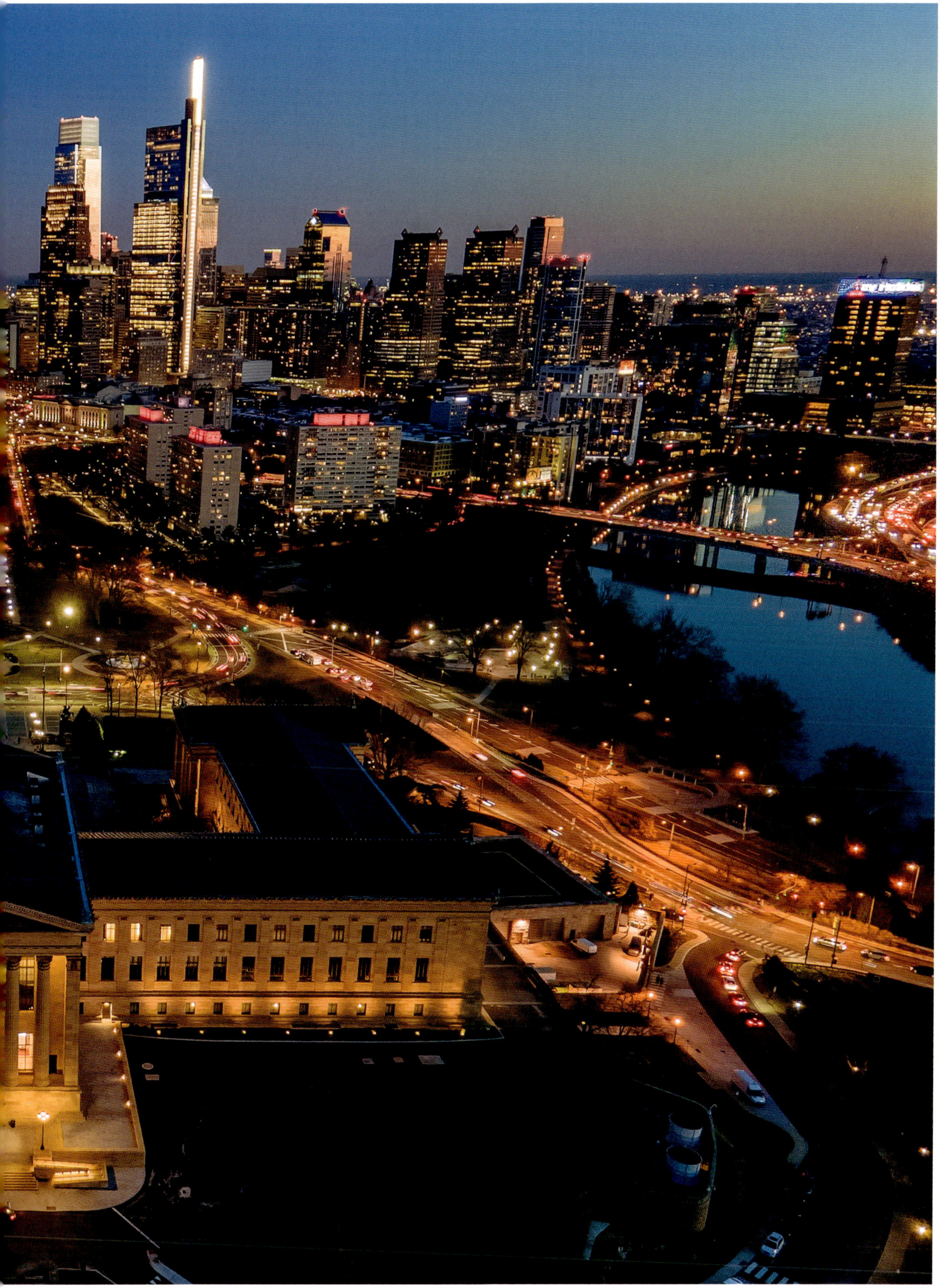

Getting Outside ★ With over 11,000 acres of green space, including parks, squares, playgrounds, and athletic fields, Philadelphia is a very livable city, offering residents countless opportunities for outdoor recreation and connection with nature. ★ Fairmount Park is one of the largest urban park systems in the country. Divided by the Schuylkill River, Fairmount Park was established in 1812 with the purchase of the Lemon Hill estate and was originally created to protect the Schuylkill River watershed, Philadelphia's main source of drinking water. Throughout the 1800s, Fairmount Park expanded significantly through the acquisitions of surrounding estates, eventually encompassing over 2,000 acres. In 1876, Fairmount Park hosted the Centennial Exposition, the first official World's Fair in the United States, celebrating the country's 100th birthday. Many of the structures built for the exposition, including Memorial Hall, still stand today. ★ Once bustling with industrial activity, Philadelphia's historic riverfront piers have been reimagined as outdoor recreation spaces. Stretching along the Delaware River, these piers provide a unique way to experience the city's waterfront with green spaces, public art, and special events. Extending into the river beneath the Benjamin Franklin Bridge, Race Street Pier features tiered seating and stunning views of the water and the boats drifting by. ★ With a passion for its professional sports teams, Philadelphia comes alive on game days. People pack bars, tailgate, and travel to stadiums to cheer on their teams. The city's deep-rooted loyalty to its teams is part of its cultural identity. Philadelphia is home to five professional teams, including the Eagles, the 76ers, the Phillies, the Flyers, and the Union. The South Philadelphia Sports Complex is the epicenter of this activity, housing Lincoln Financial Field (home of the Eagles), Citizens Bank Park (home of the Phillies), and the Wells Fargo Center (home of the Flyers and the 76ers).

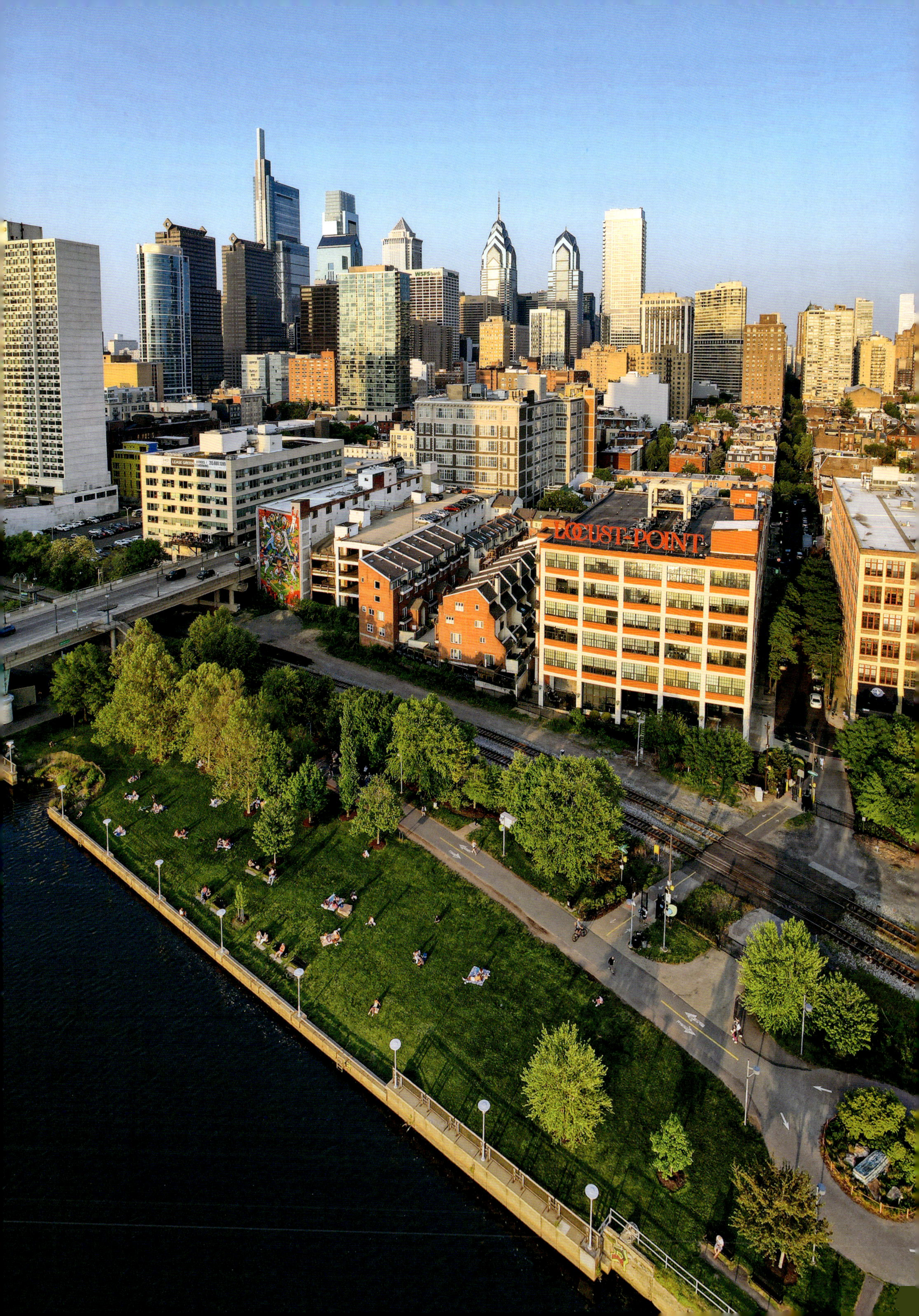
LOCUST POINT

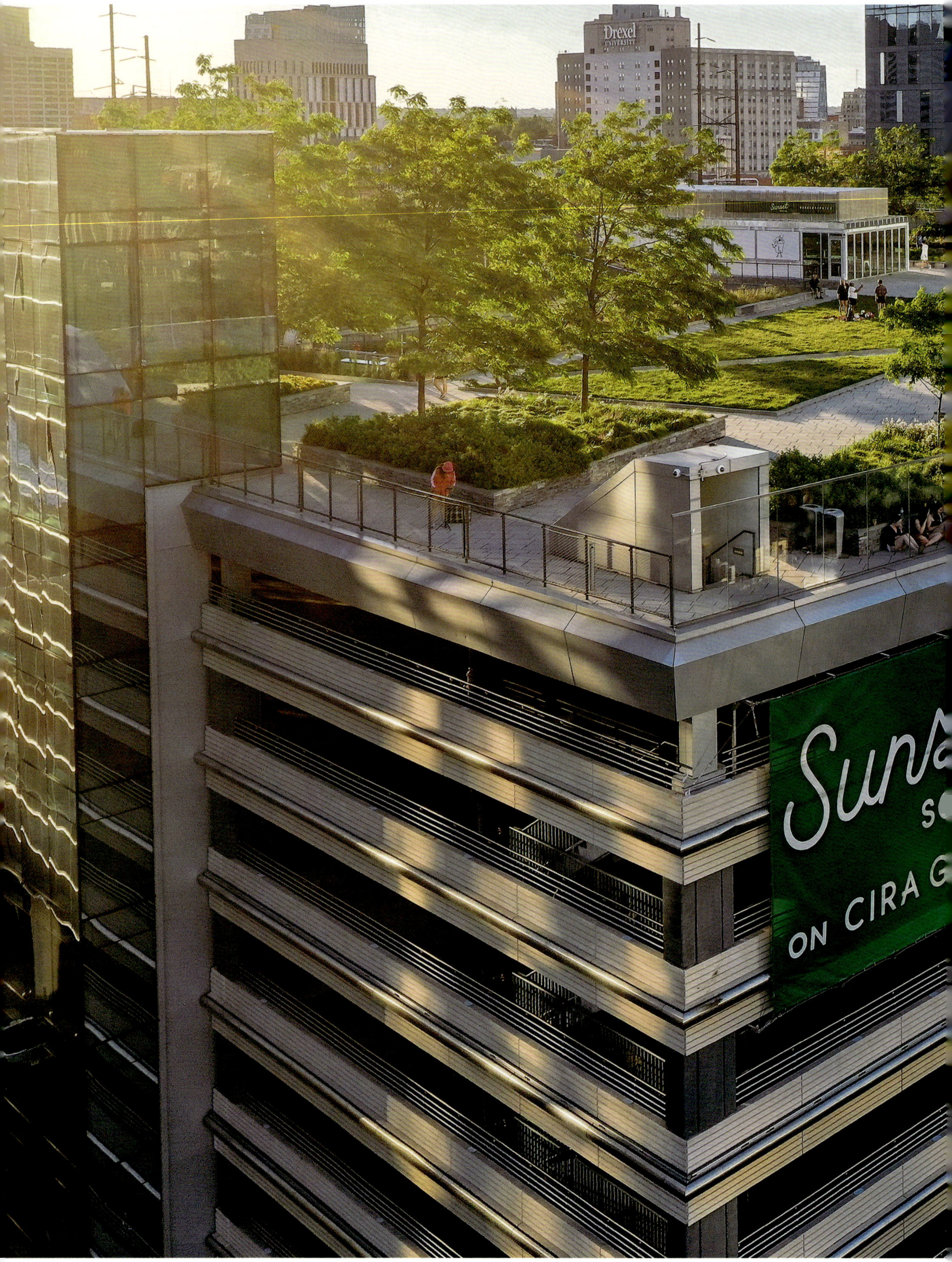
Drexel
Sun
ON CIRA G

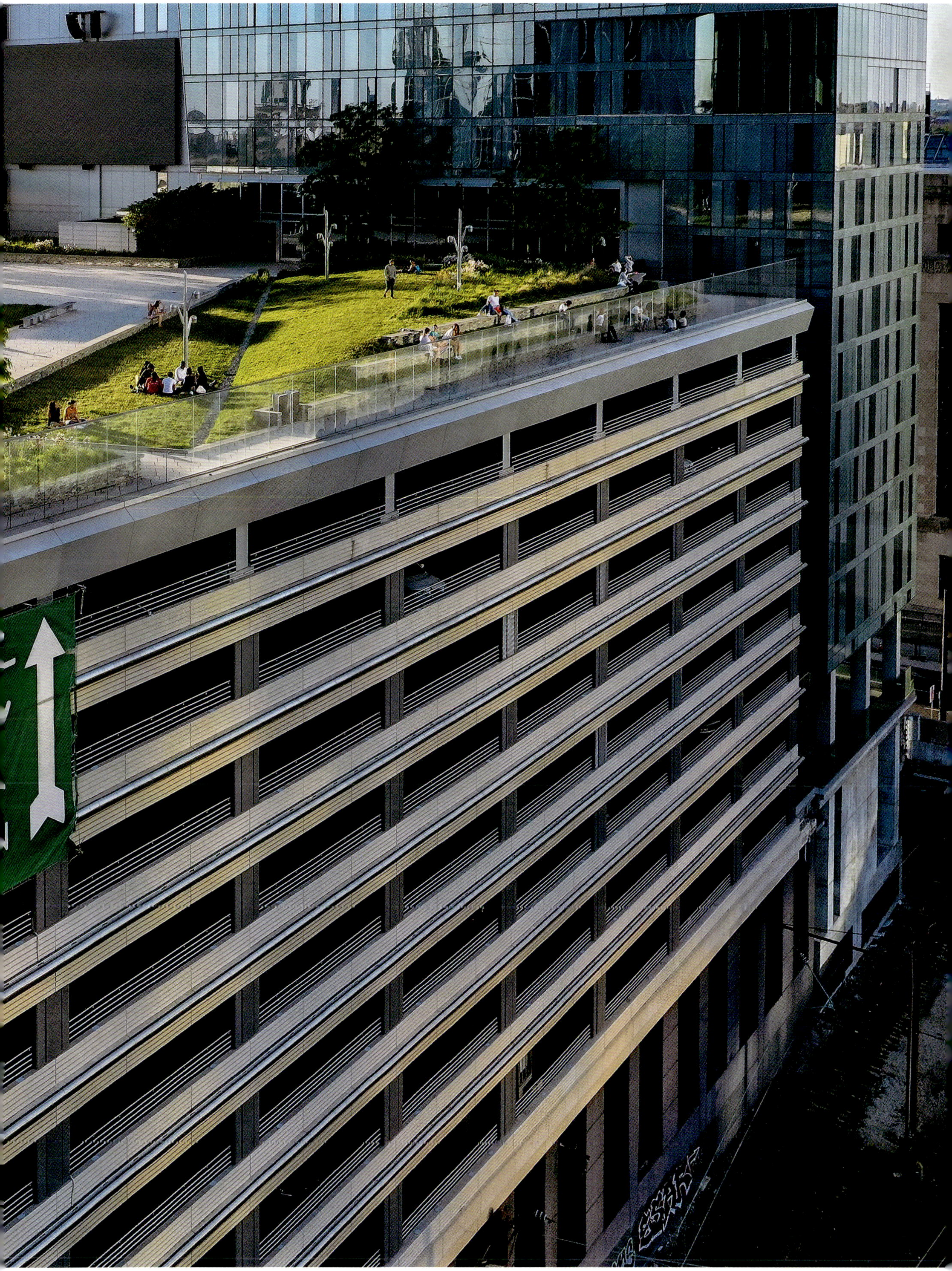

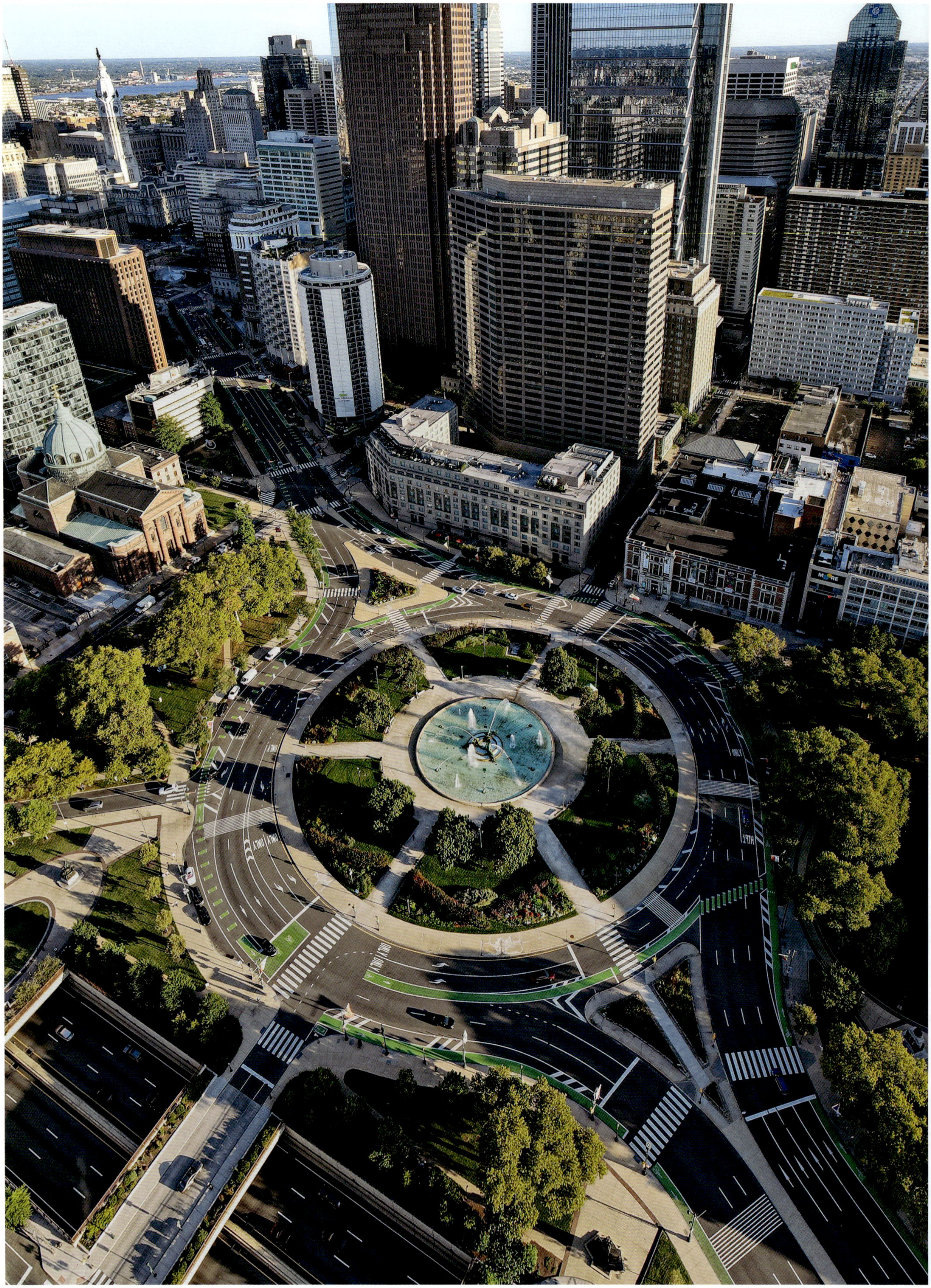

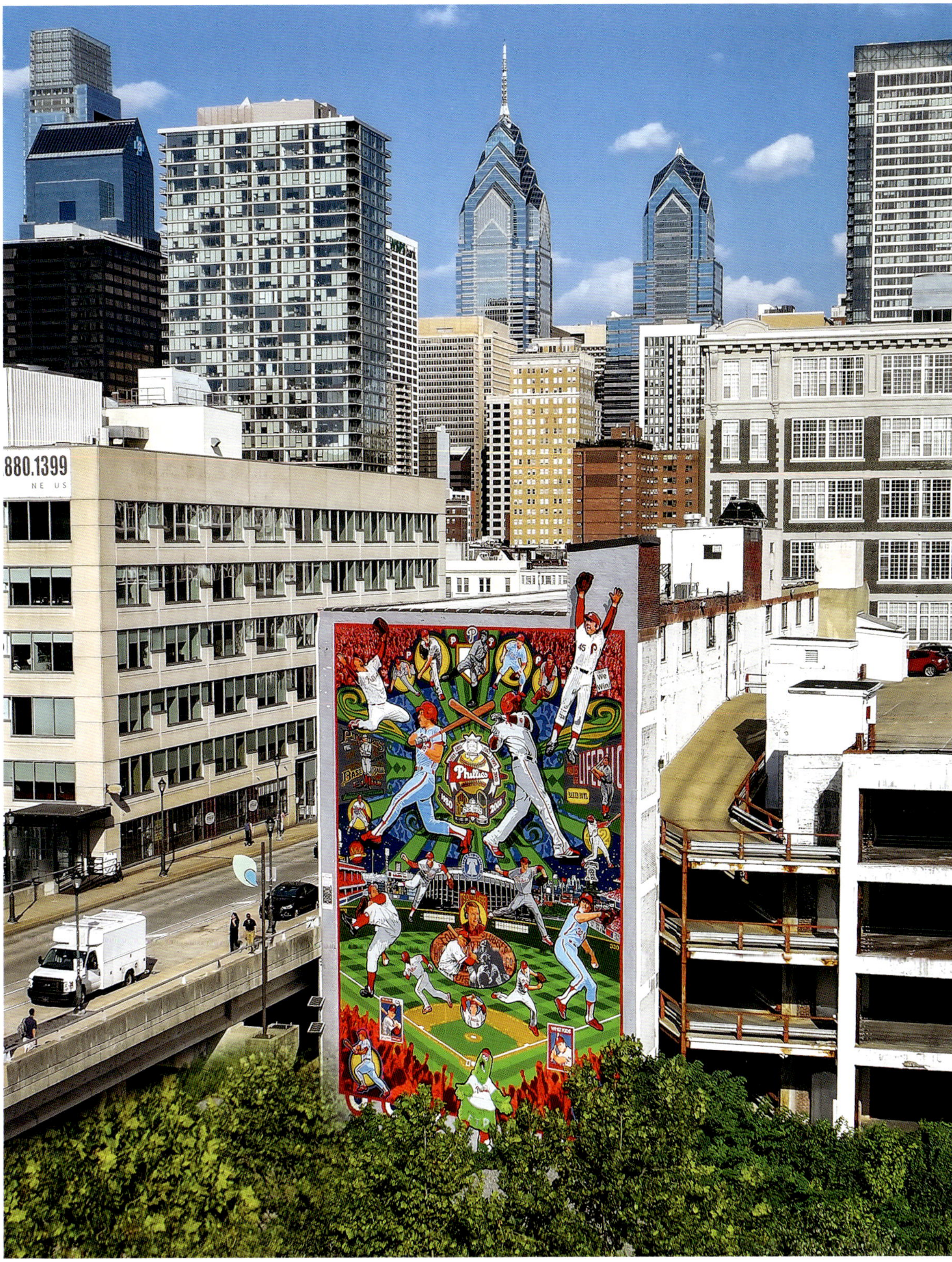
880.1399

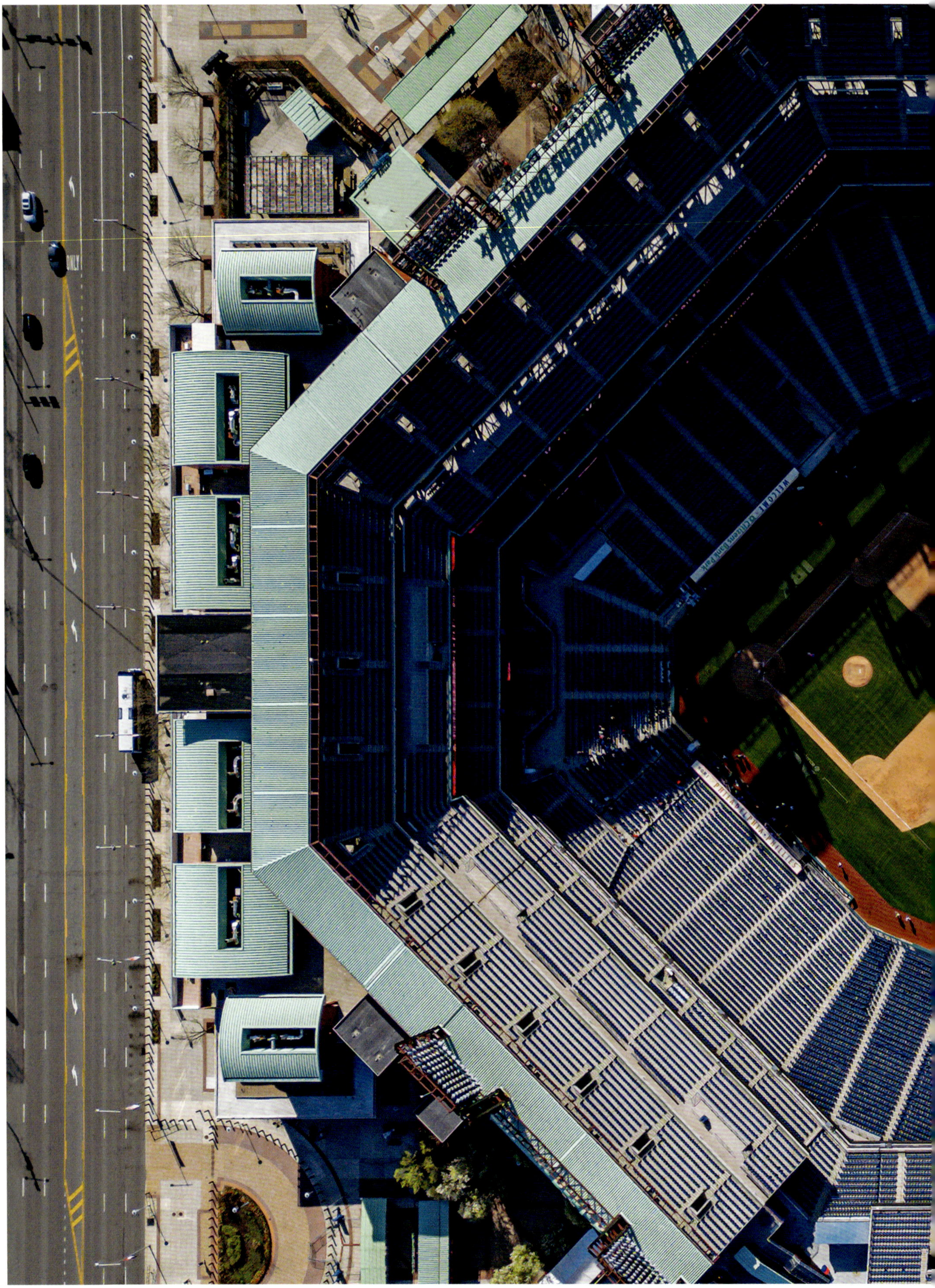

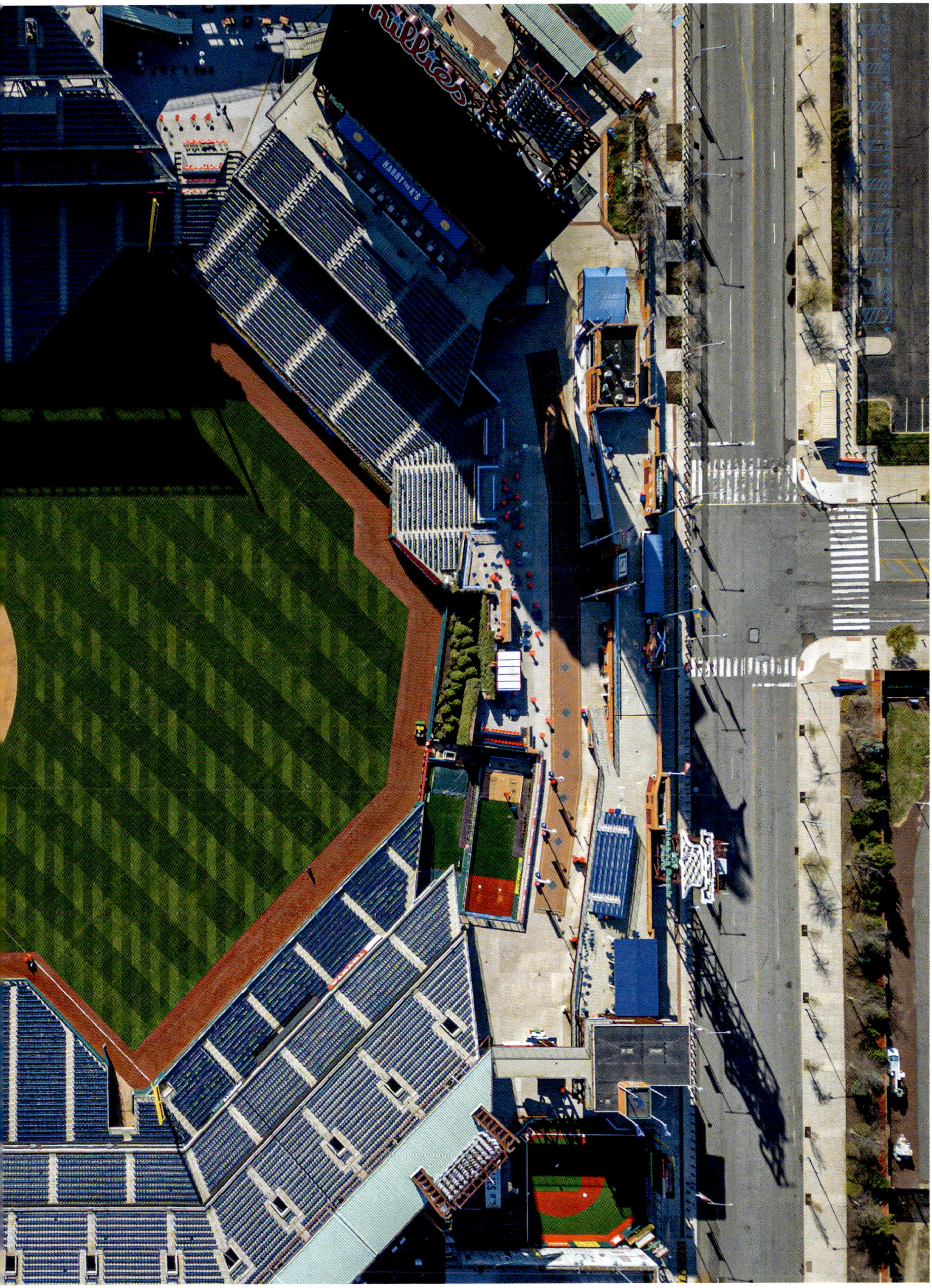

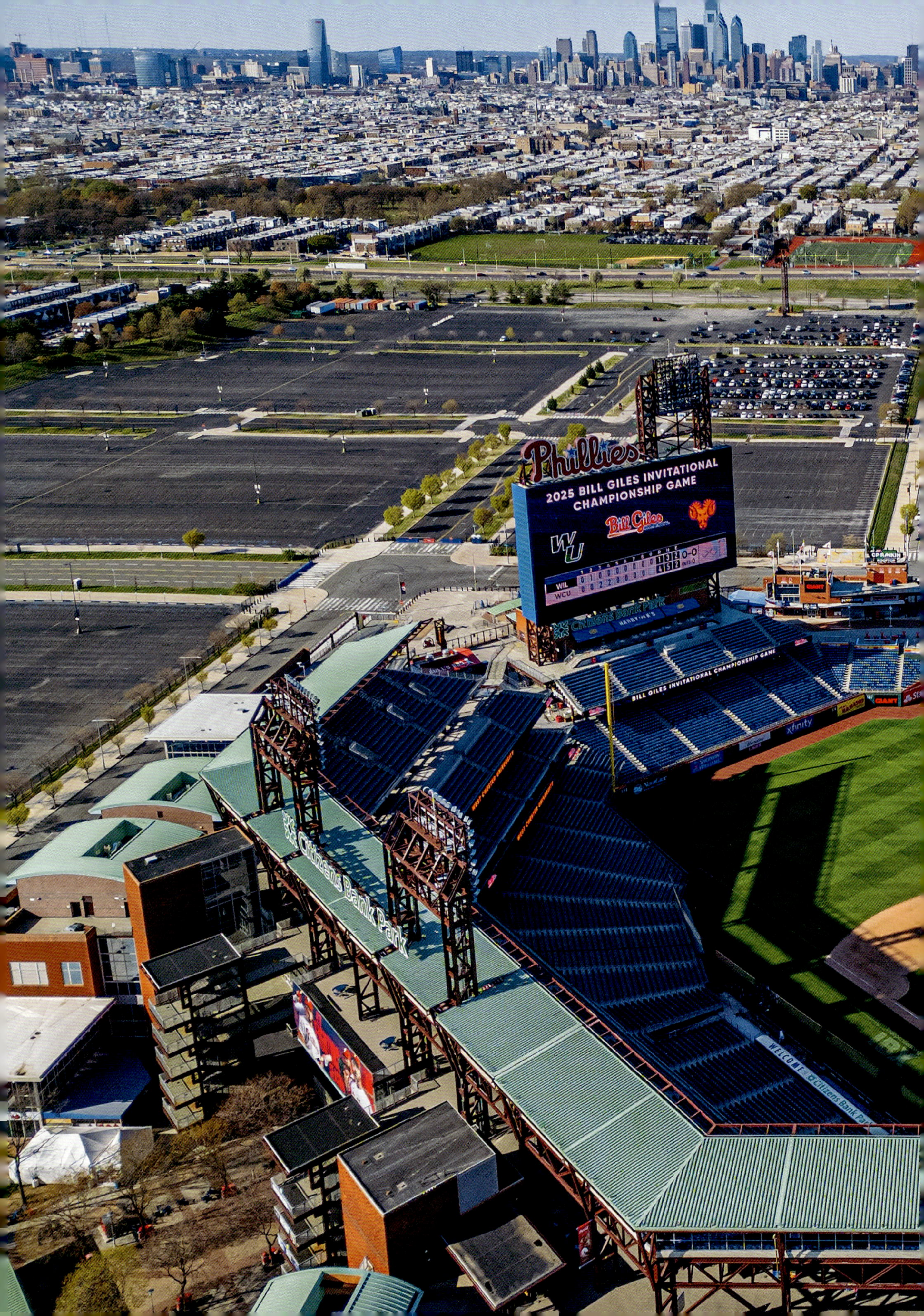
Phillies
2025 BILL GILES INVITATIONAL
CHAMPIONSHIP GAME
Bill Giles
WIL
WCU
Citizens Bank Park
BILL GILES INVITATIONAL CHAMPIONSHIP GAME
Citizens Bank Park
WELCOME Citizens Bank Park

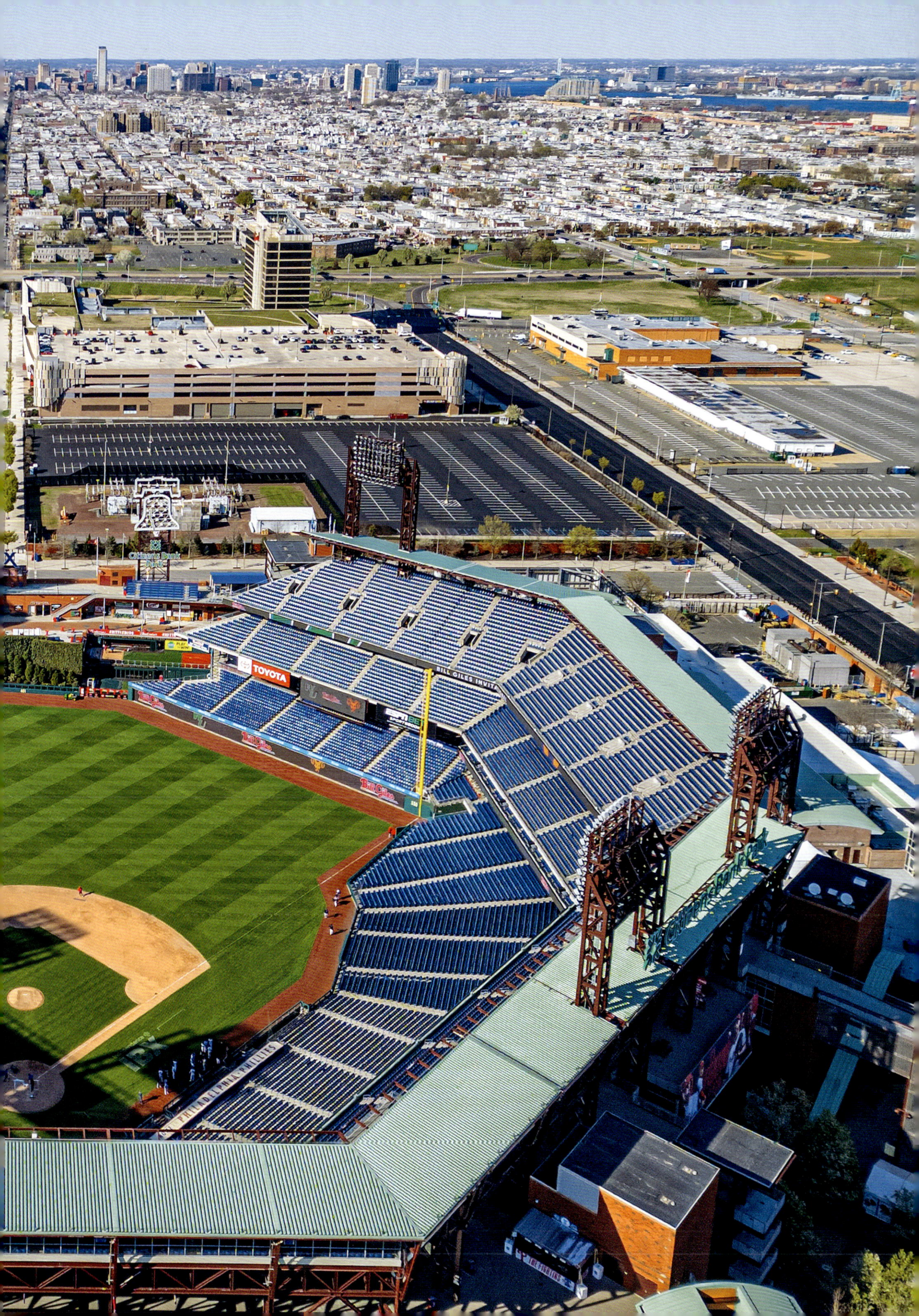
TOYOTA

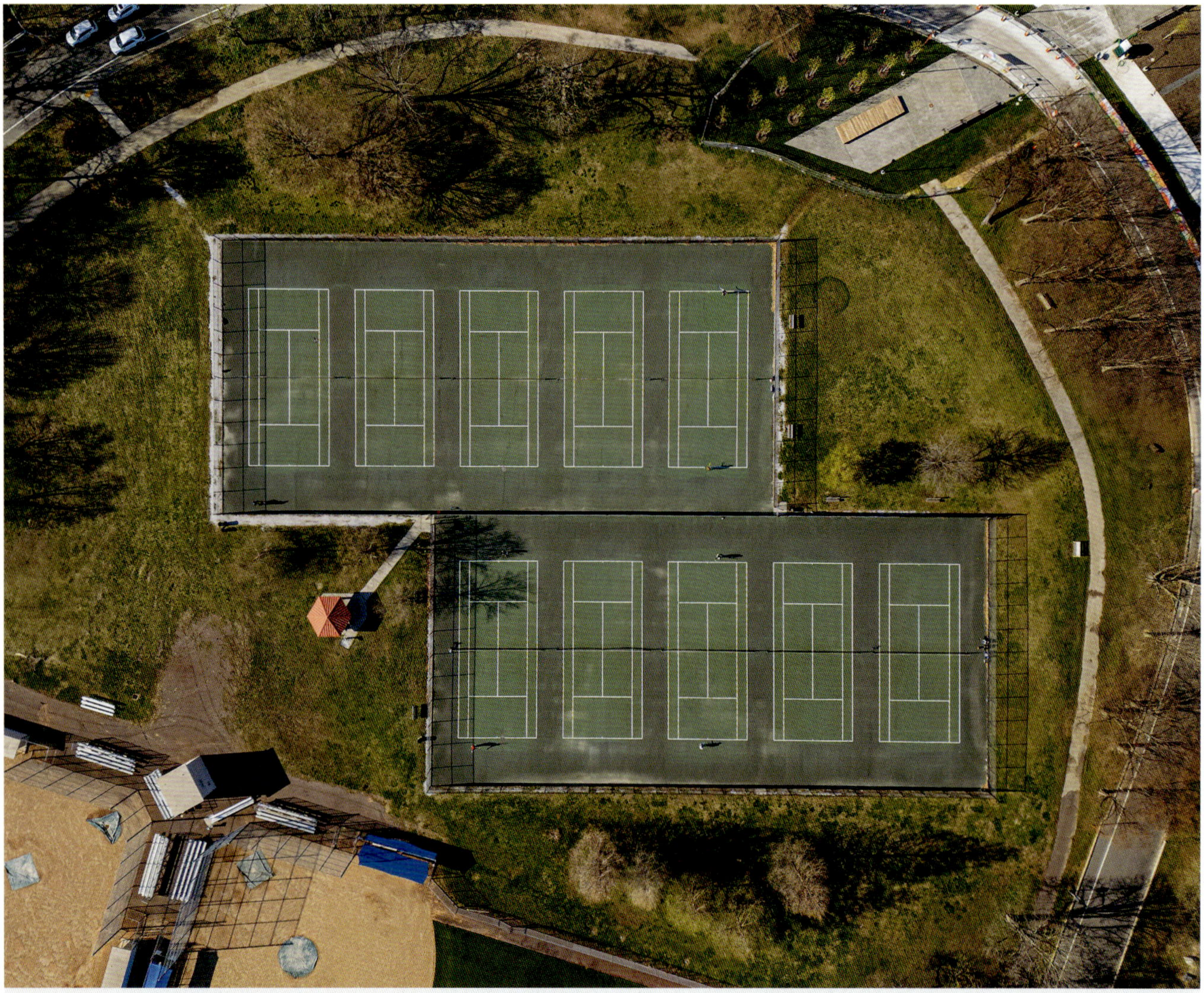

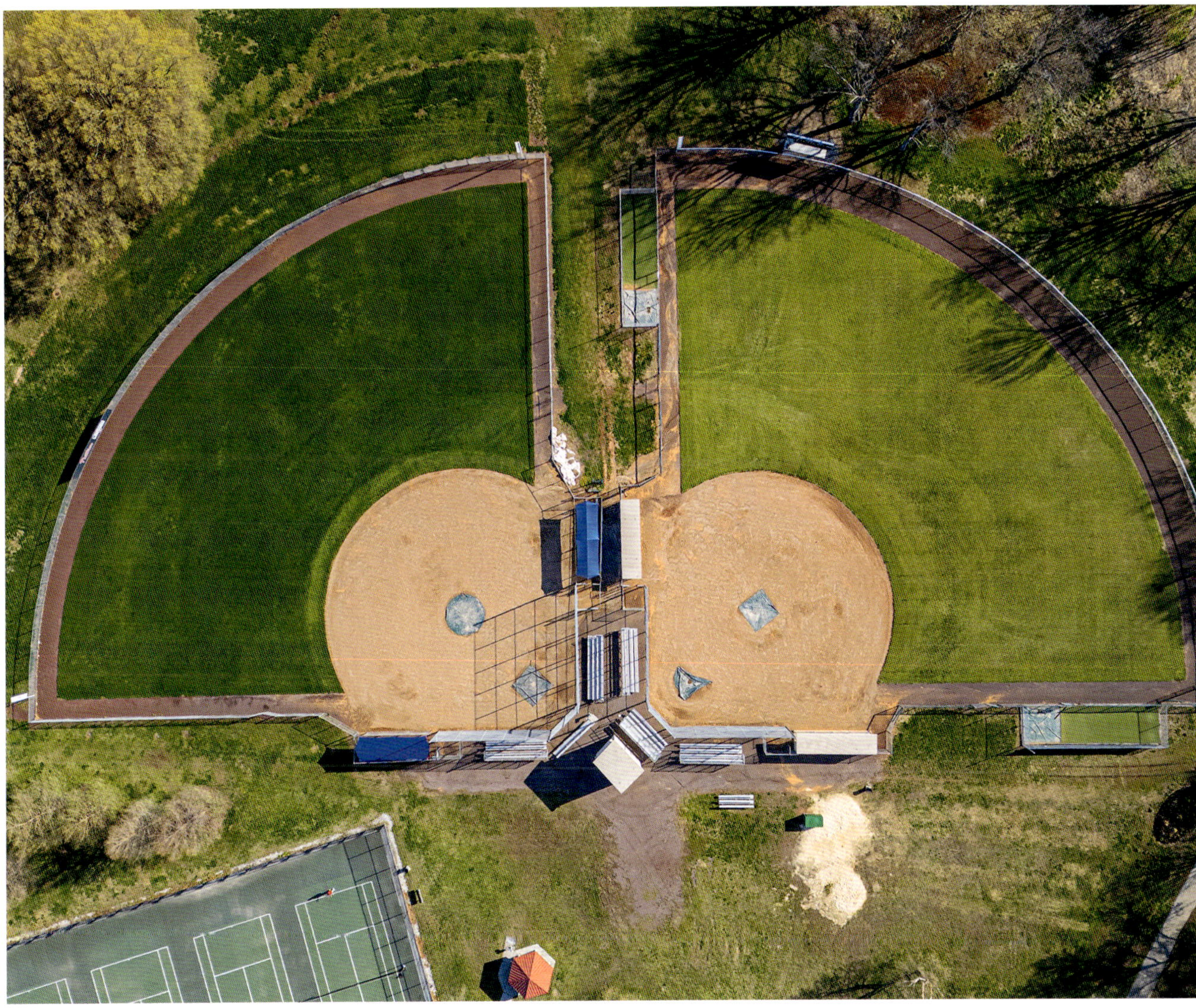

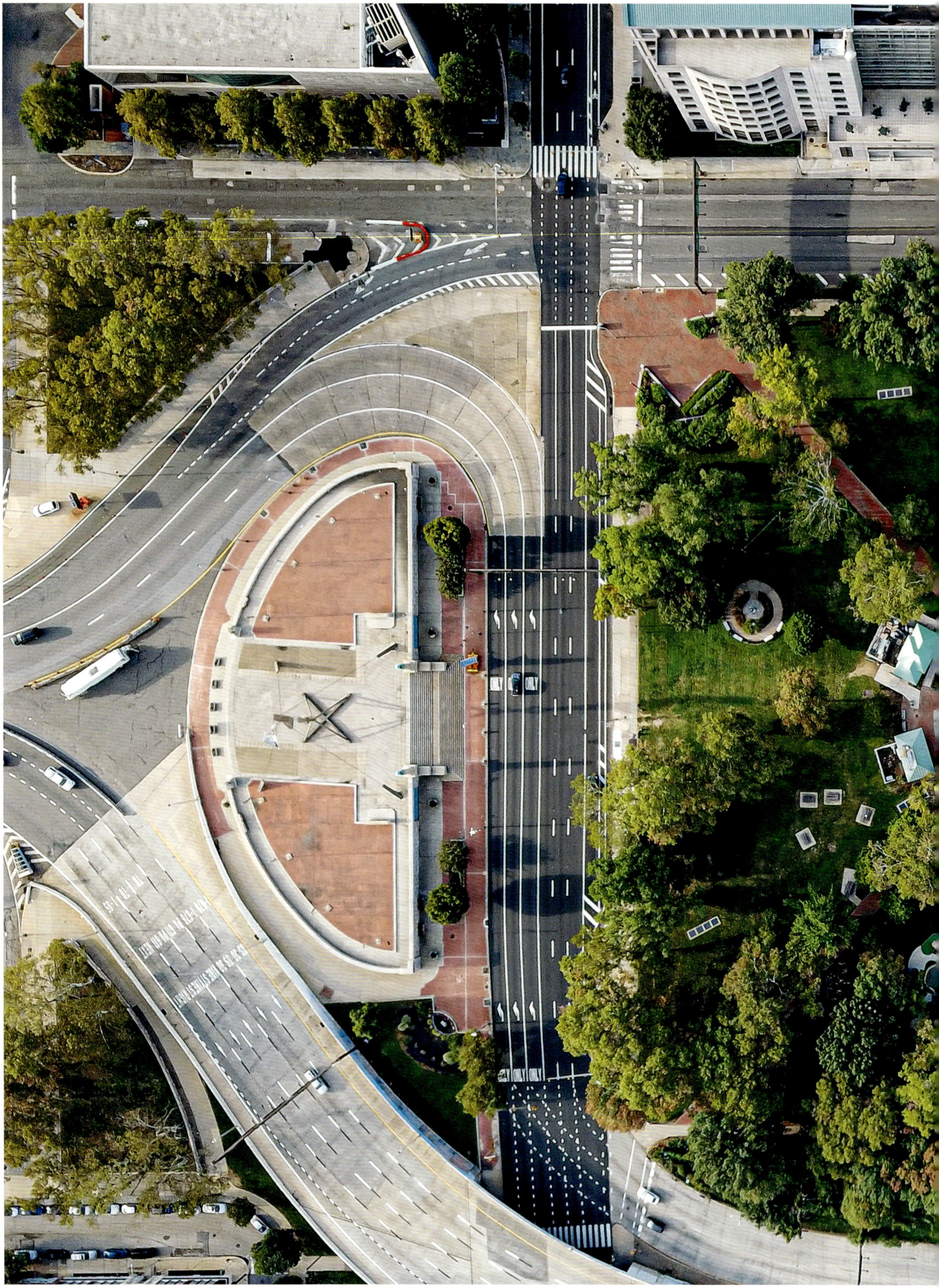

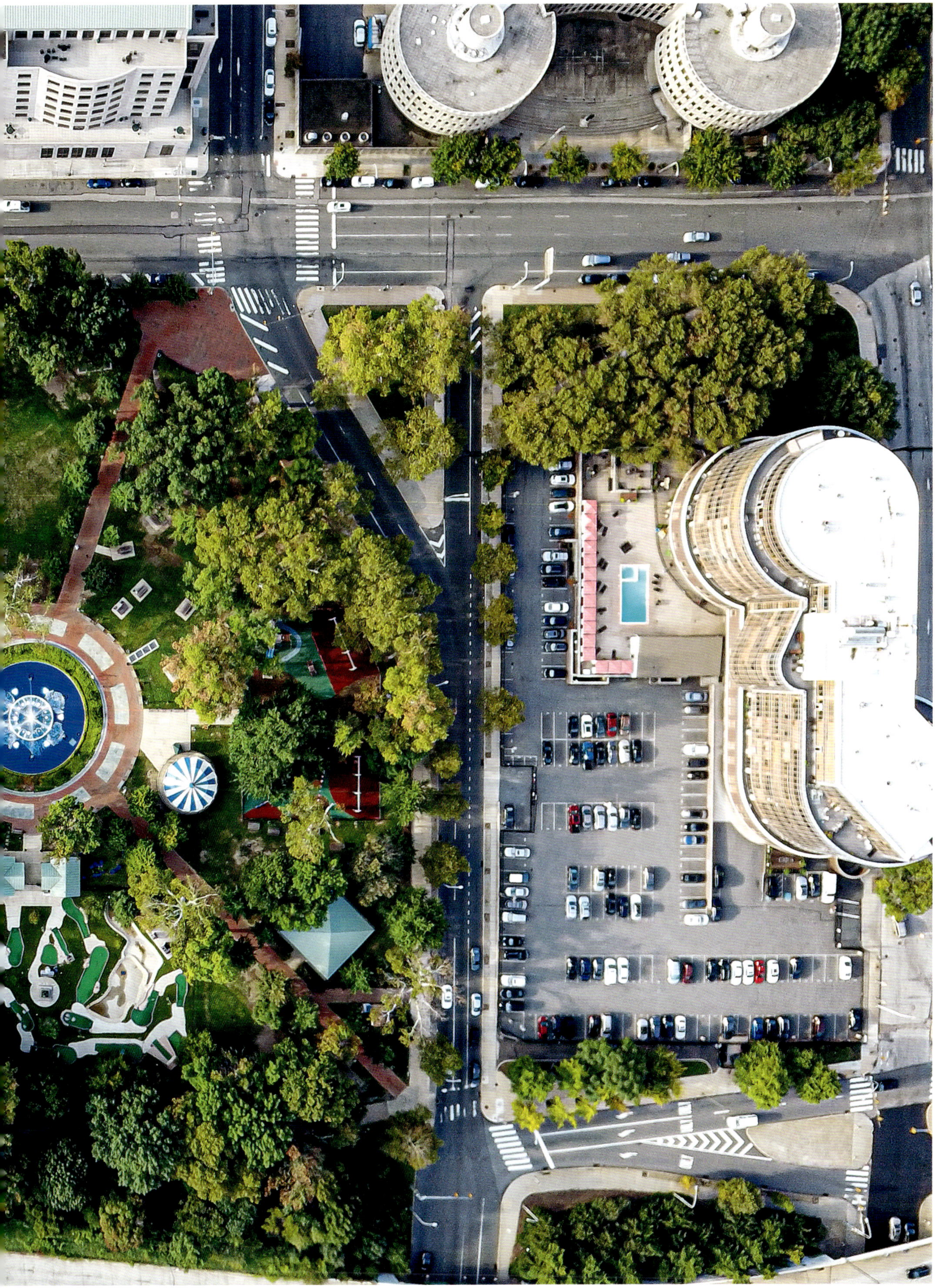

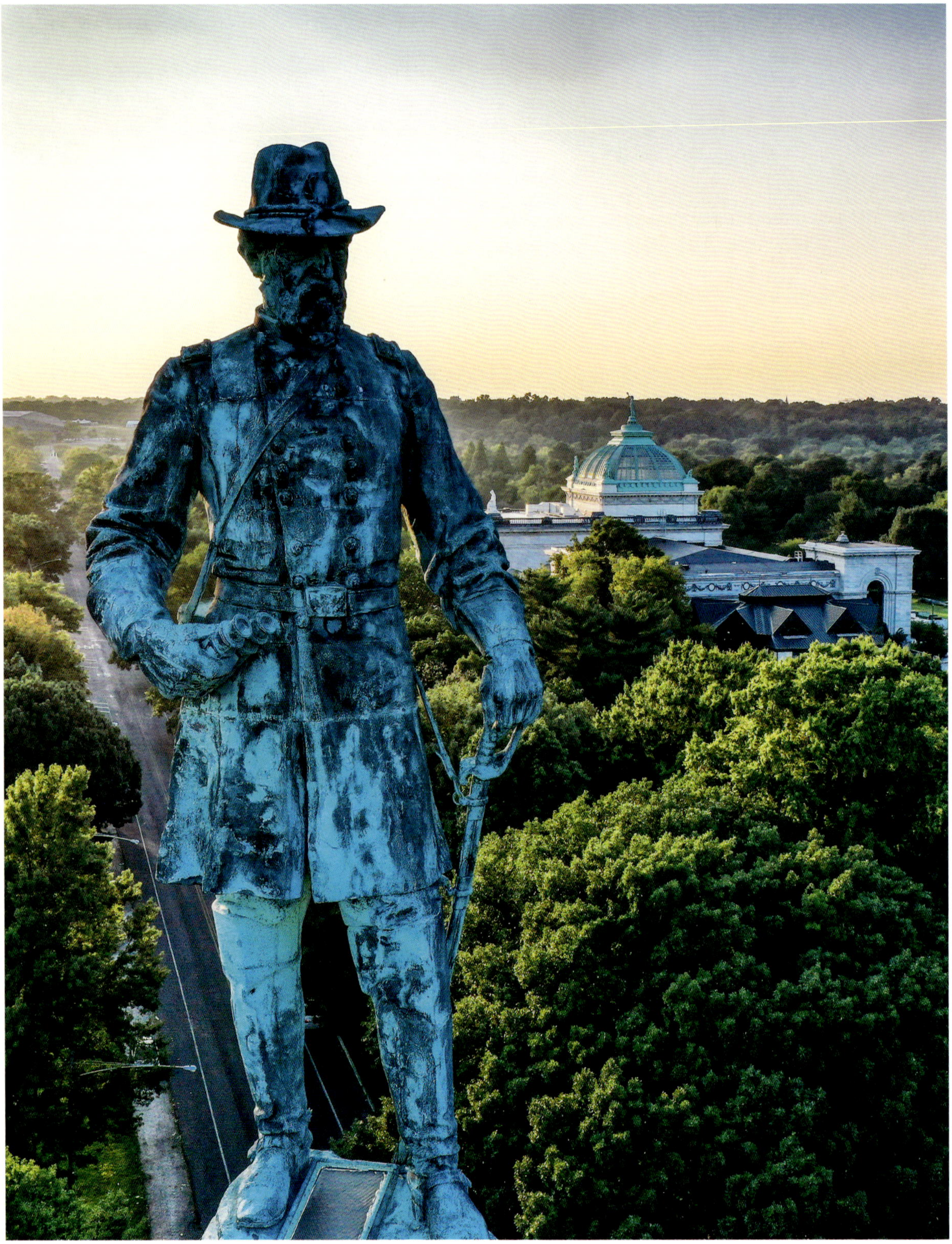

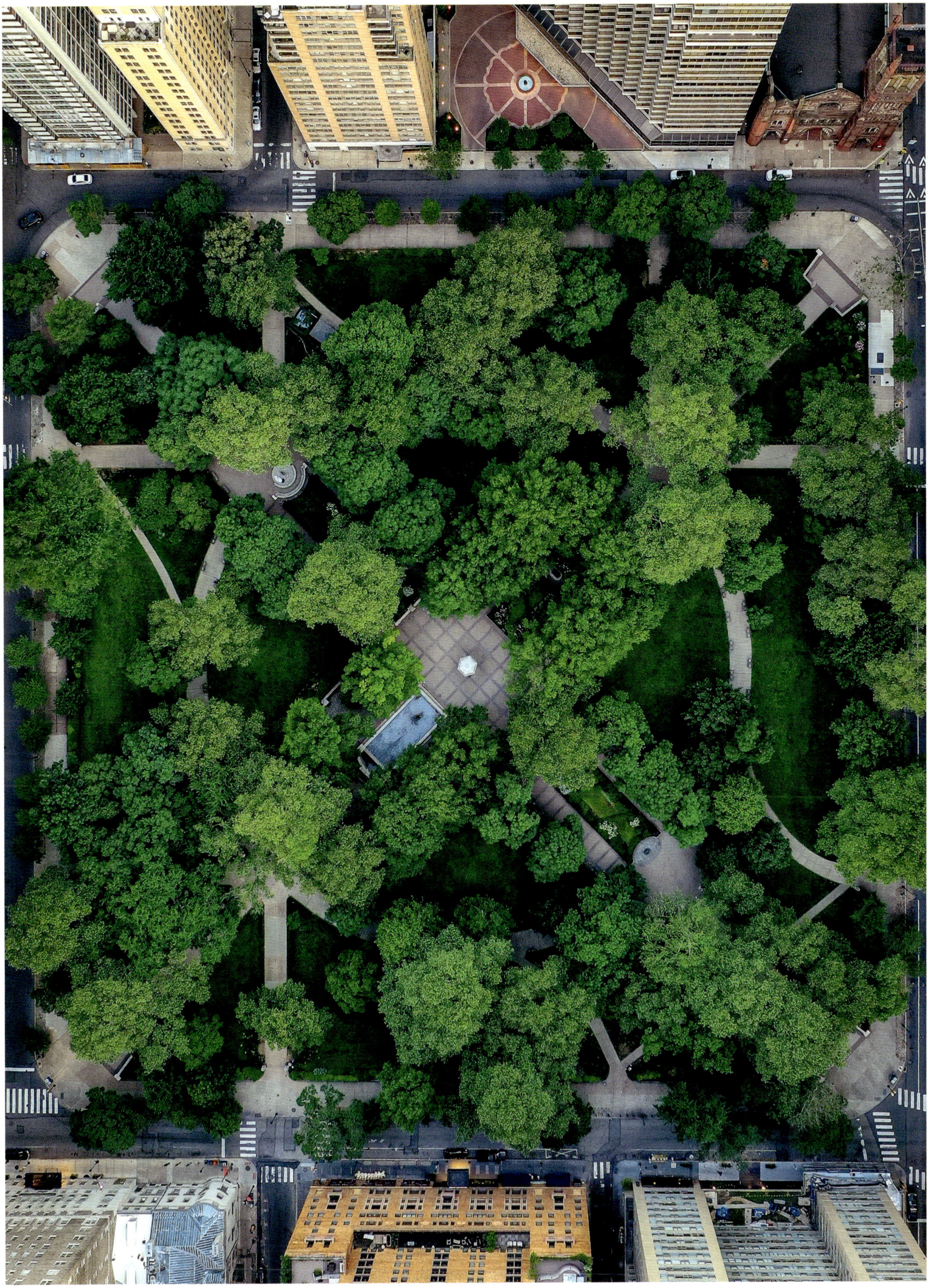

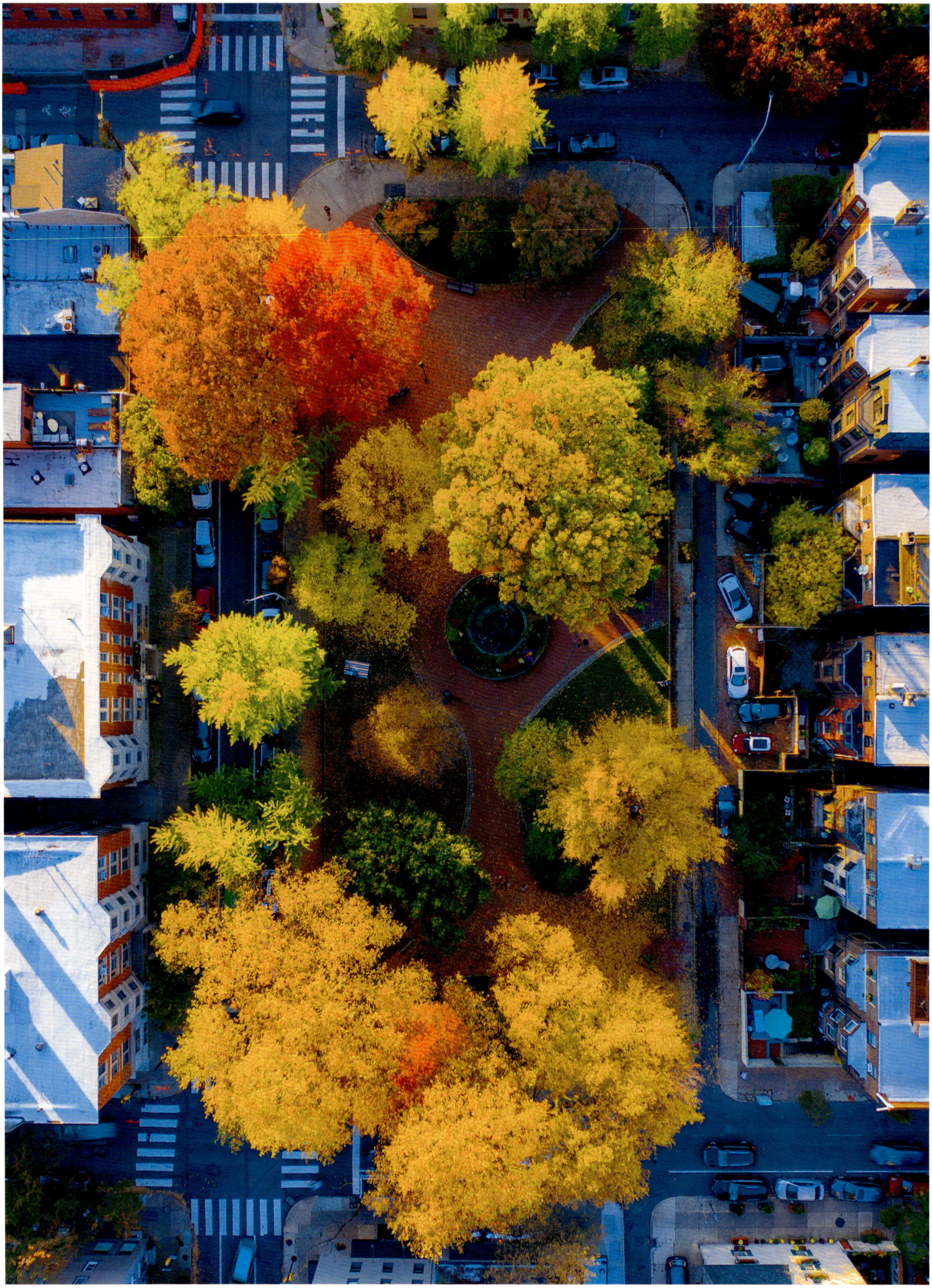

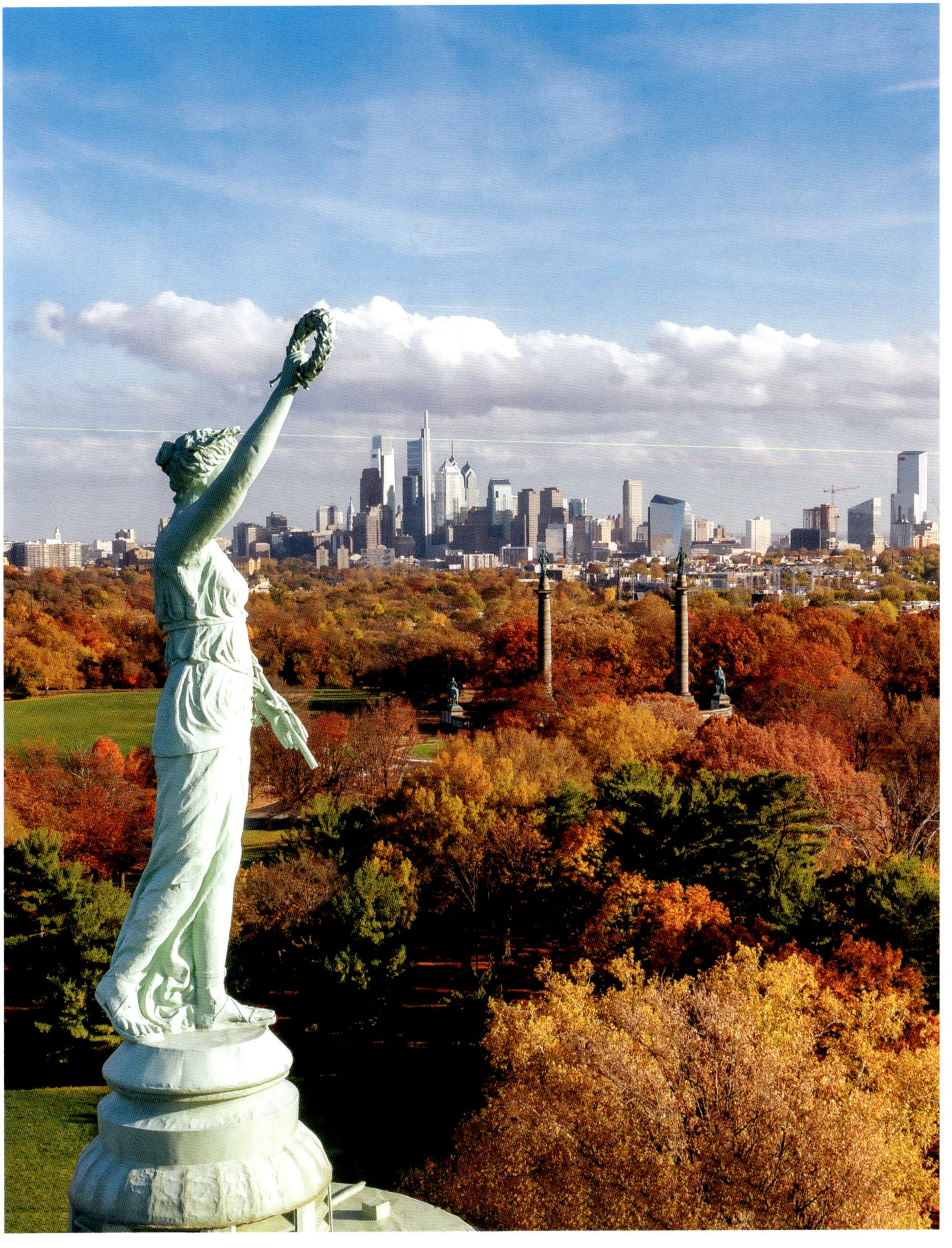

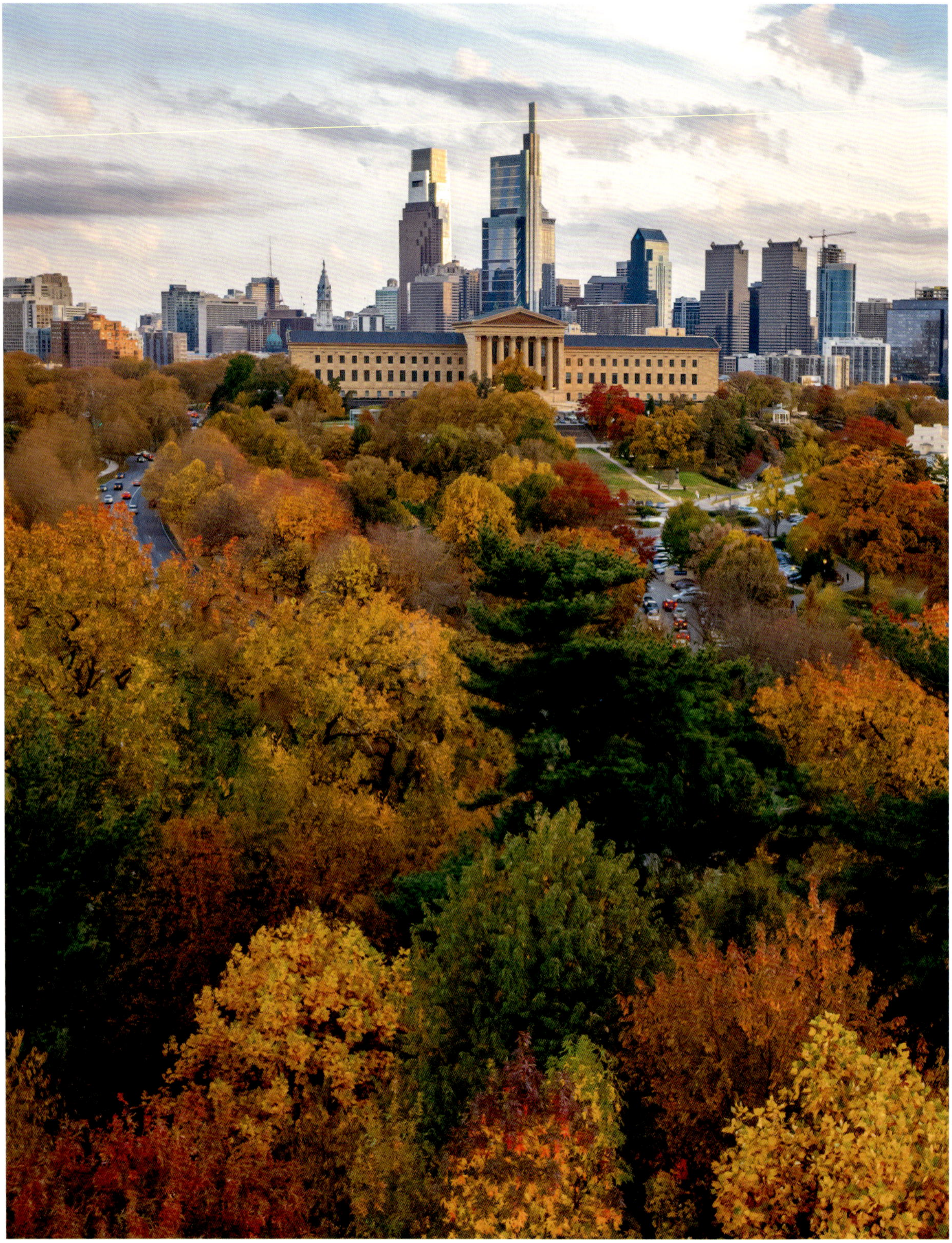

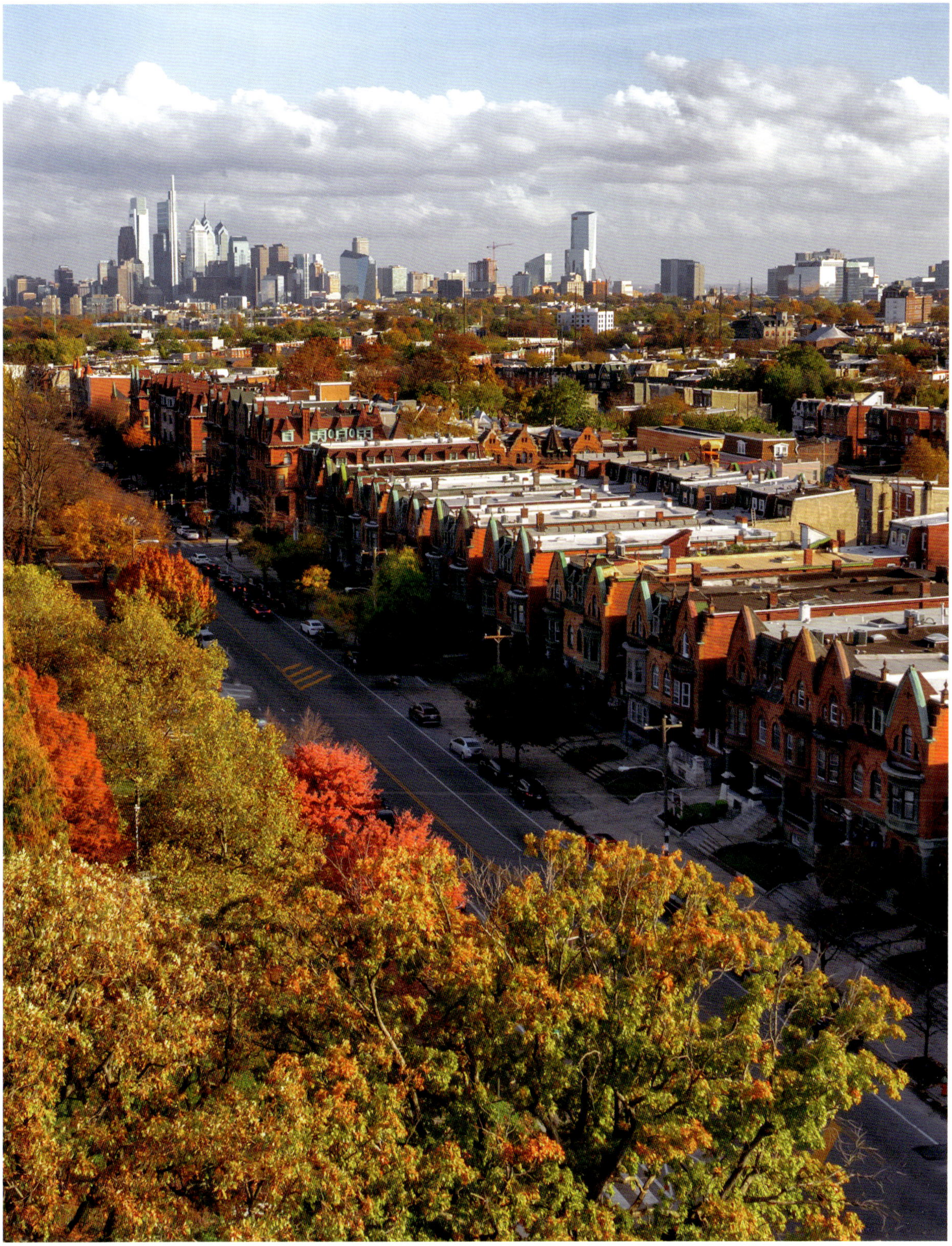

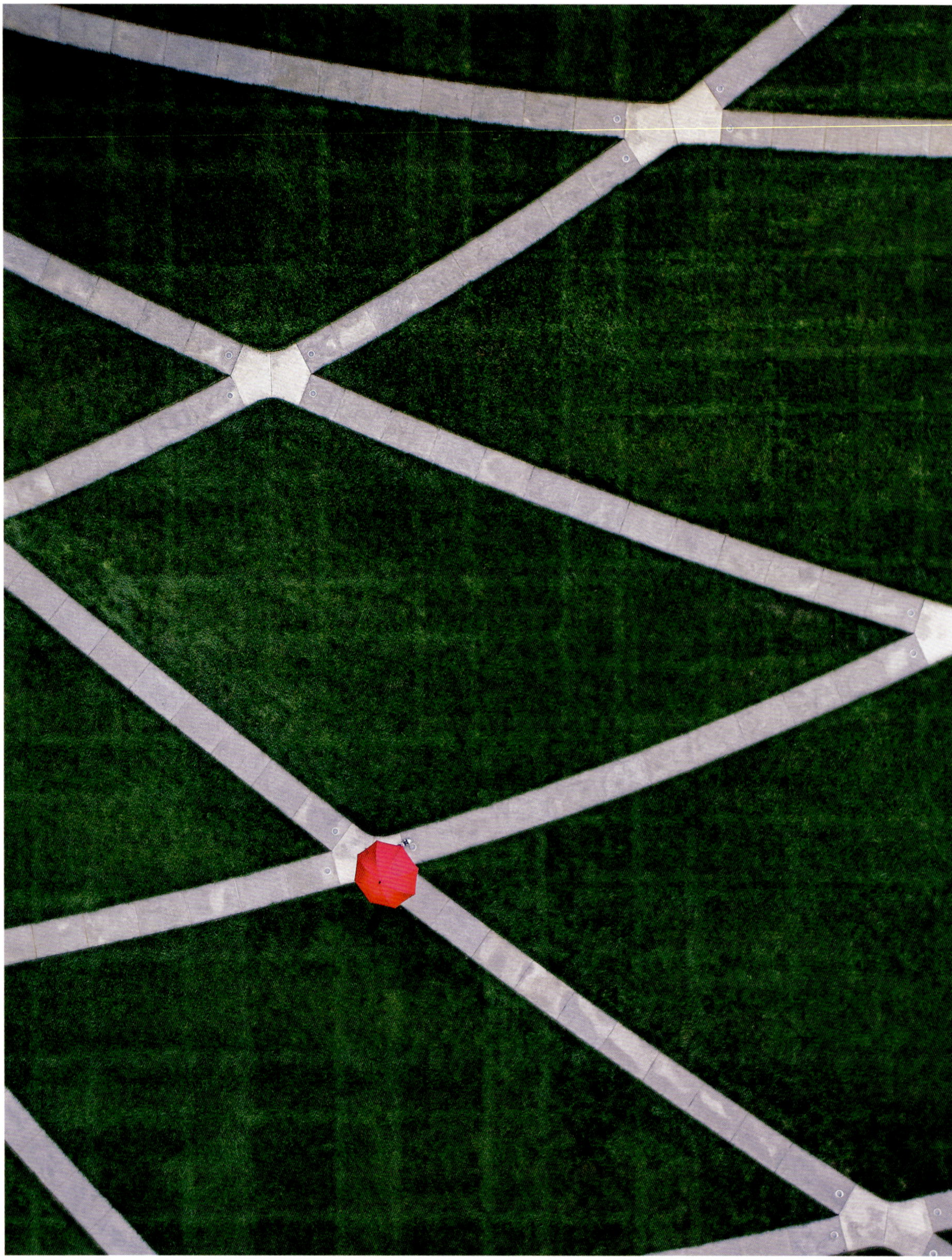

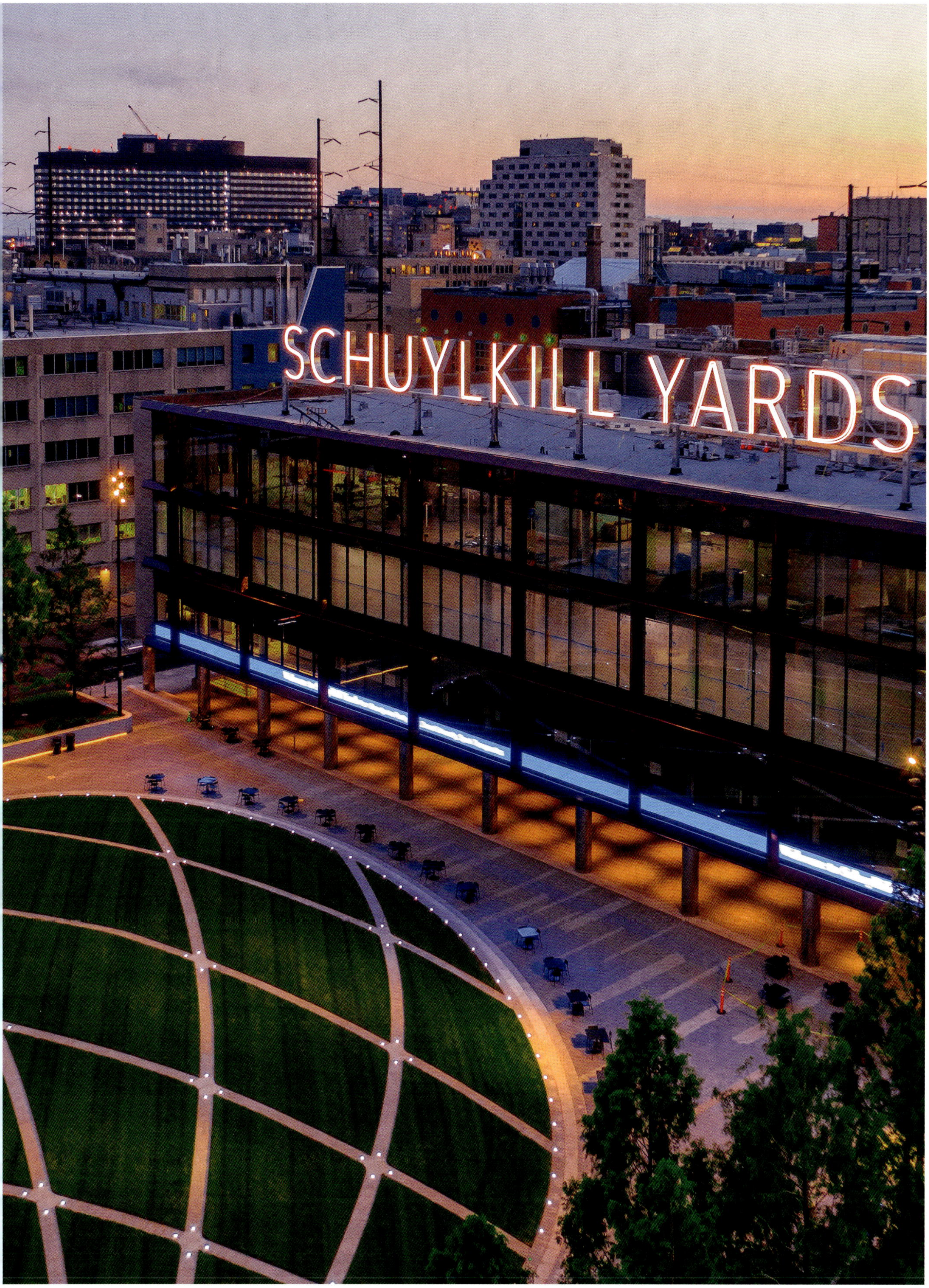
SCHUYLKILL YARDS

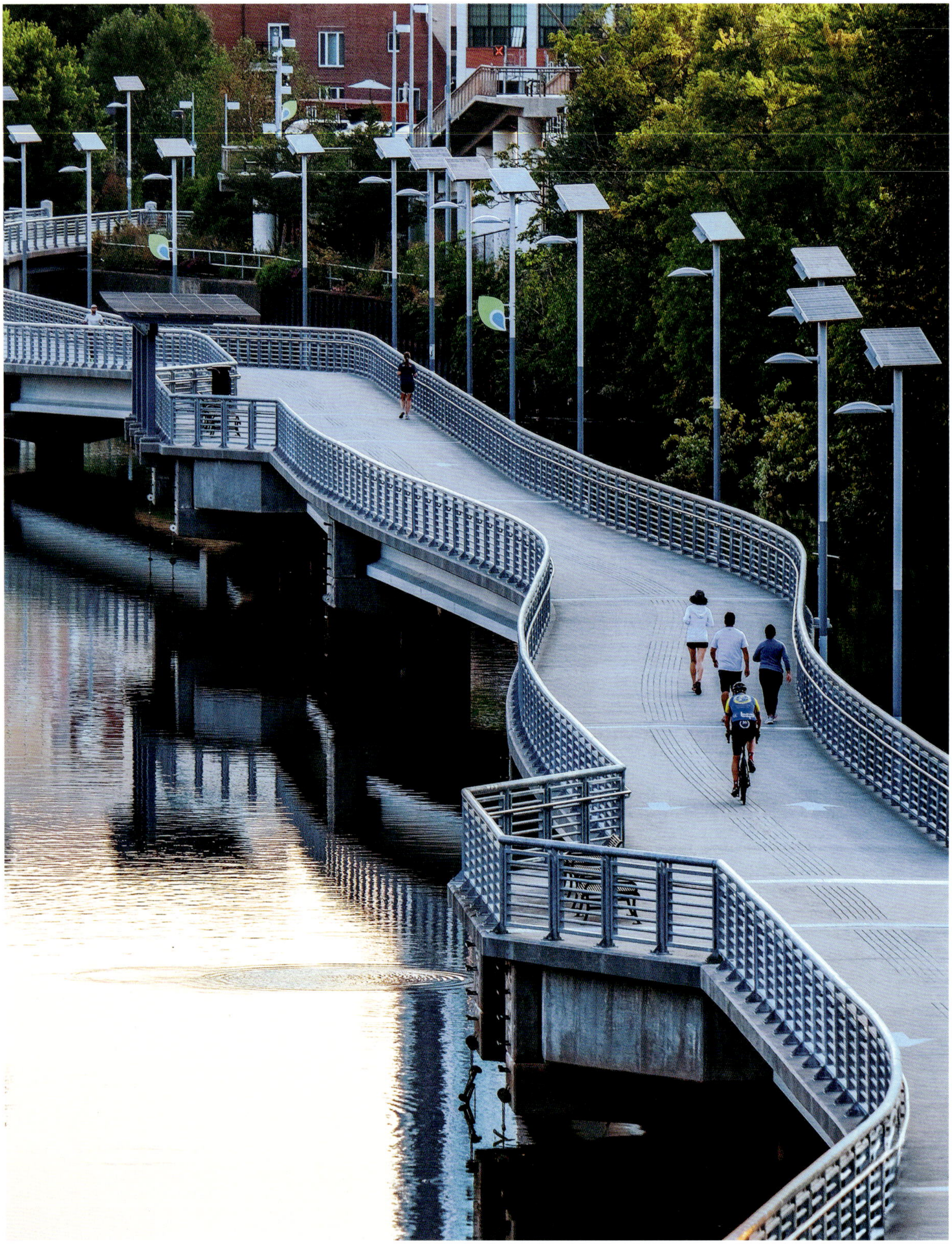

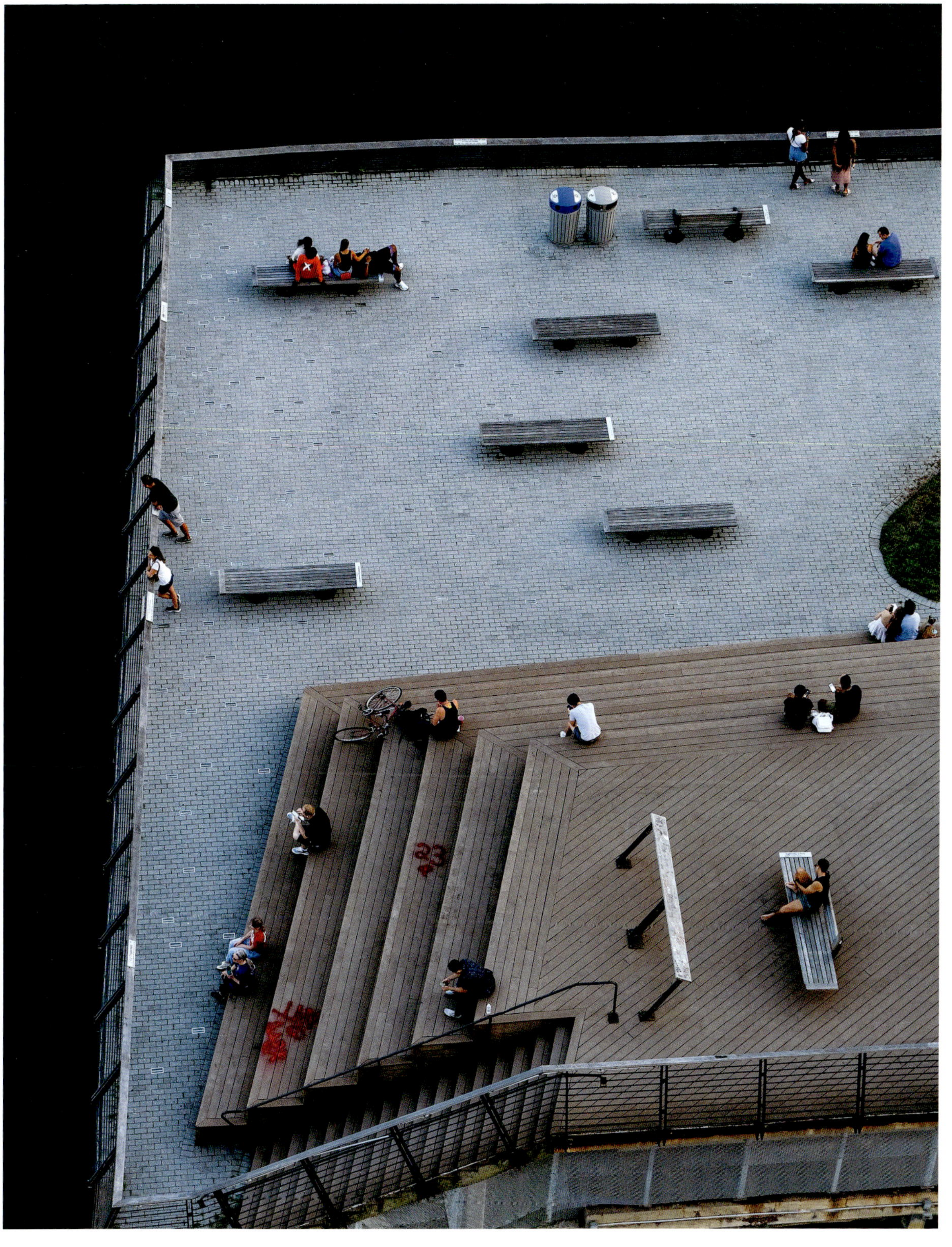

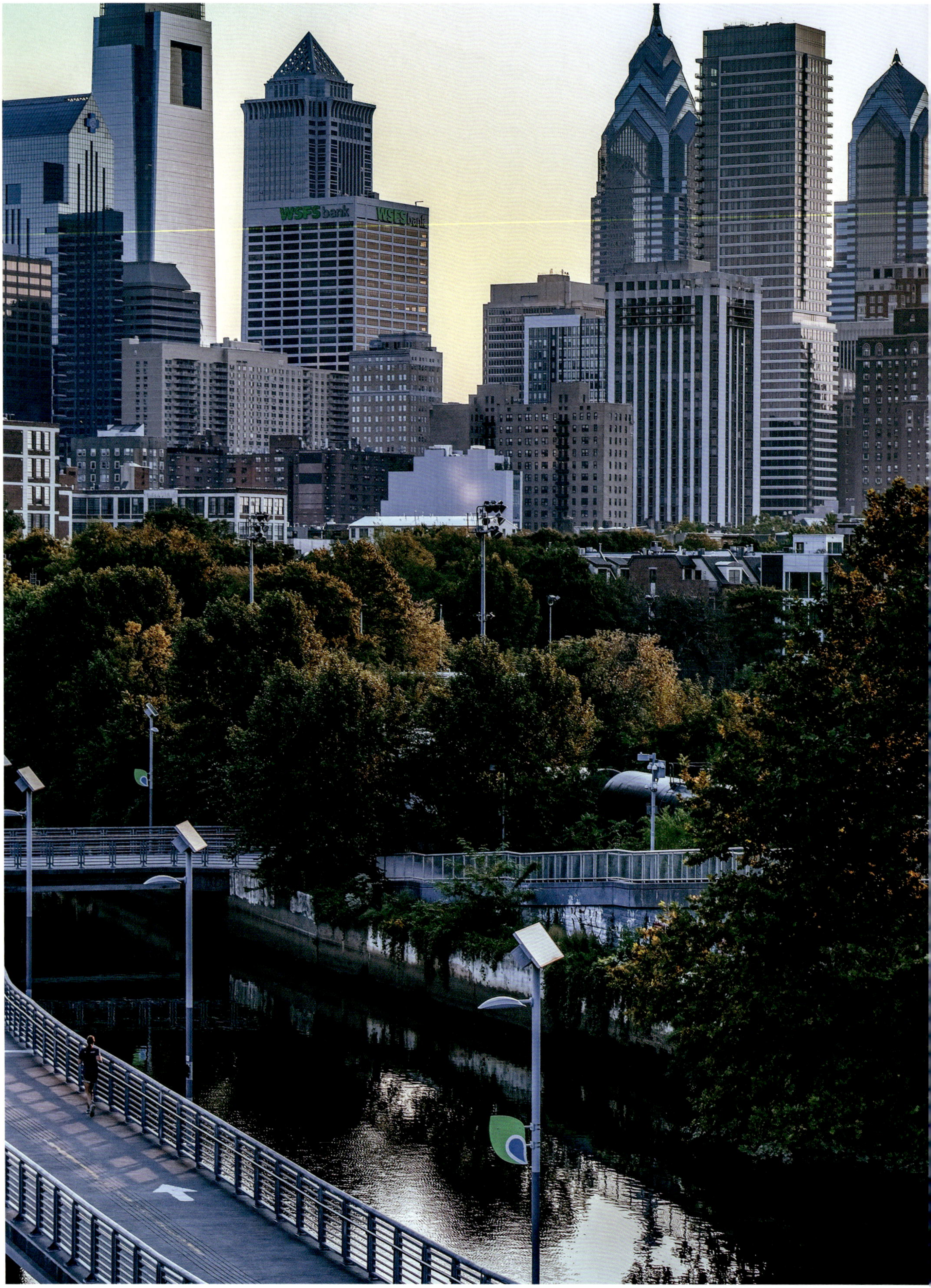
WSFS bank
WSFS bank

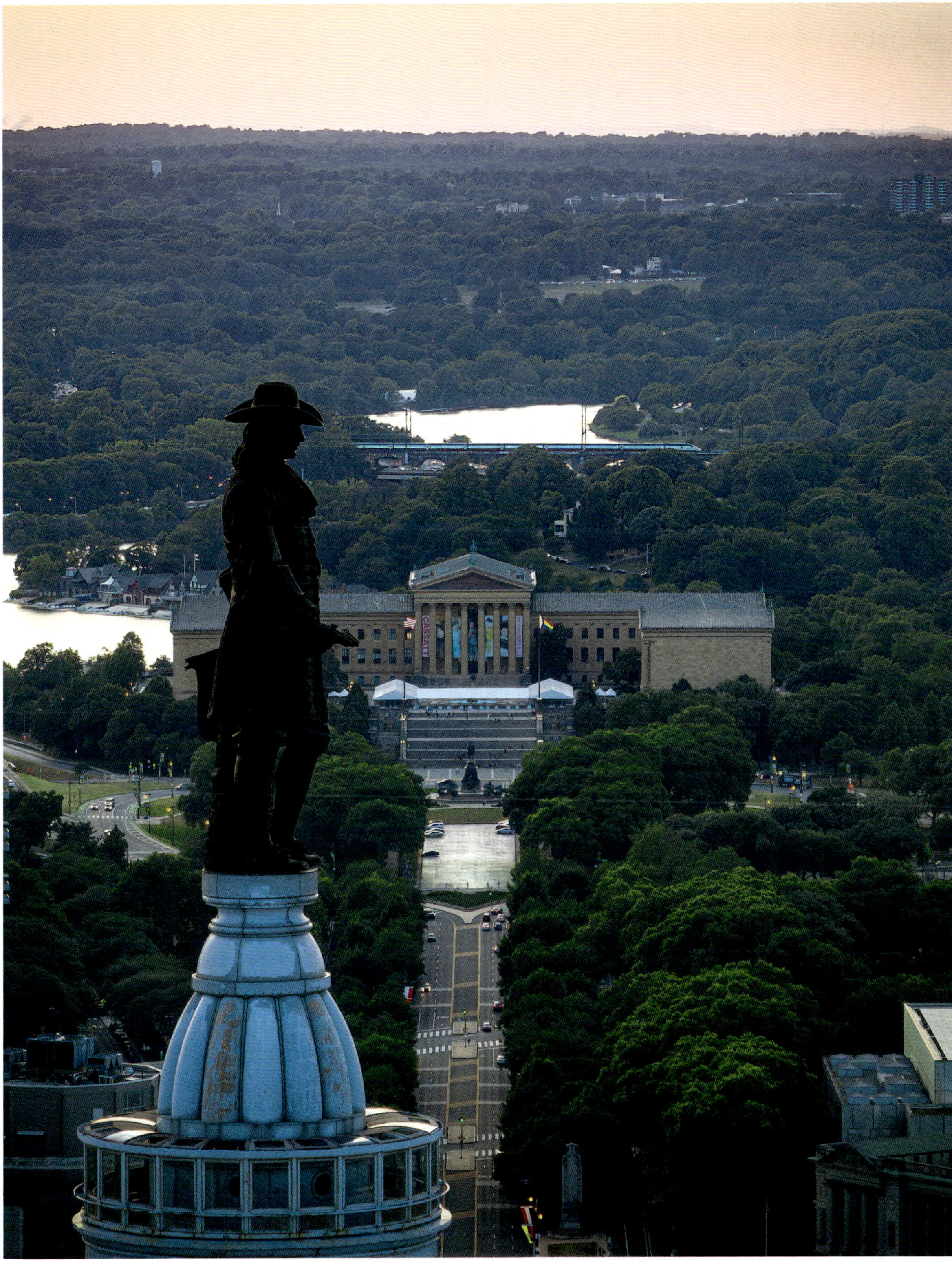

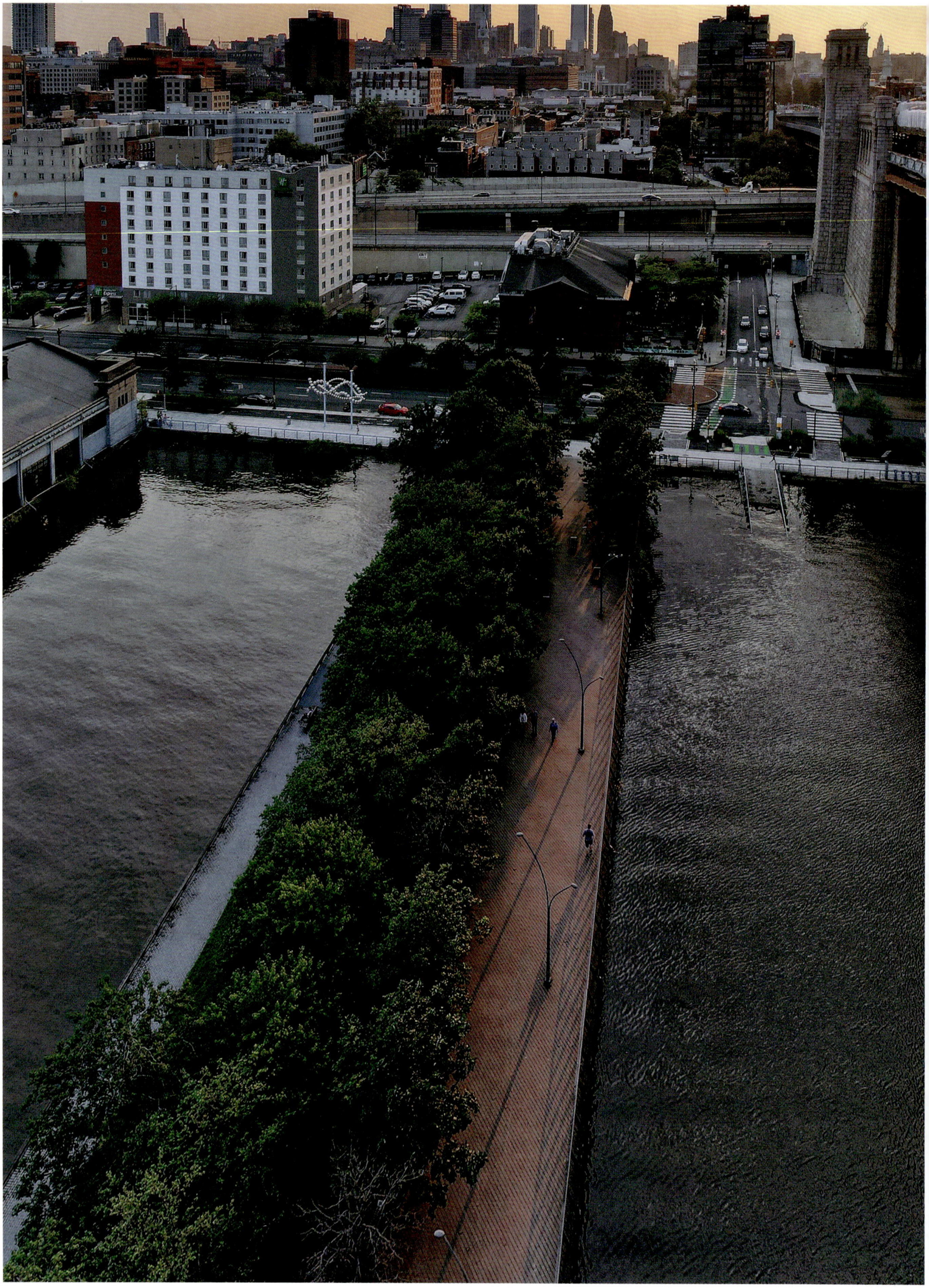

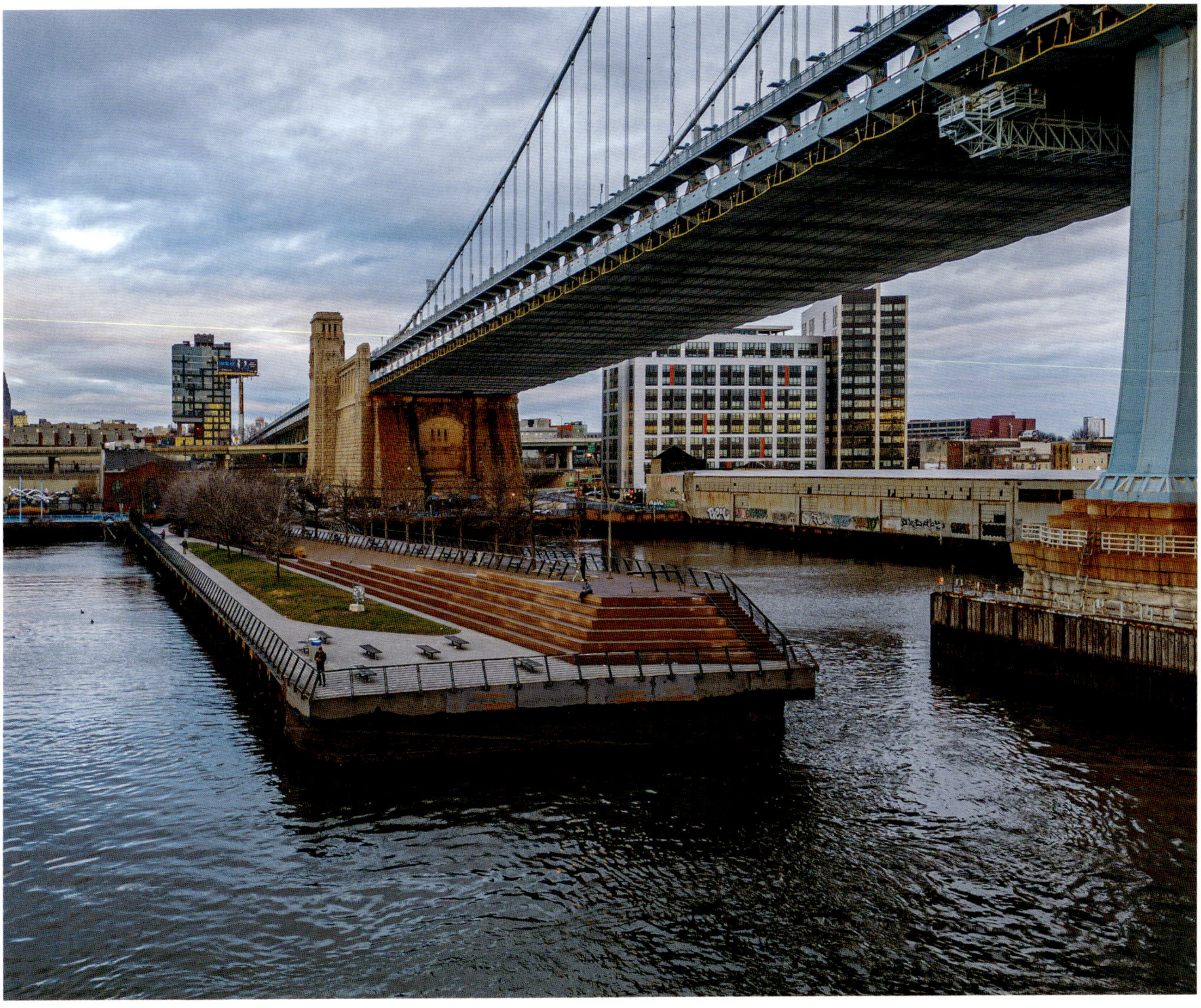

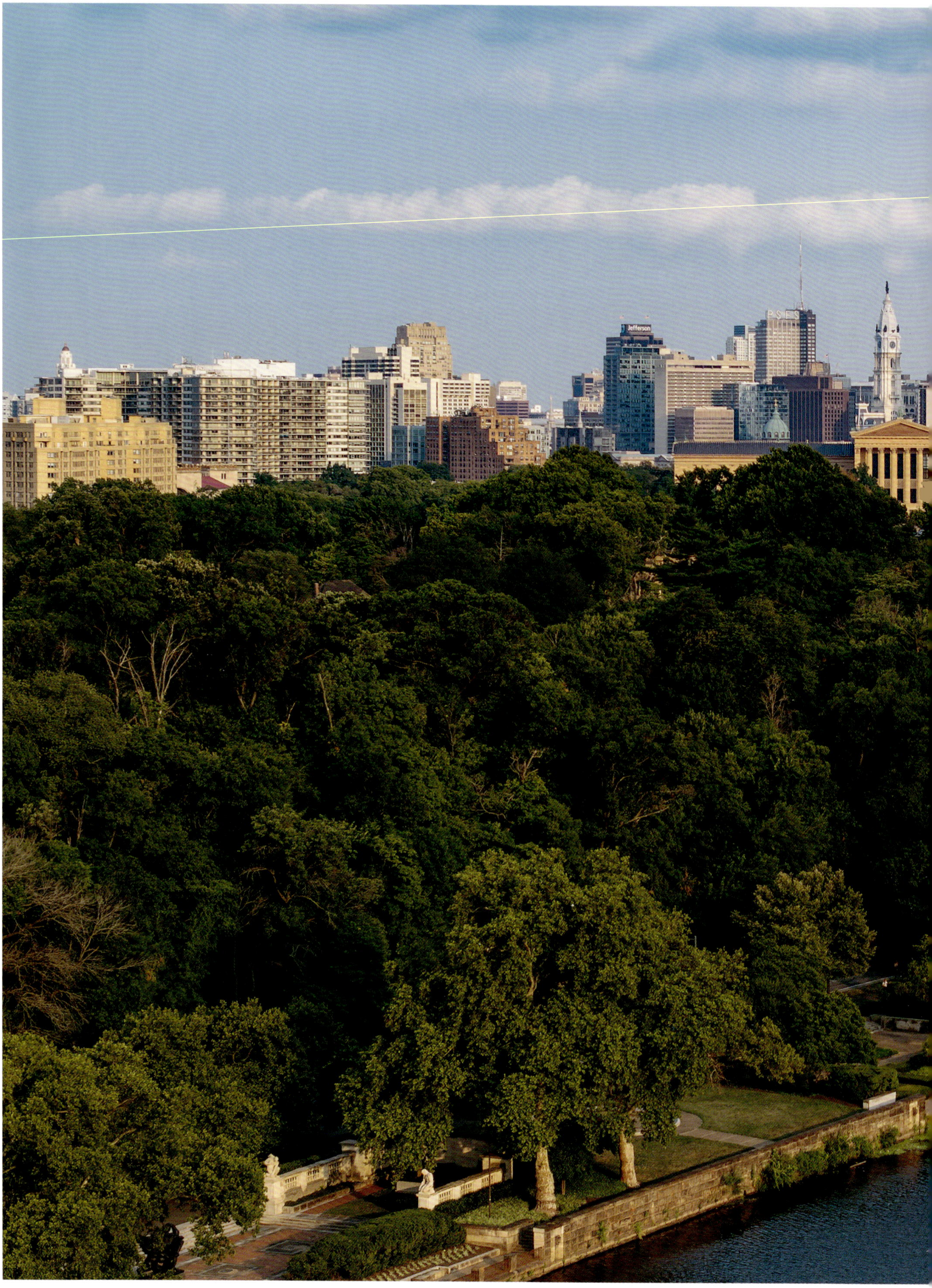

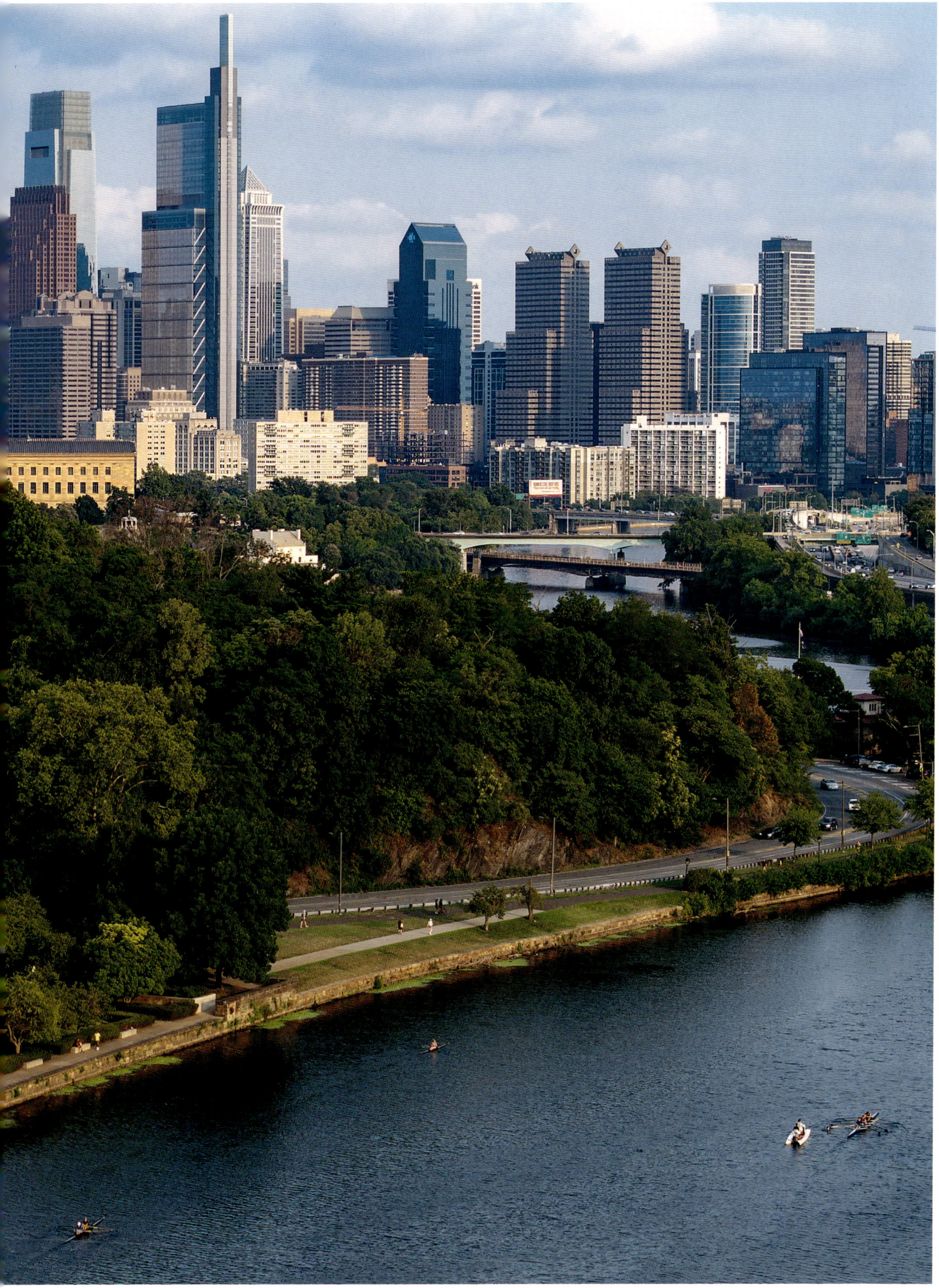

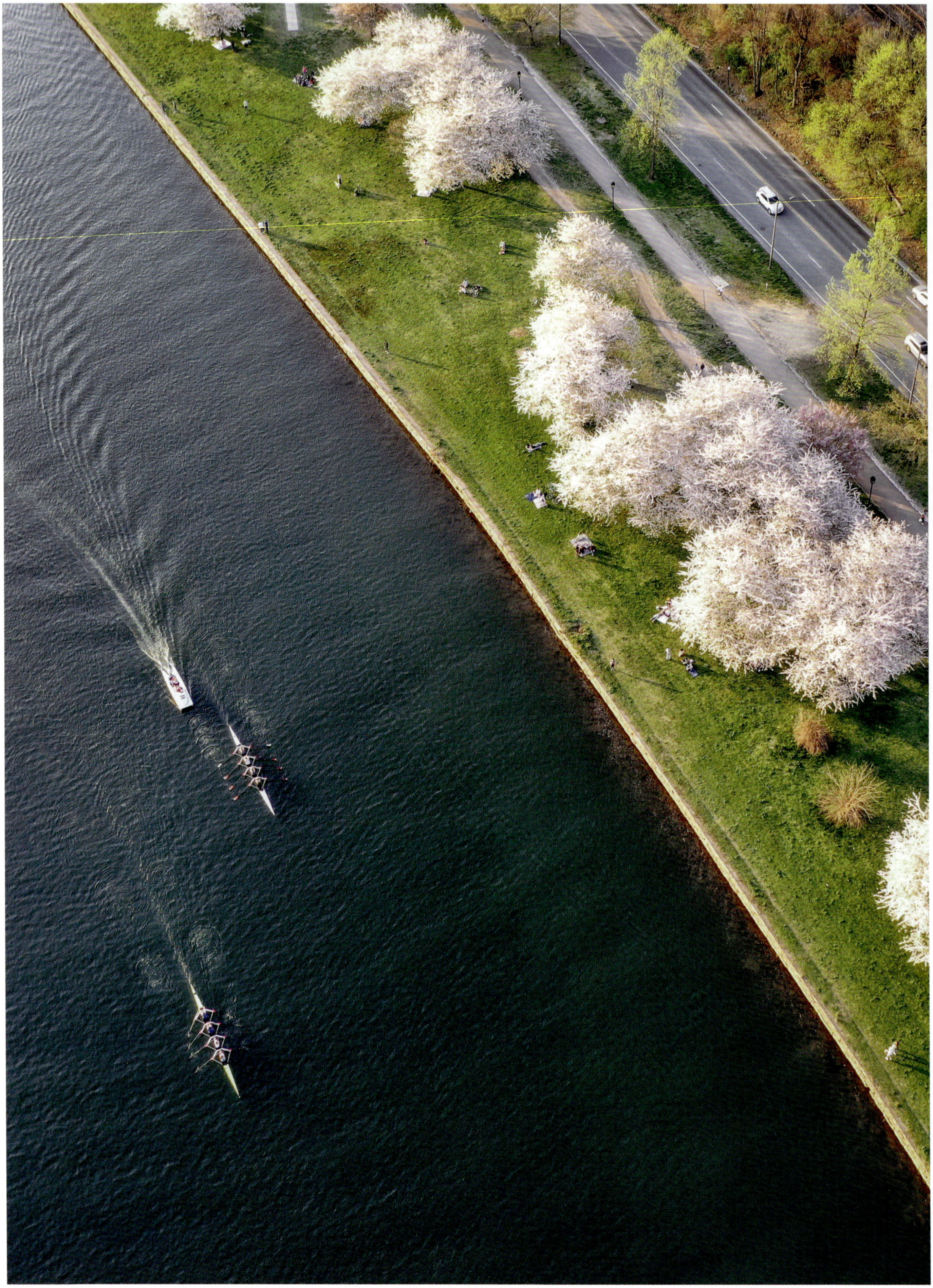

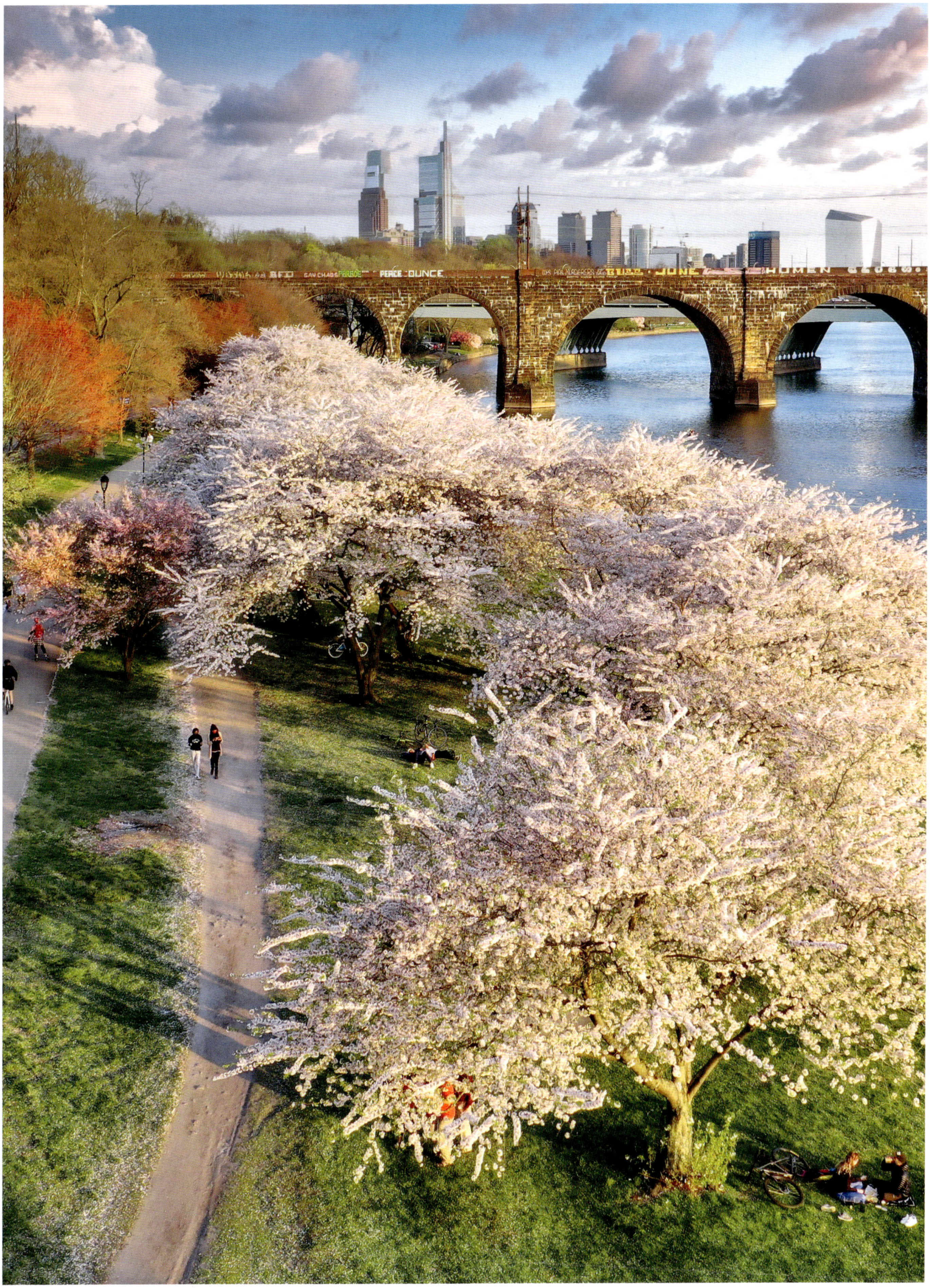

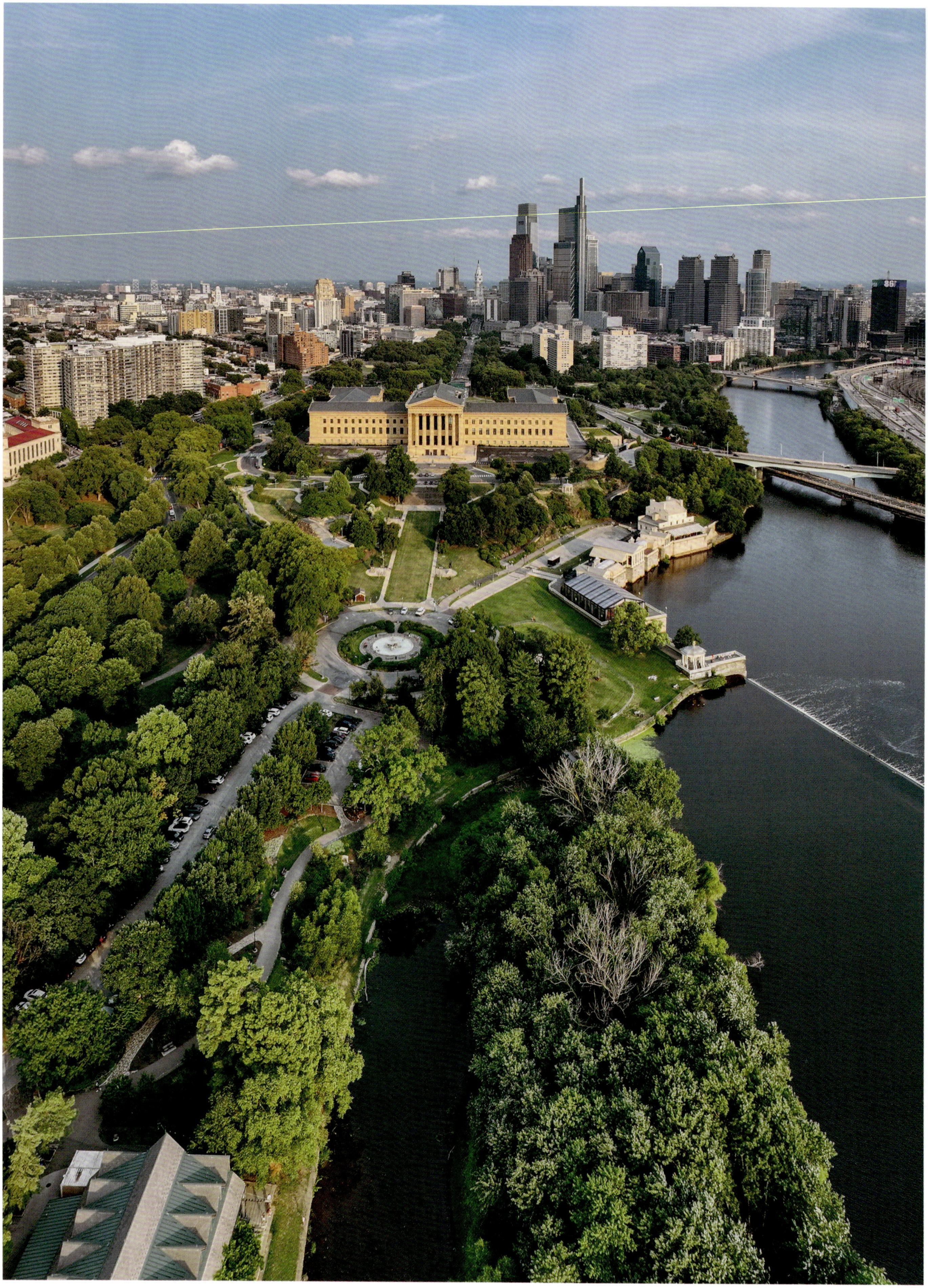

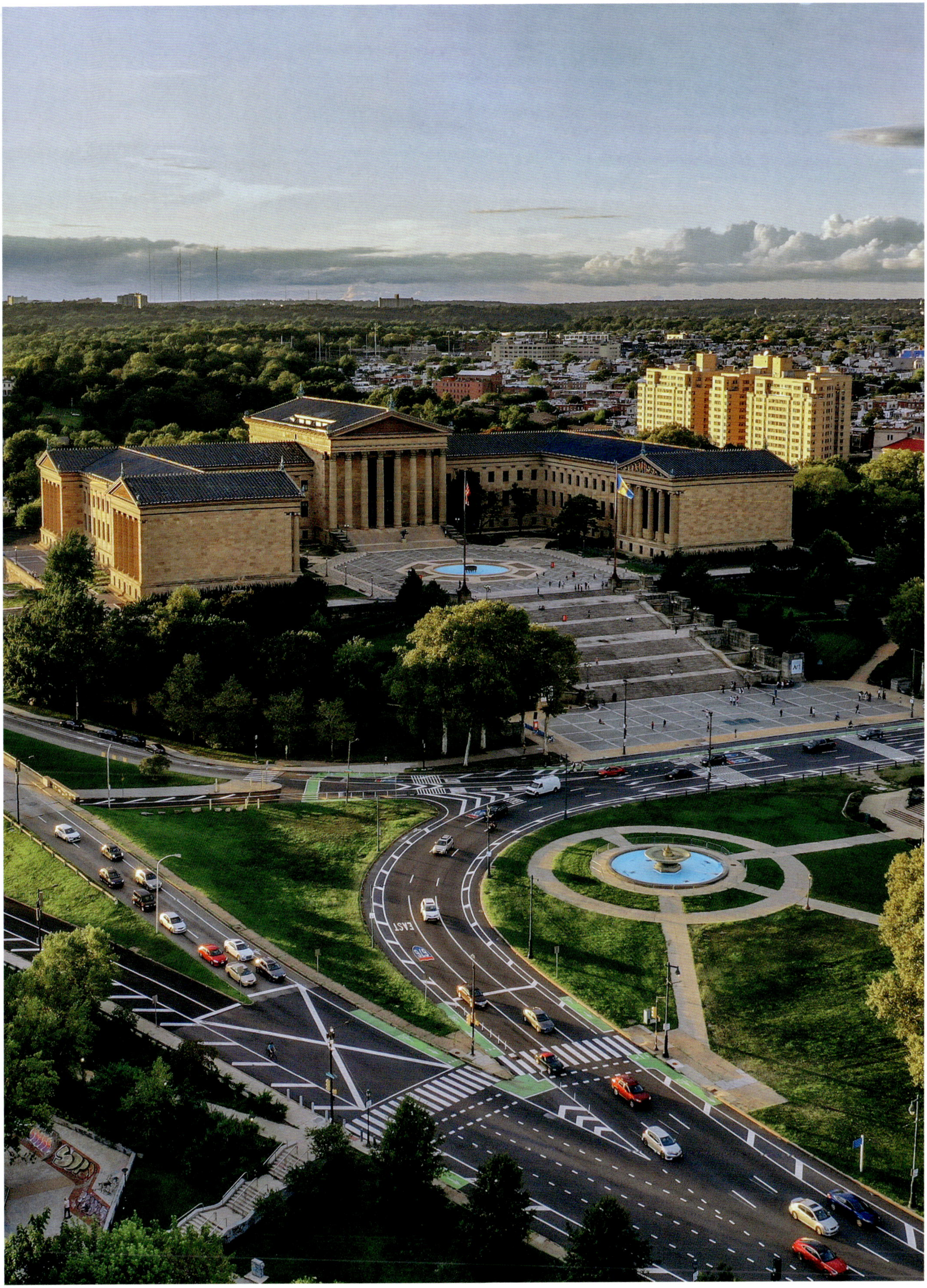

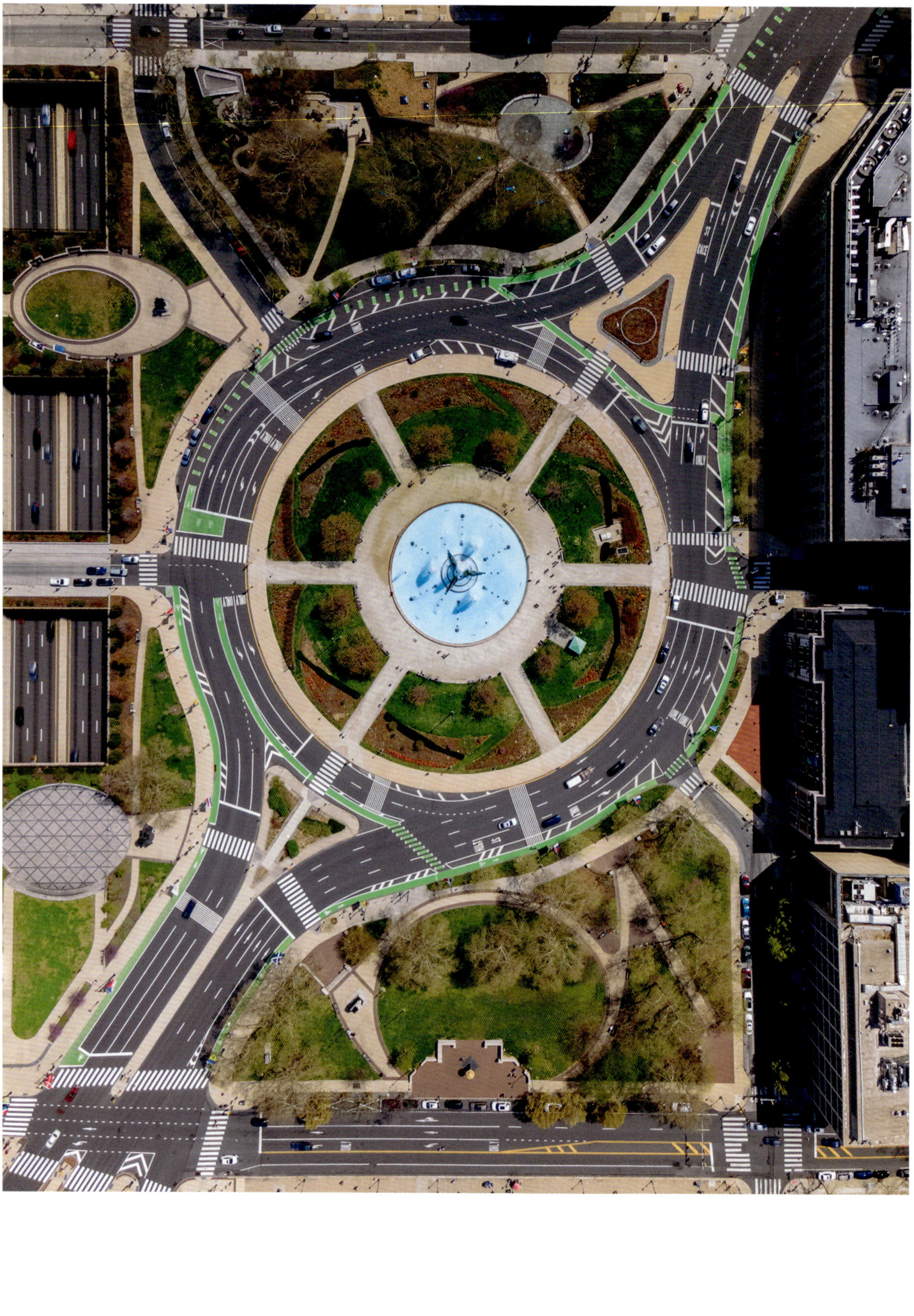

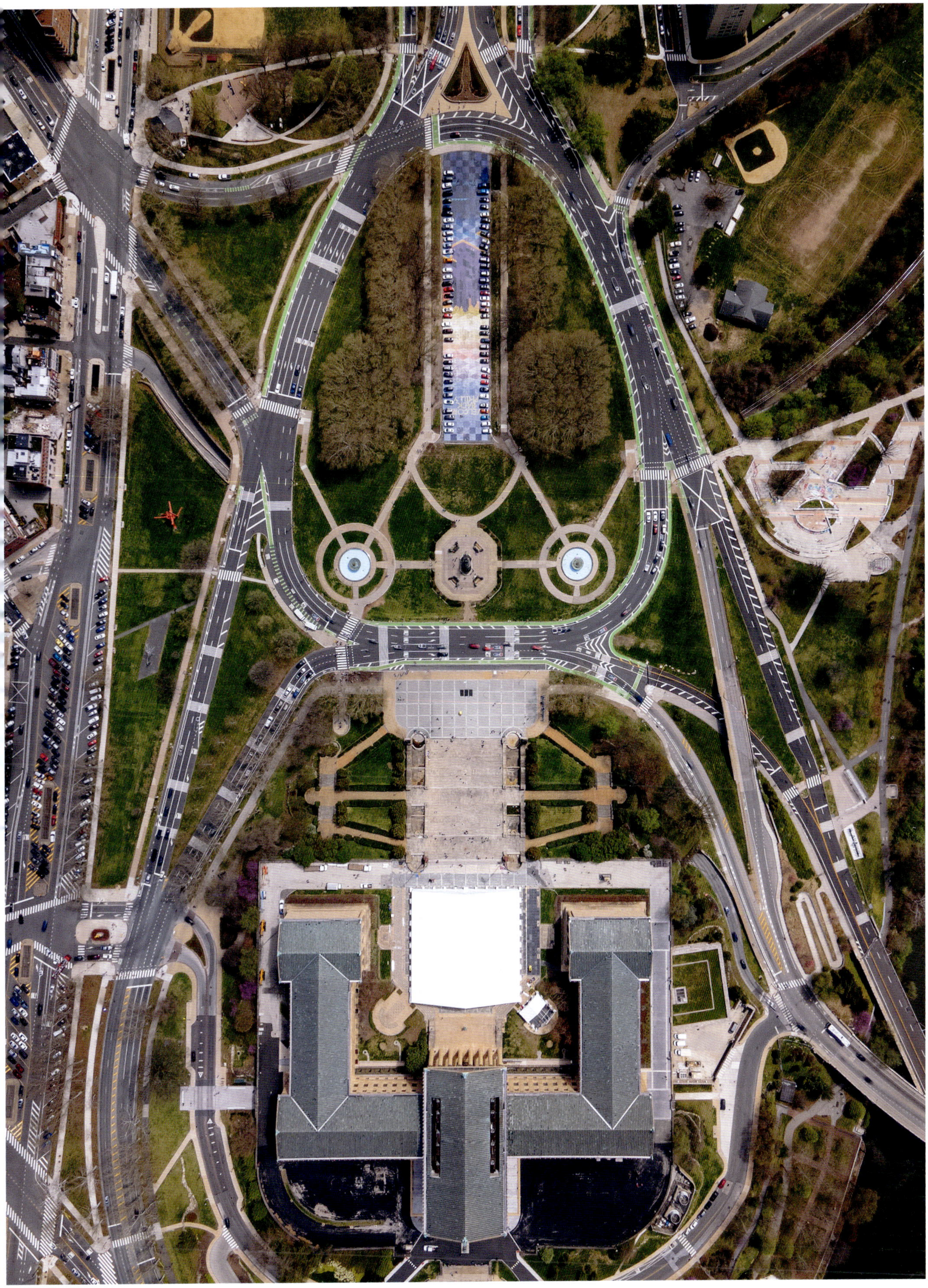

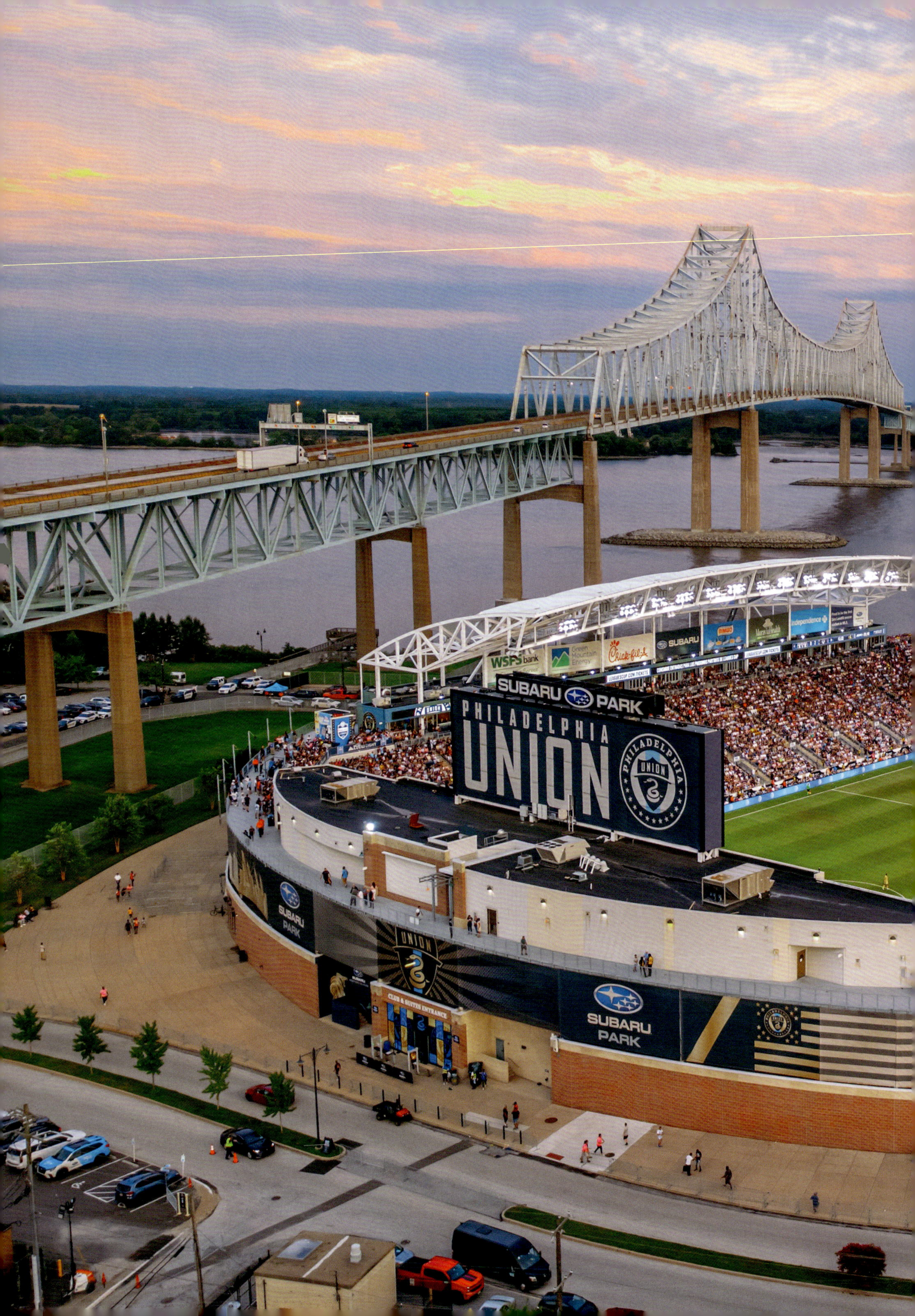
SUBARU PARK
PHILADELPHIA
UNION
SUBARU
PARK
SUBARU
PARK
CLUB & SUITES ENTRANCE

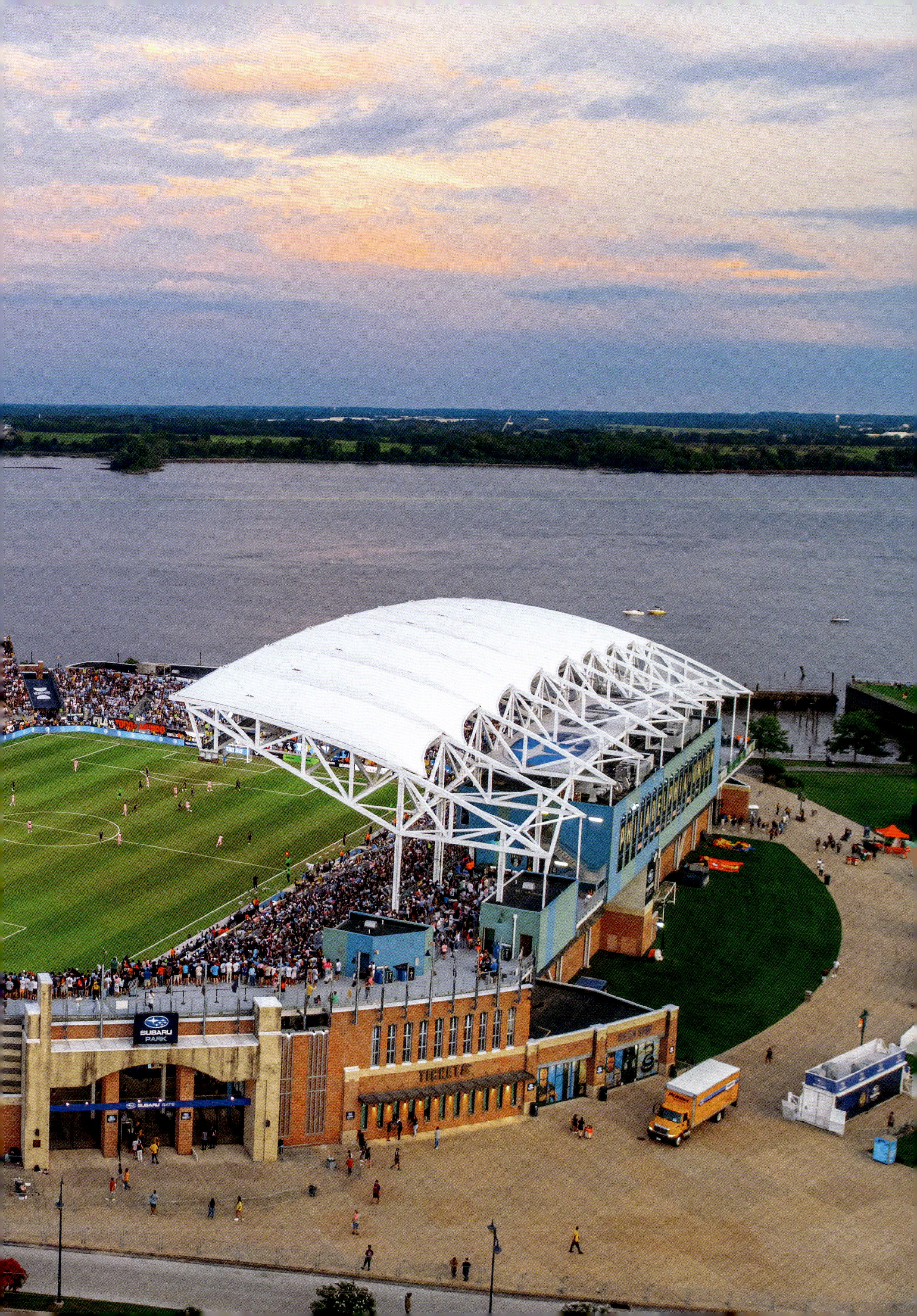
SUBARU
PARK
SUBARU GATE
TICKETS

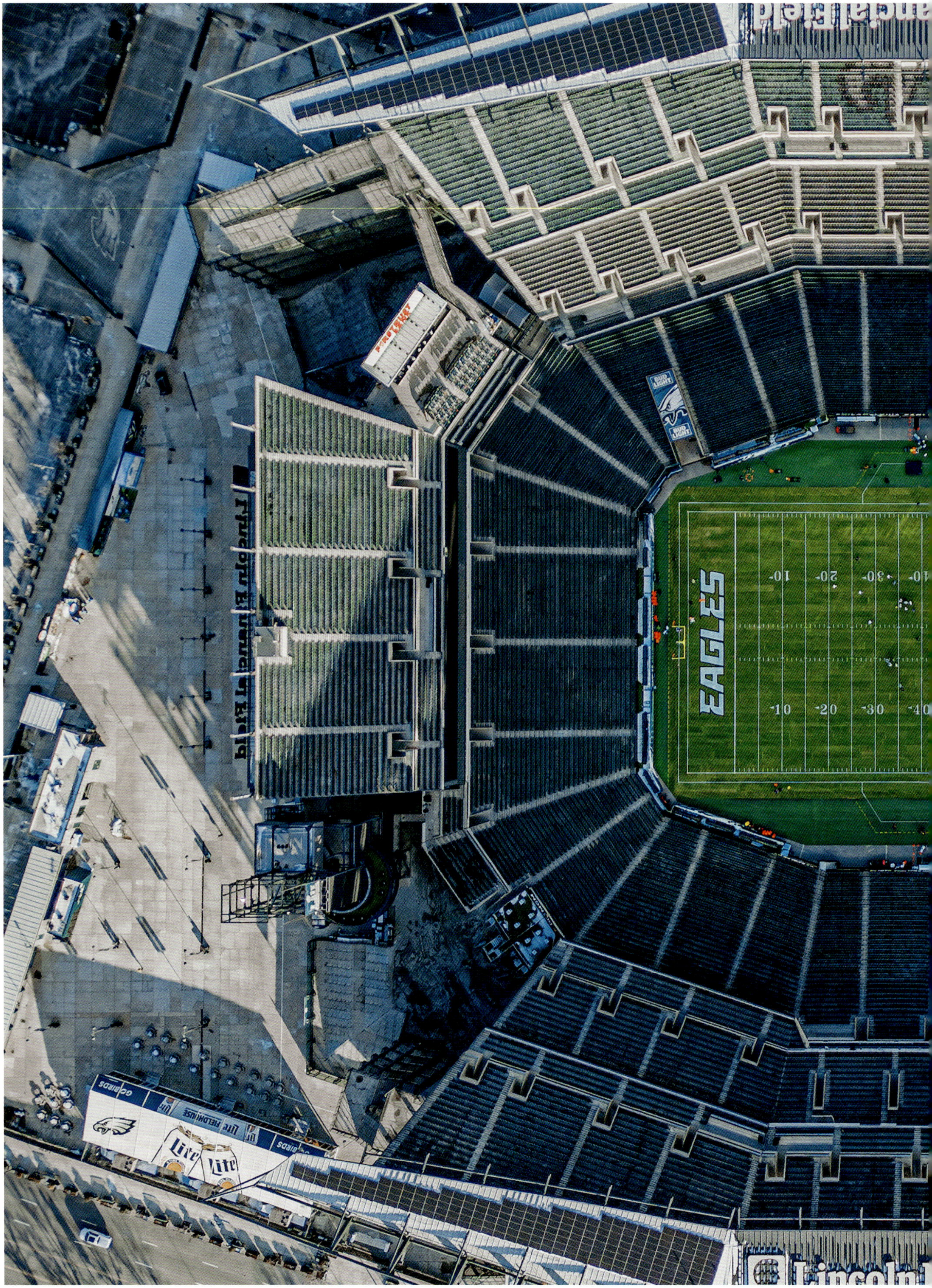
Lincoln Financial Field
EAGLES

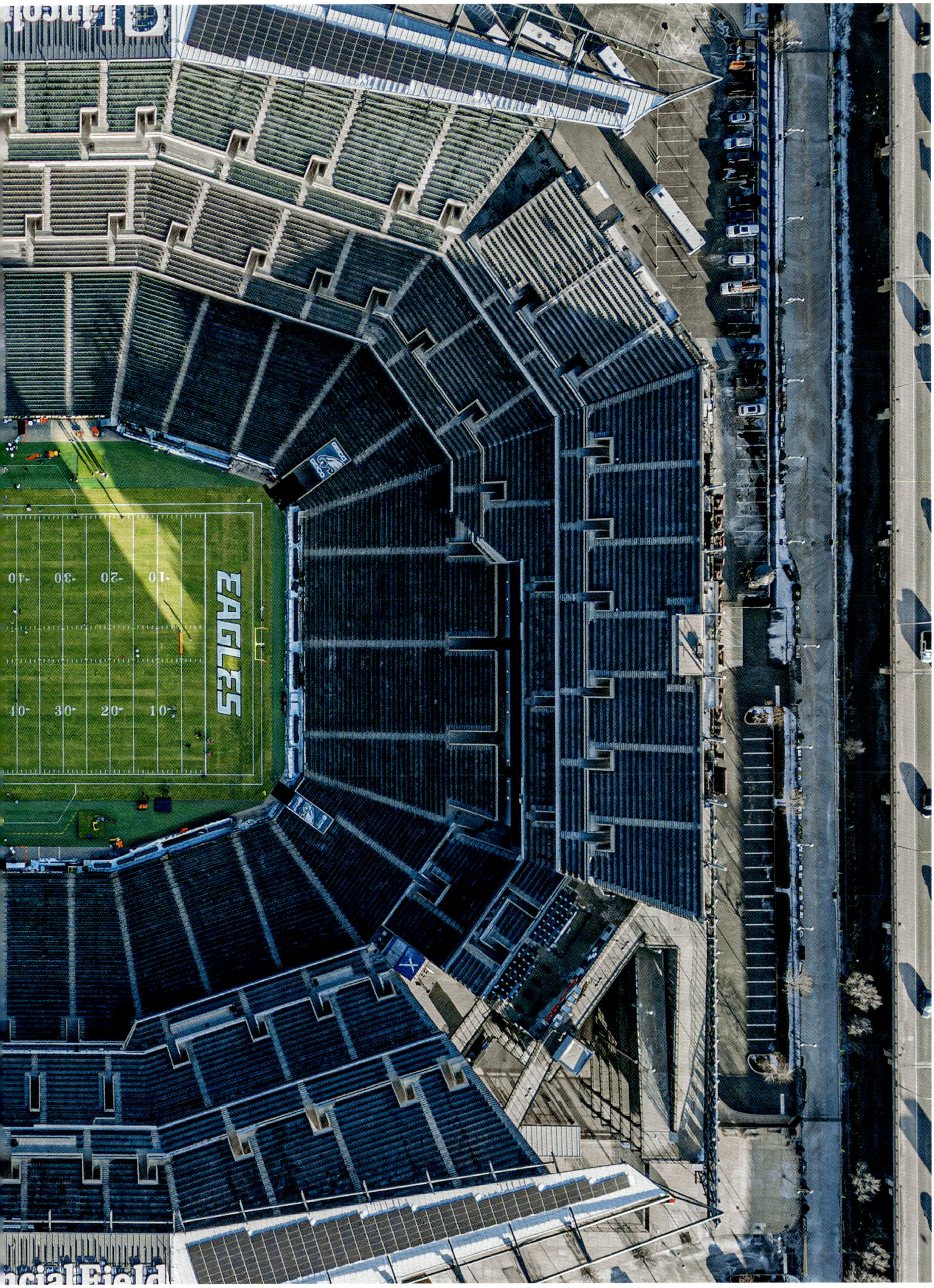
EAGLES

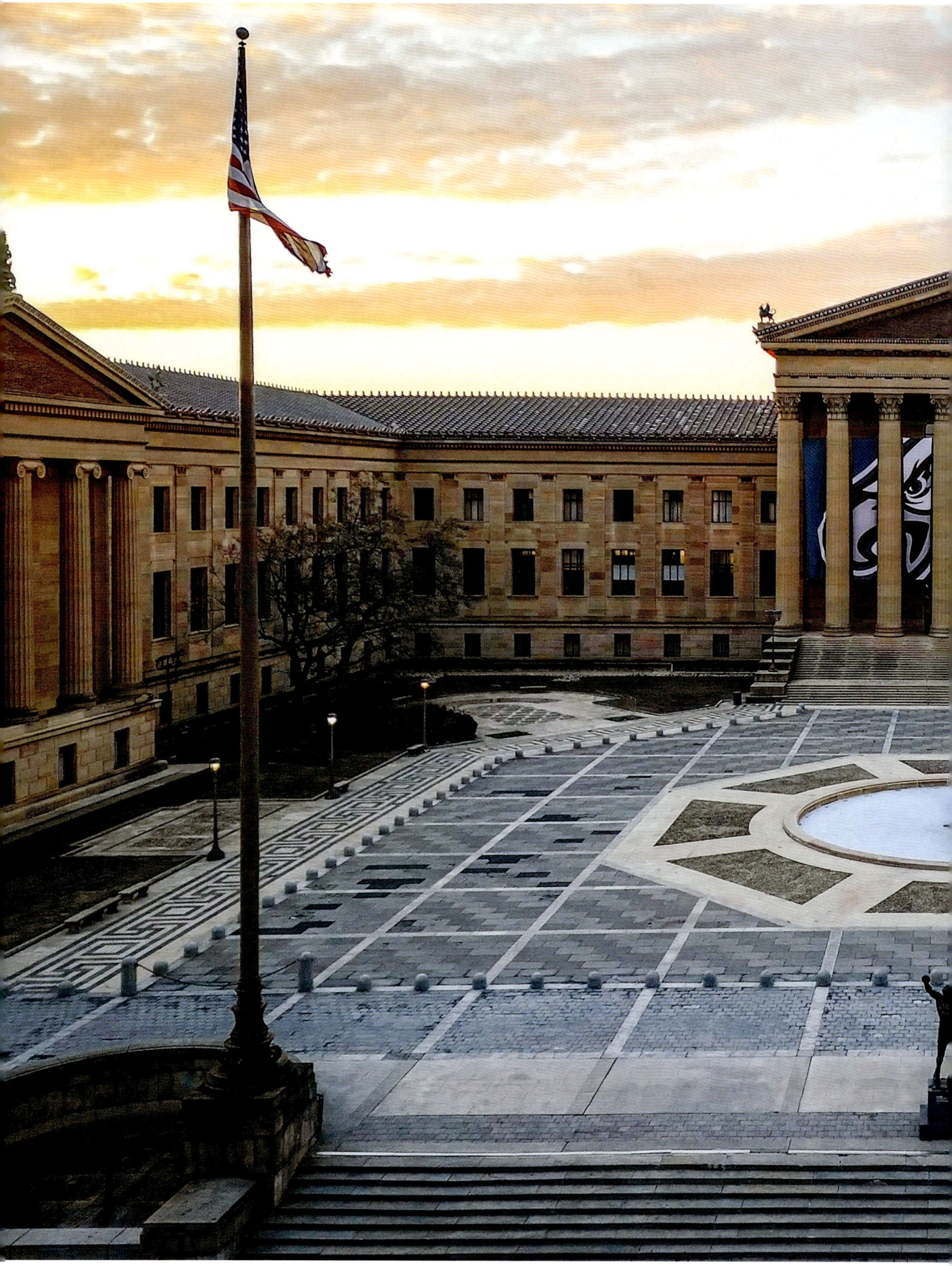

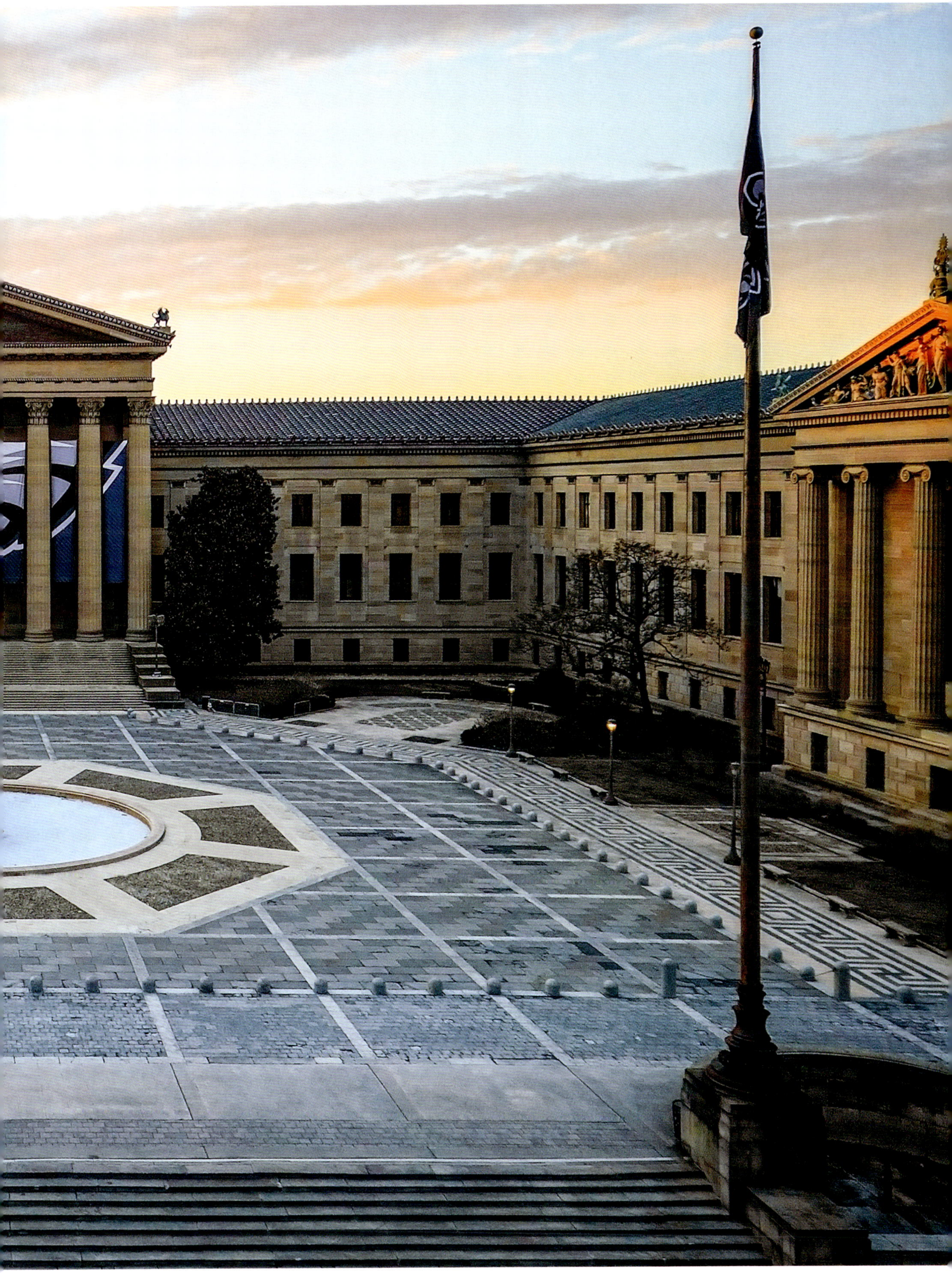

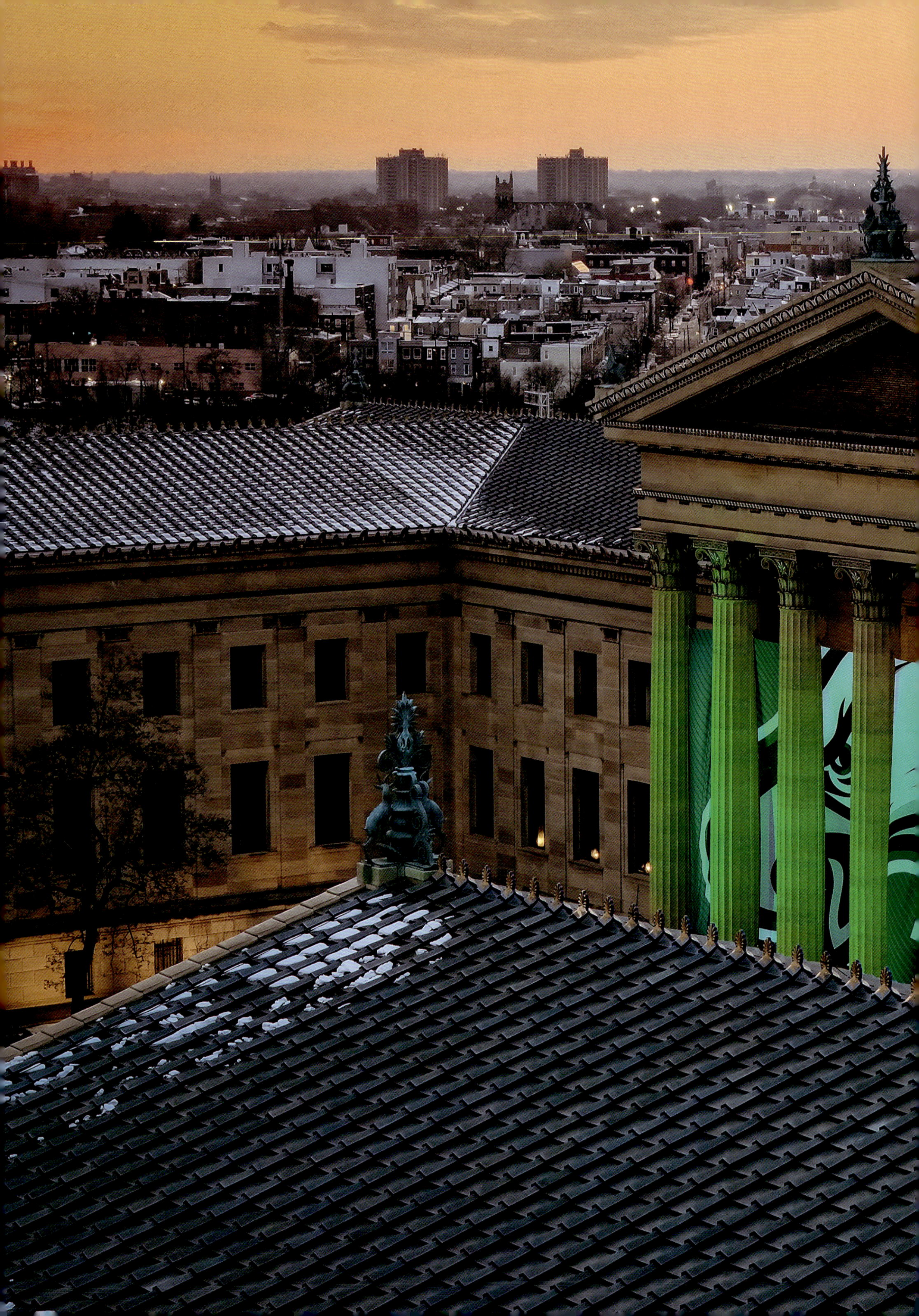

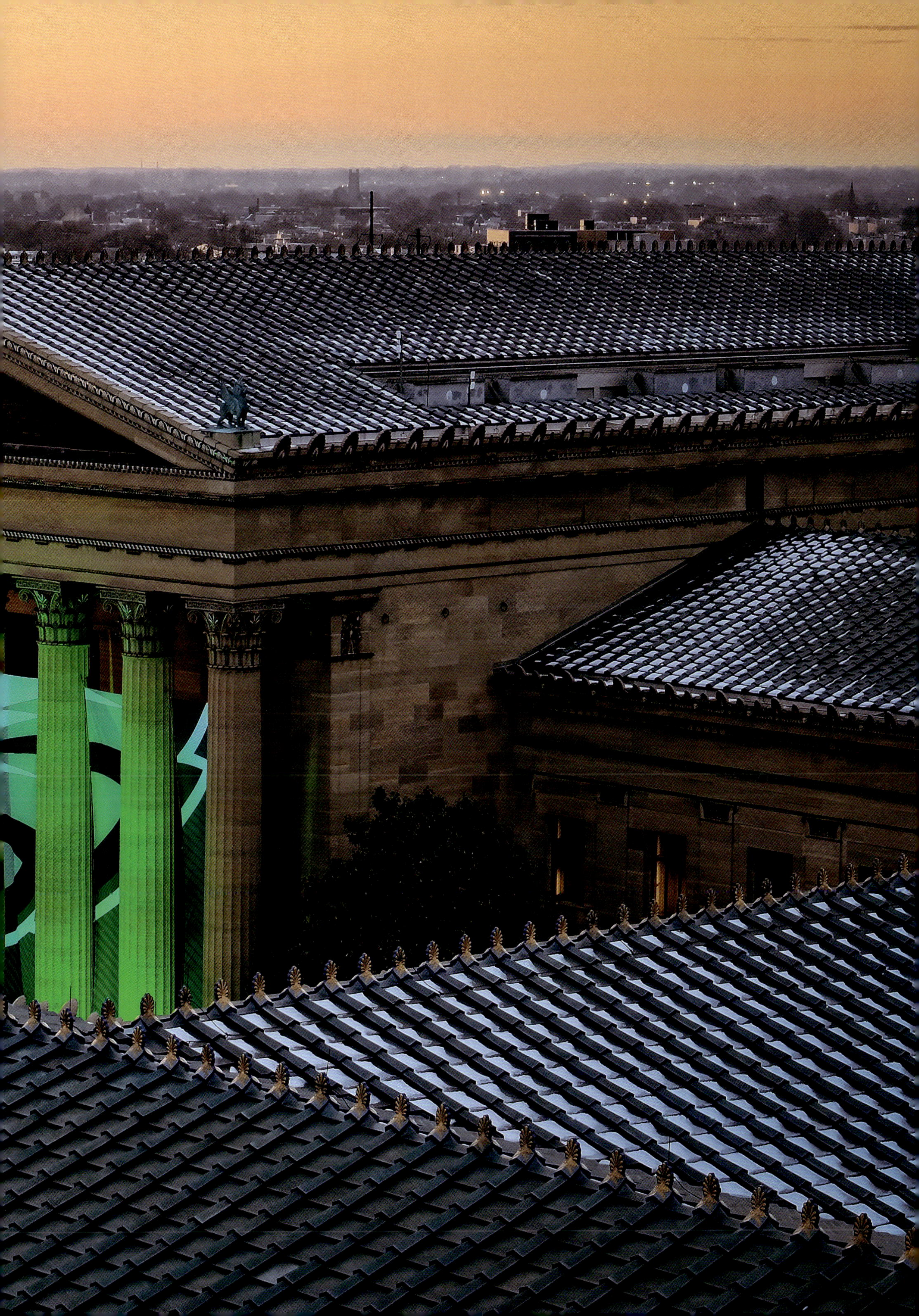

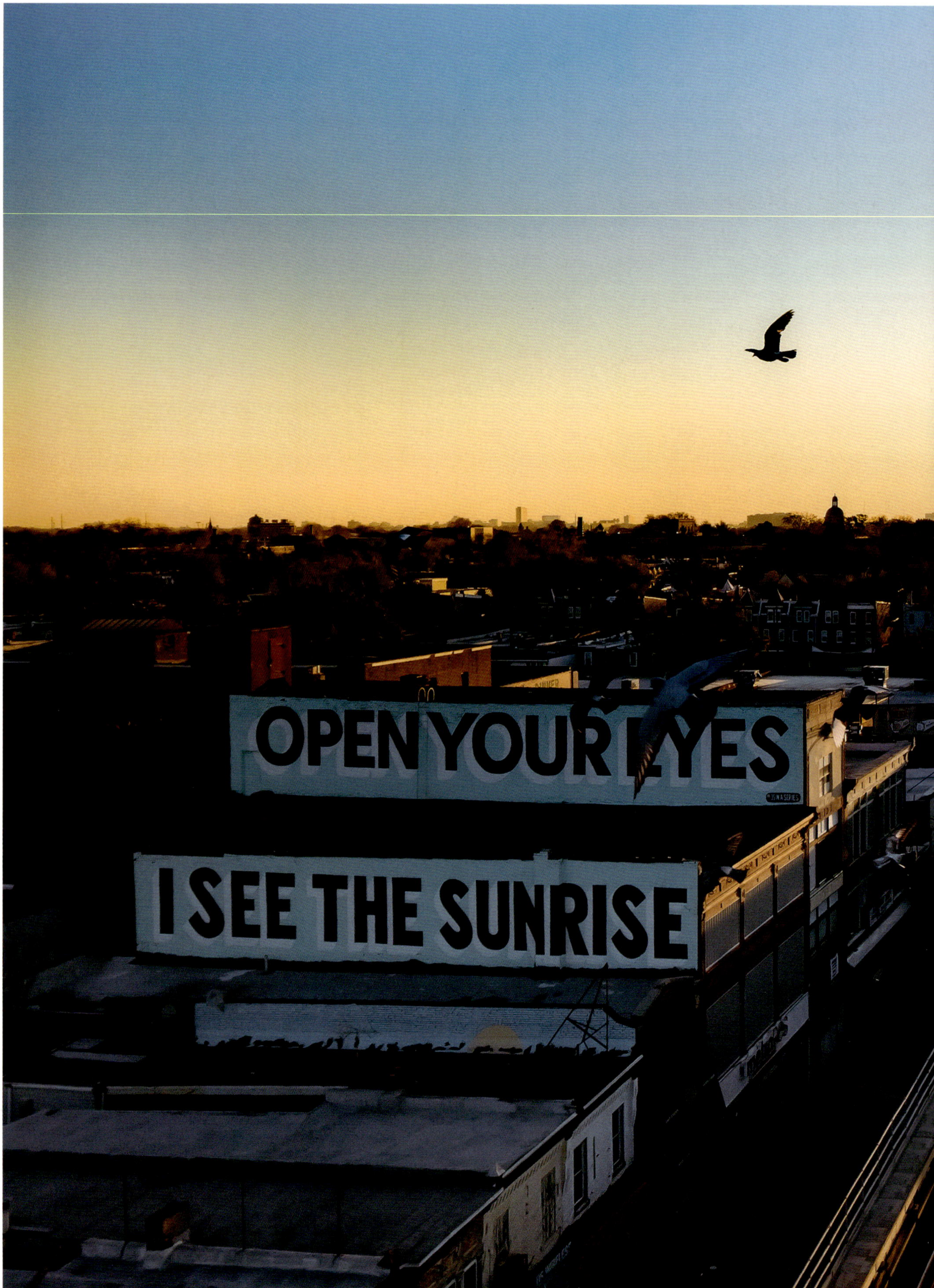
OPEN YOUR EYES
I SEE THE SUNRISE

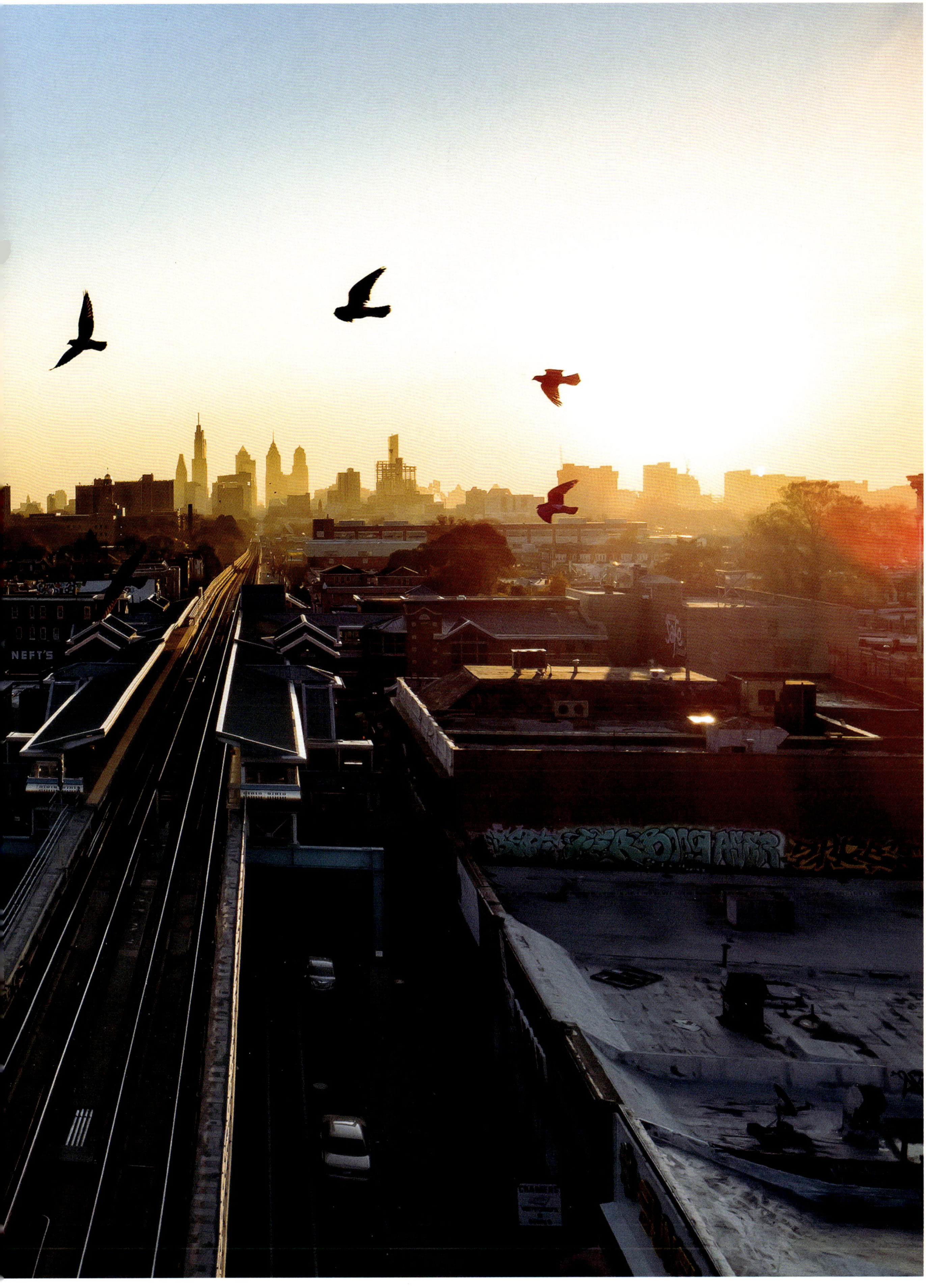
NEFT'S

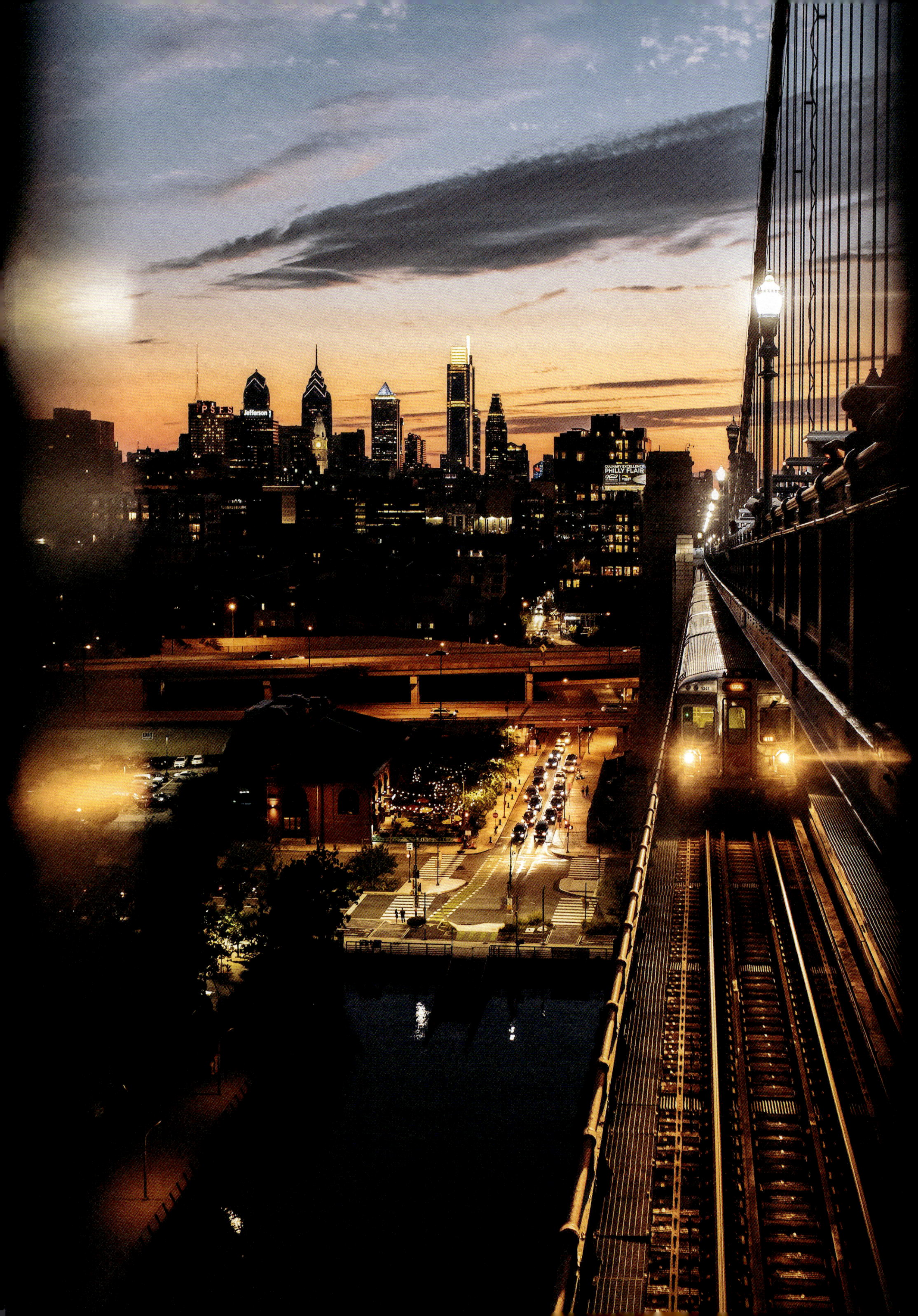
PSFS
Jefferson
CULINARY EXCELLENCE
PHILLY FLAIR

ABOVE & ACROSS

PHILADELPHIA

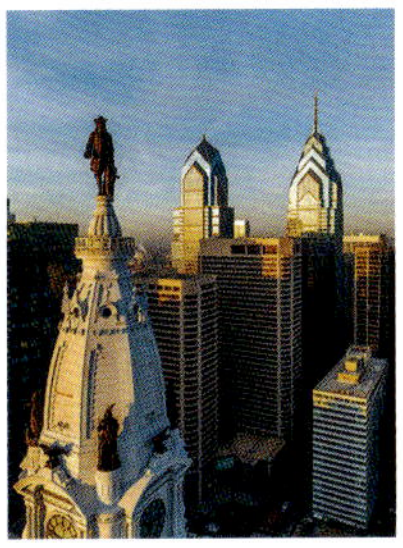

Front Cover Daniel Moreno
View of William Penn and Center City

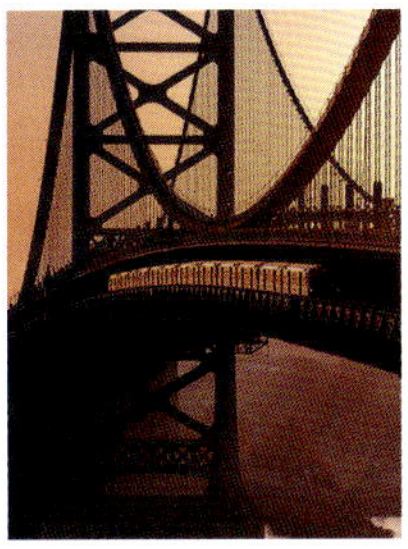

2 Trevor W. Adams
View of the Benjamin Franklin Bridge

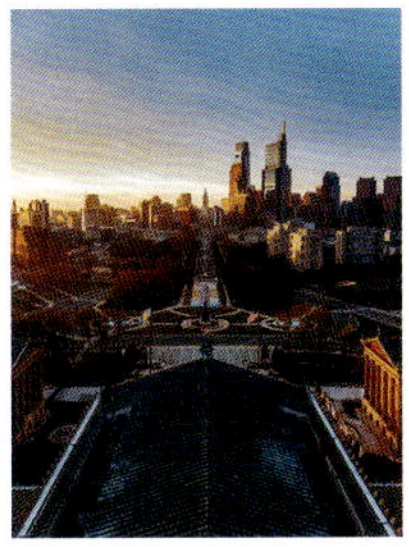

4 Greg Adams
View of Benjamin Franklin Parkway

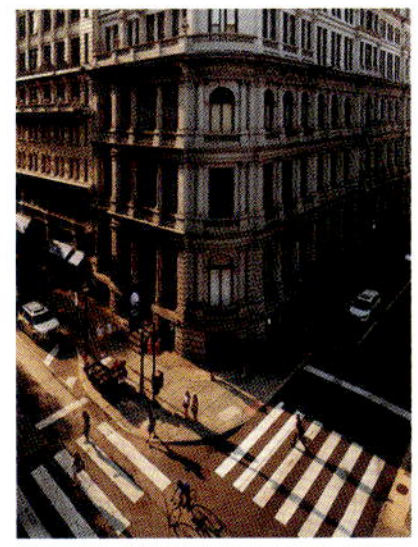

7 Trevor W. Adams
View of the Victory Building

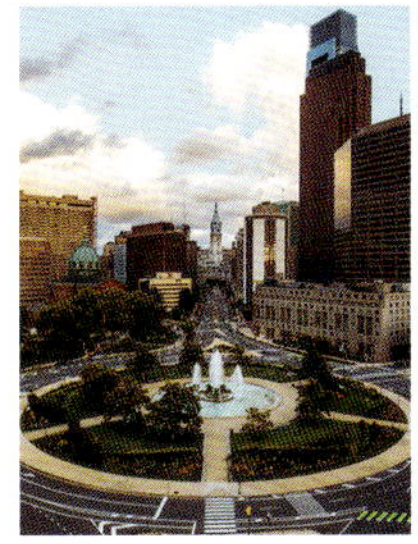

8 Greg Adams
View of Swann Memorial Fountain and Philadelphia City Hall

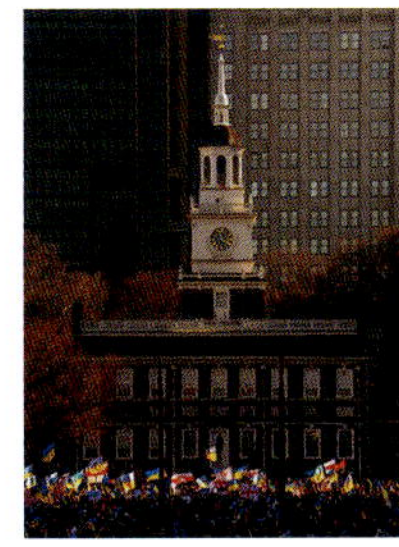

10 Trevor W. Adams
View of Independence Hall

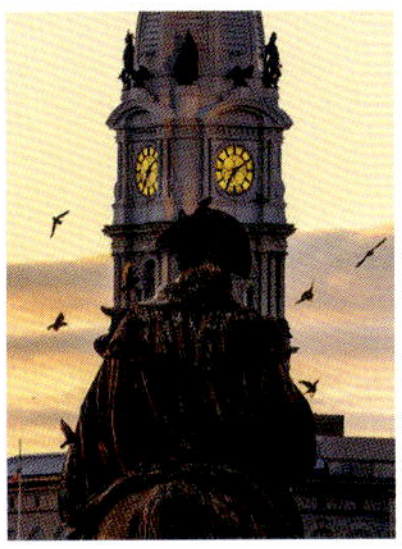

12 Trevor W. Adams
View of Philadelphia City Hall

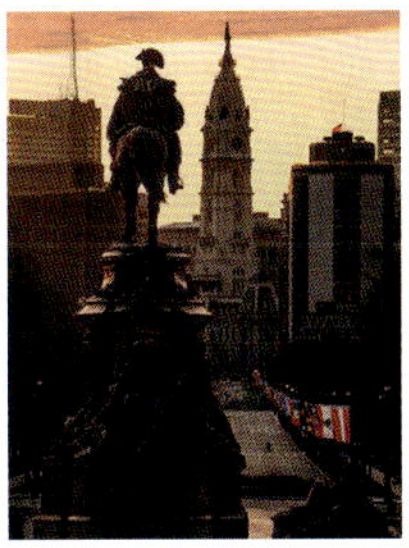

13 Trevor W. Adams
View of the Washington Monument Fountain and Philadelphia City Hall

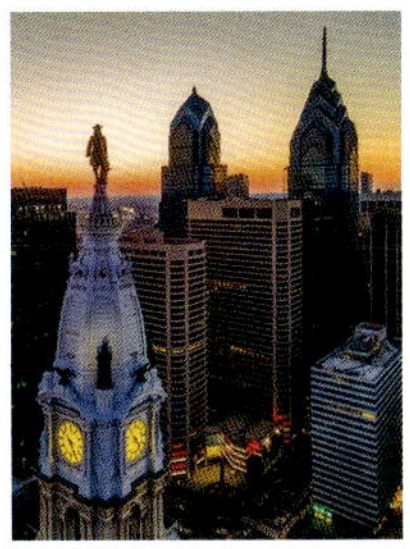

14 Daniel Moreno
View of William Penn and Center City

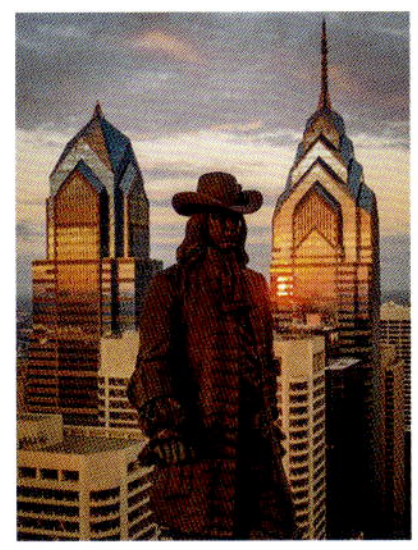

15 Brett Gross
View of William Penn

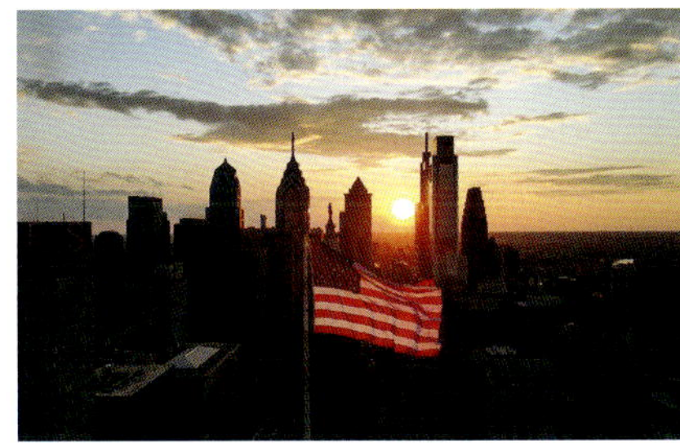

16-17 Nathaniel Bayona
View of Center City

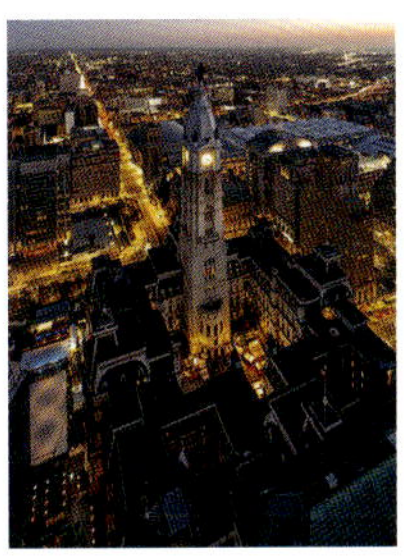

18 Trevor W. Adams
Above Philadelphia City Hall

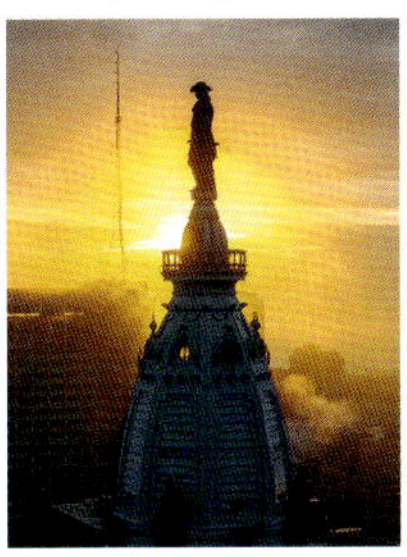

19 Daniel Moreno
View of William Penn

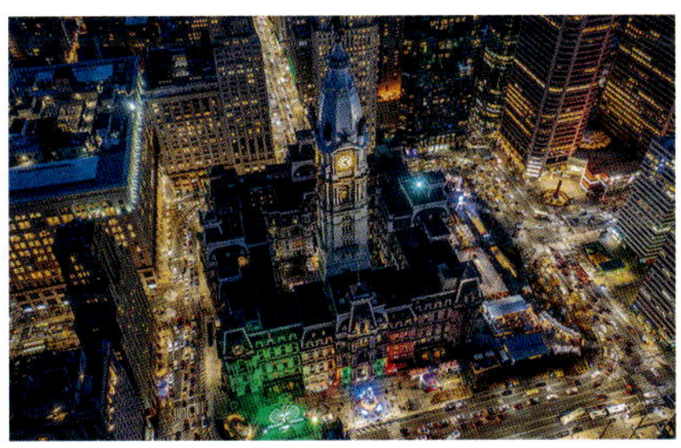

20-21 Brett Gross
Above Philadelphia City Hall

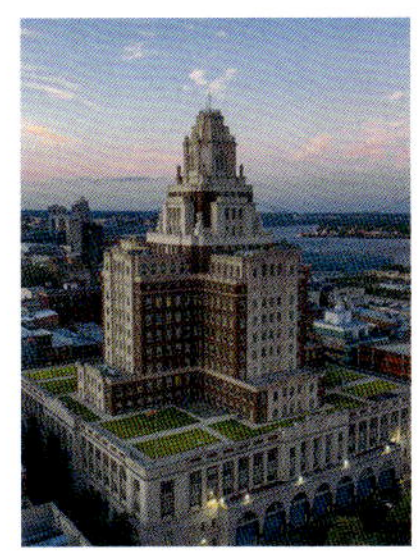

22 Brett Gross
View of the United States Custom House

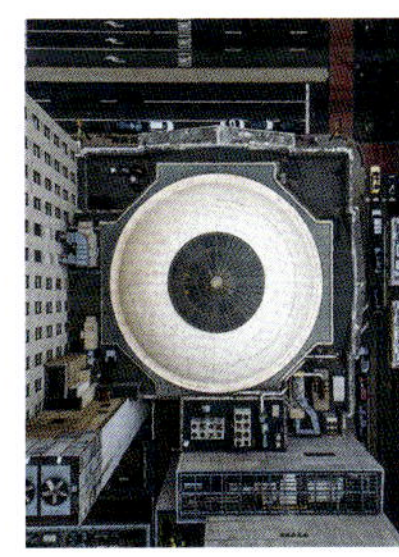

23 Luke Cuccurullo
Looking down on The Ritz-Carlton, Philadelphia

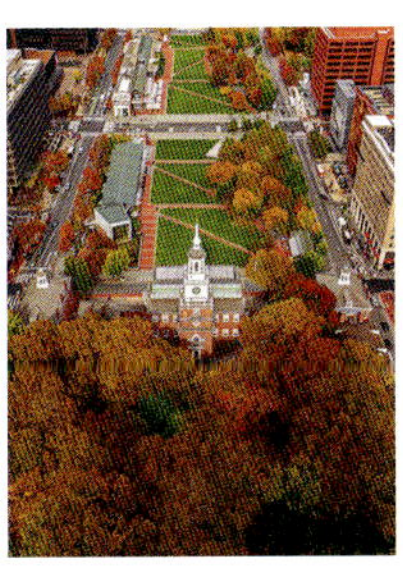

24 Brett Gross
Above Independence Hall and Independence National Historical Park

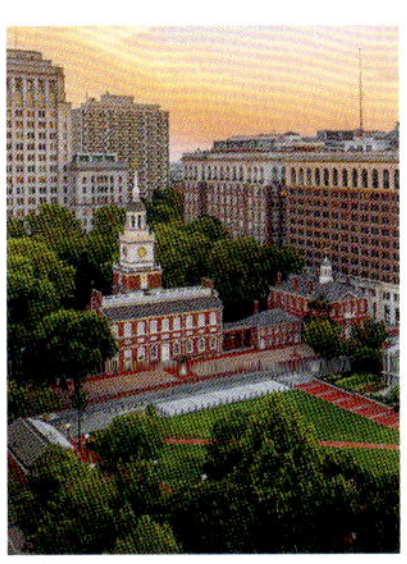

25 Brett Gross
View of Independence Hall

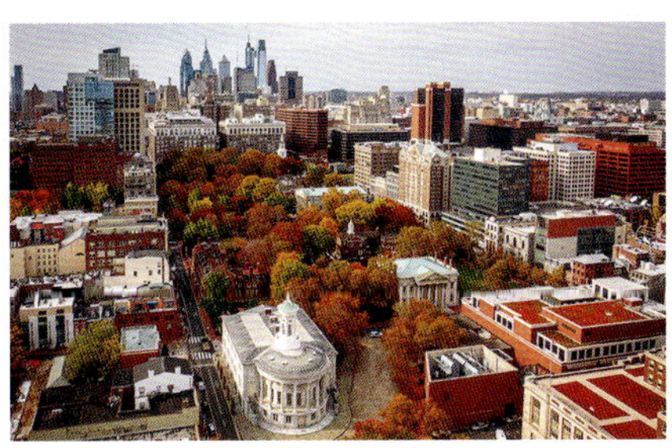

26-27 Brett Gross
View of the Merchant Exchange Building and Walnut Street

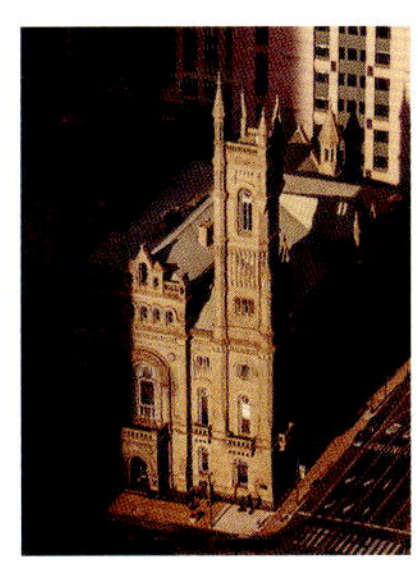

28 Trevor W. Adams
View of the Masonic Temple

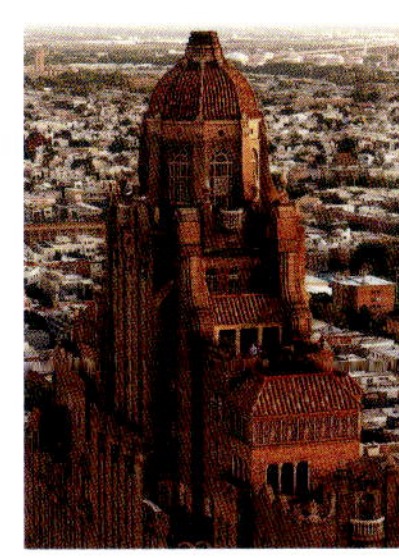

29 Trevor W. Adams
Above The Drake

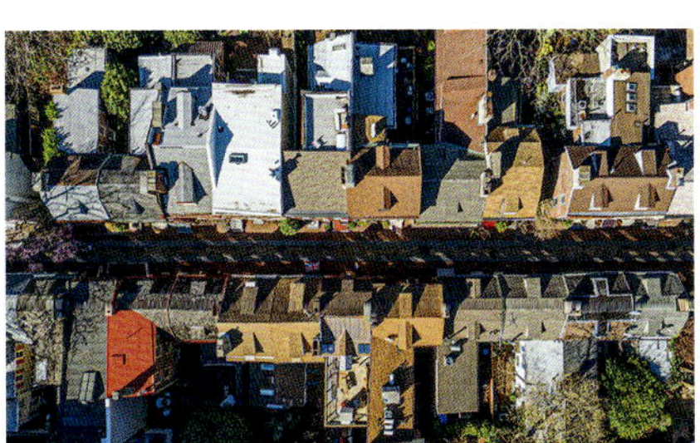

30-31 Luke Cuccurullo
Looking down on Elfreth's Alley

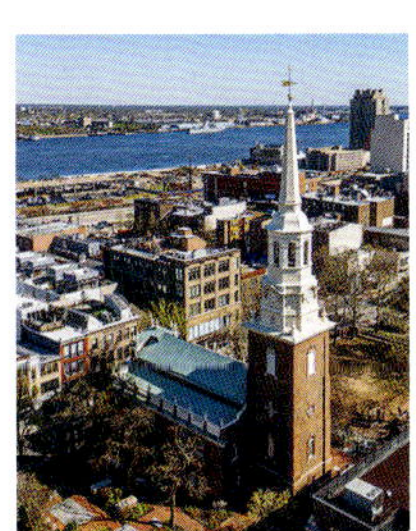

32 Luke Cuccurullo
View of Christ Church

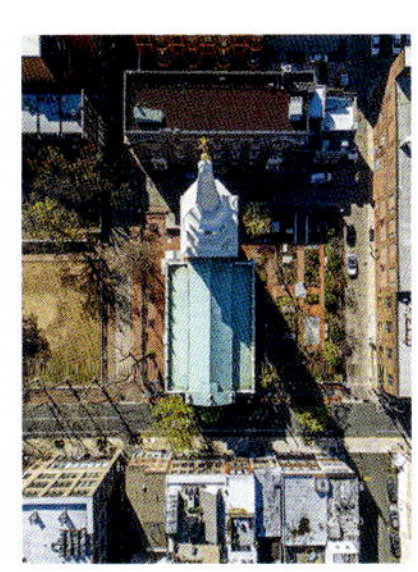

33 Luke Cuccurullo
Looking down on Christ Church

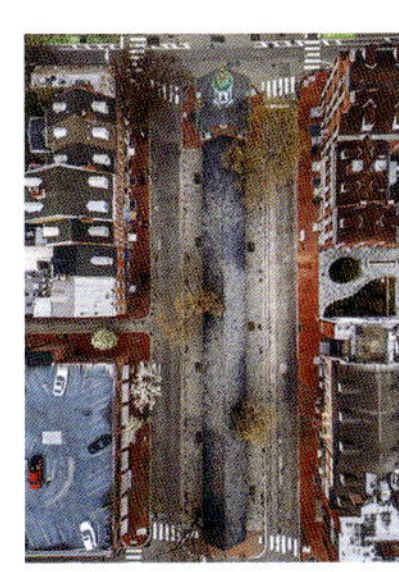

34 Luke Cuccurullo
Looking down on Headhouse Market

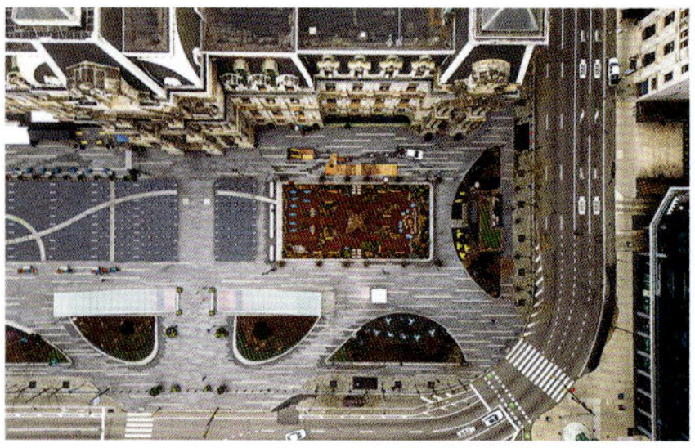

35 Luke Cuccurullo
Looking down on Dilworth Park

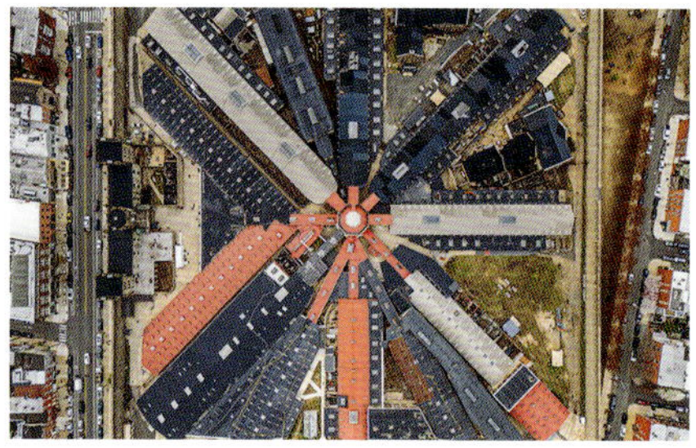

36-37 Luke Cuccurullo
Looking down on Eastern State Penitentiary

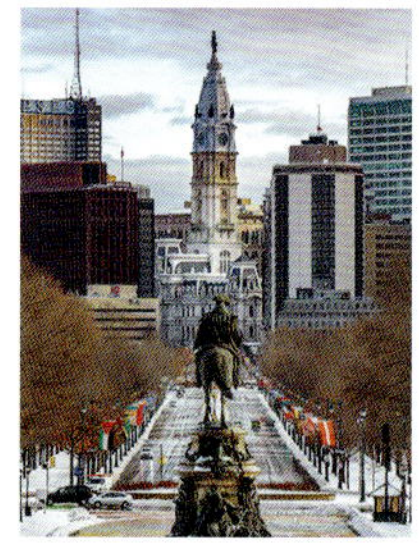

38 Thom Carroll
View of the Washington Monument Fountain and Philadelphia City Hall

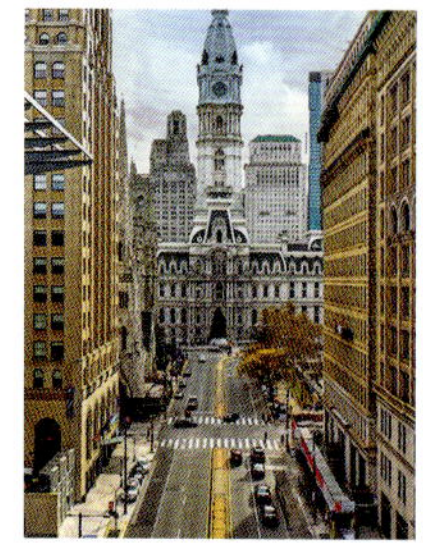

39 Andy D'Angelo
View of Philadelphia City Hall

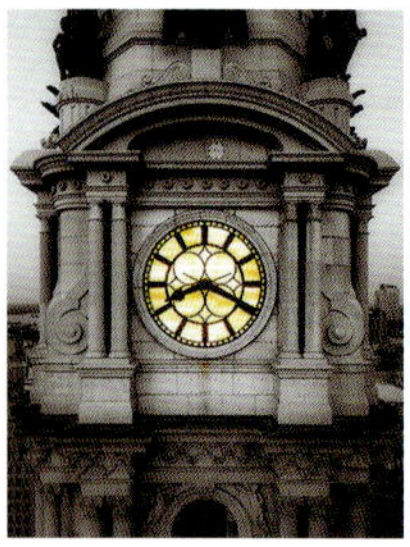

40 Greg Adams
Detail of Philadelphia City Hall

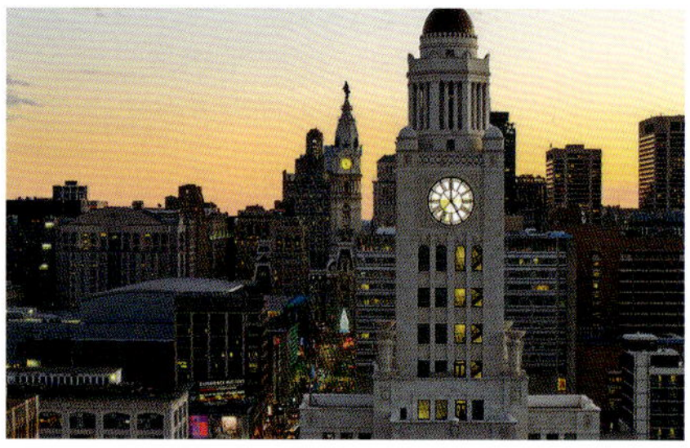

41 Nathaniel Bayona
View of the Inquirer Building

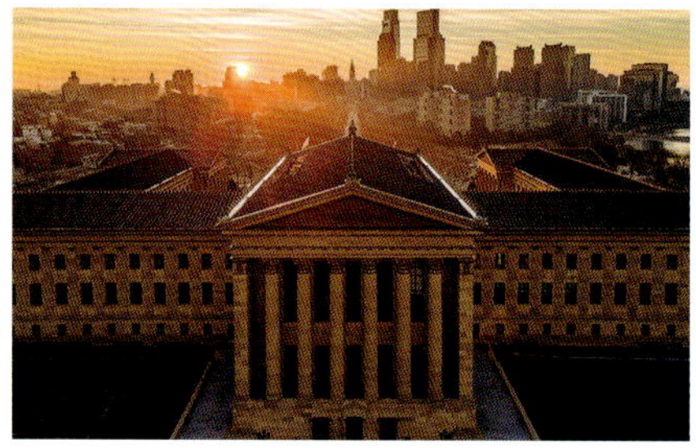

42-43 Daniel Moreno
View of the Philadelphia Museum of Art

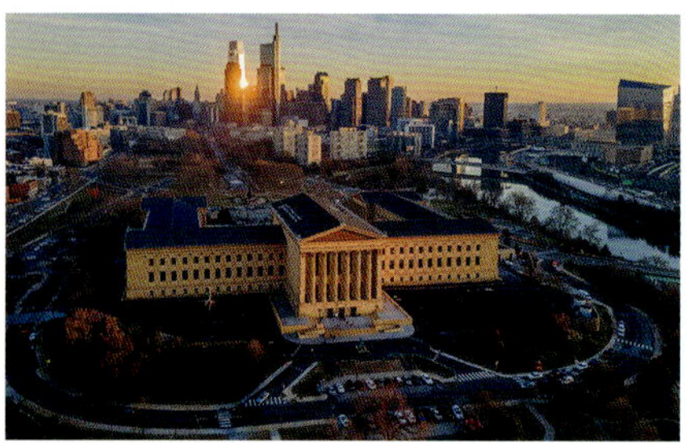

44-45 Daniel Moreno
View of the Philadelphia Museum of Art

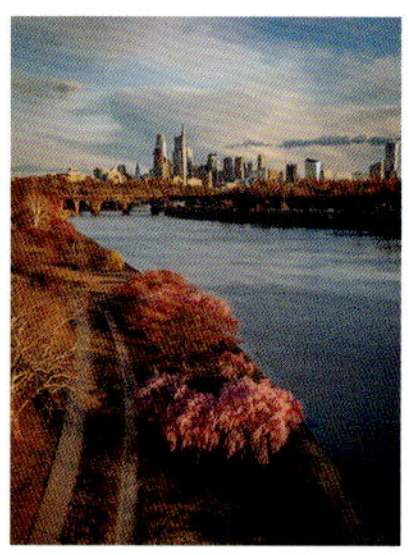

47 Brett Gross
View of the Schuylkill River

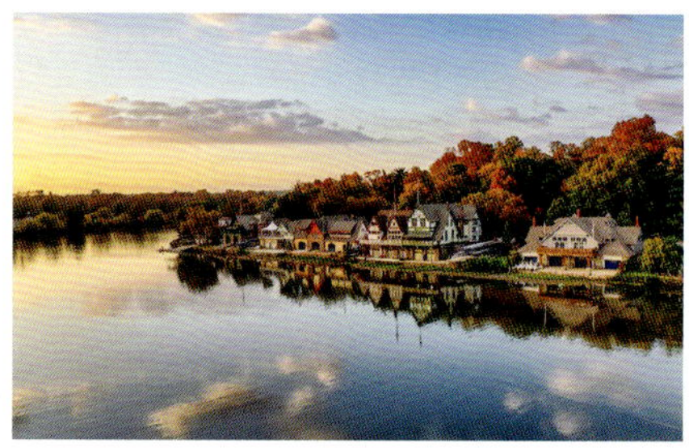

48-49 Andy D'Angelo
View of Boathouse Row

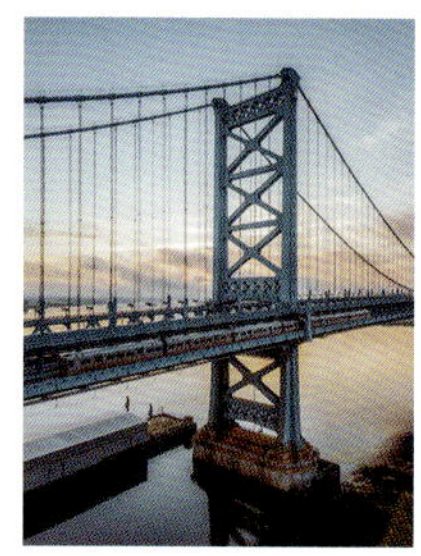

50 Greg Adams
View of Benjamin Franklin Bridge

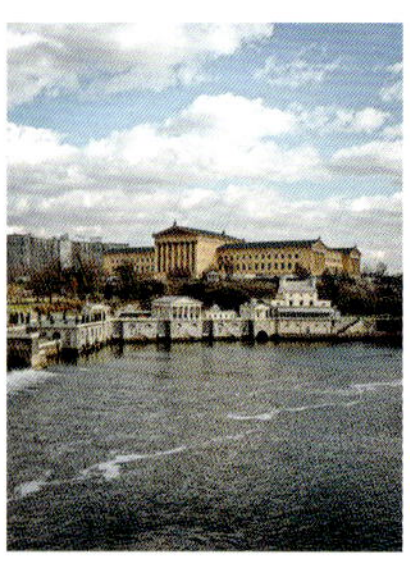

51 Andy D'Angelo
View of Fairmount Water Works and the Philadelphia Museum of Art

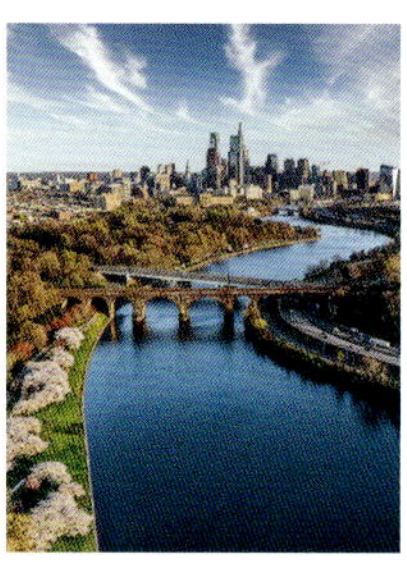

52 Andy D'Angelo
View of the Schuylkill River and Center City

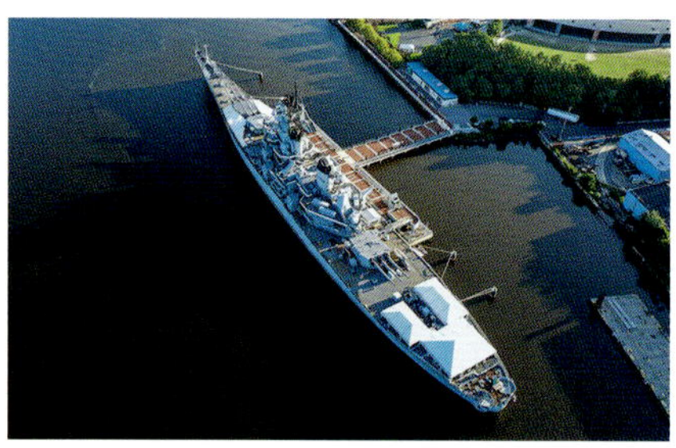

53 Andy D'Angelo
Above the Delaware River and Battleship New Jersey

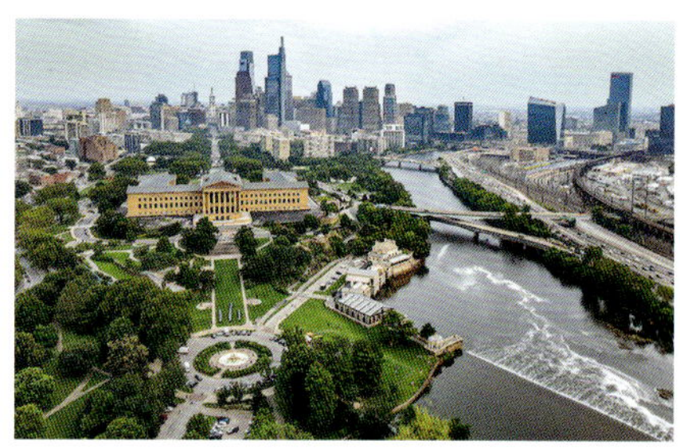

54-55 Thom Carroll
View of the Philadelphia Museum of Art and Center City

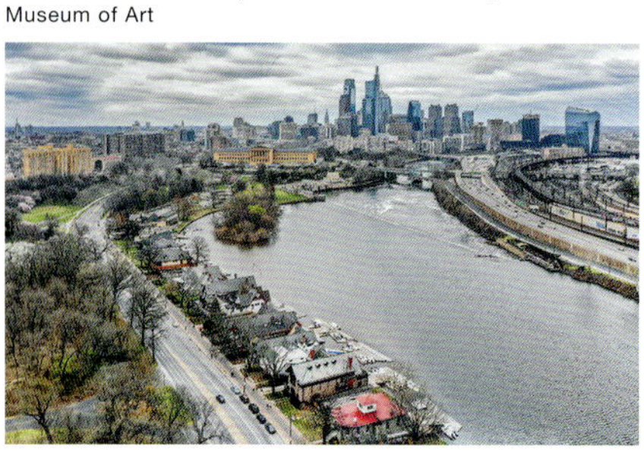

56-57 Lichao Liu
View of Boathouse Row and the Schuylkill River

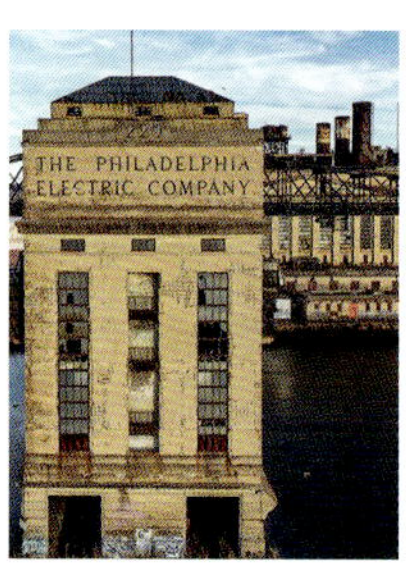

58 Andy D'Angelo
View of the Delaware Station

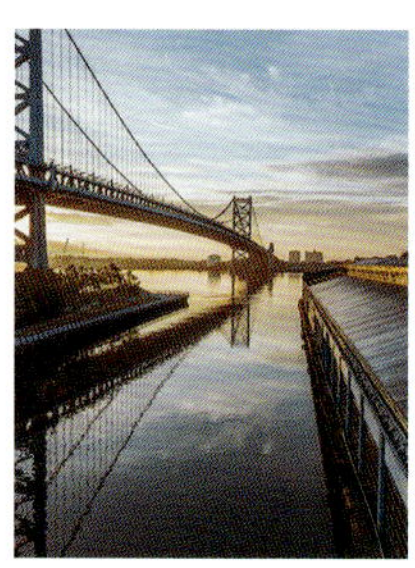

59 Greg Adams
Across the Delaware River and the Benjamin Franklin Bridge

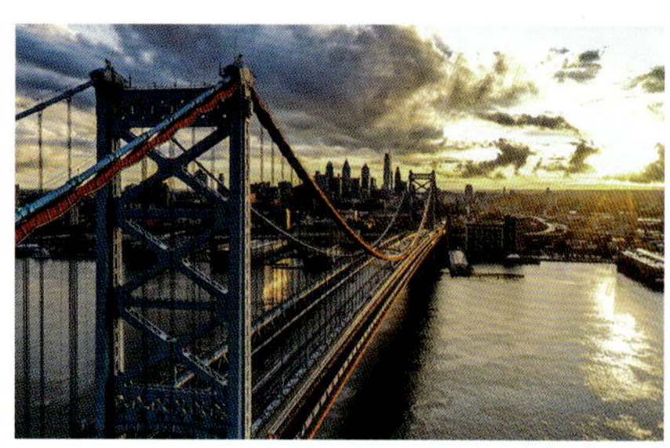

60-61 Andy D'Angelo
View of the Benjamin Franklin Bridge

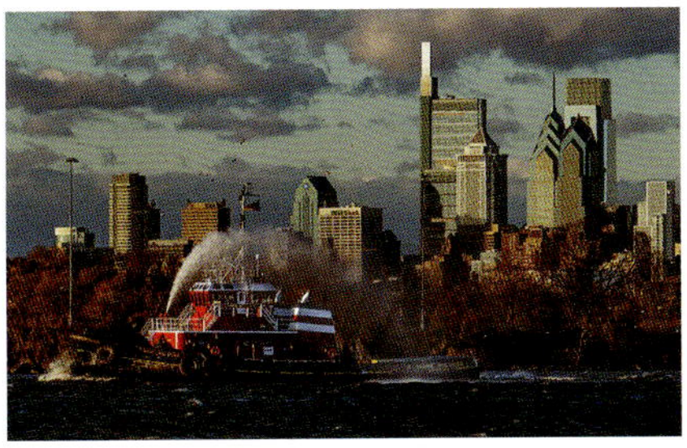

62-63 Brian Fishman
View of the Schuylkill River and the Philadelphia skyline

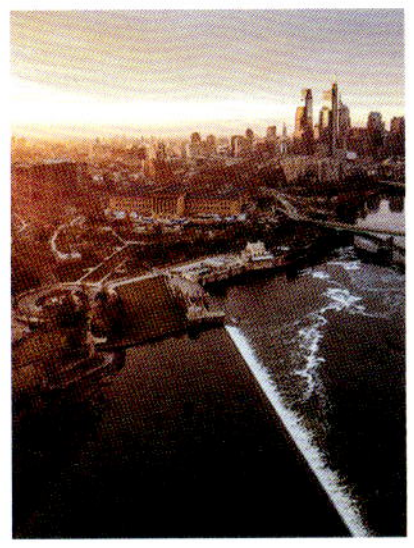

64 Greg Adams
View of the Philadelphia Museum of Art

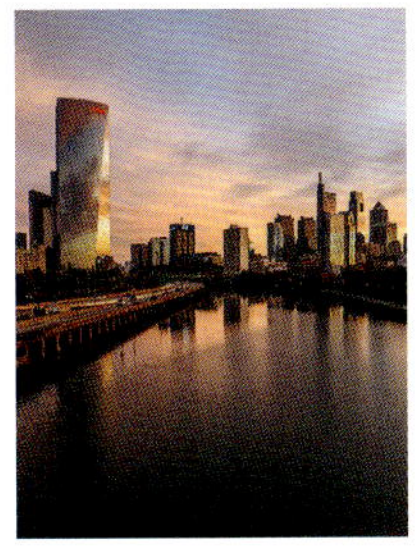

65 Kim Slouf
View of the Schuylkill River

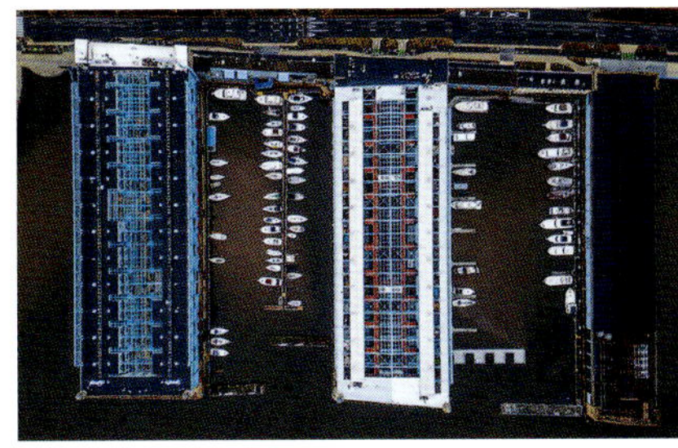

66-67 Luke Cuccurullo
Looking down on Cherry Street Pier

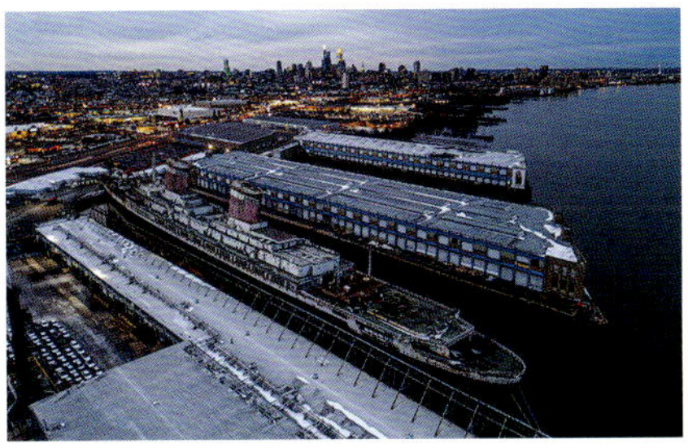

68-69 Luke Cuccurullo
View of the USS United States

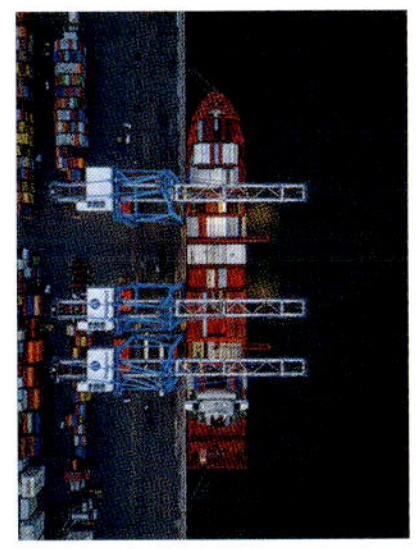

70 Luke Cuccurullo
Look down on the Delaware River

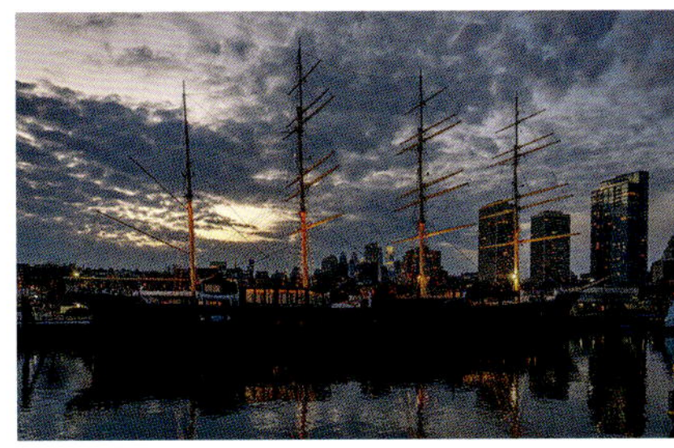

71 Luke Cuccurullo
View of restaurant on the Delaware River

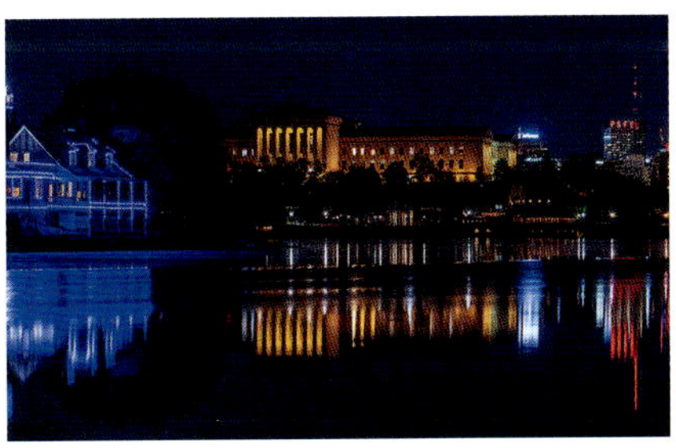

72-73 Brian Fishman
View of the Philadelphia Museum of Art

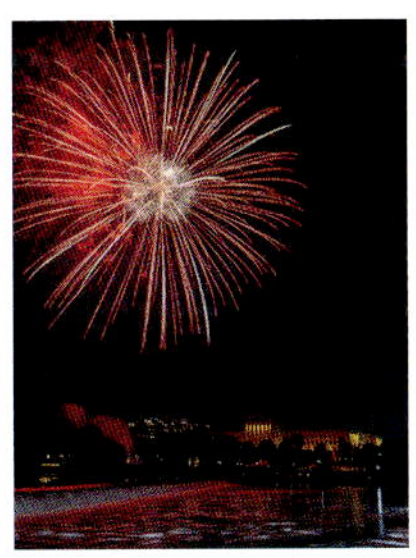

74 Brian Fishman
View of the Philadelphia Museum of Art and the Schuylkill River

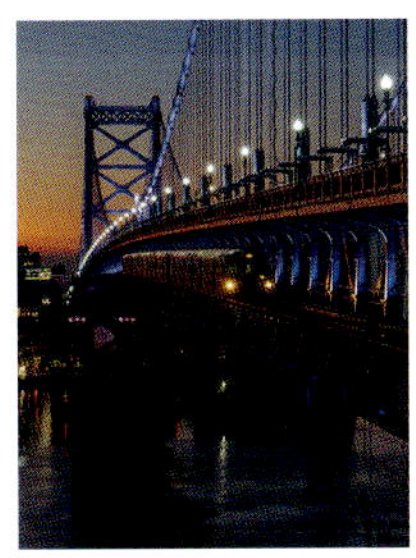

75 Daniel Moreno
Across the Benjamin Franklin Bridge

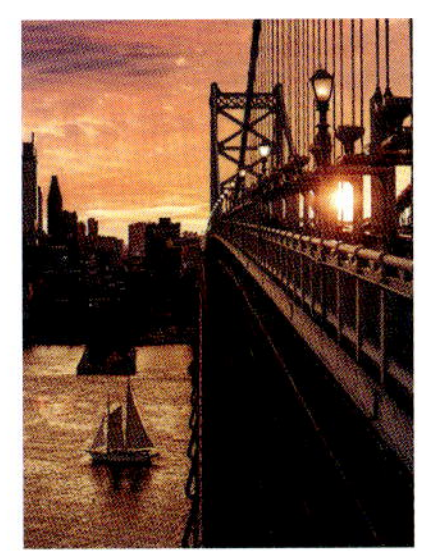

76 Trevor W. Adams
Across the Benjamin Franklin Bridge

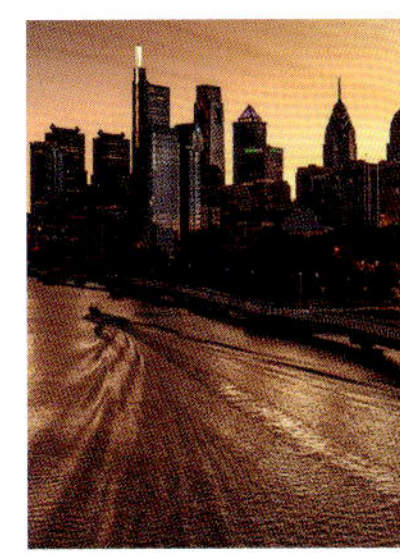

77 Trevor W. Adams
View of the Schuylkill River and the Philadelphia skyline

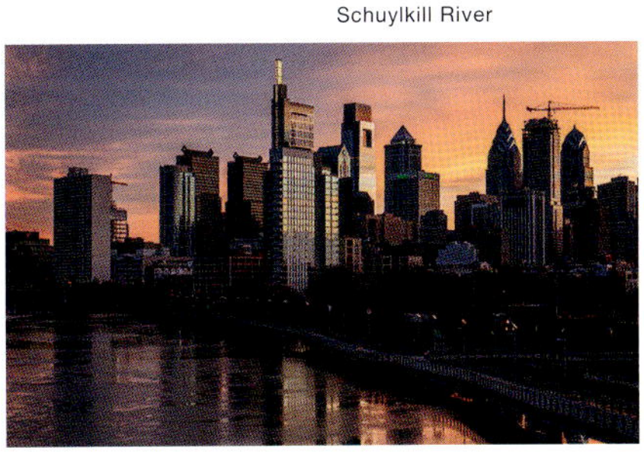

78-79 Brian Fishman
View of the Philadelphia skyline

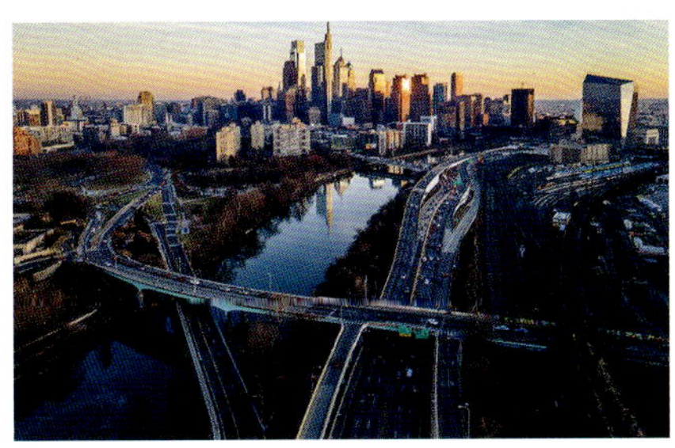

80-81 Daniel Moreno
Above the Schuylkill Expressway

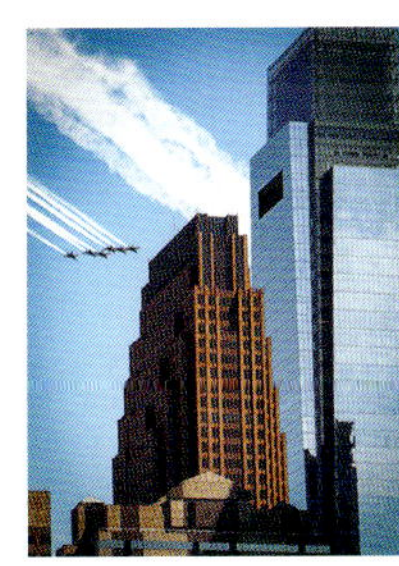

82 Andy D'Angelo
View of the Comcast Center and Three Logan Square

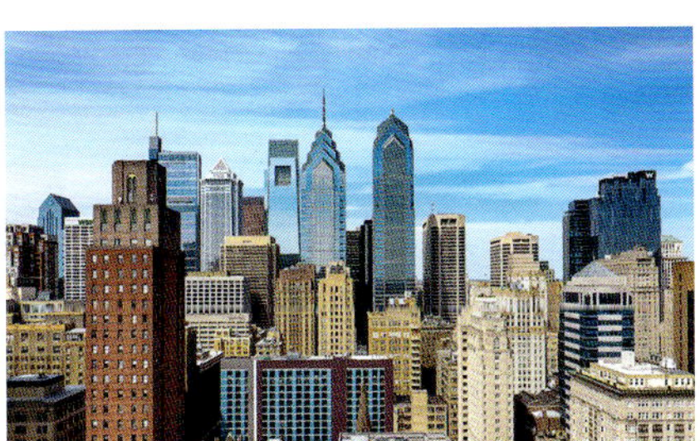

84-85 Andy D'Angelo
View of Center City

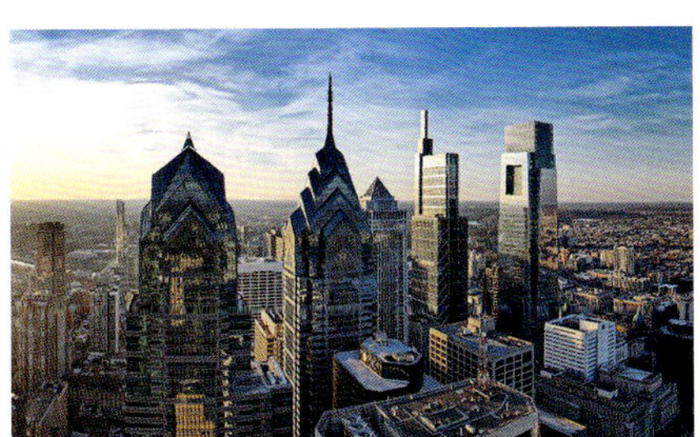

86-87 Nathaniel Bayona
Above Center City

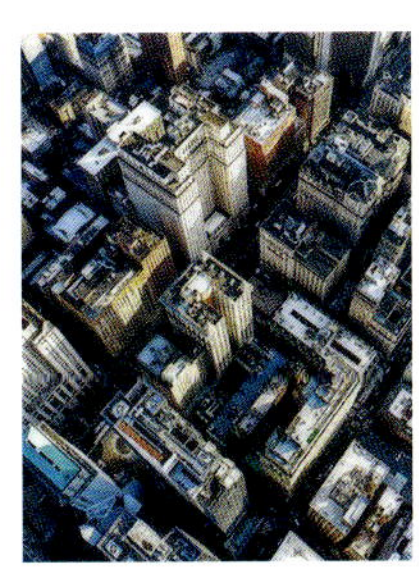

88 Andy D'Angelo
Above South Broad Street

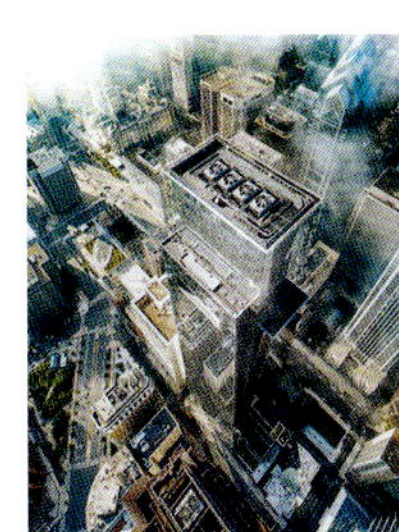

89 Andy D'Angelo
Above the Comcast Center

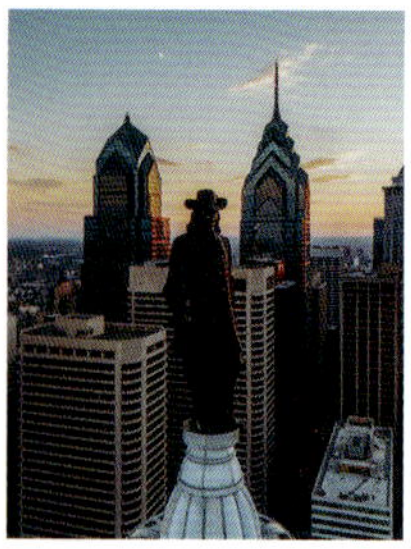

90 Greg Adams
View of William Penn

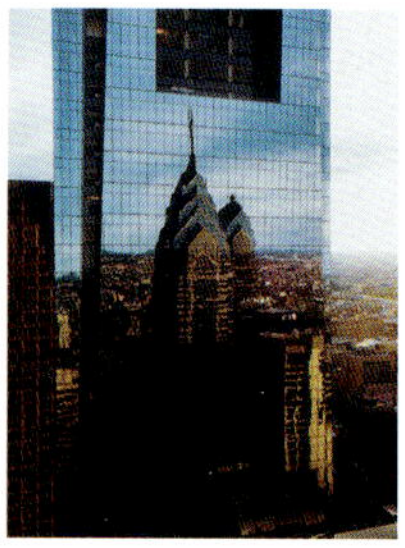

91 Greg Adams
View of One Liberty Place reflected on the Comcast Center

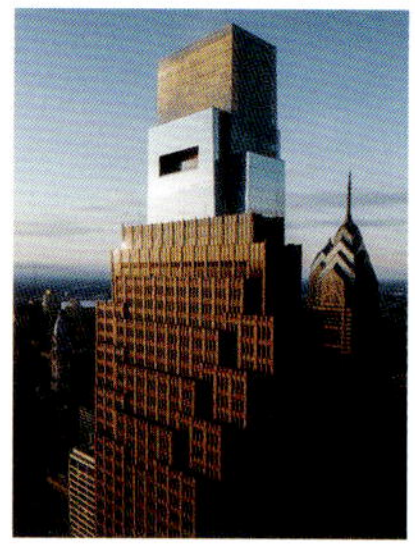

92 Greg Adams
View of Three Logan Square

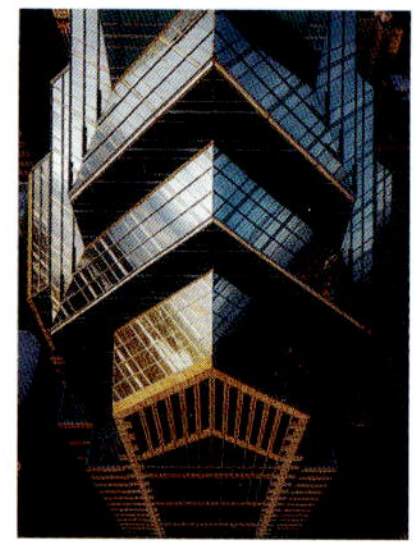

93 Greg Adams
Detail of One Liberty Place

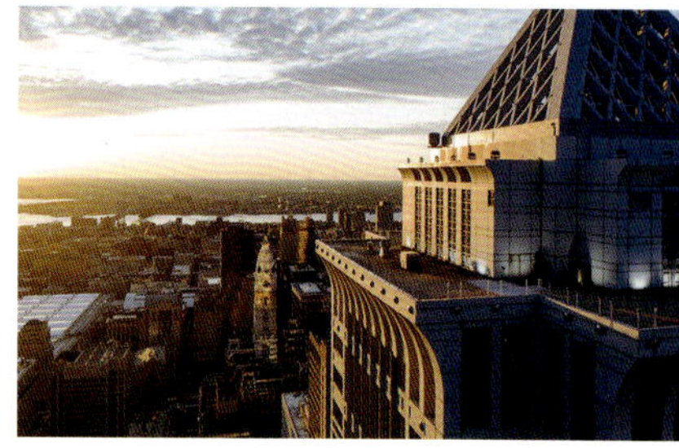

94-95 Andy D'Angelo
View of the BNY Mellon Center

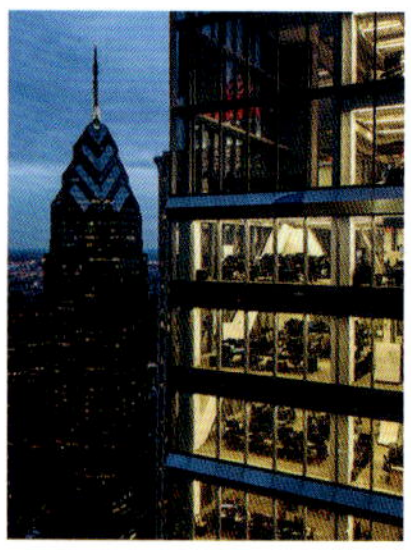

96 Andy D'Angelo
View of the Comcast Center and One Liberty Place

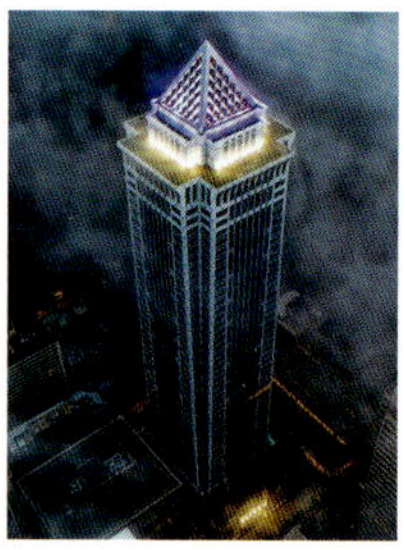

97 Andy D'Angelo
Above the BNY Mellon Center

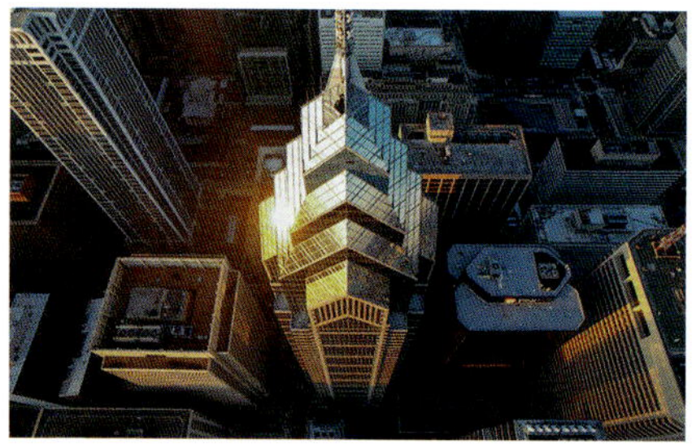

98-99 Nathaniel Bayona
Above One Liberty Place

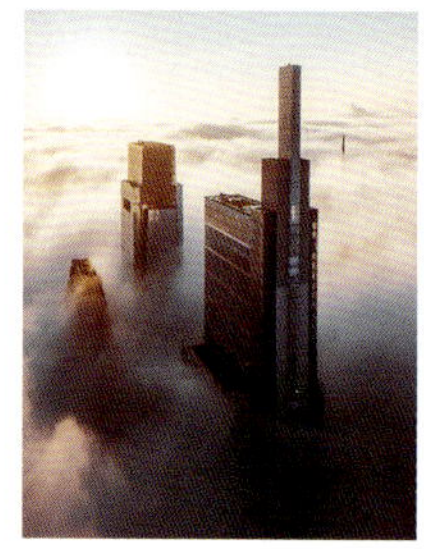

100 Greg Adams
View of the Four Seasons Hotel Philadelphia and the Comcast Center

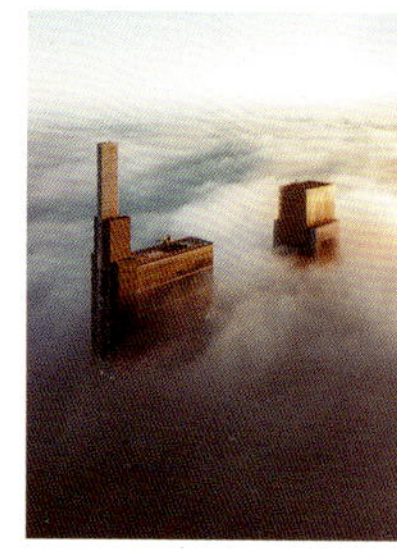

101 Greg Adams
View of the Four Seasons Hotel Philadelphia and the Comcast Center

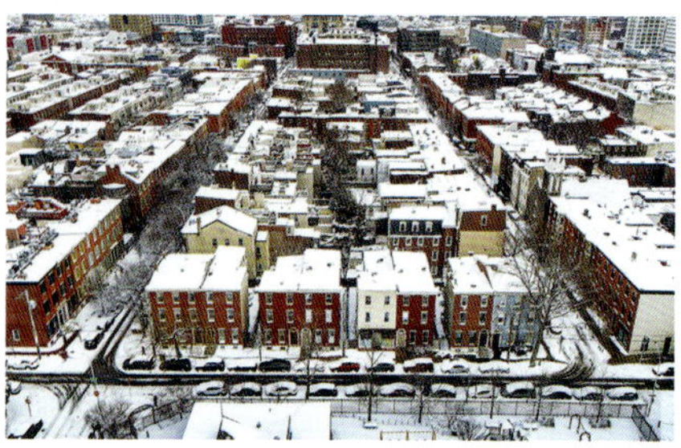

102 Thom Carroll
Above Fairmount

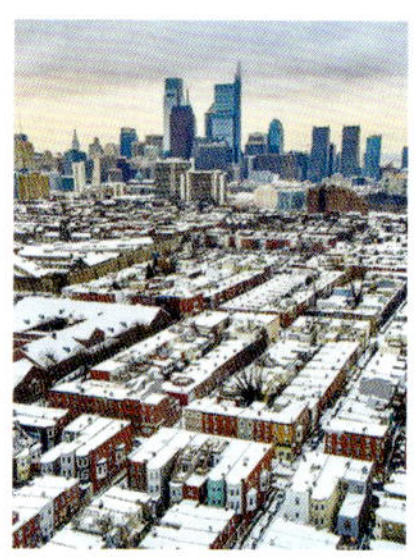

103 Thom Carroll
Above Fairmount

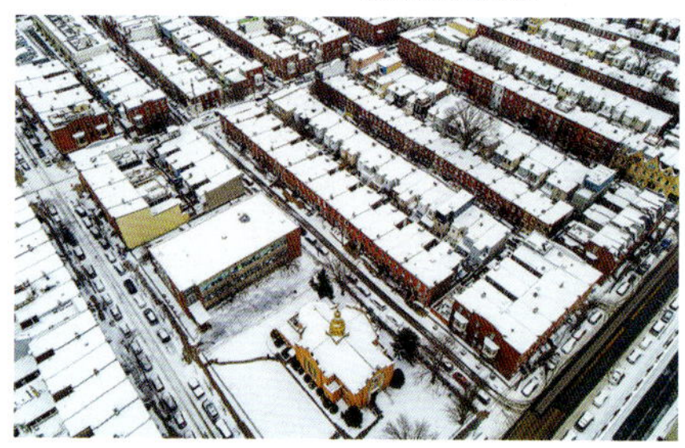

104-105 Thom Carroll
Above St. Nicholas Ukrainian Catholic Church

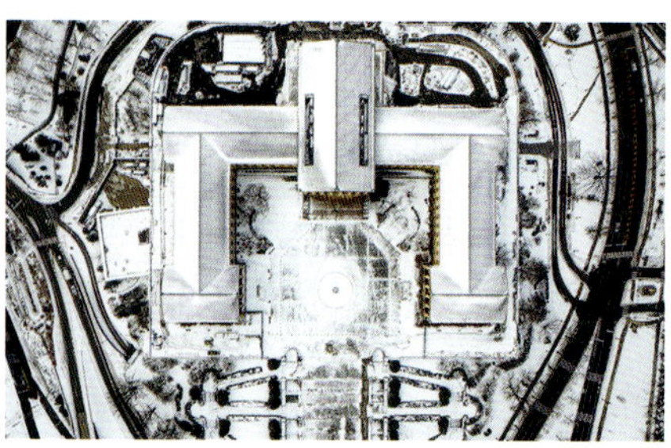

106-107 Brett Gross
Looking down on the Philadelphia Museum of Art

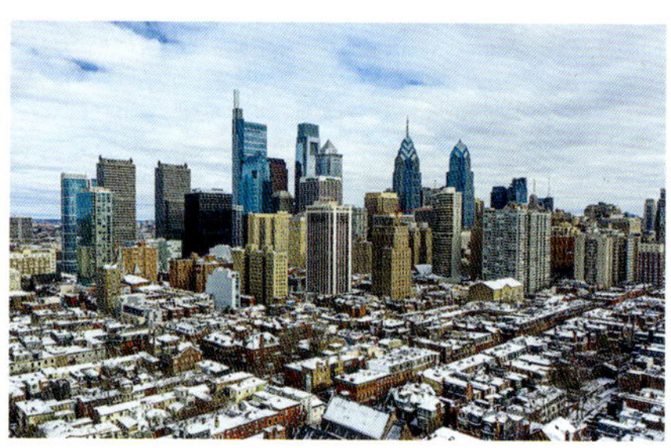

108-109 Brett Gross
View of the Philadelphia skyline

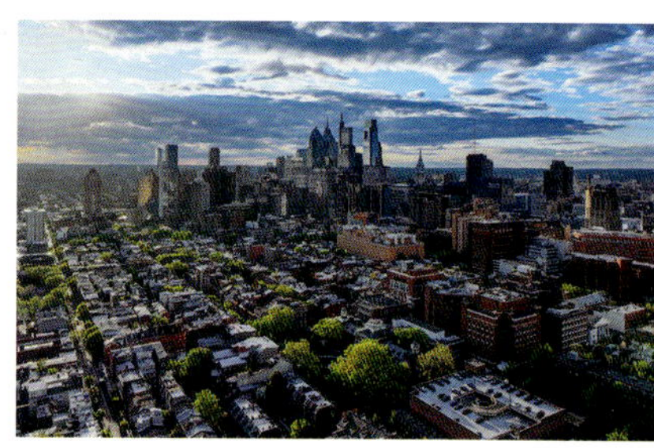

110-111 Nathaniel Bayona
View of the Philadelphia skyline

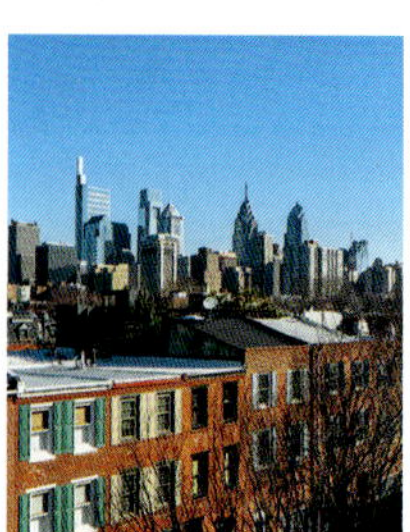

112 Andy D'Angelo
View of the Philadelphia skyline from Southwest Center City

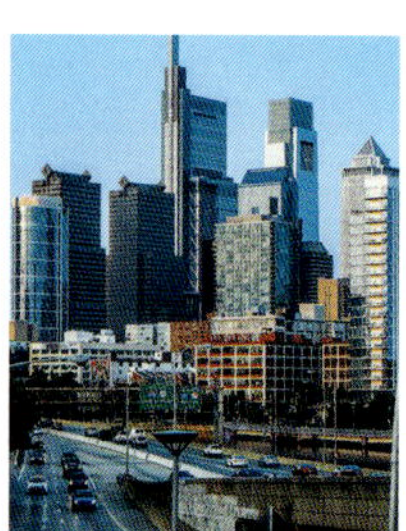

113 Kim Slouf
View of the Schuylkill Expressway and Center City

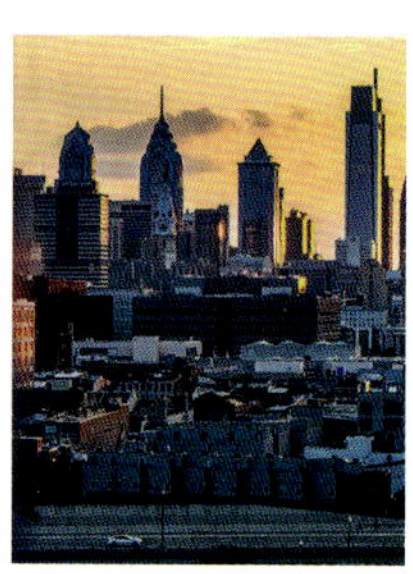

114 Kim Slouf
View of Center City

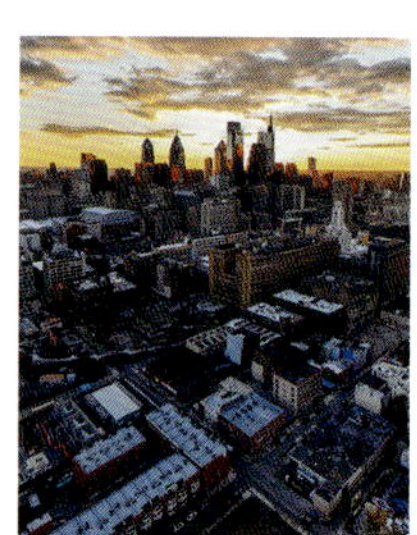

115 Nathaniel Bayona
Above Button Street and North 12th Street

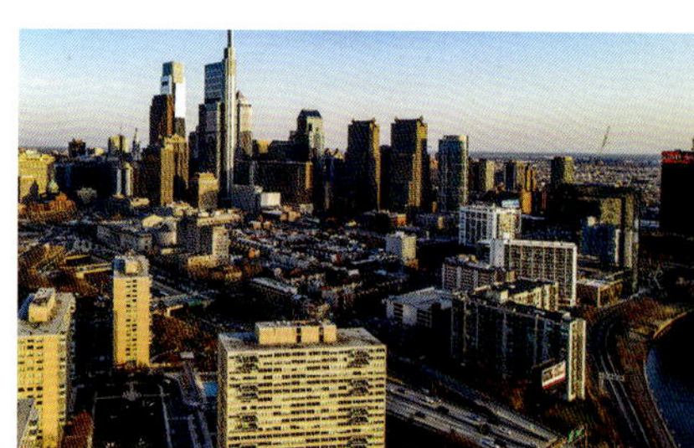

116-117 Thom Carroll
View of the Philadelphia skyline

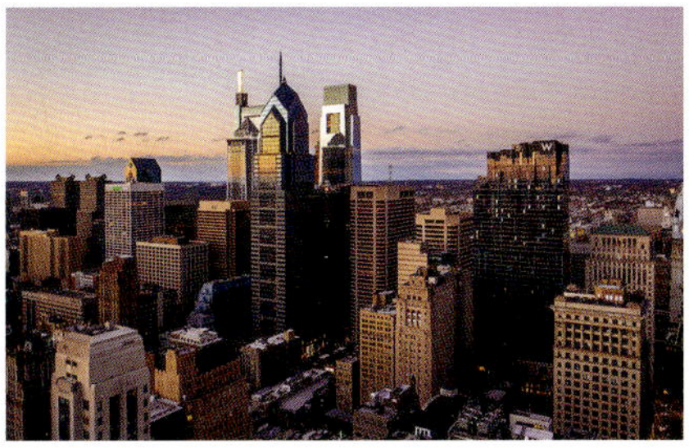

118-119 Brett Gross
View of One Liberty Place and Center City

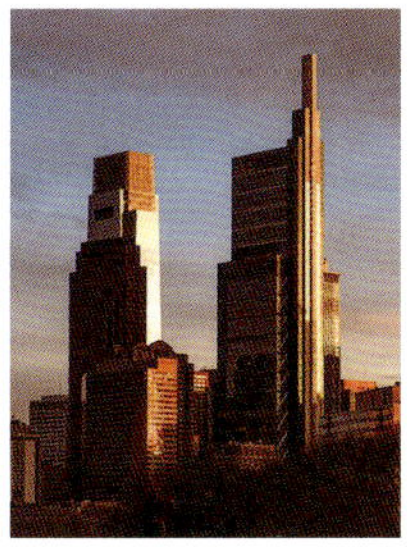

120 Greg Adams
View of the Four Seasons Hotel Philadelphia and the Comcast Center

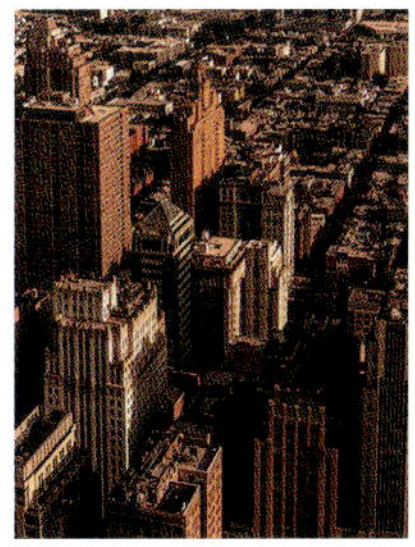

121 Trevor W. Adams
Above South 16th Street

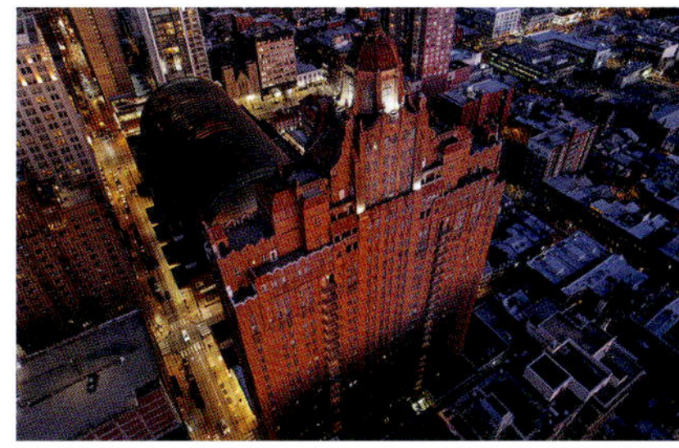

122-123 Nathaniel Bayona
Above The Drake

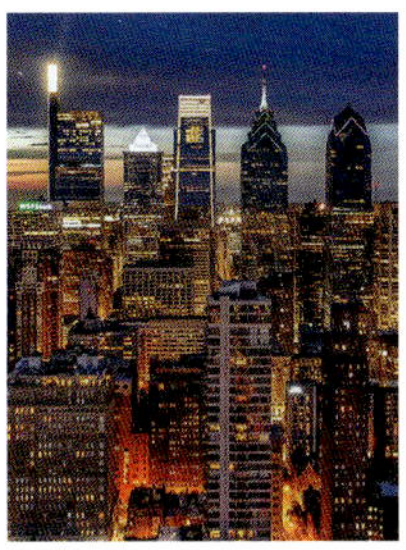

124 Andy D'Angelo
View of Center City

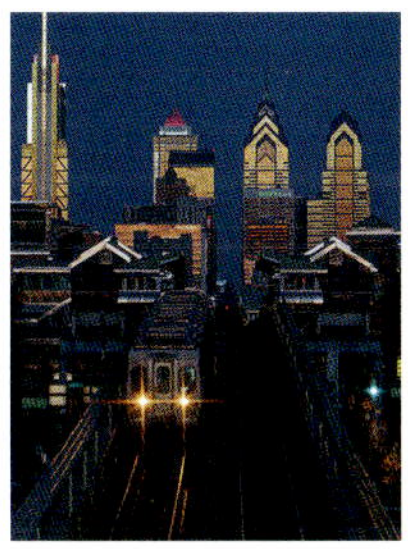

125 Brian Fishman
View of train approaching 30th Street Station

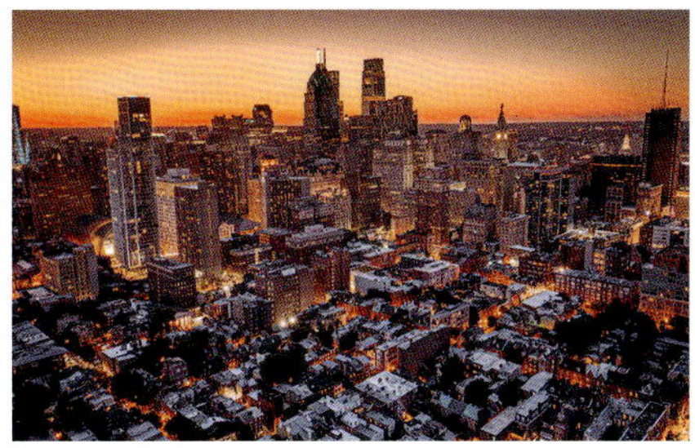

126-127 Brett Gross
View of Washington Square West and Center City

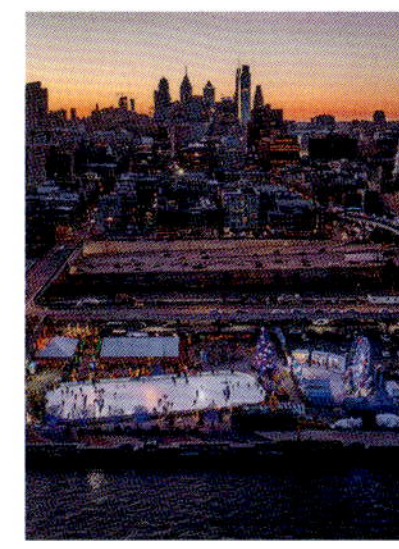

128 Brett Gross
View of Independence Blue Cross RiverRink

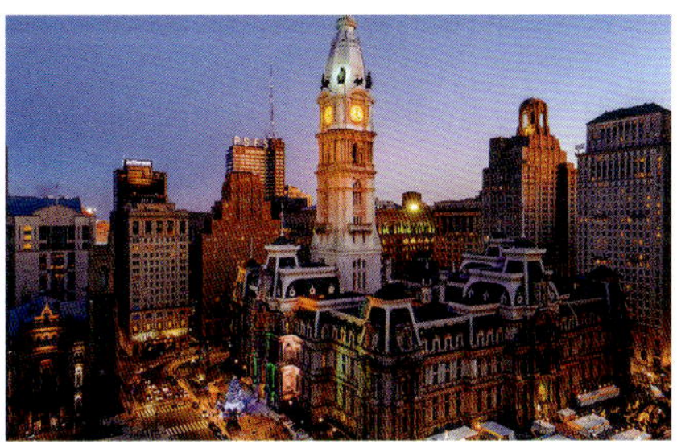

129 Daniel Moreno
View of Philadelphia City Hall

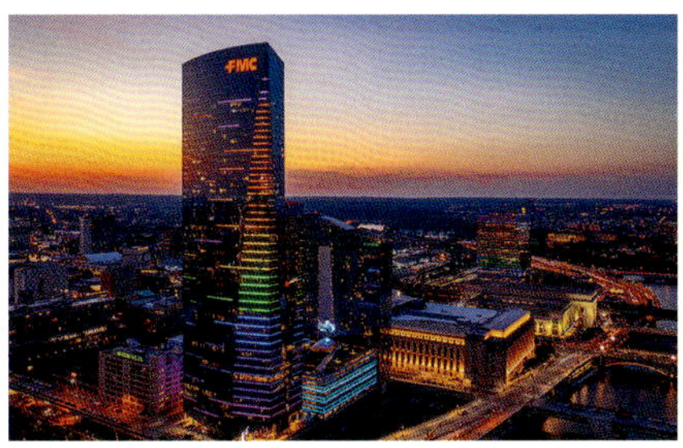

130 Brett Gross
View of the FMC Tower

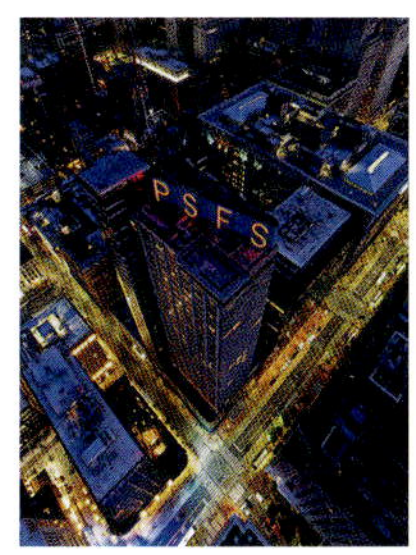

131 Nathaniel Bayona
Above the Loews Philadelphia Hotel

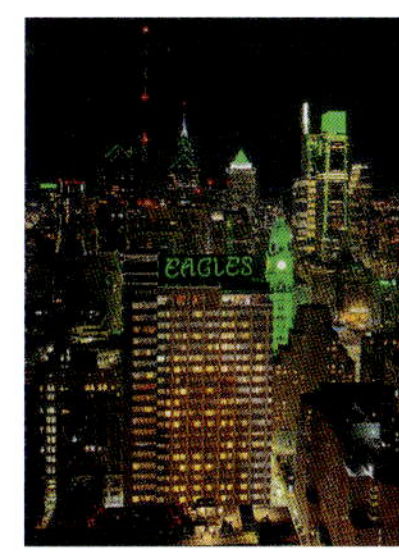

132 Nathaniel Bayona
View of the Loews Philadelphia Hotel

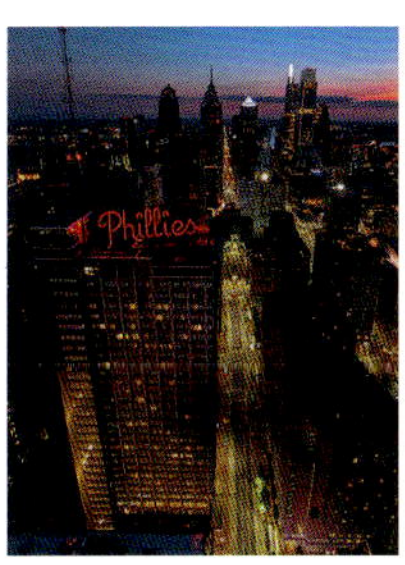

133 Nathaniel Bayona
Above the Loews Philadelphia Hotel and Market Street

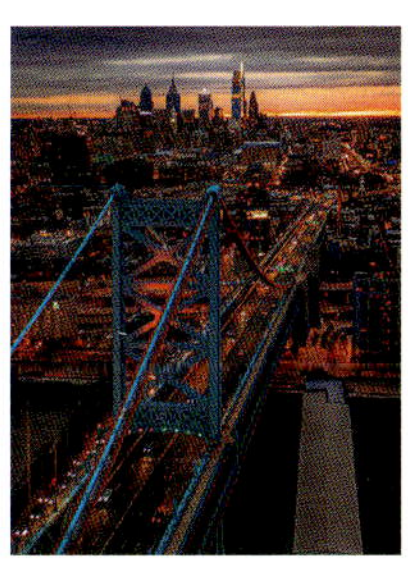

134 Brett Gross
View of the Benjamin Franklin Bridge

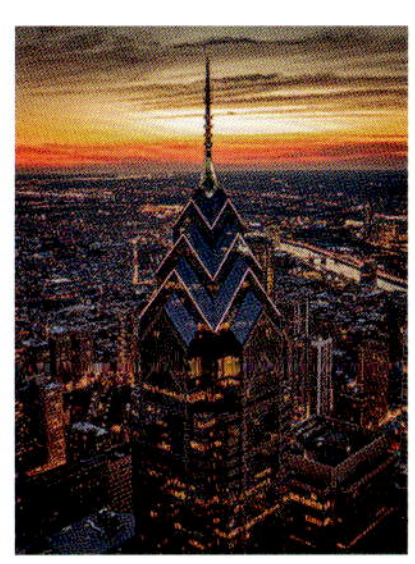

135 Brett Gross
View of One Liberty Place

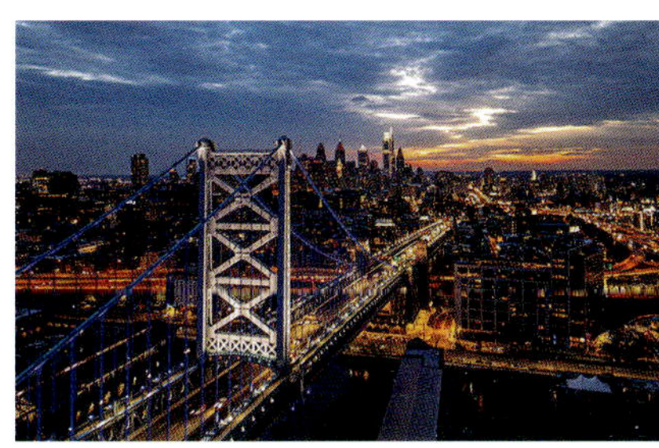

136-137 Luke Cuccurullo
View of the Benjamin Franklin Bridge

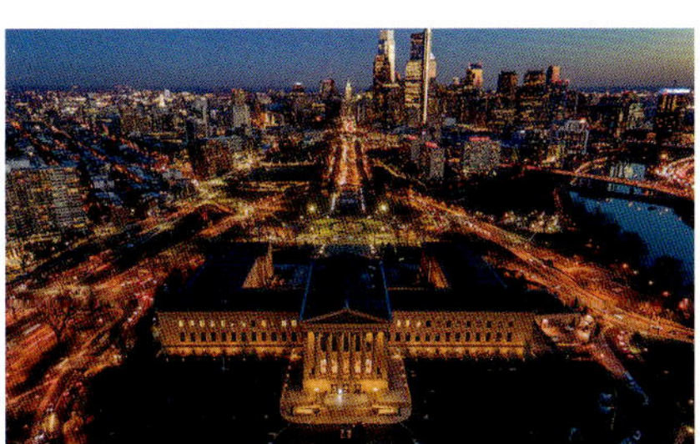

138-139 Daniel Moreno
Above the Philadelphia Museum of Art

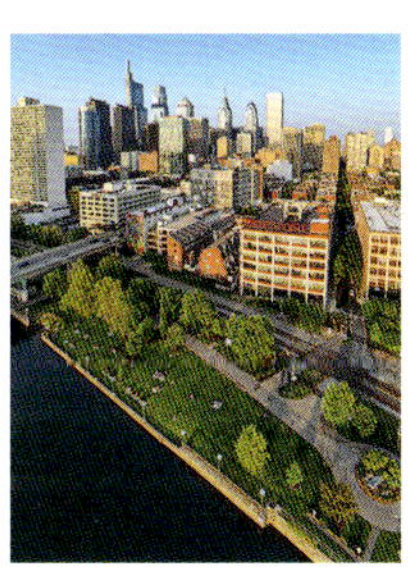

141 Nathaniel Bayona
View of the Schuylkill River Trail

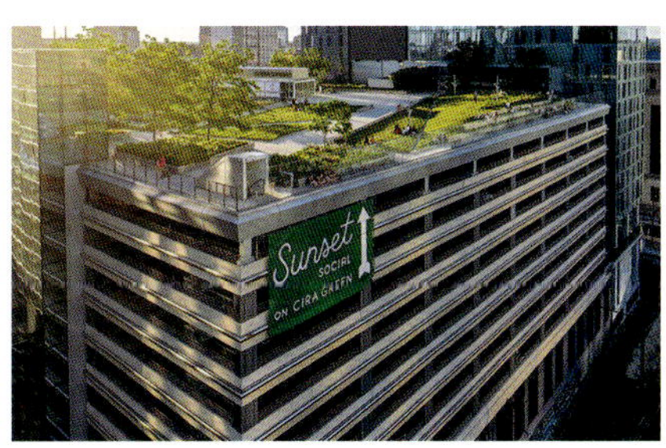

142-143 Andy D'Angelo
View of Cira Green

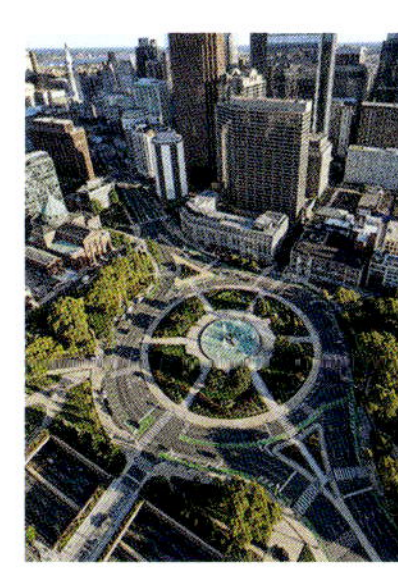

144 Nathaniel Bayona
Above Swann Memorial Fountain

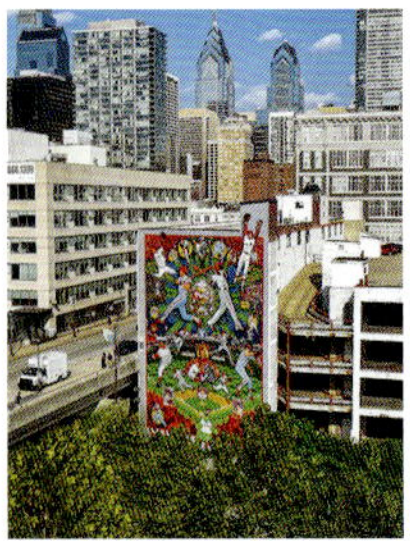

145 Nathaniel Bayona
View of Walnut Street

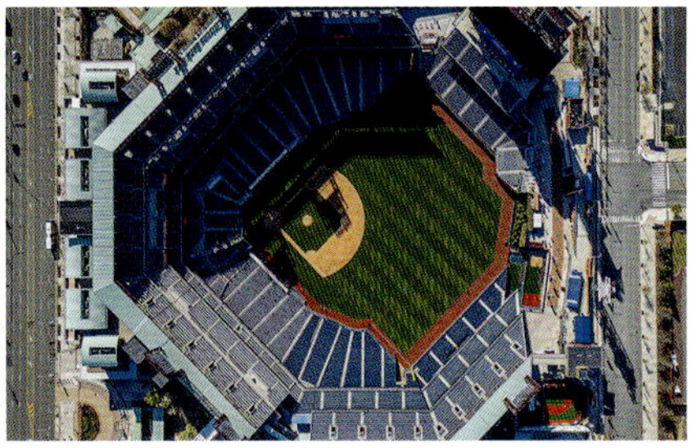

146-147 Luke Cuccurullo
Looking down on Citizens Bank Park

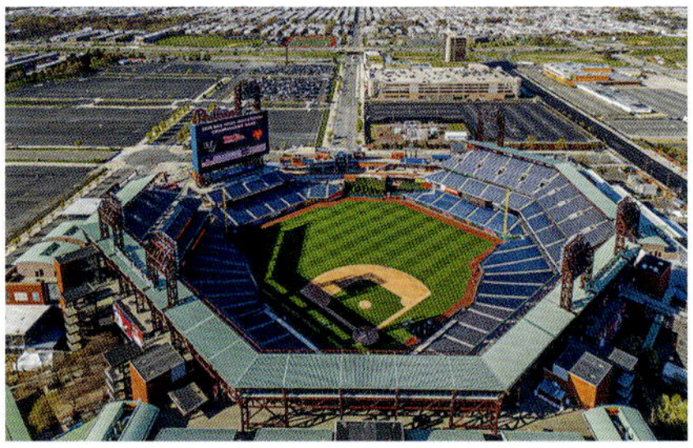

148-149 Luke Cuccurullo
View of Citizens Bank Park

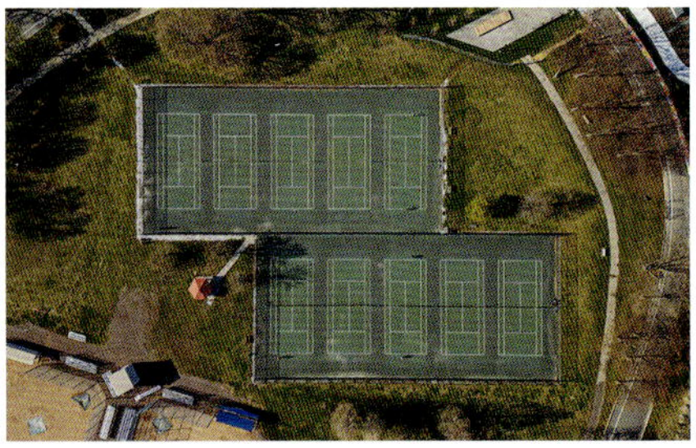

150 Luke Cuccurullo
Looking down on FDR Park

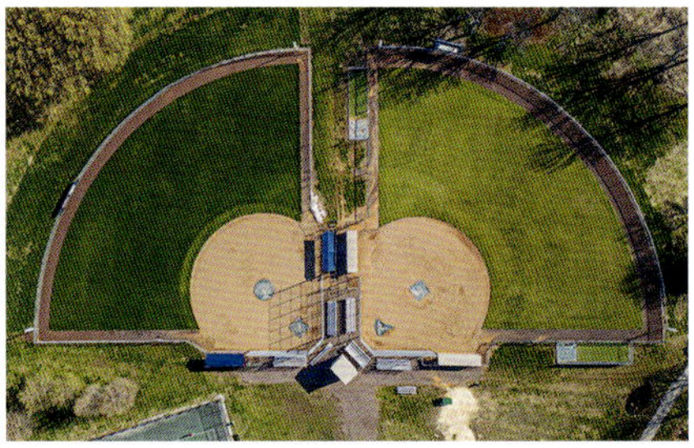

151 Luke Cuccurullo
Looking down on FDR Park

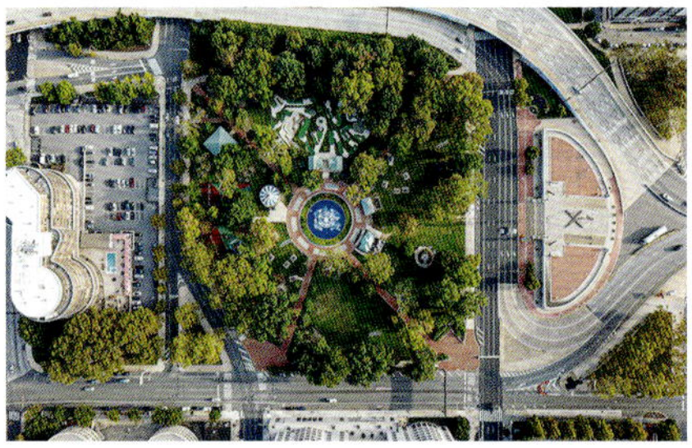

152-153 Andy D'Angelo
Looking down on Franklin Square

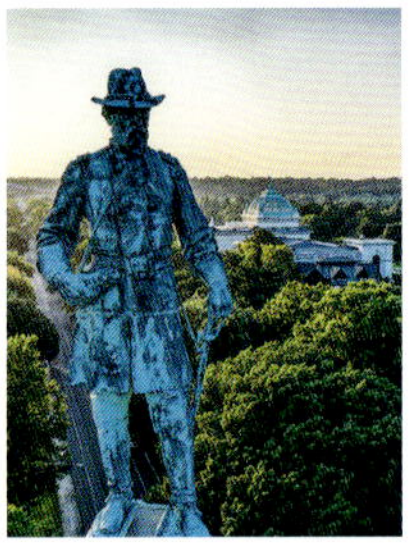

154 Andy D'Angelo
Across Fairmount Park

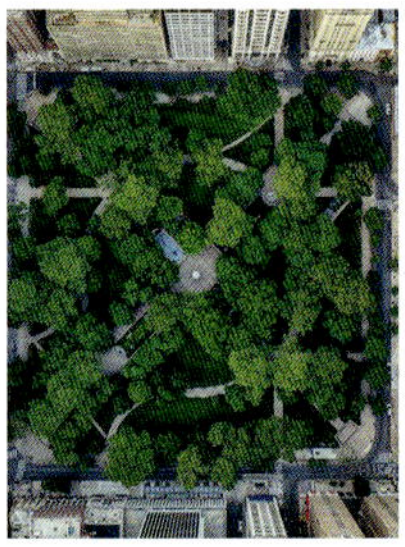

155 Andy D'Angelo
Looking down on Rittenhouse Square

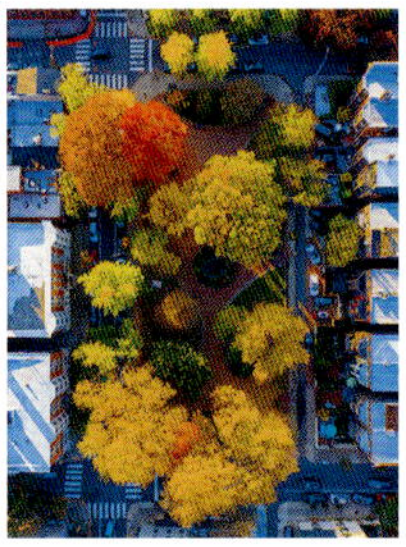

156 Brett Gross
Looking down on Fitler Square

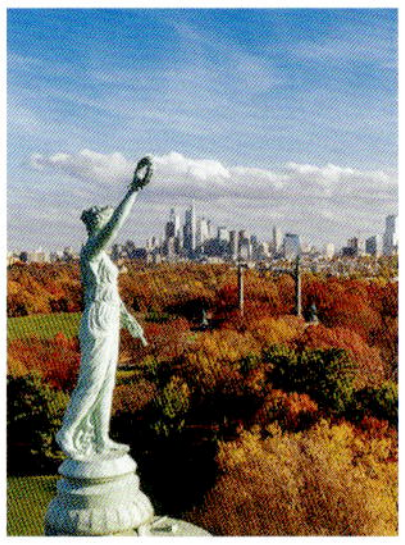

157 Andy D'Angelo
Across Fairmount Park

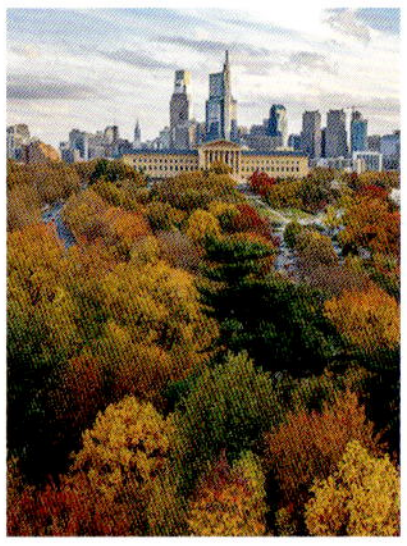

158 Brett Gross
Across Lemon Hill Park

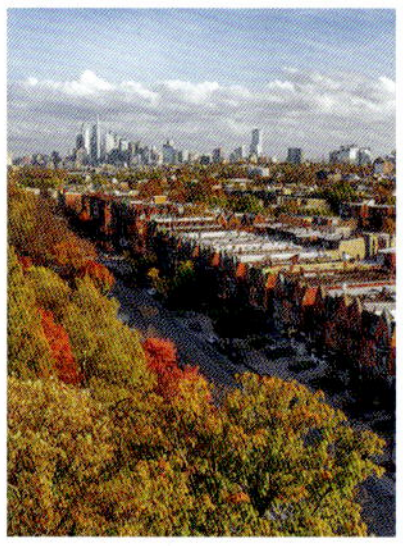

159 Andy D'Angelo
View of West Philadelphia and Parkside Avenue

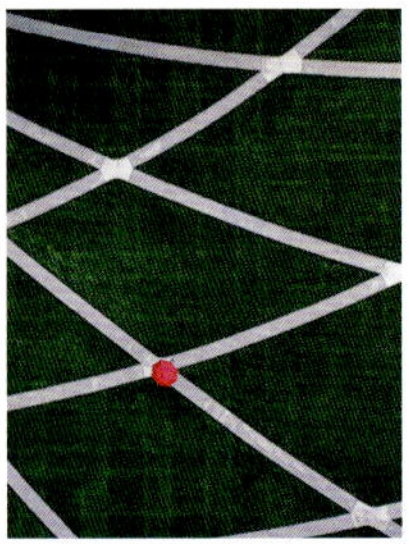

160 Greg Adams
Looking down on Drexel Square

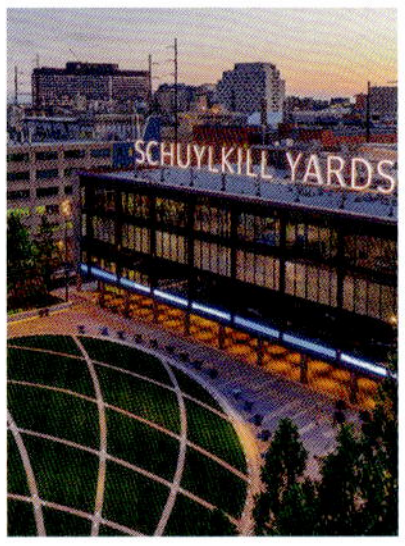

161 Brett Gross
View of the Bulletin Building and Drexel Square

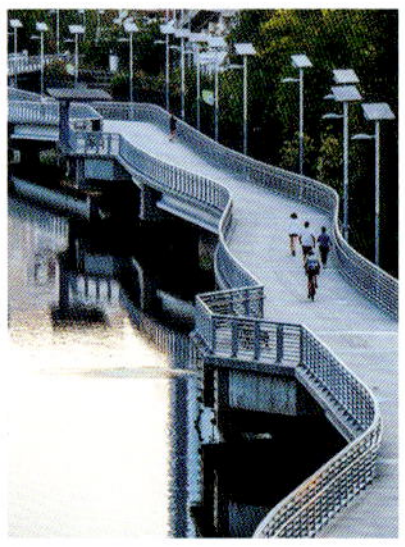

162 Kim Slouf
View of the Schuylkill River Trail

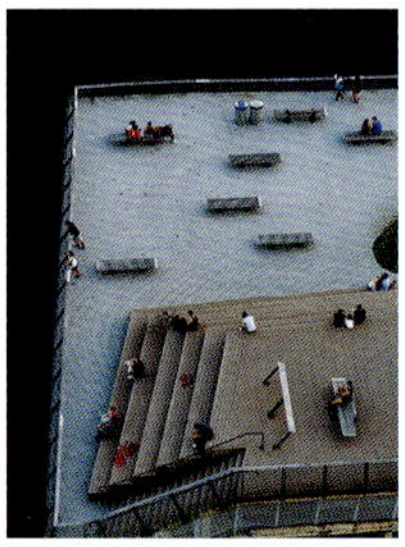

163 Kim Slouf
Above Race Street Pier

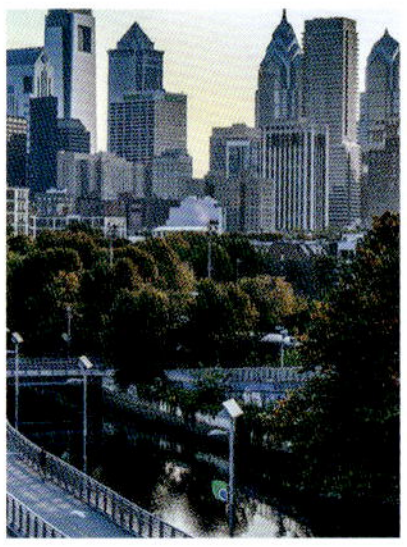

164 Kim Slouf
View of the Schuylkill River Trail and Center City

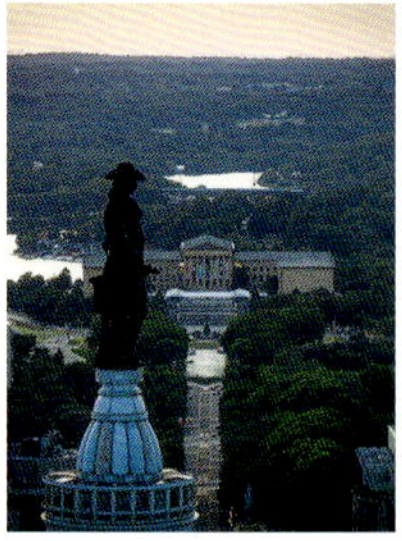

165 Nathaniel Bayona
View of William Penn and the Philadelphia Museum of Art

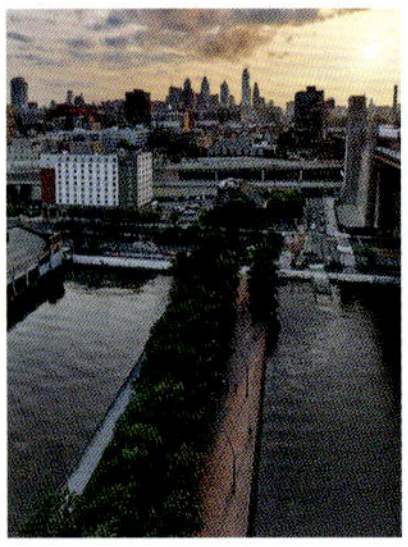

166 Nathaniel Bayona
View of Race Street Pier

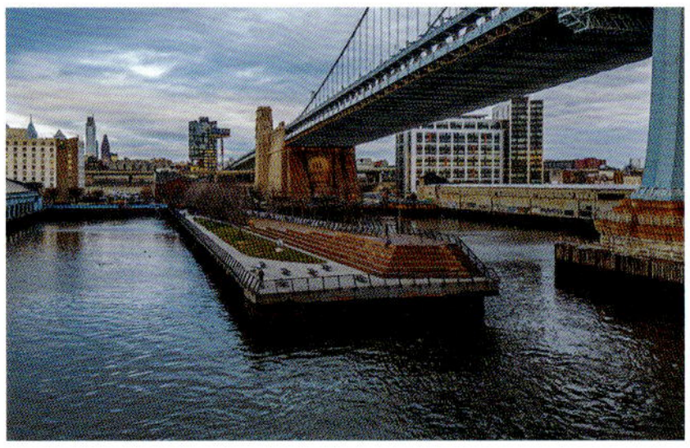

167 Luke Cuccurullo
View of Race Street Pier

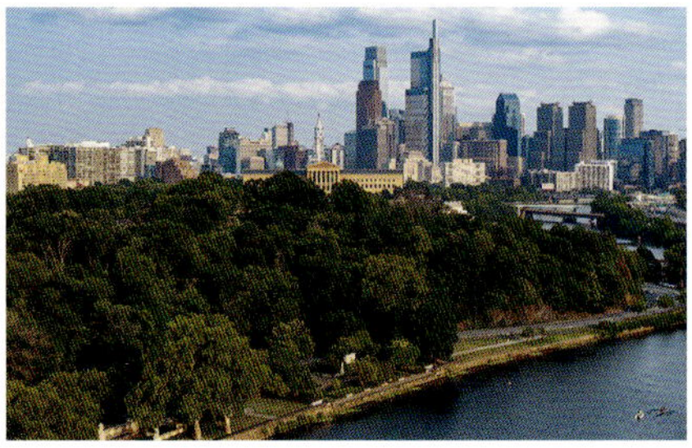

168-169 Nathaniel Bayona
View of Lemon Hill Park

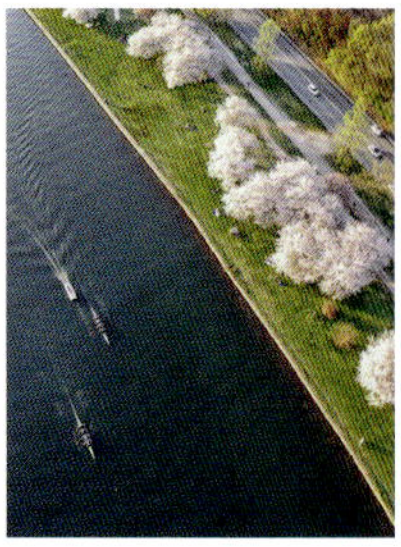

170 Andy D'Angelo
Above the Schuylkill River

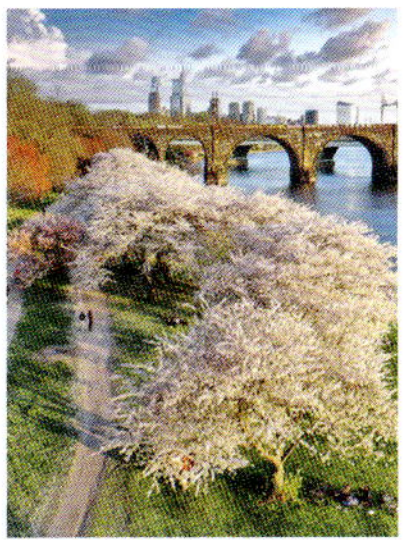

171 Andy D'Angelo
View of the Schuylkill River Trail

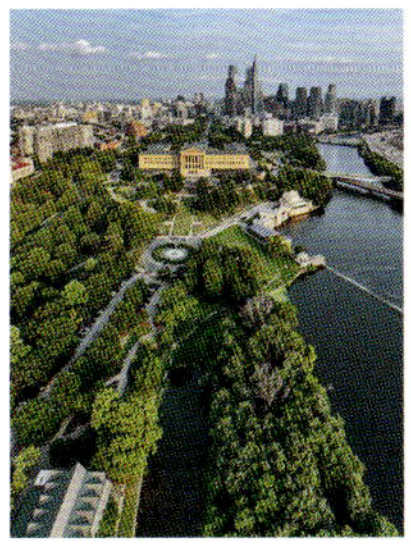

172 Nathaniel Bayona
View of the Philadelphia Museum of Art

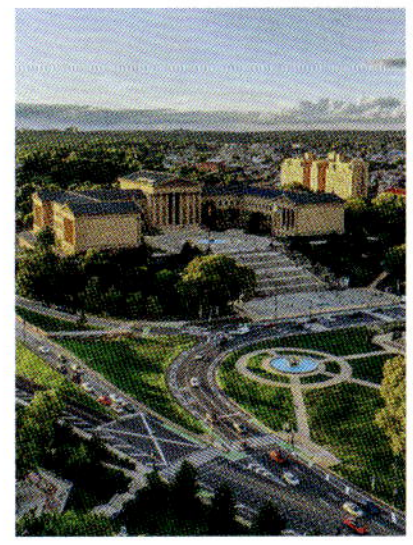

173 Trevor W. Adams
View of the Philadelphia Museum of Art

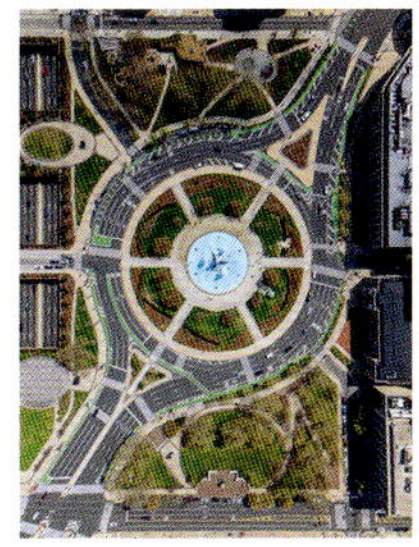

174 Daniel Moreno
Looking down on Swann Memorial Fountain

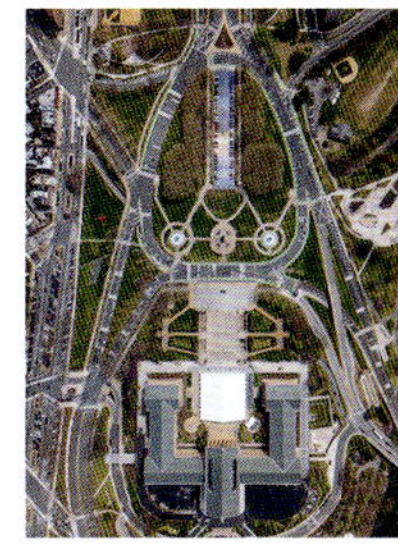

175 Daniel Moreno
Looking down on the Philadelphia Museum of Art

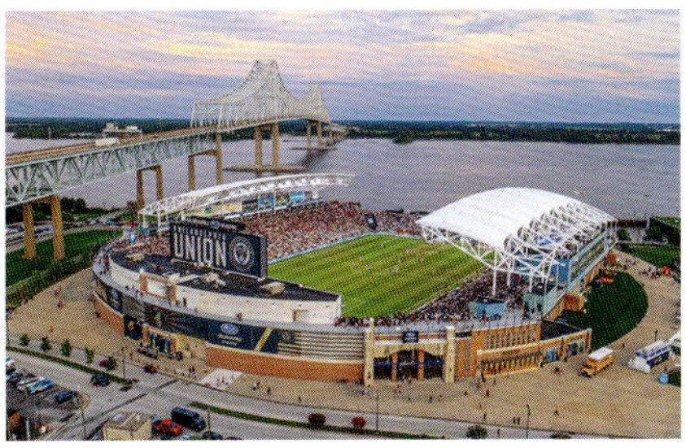

176-177 Brett Gross
View of Subaru Park

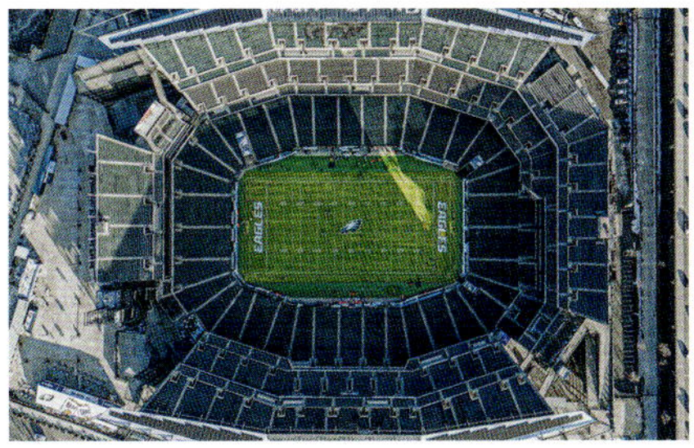

178-179 Luke Cuccurullo
Looking down on Lincoln Financial Field

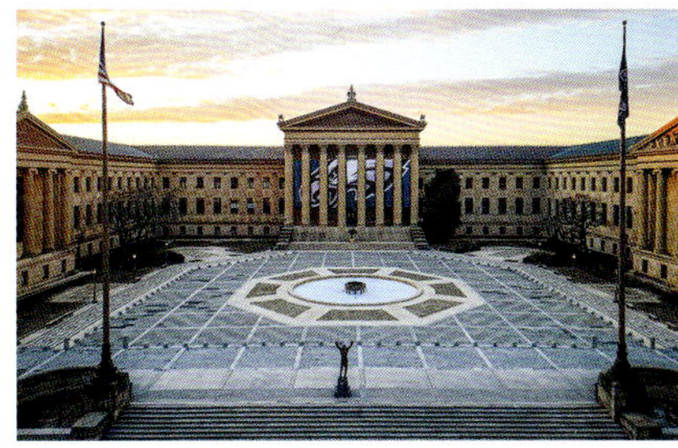

180-181 Luke Cuccurullo
View of the Philadelphia Museum of Art and the Rocky Statue

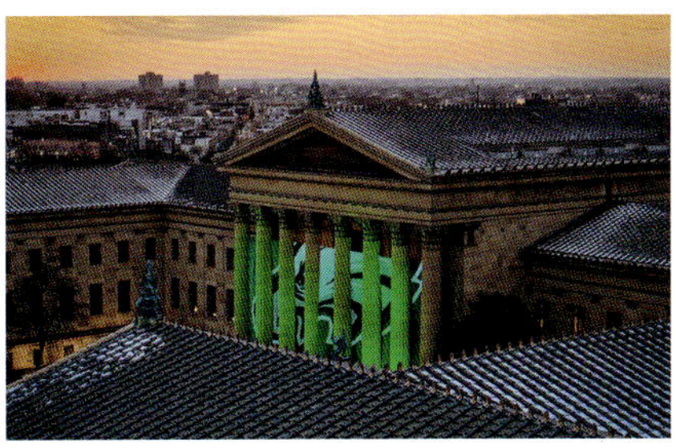

182-183 Nathaniel Bayona
View of the Philadelphia Museum of Art

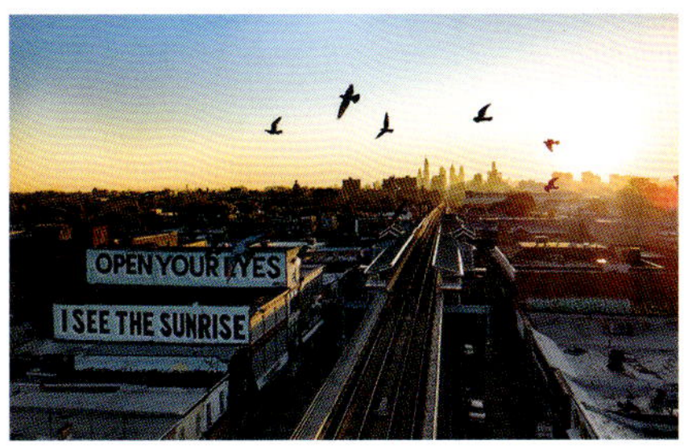

184-185 Andy D'Angelo
View of the 52nd Street Station

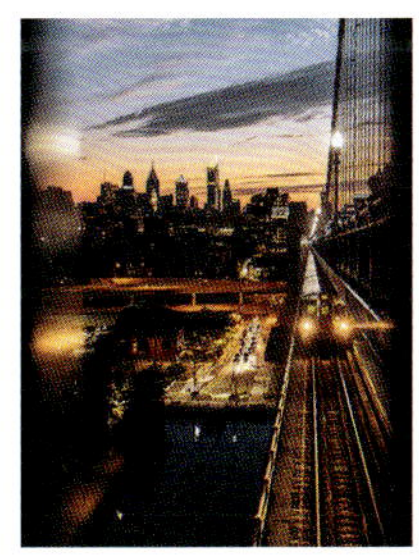

186 Greg Adams
View of the Benjamin Franklin Bridge

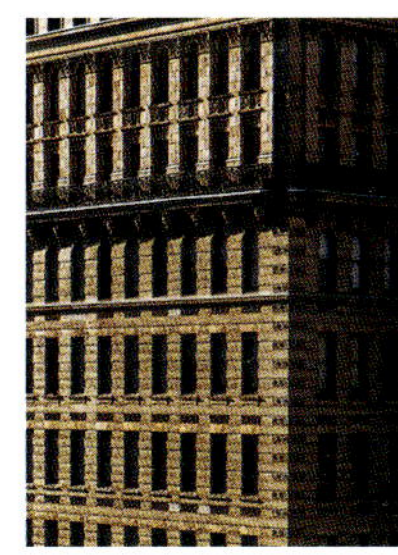

196 Greg Adams
Detail of One City building

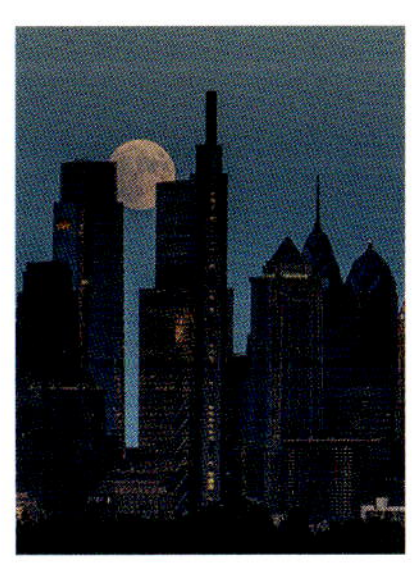

198 Brian Fishman
View of the Philadelphia skyline

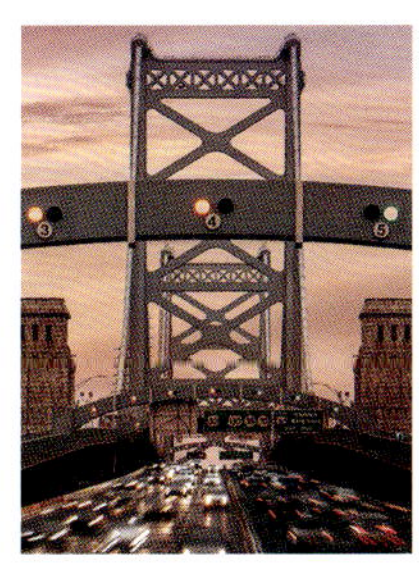

200 Trevor W. Adams
View of the Benjamin Franklin Bridge

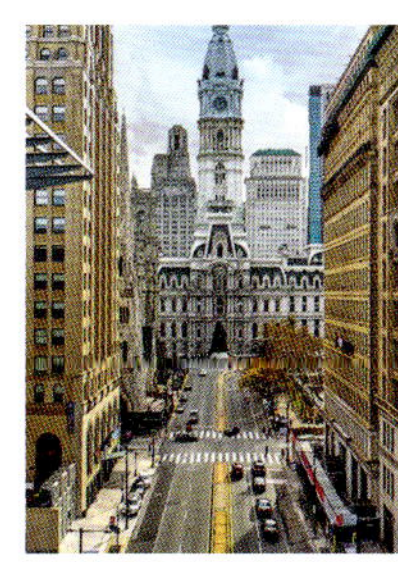

Back Cover Andy D'Angelo
View of Philadelphia City Hall

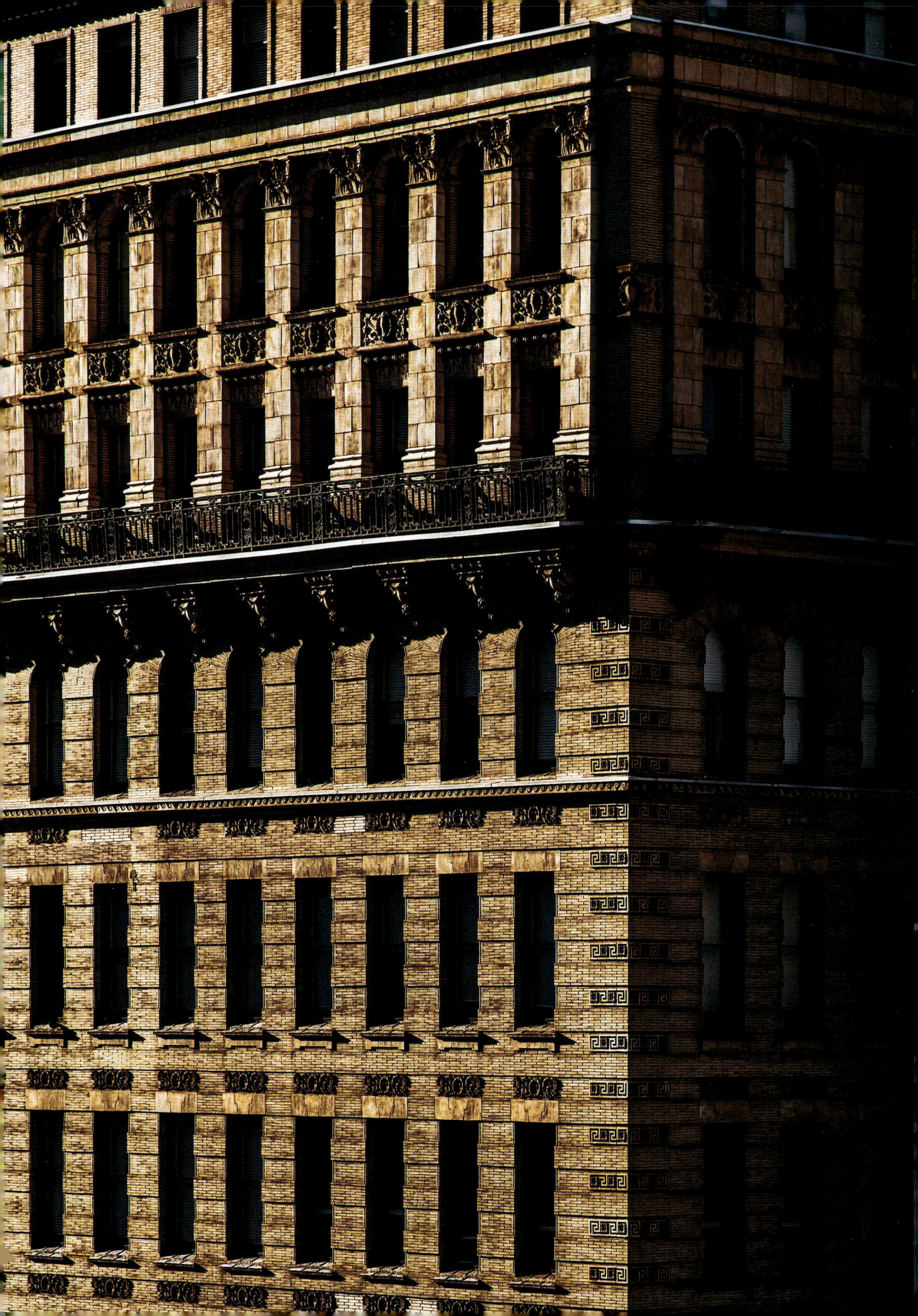

PHOTOGRAPHERS

+ ANDY D'ANGELO
Andy D'Angelo is an aerial and street photographer based in Philadelphia.
@DAngelo.Foto

+ BRETT GROSS
A Philadelphia native who has been flying drones creatively since 2019, Brett Gross enjoys traveling, sports, and music.
@bgrophoto

+ BRIAN FISHMAN
Brian Fishman is a criminal defense attorney born and raised in Philadelphia with a passion for night, moon, and reflection photography.
@brianfishman

+ DANIEL MORENO
Daniel Moreno is a Chicago-based photographer whose fascination with film and audiovisual media helped him discover his love for photography.
@daedmorgon

+ GREG ADAMS
Greg Adams is a drone enthusiast and Philly native with an eye for composition, light, and symmetry.
@gregsframes

+ KIM SLOUF
A digital strategist and self-taught hobby photographer, Kim Slouf's street style photography captures the stories of everyday life in Philadelphia.
@kslouf

+ LICHAO LIU
Lichao Liu is an architect who views photography as a form of frozen art that turns any fleeting moment into a tangible and lasting memory.
@jennylichao

+ LUKE CUCCURULLO
Luke Cuccurullo is an aerial, landscape, and street photographer raised in New Jersey, working out of Philly.
@Lukecukes

+ NATHANIEL BAYONA
Nathaniel Bayona is a passionate aerial photographer and videographer from New Jersey with a love for travel and sports.
@nathanielbayona

+ THOM CARROLL
Thom Carroll is a commercial outdoor and adventure photographer, photojournalist, and drone pilot.
@thom_carroll

+ TREVOR W. ADAMS
A graphic designer from Longview, Texas, Trevor Adams relocated to Philadelphia in 2018. Driven by a desire to elevate his design work, he developed a strong proficiency in photography blending architectural elements with street photography.
@trev.takes.photos

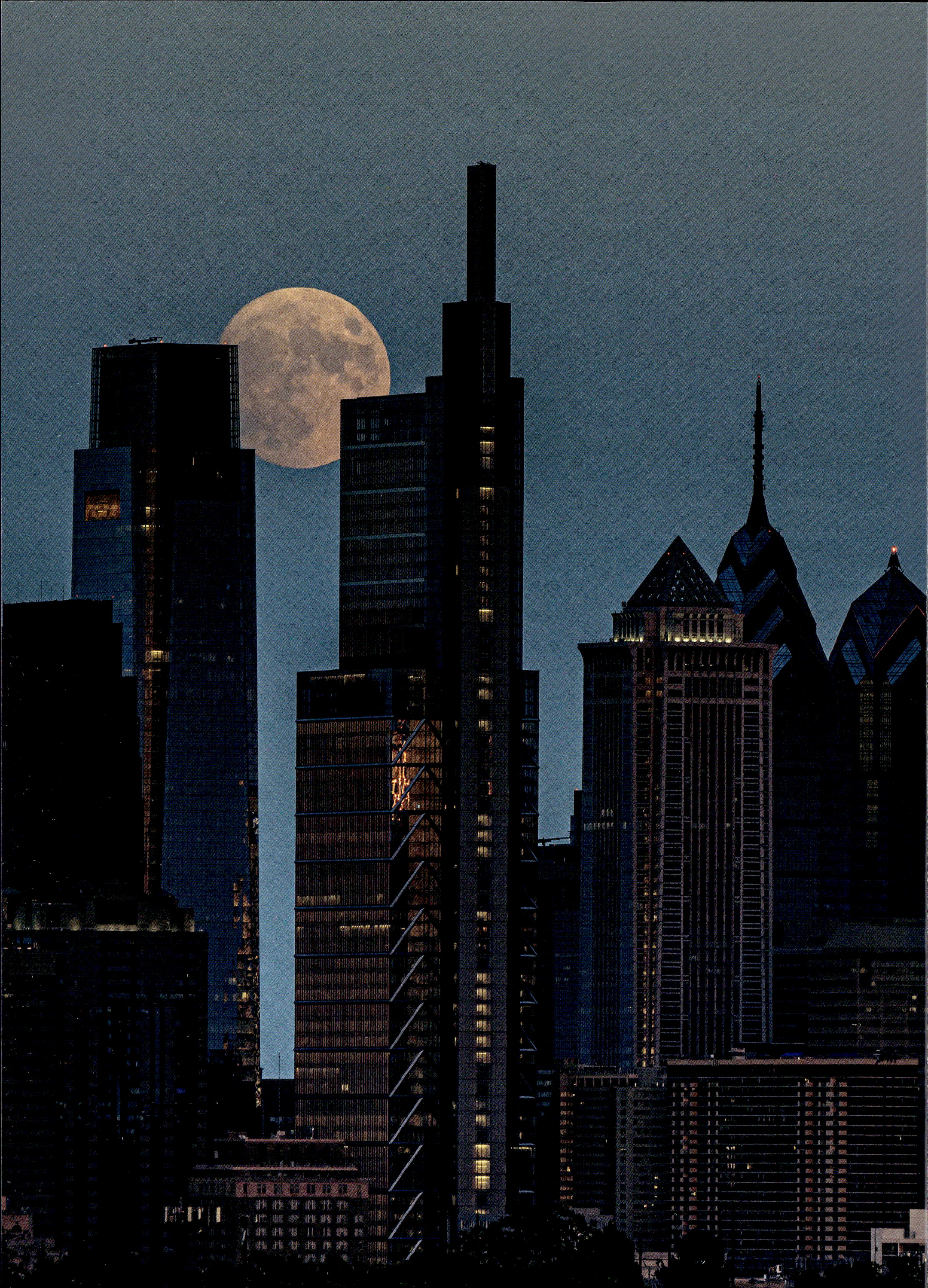

ACKNOWLEDGEMENTS

SPECIAL THANKS

+ We would like to thank all of the photographers who have generously donated their time and allowed us to use their images to create *Above & Across Philadelphia.*

Additionally, we thank the following individuals who worked tirelessly through the production of *Above & Across Philadelphia.*

+ SAM LANDERS
+ KATE LANDERS
+ JACK VAN BOOM
+ LUKE CUCCURULLO

ABOUT THE EDITORS

+ MICHELLE FITZGERALD
Michelle Fitzgerald is the Associate Publisher at Trope Publishing Co. and served as editor for *New York*, *Paris*, *Los Angeles*, and *Rome*, part of Trope's City Edition series, as well as the other titles in Trope's Above & Across series. A veteran of the book publishing industry, Michelle is a fierce advocate for books and is passionate about sharing them with the widest audience possible.

+ KENDRA HUSPASKA
Kendra is a Chicago-based designer and illustrator with a passion for editorial and publication design. As the Senior Designer at Trope Publishing Co., she has an unwavering dedication to the tactile and timeless nature of print.

LCCN: 2025937444
ISBN: 978-1-951963-45-3

Printed and bound in China
First printing, 2025

The photographs from *Above & Across Philadelphia* are available for purchase. For inquiries, email the gallery at info@trope.com

+ INFORMATION:
For additional information on our books and prints, visit WWW.TROPE.COM

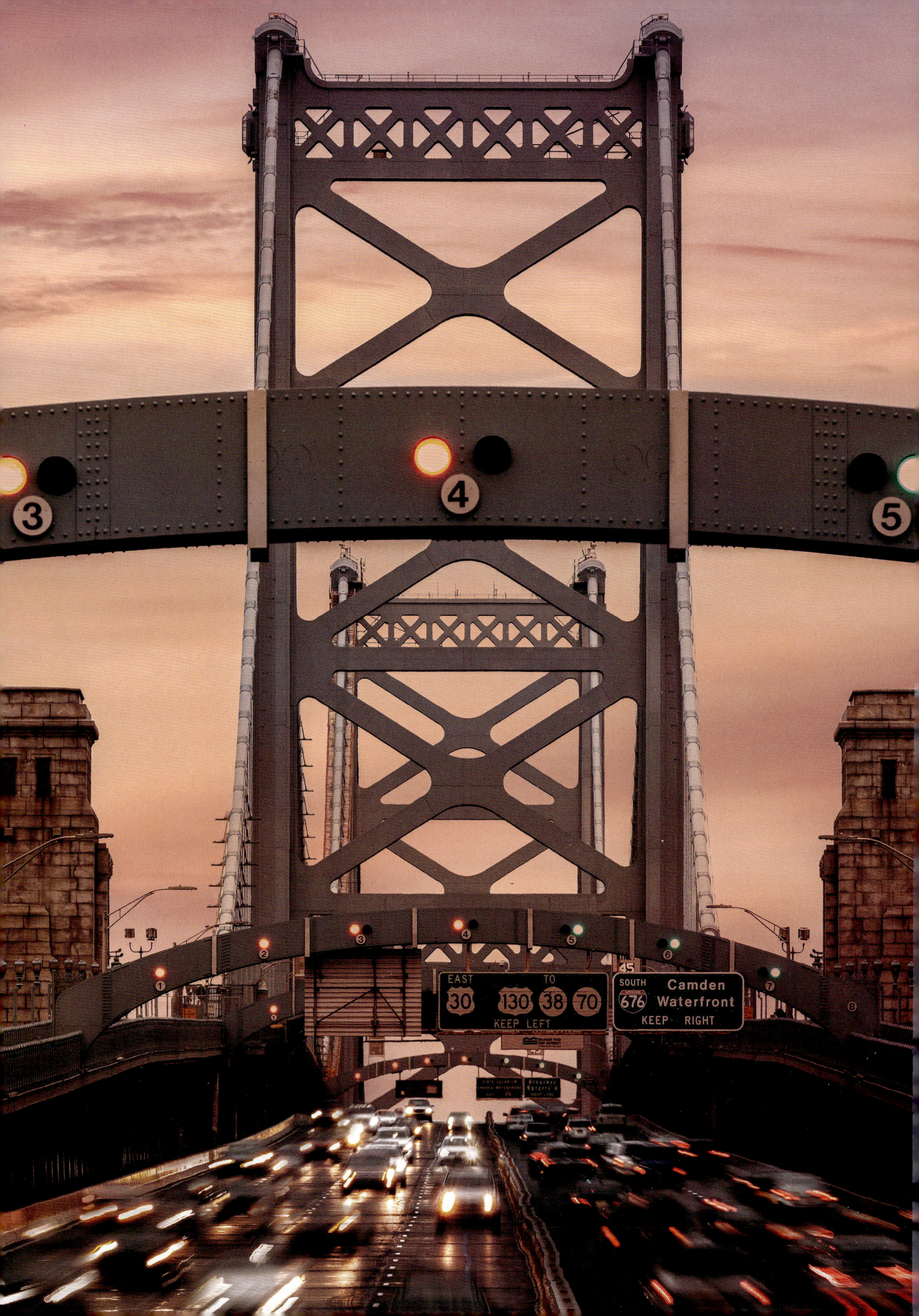
3
4
5
EAST 30 TO 130 38 70
KEEP LEFT
SOUTH 676 Camden Waterfront
KEEP RIGHT